IRA GERSHWIN

IRA GERSHWIN

A Life in Words

MICHAEL OWEN

Liveright Publishing Corporation

A Division of W. W. Norton & Company
Independent Publishers Since 1923

For information about permission to reproduce selections from this book, write to
Permissions, Liveright Publishing Corporation, a division of W. W. Norton & Company,
Inc., 500 Fifth Avenue, New York, NY 10110

For information about special discounts for bulk purchases, please contact
W. W. Norton Special Sales at specialsales@wwnorton.com or 800-233-4830

Manufacturing by Lakeside Book Company
Book design by Brooke Koven
Production manager: Anna Oler

ISBN 978-1-324-09181-3

Liveright Publishing Corporation
500 Fifth Avenue, New York, N.Y. 10110
www.wwnorton.com

W. W. Norton & Company Ltd.
15 Carlisle Street, London W1D 3BS

10 9 8 7 6 5 4 3 2 1

This book is dedicated to Mike Strunsky (1934–2024),
who gave me the opportunity to manage Ira's archive
and who believed that I could tell Ira's story

TABLE OF CONTENTS

PART ONE

The Floating Soul

CHAPTER 1

IRA GERSHWIN'S PARENTS emigrated to the United States from Saint Petersburg, Russia, in the early 1890s. His grandfather, Yakov Gershovitz, was raised in a small town near what is now Vilnius, in Lithuania. After he was taken from his home at the age of ten for military service under the czar, Yakov became a mechanic. This highly prized skill resulted in Yakov being awarded the right for him and his descendants to live unmolested anywhere in Russia; he chose the town of Shlisselburg, east of Saint Petersburg—the "gateway to Europe"—which had been, for nearly two centuries, the capital of Imperial Russia.

Yakov was "a beloved man despite all his negative sides," whose excessive drinking led to "misery for quite a period."[1] He married a young woman named Sara Greenstein, and the couple had two children: Ira's father, Moishe, and Moishe's younger sister, Mary.[2] After Sara's death, Yakov remarried at least three times and had two more sons, Kolya and Aaron.[3] Moishe was trained in another highly prized skill: making uppers on ladies' shoes; but losing large sums of money at billiards often took precedence over work. At the age of eighteen, when his own military service was to begin, Moishe decided that decades of work dedicated to Czar Alexander III, who had obliterated the Haskalah ("Enlightenment") reform movement instituted under his father, Alexander II, was not for him. He joined the wave of Russian Jewish immigrants to the United States, who "for the first time could suppose there was someplace else to go, a new world perceived as radically different from the one in which they lived."[4]

Ira's father arrived in New York Harbor aboard a steamship in August 1890, his most important possession—a piece of paper containing the

Brooklyn address of his uncle Barnet Greenstein—tucked into the brim of his hat. But when he leaned over the portside railing of the ship to catch a glimpse of the Statue of Liberty, a gust of wind lifted the hat into the air, depositing it and the precious piece of paper into the waters of the Upper Bay. The plucky young man was unperturbed; after clearing immigration at Castle Garden on the Battery, he spent the night in the Bowery, pestering locals in a mixture of Russian and Yiddish as to where he might find Mr. Greenstein. His love of billiards won him 30 cents, enough money for a trip across the Brooklyn Bridge to Brownsville, where he tracked down his uncle.[5]

Moishe anglicized his name to Morris and quickly settled into a new way of life that became complete when he was reunited with Rosa (later Rose) Bruskin, an attractive, well-dressed young woman with whom he had been friendly in Saint Petersburg. Morris's fondness for her was obvious, and he ingratiated himself to the family by playing cards with Rose's father, a prosperous furrier.[6] Unlike Morris, the Bruskins' emigration was the product of financial opportunities in the New World rather than fear of the future; when Rose, her parents, and her two younger siblings arrived in New York Harbor in February 1892, they had not crossed the Atlantic in steerage.[7] Morris's success as the foreman at a factory that manufactured ladies' fancy shoe uppers convinced Rose's father of his prospects, and on July 21, 1895, the young couple were married in a Houston Street rathskeller.

THEY WERE among the more than two million Eastern European Jews who emigrated to the United States in the late nineteenth century and changed the demographics of the cities in which they lived. In 1870, there were only sixty thousand Jews in New York City, or less than 1 percent of a total population of 1.2 million; forty years later, there were 1.1 million Jews, or 23 percent of the population of 4.8 million.[8] Morris and Rose were better prepared "for urban life than . . . most of the other immigrants from eastern and southern Europe."[9] Morris's profession kept him away from the sweatshops and pushcarts of the Lower East Side and gave him the money to live in reasonable apartments rather than squalid tenements.

Ira's parents settled in Manhattan's Lower East Side, an area of less than one square mile packed with 455,000 residents by the turn of the twentieth century. The Lower East Side was the scene of never-ending cycles of change. The Irish and German immigrants who had populated the area through the 1870s had been displaced by Eastern European Jews, many who would never entirely assimilate; the Gershwin family was not among them. Morris and Rose, and their four children, were eager to become part of their new country and its culture and to be successful—in short, to become Americans.

Before the birth of their first child, the couple rented a walk-up apartment above Simpson's Pawnshop in a building at the corner of Eldridge and Hester Streets. It was here that Israel Gershovitz was born on Sunday, December 6, 1896.[10] His given name was quickly replaced by Isidore and typically abbreviated to Izzy or Iz; it was the name by which his family and friends knew him until the early 1920s, when he adopted the Ira moniker.[11] When Ira's father applied for American citizenship in December 1897, his last name was listed as "Gershvin," which was soon modified to Gershwin.

Morris Gershwin liked to live within walking distance of his place of business, and in late 1897, he relocated to the Brownsville section of Brooklyn, "then regarded as a pastoral village" for Jews, to pursue a better opportunity.[12] He rented an apartment in a two-story house on Snediker Avenue, and his weekly salary of $35 made him "the most prosperous member of his lodge in those days." The Gershwins had a front room, a dining room, and a kitchen, with three or four "smallish but comfortable enough" upstairs bedrooms.[13] The neighborhood was rife with open spaces, and trees bordered both sides of the house, where a fenced-in yard was used for growing grapes.[14]

The most notable event of the Brooklyn sojourn was the birth of the couple's second son, named Jacob after his paternal grandfather, on September 26, 1898. Ira, not yet two years old, was blissfully unaware of the arrival of the new addition, whose given name was quickly Americanized to George.[15] By 1900, they had moved to the more desirable Park Slope neighborhood; for a time, their residence was just a block from idyllic Prospect Park, where Rose and her three sons (Arthur having arrived in March of that year) were often found picnicking with the family maid, a sign that the Gershwins were financially secure, if not well-off.[16] But Brooklyn lacked culture and friends, and an offer from Rose's parents for Morris to become part owner of a Turkish bathhouse in Manhattan could not be resisted.[17] With that move, Morris became part of the Lower East Side immigrant "middle class of independent businessmen" in search of the American dream of freedom and prosperity.[18]

IRA'S MOTHER clothed him in "starched dresses and long golden curls" until the age of five. It was "quite the style for little boys." Fortunately, for his reputation, when he began kindergarten, he was sans dresses and curls.[19] A year later, he was promoted to Public School 20, and the recently established school provided a welcome antidote to the subpar educational facilities of the Lower East Side. It was at P.S. 20 that Ira and his classmates were taught the alphabet "by learning the cute sixteen-bar tune that it was set to," an early indication of his ability to match syllables to melodies.[20] As an adult, when stumped to remember a particular tune his brother had written, Ira would "draw an approximation" of its movements in the air.[21]

When he started school at P.S. 20, the Gershwin family lived a block away at 138 Forsyth Street.[22] This period coincided with the construction of the Williamsburg Bridge, connecting the Lower East Side to the Williamsburg neighborhood of Brooklyn, and Ira witnessed the 1902 fire that damaged part of the tower on the Brooklyn side of the span.[23] By 1905, he was at another public school, at 125th Street near Third Avenue in Harlem,[24] part of a neighborhood between 97th Street and 142nd Street to which Jews had moved in large numbers by the turn of the century.[25]

MORRIS FOUND NO success with the Turkish baths and moved on to run a small restaurant on Third Avenue near the Harlem River with his sister Mary's husband, Harry Wolpin.[26] Proximity was again a deciding factor: the location was only two blocks from the Gershwin apartment on East 126th Street.[27] This was the first of several restaurants to have the Wolpin/Gershwin name attached to it over the ensuing two decades and was bordered on one side by the massive Third Avenue trolley barn and on the other by a theater whose doorman was a customer at the restaurant. Occasionally, Ira and his father were admitted through the theater doors to stand at the back and watch and listen to the performers.[28] There was also the occasional Sunday when Morris held the reins on a bakery wagon horse he had tied to a "buggy hired for the occasion from the livery stable around the corner" and led his young son on a journey around the neighborhood.[29]

Life was "full of surprises but often bewildering and fatiguing." His brother George was more adaptable, "constantly absorbing new experiences."[30] George "would get into street fights and come home with black eyes. . . . He had his own life, and I had mine. We were in two completely different worlds."[31] Harlem was soon abandoned for a return to the Lower East Side. The new establishment was small—one waiter and a busboy—but business was good, "for in addition to our regular customers we supplied through an opening in the wall the hungry in adjacent Wolpin's Turkish Baths."[32] Each week, Ira earned a quarter serving water to the customers after school, supplemented by the dollar he made purchasing the playing cards and delicatessen fare for his mother's weekly poker games.[33] With money in hand, and little parental supervision, Ira began to explore the world around him.

It was a world of smells and tastes: the epicurean delights of a Lower East Side childhood included Chinese nuts, polly seeds (a name for sunflower seeds in New York City), boiled chickpeas known as "Hot Arbis," sweet potatoes, lollypops, cotton candy (known as "candy floss"), and half-sour pickles.[34] It was also a world of noise and visually arresting sights: the sound of horses' hooves and the rattle of the wagons they led, the rumble of the electrified trolleys on their tracks, the metal-on-metal grating of the elevated railway, the shouts of peddlers selling every item imaginable from their pushcarts—all these could set your ears abuzz. It was invigorating to realize that you lived in an exciting city that was the center of a newly urbanized America. But it was a dangerous city: the "affable young men who used to hang around" the neighborhood and encourage Ira in roller skating contests "turned out to be, some years later, Young Frenchy, Gyp the Blood, and Leftie Louie."[35] Ira's grade school was not exempt from a mention in the annals of crime. In 1905, the gangster Benjamin "Dopey Benny" Fein was sent to prison for recruiting students at P.S. 20 for his gang of pickpockets.[36]

Through the bustling, crowded streets he walked; by the age of twelve, he could, with a sense of pride, claim that if he wasn't "the smartest boy" in his class, he was certainly "the best informed about New York and its landmarks."[37] It was during these peregrinations that Ira discovered a love for words. Primary school readers did not fill his needs; his fascination for adventure stories with their bright covers often had him huddled in a chair by the warm stove poring over the thin narratives. Keenly aware of the disreputable reputation of these poorly bound and disposable pulp magazines, he hid them under the edge of the carpet if anyone other than members of his immediate family knocked on the door.[38] But once he became aware of the existence of public libraries and their more diverse—and more enlightening—selection of books that did not have to be hidden away from disapproving eyes, he became an even more obsessed reader who, as an adult, owned a library of thousands of volumes.

Although he cannot be identified as being a member of the crowd that lined up outside the new Beaux-Arts main branch of the New York Public Library on Fifth Avenue on May 23, 1911, he surely would have been there soon after. He later patronized the Ottendorfer Branch on lower Second Avenue, the first free public library in New York City, spending many hours there poring over literary magazines like *The Bookman*, *The Century*, and the *London Illustrated News*.[39] Even the arrival of his sister Frances—born ten years to the day after Ira—was connected to literature; his only recollection of that time was that by Christmas of 1906, he had acquired his first hardcover book, Sir Arthur Conan Doyle's Sherlock Holmes novel *A Study in Scarlet*.[40]

Soon he began to keep records of the books he devoured—ten in 1909, fifteen the following year; he filled three-quarters of a page with the titles of books he read in 1911 and reached two full pages' worth for 1912—and to create scrapbooks of items clipped from the *Literary Digest* and the *World Almanac*.[41] Interspersed among the clippings were his colorful drawings and sketches, many done in the style of the popular contemporary illustrator Charles Dana Gibson, of Gibson Girl fame. What was the source of this passion for words? No literary genes have been noted in the Gershwin or Bruskin families, but the freedom Ira's parents gave him to wander the city exposed him to the thoughts of the new American century and drew him away from the culture of his ancestors.

THE RELIGIOUS and cultural assimilation of the Gershwin family was typical of its time; to many of the Russian Jews who had emigrated to the

United States, becoming Americans was more important than remaining faithful to their traditions. "To be an American, dress like an American, look like an American . . . became a collective goal, at least for the younger generation."[42] Even if Rose Gershwin occasionally held a seder, particularly at important Jewish festivals like Passover that featured six or seven courses of food (which Ira thought "entirely too plentiful" for one evening's consumption),[43] the Gershwins were resolutely secular and Ira himself largely ignorant of the rituals and traditions of his people. But as the eldest son in a Jewish family, the tradition of a bar mitzvah could not be ignored. Shortly after he turned thirteen, his family and relatives gathered on the Sabbath at a nearby synagogue for the ritual rite of passage that signaled a young Jewish man's arrival at the moral responsibilities of adulthood.[44] Ira awkwardly tied the tefillin, a pair of black leather boxes containing Hebrew parchment scrolls, around his forehead and left arm as prescribed.[45] But because he could not read Hebrew,[46] he needed assistance when he forgot some of the scripture.[47] The solemn ceremony was followed by an elaborate feast at Zeitlin's, a Grand Street café and popular gathering place for actors and playwrights of the Yiddish theater.[48] The next day, Ira discarded the trappings of his bar mitzvah on his way to school.[49] From that day forward, he participated in Jewish culture rather than its religion.

HIS TRUE RELIGION was words, abetted by an unfettered, unstructured exploration of the streets of New York City and its environs. By the age of ten, Ira was working at his uncle Barney Bruskin's "Postals While You Wait" stand at Brighton Beach in Brooklyn, a job he held for several years, progressing from greeting customers and going out for sandwiches to taking and processing his own photographs.[50] Among his subjects was an advertisement for a vaudeville mind reading act that performed near the studio. Brighton Beach was the venue for the touring 101 Ranch Wild West Show, a popular circus and sideshow to which he was taken by "a sweet and mild man" named Golding who owned a saloon on the corner of 112th Street.[51] It was also where Ira and George first saw the vaudeville act of two young performers from Nebraska: Fred and Adele Astaire.[52]

In the fall of 1910, Ira entered Townsend Harris Hall, the prestigious, selective, and accelerated three-year preparatory school for the College of the

Young Ira at his Uncle
Barney's photography
studio, Brighton
Beach, Brooklyn, New
York, ca. 1907.

City of New York (CCNY). Founded in 1847, the college was the brainchild
of Townsend Harris (1804–1878), a native New Yorker who successfully led
the fight for taxpayer-funded higher education in his state and later became
the first US envoy to Japan. Attendance at CCNY and Townsend Harris
Hall grew exponentially through the nineteenth century, and by 1908, all
the college students and all the high schoolers who lived on the East Side
of New York above 110th Street had transferred to a new campus in Washington Heights. Ira was among the group of boys who matriculated in the
original building near Gramercy Park on East 23rd Street known as the
Annex, an imposing Gothic Revival–style structure of red brick covered
with a reddish-brown stucco finish designed by James Renwick Jr., who
numbered the first Smithsonian Institution building in Washington, DC,
and St. Patrick's Cathedral in New York among his projects. But the building's "distracting outlook upon one of the busiest thoroughfares in the city"
and its "gloomy corridors with their dusty pictures and mustier trophies"
created an almost second-class feeling among its remaining occupants.[53]

Ira's enrollment at Townsend Harris was the result of a recommendation from his principal at P.S. 20 and his successful results in the school's rigorous admission examination in spelling, reading, writing, English grammar, geography, arithmetic, and United States history.[54] By the age of fourteen, Ira was already more of a modernist than a classicist, and he opted to study the romance languages of French and German, which made up part of the science path at Townsend Harris, but the heavy academic workload of languages, mathematics, English, history, drawing, physics, and physiology proved too much for him: he failed the Lower C French class of Professor G. Lafayette Cram, who "used to pick his nose" in class, second-semester plane geometry, and third-semester analytical drawing.[55] If the lack of academic success were not enough, he also finished last in a school swimming contest.[56]

If proscribed academic study failed to hold Ira's attention, Townsend Harris did offer encouragement for his literary and artistic ambitions. During his first term, he spent twenty-six Saturdays writing and illustrating *The Leaf*, a homemade, one-page, four-column periodical written in India ink on laundry shirt cardboard that consisted of "cartoons, fables, news items and advertisements concerned with the good things the solitary reader [Ira's older second cousin, Morris Lagowitz] might expect in next week's issue."[57] The immature style of *The Leaf* was influenced by Ira's enthusiasm for comic newspaper supplements. Many pages of favorites were saved—from his first perusal of F. M. Howarth's pioneering *Lulu and Leander* to "the stupidities of good-natured Happy Hooligan, the perennially forgetful 'Jimmy' and his pals. The revengeful Maude and her boisterous 'Hee-Haw,' the stratagems of 'Foxy Grandpa,' the incorrigibly pranky and cold-blooded Hans and Fritz Katzenjammer, the beatific and angelic Buster Brown and Tige, 'Little Nemo' and the glorious panoramas and vistas of Winsor McCay"—only to be discarded when a preference for words took hold.[58]

By the second decade of the twentieth century, New York had a plethora of newspapers: the *Tribune, Herald, World, Telegram, Journal, Sun, Times, Post,* and *Mail.* Ira devoured their contents as a source of entertainment and as a model for his own nascent literary style. There were plenty of bookstores, too, and every spare dollar gave him the opportunity to "walk from Second Avenue and 7th Street to the old Dutton bookshop on 23rd Street to buy various volumes in the catalog of Everyman's Library." For less than

$1.50, he could purchase classics like the four-volume hardcover edition of *The Spectator*.[59] All this reading took its toll on his eyesight, and at the age of sixteen he started wearing glasses.[60]

John Finley, the president of CCNY from 1903 to 1913, was reported to have advised his students to "take a long walk, read a good book [and] make a new friend" when they embarked on their vacations.[61] Ira needed little encouragement to walk or read; he discovered a new friend sitting next to him in class at Townsend Harris. Isidore Hochberg—who later changed his name to Yip Harburg—grew up poor on the Lower East Side and shared Ira's ambitions and diversions. One day, he brought a copy of W. S. Gilbert's *Bab Ballads* to class. Ira was thrilled and asked if Yip knew that many of the ballads had been set to music. He invited him to what Harburg described as the Gershwins' "swank" apartment on Second Avenue, where Ira played some of the family's Gilbert and Sullivan records on the Victrola.[62]

United in their hatred of algebra, the two young men ignored their studies to work on a small amateur paper, the *Daily Pass-It*, where they practiced their versifying and Ira sketched cartoons for an audience of their classmates.[63] The pair graduated to sanctioned work in 1913, shortly after the Townsend Harris Annex class moved to the CCNY campus in Washington Heights, when they wrote and illustrated "Much Ado," a column in the school newspaper, the *Academic Herald*. "Much Ado" borrowed its style from the popular "Always in Good Humor" and "The Conning Tower," newspaper columns of Franklin P. Adams, more familiarly known by the initials F.P.A.

It seemed that almost everyone in New York read F.P.A., the author of the first daily literary column in an American newspaper, and every aspiring writer wanted to contribute items to it.[64] Ira was no exception. His fondest wish was to join the ranks of those accepted by the glorious Adams, who "as much as anyone," in the words of F. Scott Fitzgerald, "guessed the pulse of the individual and the crowd, but shyly, as one watching from a window."[65] To Ira, to be a columnist was to combine the qualities of "a light versifier, engaging table talker, humorous commentator and genial philosopher all rolled into one."[66] The influence of F.P.A., whose light verse "sparkled with the irresistible wit of the self-deprecator," was obvious on Ira's early writing.[67] An entry from his 1917 diary captures his sense that he had yet to fully express himself with his pen:

A page of clear white paper.
To put some verse form upon it.
Triolet, quatrain, sonnet, blank verse etc.?
Something pretty, sweet dainty (see Thesaurus)
To put some article upon it.
Definite, indefinite, worldly, authoritative, statistical,
To essay upon it.
Light, bright, slight, right, blithe, philosophical, egotistical,
To humor it,
Tickle it, trickle it, Georgeadeit, Mark Twainit,
To vers libre it
To cut it up in short snappy.
Lines.
To leave it alone
A page of clear white paper.
Or just to spoil it.
Like a vandal or something.[68]

Ira (*top row, far left*) with the staff of the *Academic Herald*, Townsend Harris High, February 1914.

Ira eventually became the literary and art editor of the *Academic Herald*, and by his final term at Townsend Harris, the newspaper had become larger (doubling in size to thirty-two pages), popular (quadrupling its circulation to two thousand copies),[69] and so profitable that it earned enough money for its chief editor to have gold medals struck off "for himself and four or five of the more important editors" and to spend the balance on lavish meals for the entire staff. Ira "felt rather devilish that night—Chianti was served, even cigars—but most of us were home by ten p.m."[70] The self-styled "Second Avenue Boy"[71] retained vivid memories of this period of his life, as he revealed in a letter written when he was nearly seventy years old:

> *In those non-affluent days there was little, if any, dating—nothing but school and homework. Next in importance was looking forward to jobs in vacation time. (I don't recall having a job those summers; mostly I spent time drawing, reading at the Ottendorfer Branch of the Public Library, going to the movies, etc. But then we were considered well-off because not only did we live on Second Avenue in a $40-a-month flat but I had an extra suit.)*
>
> *Kissing and smooching at that time? Save the mark! Once you kissed a girl, there was no question or argument about that; she was the girl you were going to marry as soon as you could graduate City College and make a living (expectedly as a teacher or accountant).*
>
> *I recall too that when classmate Goldberg (this was 1915 or '16, C.C.N.Y.) told us he had been to a whorehouse on East Broadway, not one of us believed him. Not that we weren't aware of prostitutes: in our first two years at Townsend Harris—before we were moved uptown—a half-dozen-or-so of us would walk home from 23rd Street by way of 3rd Avenue, and we soon became used to being solicited by shabby street-walkers yelling above the noise of the El, 'Only 25¢, boys!' 25¢ in those days meant not only lunch but transportation too if it rained or snowed. But even in the unlikely chance that 25¢ could be spared, I never knew any of us to give those poor old drabs a second glance.[72]*

CHAPTER 2

BY THE EARLY TWENTIETH CENTURY, children "pounding on pianos" and melodies from hand-cranked Victrolas were common sounds in most US neighborhoods.[1] Morris and Rose, eager to keep up with their neighbors after moving to a new apartment on Second Avenue, acquired both a piano and a Victrola. Ira was content to limit his "musical activity" to cranking the handle of the Victrola to play his father's collection of opera and light classical recordings,[2] but his parents had a more formal musical education in mind for him. Rose's younger sister, Kate Wolpin, was both geographically and emotionally close to her nephews and niece—she was only six years older than Ira and lived around the corner from the Gershwin home—and agreed to give Ira piano lessons.

Although Ira's proficiency at the piano never reached beyond the level of simple duets,[3] in the spring of 1917 he supplied the accompaniment for dancers at the Finley Club—a CCNY literary society he had cofounded with Yip Harburg—with the waltzes and simple folk tunes plunked out with one finger of his right hand and three fingers of his left.[4] The extent of Ira's pianism was exposed on the day an upright piano was hoisted into the Gershwins' front room. Although the instrument was meant for Ira, George raced to the piano bench and proceeded to play a popular contemporary melody—fluently and melodically, with an adept left hand in the bass that mightily impressed his older brother.[5] Overjoyed, Ira happily ceded the piano to his brother and returned to words and to exploring the world around him.

The brothers, whose lives had, to this point, largely diverged, would spend the next decade in "a shaky parallel, with now and then a momentary intersection."[6] Ira's nascent literary efforts were quickly overshadowed by George's burgeoning, prodigious musicality. Ira proudly recalled that he was partially responsible—as a member of the arrangement committee of the Finley Club in March 1914—for his brother's public debut as a pianist and composer.[7] Soon, George was hired by the music publishing firm of Jerome H. Remick as a Tin Pan Alley song plugger, and Ira reported that the sixteen-year-old was earning $15 a week by the end of the year.[8]

One thing they had in common was a passion for popular entertainment; the brothers spent many of their evenings at Manhattan vaudeville theaters, where, in their 25-cent gallery seats, they were alternately entertained or bored.[9] George's new connections allowed him to secure balcony seats for the opening night of Irving Berlin's first Broadway musical comedy, *Watch Your Step*. George had brought home copies of the show's sheet music, so Ira already knew parts of the score, but it was his first experience of a Broadway production.[10] The moment stayed with him: a few months later, he looked out of the window of their Second Avenue apartment and heard a man whistling the tune to Berlin's "Settle Down in a One-Horse Town." Ira identified the whistler as an uptown resident; few people on the Lower East Side would have been familiar with the songs from a recent Broadway show.[11]

IRA BEGAN CLASSES at the City College of New York in 1914 as one of the nearly 450 students in the class of 1918.[12] The Gothic-style buildings of CCNY, built of local gray stone and ornamented in white terra cotta, were elevated in splendid pseudo-isolation and gave Ira a sense of space that was a welcome contrast to the overcrowded feel of the Lower East Side. His journeys uptown were opportunities to see and hear the idiosyncrasies of his fellow New Yorkers.

He continued the path he had established at Townsend Harris, with classes that would lead to a bachelor of science degree; more vitally, he continued his literary partnership with Yip Harburg. They contributed to *The Campus*, the weekly college newspaper, typically under the joint byline Yip–Gers. The thrill of seeing his name in print stoked Ira's need for further literary recognition. To have a short squib or a piece of verse—even if unpaid—published in one of the many columns to be found in the major New York newspapers was a "consummation devoutly to be wished." His first accepted contribution appeared in C. L. Edson's "Always in Good Humor" column in the *New York Evening Mail* on September 26, 1914: "Tramp jokes, writes Gersh, are 'bum comedy.'"[13] On consecutive days in October, the *Mail* published a three-quatrain poem, "Advice to a Colored Pugilist," and "A Feature Story." The references in the former to color show Ira's early fascination with the subject, while the play on words of the latter's title shows his early attempts at humor:

> A classic Grecian nose had Bill,
> A chin to tempt the sculptor's skill;
> But on his beak last week he fell
> And now, until his nose gets well,
> An awful face disfigures Bill;
> And, if he's no Adonis, still,
> In justice this I must admit:
> He comes within a nose of it.[14]

Although Ira was the most prolific contributor to the semiannual humor edition of CCNY's *Cap and Bells* (one cartoon and six "pomes"),[15] the uncertainty of his family's finances led to his abandonment of full-time studies at CCNY in February 1915 and a transfer to night classes attended by other young men who worked during the day. A "rather run-of-the-mill" student, he kept writing, submitting pieces of light verse and finding occasional joy in seeing them published, under the byline Gersh or I. G., in the *Mail*, the *Evening Journal*, the *Evening Sun*, and the *Mercury*, CCNY's literary and humor magazine.[16] One example, "I Remember," describes the cacophony of noise coming from apartments in his neighborhood:

> I remember, I remember
>   Those peaceful, happy times
> When we heard no music other
>   Than distant church-bell chimes.
> That picture cannot now be drawn;
>   The flat wherein we dwell
> Alas! Of late it has become
>   A throbbing torture cell.

> I remember, I remember
>   The time when peace prevailed;
> When no budding prima donna
>   Above "Lucia" wailed;
> When the tenants living near us
>   No phonograph did own,
> To drive me to insanity
>   With its melodic tone.
>
> I remember, I remember
>   When no infernal chump
> On a pianola, down below
>   Both day and night would pump.
> Someone next door the bugle flares
>   He's blowing himself pink . . .
> They're all to music taken, Woe!
>   I think I'll take to drink.[17]

In November 1915, the first of many columns by Ira and Yip was published in *The Campus*, most appearing under a "Gargoyle Gargles" moniker derived from the ubiquitous creatures that ominously looked down from the sides of the college buildings. Fooling around with "French verse forms, such as the triolet, villanelle, and especially the rondeau—with its opening phrase taking on new meanings when repeated," became a testing ground for Ira's lyrics.[18] "Rosey," a playful piece of light verse, was printed in *The Campus*:

> Rosey smiles at me so queer,
> Can it be—my Rosie knows?
> Every time I call for beer
> Rosie smiles at me so queer
> Something must be wrong I fear
> —What it is I can't suppose?—
> Rosie smiles at me so queer,
> Can it be my rosey nose?[19]

ALTHOUGH never "poor in the sense of having to go out and sell papers," Morris Gershwin's casual attitude to money left his oldest son with an abiding diligence regarding his own bank account. He cringed when recalling his father's business failures: a hotel that was abandoned "because so many relations came and lived in it"[20] and a month as a bookmaker at Belmont Park, given up when "too many favorites won."[21] Even Morris's chain of restaurants—his most stable enterprise—collapsed under the weight of his inability to run a successful operation. A financial failure in the summer of 1914 led to the first of two moves to an apartment in Coney Island, but the location had its joys: Ira accompanied his cousin Henry Botkin on sketching trips and made a mile-long swim to Brighton Beach. "If you ask Ira about it," his brother Arthur marveled, "he may try to deny it because he's so modest. But I saw him do it."[22]

It was no surprise that by the end of 1914, Morris was forced to sell his Third and Eighth Avenue stores,[23] and by the early part of the following year, the Gershwins had moved once again, this time to 108 West 111th Street, just north of Central Park, in Harlem. The building, equipped with an elevator, had twenty-four apartments of from four to six "small and cramped" rooms. Ira noted that the German landlord and his two elderly sisters charged rents of $50 to $80 per month but were so stingy "that the elevator boys do not exist who can remain more than a few weeks at the five-odd dollars per week they are paid. And because he is very careful about wasting lights and electricity some of them do not remain more than a day or two." Their neighbors included a "well-known violin instructor" and "two young lady schoolteachers," identified as "literary" because Ira saw their copies of the *New Republic* and *The Masses* on the mail table in the lobby.[24]

Ira may have believed that his family was financially down on its luck, but his cousin Henry Botkin did not; to him, the Gershwins were prosperous, if mysteriously so. During a visit to New York in the winter of 1916–17, Botkin described his fancily dressed cousins, including Ira, who sported clothes of his own design and wore expensive jewelry and diamonds.[25]

IF HIS ACADEMIC career was flagging, Ira's dreams of a literary life were still fanned by books that featured protagonists he recognized as fellow "literary youths."[26] But how was he to follow their example? It was at this time of uncertainty that he chose to express himself in a form that gave him the space for stylistic experimentation. Oscar Wilde once asked, "Do you seriously propose that every man should become his own Boswell?"[27] Ira answered the question on September 5, 1916, when he set down the first lines in a diary that he named "Everyman His Own Boswell," a play on the idea of an Everyman character as the prototypical "man on the street." It was also a twist on James Boswell's biography of Samuel Johnson, with Ira as his own companion and the chronicler of his own activities and observations.

"Everyman His Own Boswell" strives for literary form in the manner of F.P.A.'s *The Diary of Our Own Samuel Pepys*, but Ira's slavish, sometimes strained, mimicking of Adams's style, with its descriptions of food eaten; the popular fiction, newspapers, and magazines read; the movies, vaudeville performances, and plays seen; the activities with friends; and the smallest notions in his mind or the overheard dialogue he has heard, become more like the quote Ira attributed to the humorist Don Marquis (*Archy and Mehitabel*): "Every man who keeps a diary is consciously or unconsciously lying to himself."[28] Ira's lies largely come, as they do in F.P.A., through his unwillingness to delve into the issues raised or attitudes displayed by his friends and acquaintances; like his idol, Ira kept to his "self-imposed limitations [showing] no passion, no evidence of vulnerability or serious commitment."[29]

Regardless of the archaic form and the self-conscious attitudes, "Everyman His Own Boswell" reflects Ira's life as he reached manhood and struggled with the often-conjoined subjects of work and family, charted the waters of relationships with his friends, and trod the paths of literary ambition, finding limited success and an almost constant frustration with his art and himself.

IN THE FALL of 1915, Morris Gershwin and Harry Wolpin declared bankruptcy.[30] All four of their jointly owned restaurants were lost and the Gershwins moved again to Coney Island, renting an apartment near the boardwalk before returning to Harlem the following summer when Morris and Harry and the real estate developer Israel Kobre incorporated themselves as the Lenox Arcade Company.[31] The trio took a long-term lease of the St. Nicholas Baths, at Lenox Avenue and 110th Street, near Central Park. The baths, the largest in New York City, occupied seventeen thousand square feet on two floors and included space for forty large rooms[32] as well as the street-level St. Nicholas Bar and Grill, whose owner occasionally took Ira to the races in Sheepshead Bay.[33]

The fortunes of Morris's eldest sons mirrored their divergent pursuits: Ira, without college on his mind, and with no other likely job prospects, settled into a routine as the day cashier at the baths, where he manned the switchboard from 10 a.m. until 11 p.m., settled the payroll, attended to the customers, and kept the books; George, in hot pursuit of his goals, played the piano in Atlantic City and saw the publication of two of his songs.[34] Ira enjoyed his brother's early success, yet wondered where his own future lay. The baths entailed endless drudgery but were a window into human nature that sharpened his powers of observation:

> *It is surprising to see the amount of money men deposit in the safe vault. Men from whose appearance one wouldn't expect more than a dollar or two, slip rolls into the "valuable envelopes" that contain greenbacks and yellowbacks galore. And the surprising part of it is that well-dressed men, men who look prosperous, also slip rolls into the "v.e." that contain g. and y. galore. This of course refers to men who do deposit. Men who do not, haven't, as a rule, more than the dollar for the bath. Their valuables are safe—at home.[35]*

Whether he was told that better business would come when the "season" began, that the weather—good or bad—influenced attendance, or that the rooms remained empty due to holidays or elections, Ira realized that the bathhouse would never be financially stable.[36] Within six months of its acquisition, all the masseurs at the St. Nicholas had been dispensed with, and only a few customers were passing through the doors.[37] Morris did not despair, and he and Harry Wolpin soon took over the management of the four-story Lafayette Baths and Hotel, near the Astor Place subway station.[38]

Ira transferred to the Lafayette in early 1917, but business soon proved equally "dumpy" in the new location.[39] The reason was clear: in October

1916, the Lafayette, known as a haven for male homosexuals, had been raided by agents from the New York Society for the Prevention of Vice. Twenty-five men arrested during the raid were convicted and sent to prison; the then-proprietor of the baths was charged with "maintaining a public nuisance"; and his son committed suicide in his room above the baths just days before the Wolpin/Gershwin partnership took over.[40] From the day the Lafayette reopened, it operated under a cloud of suspicion. Policemen were stationed outside, and a trial was held to determine whether the business should be shut down.[41] It came off successfully: city officials "admitted there was nothing against us, nor had anything occurred at the Baths since our arrival that might be in any way against the law. The police were merely kept at the Baths for the moral effect they might wield over individuals who haven't been near the Baths since the night of the raid."[42]

The baths continued to be awash in debt; "where it will end the Lord only knows." The day came when six creditors simultaneously arrived on the premises, only to be told there was "no money in the bank" to pay them, which led to Ira loaning his father and uncle $200 from his savings for college. "Squeezed on all sides," he wrote.[43] By early July 1917, the Lafayette Baths were placed in the hands of a receiver, and Ira was out of a job.[44] Once again, Ira's father seemed unaffected and promptly investigated a dry cleaning establishment in Connecticut.[45]

THE BRIEF SOJOURN at the Lafayette Baths had one positive result: Paul M. Potter, a journalist for the *New York Herald* and the author of the popular theatrical adaptation of George du Maurier's novel *Trilby*, had fallen on hard times and was living in one of the apartments above the baths. Potter recognized Ira's desire to be a writer; he also saw that the young man was struggling to find his own voice, so enslaved was he to the styles of his favorite authors. Their initial interaction was limited to Potter giving Ira copies of magazines—the *Atlantic Monthly*, *The Century*, *Cosmopolitan*, and the *Green Book Magazine*—filled with prose, verse, essays, and humor that provoked such a "gamut of emotions" in Ira that he was "unable to sit down to work [or] concentrate." Soon Potter became a kind of literary mentor, encouraging Ira to persist in polishing his writing and offering him the most important piece of advice he ever received: to learn "your American slang" and remember that "a writer doesn't necessarily have to experience everything he writes about, but by being an attentive listener and observer, can gain a good deal by second hand experience."[46] Not for Ira was the French poet Arthur Rimbaud's theory of "making your way to the unknown by a derangement of *all the senses*" that led to visions and thus to inspiration.[47] He would be an observer, not a doer, a writer who heard the world around him, who listened "to the argot in everyday conversation."[48]

THE FIRST FRUIT of Potter's advice was "The Shrine," a short piece credited to "Bruskin Gershwin" that was published in the February 1918 issue of *The Smart Set*, alongside works by established writers such as Ben Hecht, Maxwell Anderson, and the magazine's editors, the critic George Jean Nathan and the journalist and essayist H. L. Mencken:

> Fascinated, he would stand before it, glorying. At such times, a sublime shivery sensation . . . an incomprehensible wonder at the beauty of it all. Reverent before it, he felt invigorated with the spirit of eternal youth and happiness. Such soul absorbing devotion to the embodiment of an ideal was unprecedented. . . .
>
> And one day it fell and lay shattered in a thousand sharp, jagged fragments.
>
> Panic-stricken, ashen-hued, he was scarcely able to mutter, "Gawd! Seven years' bad luck!"

Ira needed every ounce of courage to slide "The Shrine" into Potter's mailbox with "a little note asking for his opinion."[49] The older man suggested its submission to the popular and well-respected "Magazine of Cleverness"; five months later, Ira was greeted by a letter with the return address of *The Smart Set*. He opened the envelope with trepidation and removed the contents. The editors "liked my little filler, would send me a cheque and wanted to read more of my stuff." He felt elated but it was "nothing of the supreme delight I had always coupled in imagination with the realization of my 'fondest dreams.'" The arrival of the "munificent honorarium" of a dollar did not improve his attitude: "I will not, I cannot in all honesty,

declare that I was wildly happy—yet I didn't feel quite bad either—in fact
dissecting my emotions at the moment I think joy partially anyway pre-
dominated."[50] But he cashed the check: "I needed the money."[51]

The publication of "The Shrine" was a "lucky strike," he declared in
tones of the last century: "Wherefore I must bide my time and try to attain
a certain standard and distinction in all I contribute."[52] By this time, his college career had sputtered to a close. Through the spring of 1917, he attended
evening courses at CCNY without a sense of purpose or accomplishment.
His absences became more frequent, whether due to the nonappearance of
a relief cashier at the baths, the attraction of attending rehearsals of a play
at the Finley Club, or ennui.[53]

In March of 1917, the war that had been raging in Europe for the past
three years made its presence felt at the corner of 116th Street and Lenox
Avenue, and Ira observed in his diary "any number of what were evidently
Russian revolutionists, or at any rate, Russian Jews of the thinking class."
He also noted the protest by a large group of CCNY students over the
suspension of a fellow student who had written an editorial in the college
newspaper advocating the mere discussion of pacifism.[54] Ira became aware
of the increasing number of conversations about, and displays of, patriotism:
"Not a store, not a fence, not a truck or wagon, not a lapel, not an auto, not
a building, but that it shows some sign of patriotism[;] from it waves a flag,
or flaunts a poster 'Your Country Calls' or some other appeal to patriotism. Not a few minutes' walk on the streets but you meet several in khaki,
yet things go on as usual, and if the war [is] discussed it is only casually."
Eventually, the trend reached his own household. Paul Potter's best friend
and patron, the theatrical producer Charles Frohman, had died aboard the
British ship *Lusitania* when it was sunk by a German submarine in 1915.
Potter told the Gershwins that it was necessary to show support for the war
by raising an American flag on the roof of their building. It was left to Ira
to accomplish the task.[55]

In May 1917, the Selective Service Act was passed; it required all men
between the ages of twenty-one and thirty to register for the military
draft. Because Ira's twenty-first birthday did not occur until December,
his registration occurred the following May, but he did receive a notice

from the state of New York for possible service in the state militia.[56] It was a time of anti-war fervor among American isolationists, who believed that the United States should not be involved in foreign conflicts. Ira dabbled in organizations dedicated to keeping America on the sidelines, but he was a patriot at heart and could not truthfully state any exemptions to military service were it to become necessary "after the present draft is petered out."[57]

After successfully completing his exams in June 1917, Ira pondered a world caught in a great war that hovered over the lives of draft-eligible young American men like himself. Should he invest in the future of his country and purchase a Liberty Bond to support the war effort or invest in himself and save "every bean and bone" for the fall, when he might enter Columbia? His diary increasingly includes references to uncertainty and despondent evenings spent walking alone through Harlem.[58]

THERE WERE OTHER reasons for unhappiness. While George had started chasing girls at the age of nine,[59] Ira was reticent when it came to the opposite sex, a late bloomer who was very much a product of a more innocent time, when "kids on the East Side in the early 1900's . . . were brought up to have a great respect for women."[60] He showed little interest in the opposite sex other than as "good pals."[61] A rare exception to this rule was his relationship with a young Jewish woman named Rose Eisen.

In his early twenties, Ira had a revolving group of male friends. Their excursions to the movies, vaudeville, musical theater, dramatic performances, museums, and art exhibitions were often followed by earnest conversations about what they had seen and the state of the world. They expressed the sheer enjoyment of being alive at a time when all around them seemed hazy and changing. Among this "informal group of embryo artists and human beings"[62] was Arthur Eisen, a CCNY classmate, whose "very pretty" younger sister, Rose, was an aspiring classical pianist.[63] The Gershwin and Eisen families had been neighbors since the early 1910s, when they lived on the same block of Second Avenue. Rose was born in 1898, not far from Ira's birthplace, and when the Gershwins moved to Harlem in 1915, the Eisen family followed suit. The friendship between George and Ira and Rose and Arthur blossomed, with the Gershwin brothers becoming frequent visitors to the Eisen household on Lenox Avenue, where they often sat on the stoop, outside of the range of their elders, to talk.

Rose Eisen first appears in Ira's diary in September 1916, when he discovers her reading *Kent Knowles: Quahaug*, Joseph C. Lincoln's popular 1914 novel about a secluded writer of adventure stories. A "quahaug," Lincoln informed his readers, was "a very common form of clam, which is supposed to lead a solitary existence and to keep its shell tightly shut," a description Rose may have felt applied to her reserved young friend.[64] Their relationship appears to have been wholly innocent, and Ira knew he was not Rose's only admirer: "I used to visit them once or twice a week to drink tea and to discuss life and literature with her mother, her older brother, and with Rose (when she wasn't practicing)."[65] For her part, Rose swayed between playing the engaging companion and the unconvinced recipient of Ira's mild advances.

He wrote longingly that "when you gave me a coquettish glance now and then, my soul, heart, my entire being reverberated with exstacy [*sic*]. I felt like a being aloof. But I noticed the other day in company you were quite indiscriminate, with those glances: on others, on others; ah me! You made me feel—oh—all I gotta say is—Lady you gotta reform." Reform she did not.[66]

Ira bided his time until a propitious occasion arrived in June 1917, as he told his cousin, Ben Botkin, nearly fifty years later, in an anecdote he dubbed "Rose, Not of Washington Square":

> *One night about nine Rose, terribly worried, telephoned me. Her younger brother, sixteen-year-old Solly, was missing, and she felt he was somewhere on Coney Island, probably at a bathhouse on Surf Avenue, the owner a friend of the Eisens. The telephone there didn't answer. Would I help her find Solly? Of course I would. So I took the subway with her down to City Hall, and then the B.R.T. to Coney Island. We finally got to the bathhouse about eleven p.m. and thank goodness, after the long and worried trip we found Solly in one of the small overnight rooms. He was O.K. and wanted to stay over another day. Rose, greatly relieved, reluctantly agreed. So back to the Brooklyn Rapid Transit, back to Manhattan, and then to the Interborough Subway with R smilingly grateful to me for all the bother I'd shared with her.*

I forget whether it was R or I who suggested that if we got off at the next subway station we'd be only a short distance from Wash Sq and that it still wasn't too late to catch one of the 5th Avenue double-deck buses that ran to 110th Street. So about one a.m. we were atop a breezy bus and all was well. The night was bright and balmy, R was prettier than ever and I'd never forgotten that her mother had once intimated that R was fonder of me than of two or three other devoted admirers. By the time we reached 90th or 100th Street I was feeling more sentimental than ever about her and felt too I deserved at least a wee bit of tribute to my devotion of several years. So I reached over to hold her hand. But only for a second, because she gently lifted my hand away with, "Izzy, if you don't mean it, don't do it—and if you mean it, think of me."

And that's how Victorian some girls still were as late as the summer of 1917, and how un-Casanovanic some gents.[67]

Rose Eisen disappeared from Ira's story in the late winter of 1918.[68]

As IRA's LOVE LIFE crashed onto the shoals, his writing slowly, haltingly, progressed, and in May 1917, he turned to Don Marquis's "Sun Dial" column in the *New York Evening Sun* to find "You May Throw All the Rice You Desire (But Please Friends, Throw No Shoes)," a spoof lyric by "I. B. Gershwin." He also sent items to F.P.A. that received the "necessary quota of blue rejection slips" that marked Ira as a bona fide member of the "Not-There-Yet Literary Society." He waited weeks for an answer "in a fever of exhilaration and depression" until the morning of June 4, 1917, when upon opening a copy of the *Tribune*, he discovered a two-line squib in Adams's "Conning Tower" column, credited to "Gersh," his second contribution in two years: "One thrills with literary power—/ On finding one's stuff in the Tower."[69]

As IRA HIMSELF ADMITTED, "My career at City College could hardly be set down as felicitous. In my second year I was still taking first-year mathematics, and when I heard that calculus was in the offing, I decided to call it an education."[70] He left CCNY without a degree in the fall of 1917. That he never graduated did not deter his being awarded the Townsend Harris medal for "Distinguished Service" thirty-five years later and the college's 125th Anniversary Medal in 1973. But at the insistence of his mother, who felt that being a doctor was a better calling for a good Jewish boy than journalism,[71] Ira enrolled in extension classes at Columbia University "to brush up on some of the subjects he had studied at CCNY. Six months of this and he flunked again, this time in chemistry."[72] Ira's sister Frankie joked that her brother fainted "the first time he dissected a frog."[73] Perhaps one of the reasons for the end of Ira's formal education was the absence of an inspiring mind to guide him along, someone who could act as a substitute father figure.

Ira's father continued his meandering ways, taking a brief option on a mill in the "small dead town" of Flanders, New Jersey, in an effort to keep afloat and to get the money to start a small restaurant where "we expect to do a fairish business."[74] Soon he purchased an automobile garage. "Hope it will succeed," Ira wrote in his diary. "It's got to." But it was "not a business for Pop," and within two weeks, the concern had been sold—this time for a "fairish profit." With those funds, the family rented a "splendid" new apartment at 520 West 144th Street for $55 per month. Ira fantasized about how he would fix it up "artistically and aesthetically," a process that he ruefully noted never lasted beyond the second week of residency.[75]

AFTER THE ASSETS of the Lafayette Baths were disposed of in August 1917, Ira looked for gainful employment wherever he could, as "financial considerations at home have so intruded on family existence as to be nigh unbearable all round."[76] Through the efforts of an employee of the St. Nicholas Baths, Ira acquired a $15 per week position in the receiving department at the luxury retailer B. Altman and Co., near the Empire State Building, a position he held for six months.[77] As Ira noted in his diary, "The work of course is not one calculated to keep the brain on the alert by reason of its intellectual propensities, yet it keeps one reasonably on the go all day, and if some days it is somewhat tiring still it is not absolutely so and it has its compensations (outside the financial) in its revelation of the inside workings of a dep't store."[78]

While Ira spent his days at Altman's, George worked as a rehearsal pianist for the Broadway musical comedy *Miss 1917* by Jerome Kern and Victor Herbert. George's entrée into the world of the musical theater gave Ira what he hoped would be a door into the same world, as a critic for the *New York Clipper*, a popular weekly entertainment newspaper. Managing editor Paul C. Swinehart was skeptical of the young man's knowledge of vaudeville but offered him an opportunity to review a few shows on a trial basis after Ira successfully answered the question, "What's the difference between a sketch and a skit?"[79] Swinehart used a few of Ira's reviews but did not hire him for a staff position. Another possible opportunity on *The Billboard* similarly came to naught. This left him open to an inquiry from the St. Nicholas Baths asking if he would return to his better-paying old job. Although Ira's supervisor at Altman's offered him a transfer to the advertising department, he turned it down and said goodbye to his department store employment in March 1918.

To THIS POINT, George Gershwin had given his older brother "little encouragement" in his early efforts at writing lyrics.[80] After returning to work at the St. Nicholas, Ira had a few ideas for songs, but they rarely made it past a title. He continued to ponder the construction of lyrics and how he could make his attempts stand out from the "felicitous ignoramuses" with whom his brother had been working.[81] "Writing songs for musical comedy consumption . . . certainly gives me remarkable practice in applied penmanship." In May 1918, he "waste-basketed" three choruses of an embryonic idea, but "after several sporadic starts," this one left him feeling satisfied:

> The Great American Folk Song is a rag
>> A mental jag.
> Captures you with a pure melodic strain
> Its aboriginal odd refrain
> Has been inoculated with an ultra syncopated
>> Rhythm and with 'im,
> There's a happy, snappy, don't care a rappy sort of
> I don't know what to call it.
> But it makes you think of Kingdom Come
> You jazz it, as it makes you hum.

> Concert singers say that they despise it
> Hoary critics never eulogize it.
> Still—it's our national, irrational folk song—
>> It's a masterstroke song
>> It's a rag.

It was "passable with a good rag refrain," Ira wrote, and George liked the lyric enough to start composing a melody for it, but "unhappily the musical lines were of different length from the lyric, so after having sweated and toiled and moiled over twenty or so different versions, it now devolves upon me to start an entirely new one keeping the first two lines as a memento of a tussle strenuous and an intimation of a struggle heroic to materialize."[82]

What began life as the "*Great* American Folk Song" was reshaped through the ensuing weeks into the unconditional "*Real* American Folk Song"—a syncopated "rhythmic tonic for the chronic blues." The effort to capture his muse and transfer his thoughts to words on paper were rewarded in August 1918 when "The Real American Folk Song (Is a Rag)" was included in the first performance of *Ladies First* in Trenton, New Jersey. Ira, eager to hear how the song would go over with an audience, took the afternoon off from his job to catch the tryout. As a young man, Ira displayed a need for attention by acting the part of a dandy, decked out in "silk socks, blue double-breasted suit, brown double-breasted vest, blue silk shirt, purple knitted tie, soft collar, green velour and dark coat."[83] One of "*the great* ambitions" of his life was reached on the day he purchased a pair of black spats.[84] He adopted poses, smoking pipes and cigarettes to relieve a "somewhat restrained atmosphere" among people,[85] only to have George warn him that the "novelty" of his "Beau Brummel" pose would result in the loss of his friends.[86]

Regardless of his brother's comments, Ira boarded the train "poetically attired in a self-designed vesture consisting of purple shirt, dark blue knitted tie, and a mottled green tweed suit (with European-styled horizontal pockets in the front of the trousers)." Mistakenly disembarking at Princeton Junction, he was too embarrassed to ask for directions. Forced to detour through Princeton, he endured a "wild trolley-ride through the rugged New Jersey terrain" before arriving at the theater mere minutes before the curtain rose.[87] The star of *Ladies First* was the popular Broadway actress and vaudevillian Nora Bayes, who played a newly minted suffragette running for political office. She liked "Folk Song" well enough, but when *Ladies First* reached Baltimore, George bemoaned the fact that the song had been "ruined in its present condition" by the singer Hal Forde.[88] The number made its Broadway debut in October but, much to Ira's disappointment, was not published until the late 1950s.

As THE MONTHS PASSED during 1918, it became increasingly likely that Ira would be drafted to serve, in some capacity, during the ever-more-dire war in Europe. In June, he registered for what he called his "Invitation to the Dance." By the following month, more than a million American troops were stationed in Europe; eventually, more than 2.8 million American men were selected for service. Classified as 1a after having passed his physical, Ira's mood and lack of focus are described by what he scribbled on his classification card: "feckless" and "shiftless."[89] Also hovering over him was the specter of the massive flu pandemic, commonly referred to as the "Spanish flu," that eventually took more than 675,000 lives in the United States.[90] He expected an October call-up to report to Camp Wadsworth in Spartanburg, South Carolina, a National Guard training facility to which many New York State residents were sent for basic training. When he arrived at the initial reporting point at the public library on 145th Street, clutching the required half dozen pairs of socks, he was looking forward to the journey. The recruits were instructed to wait for transportation to Penn Station, then were told that a flu epidemic at Wadsworth would postpone the trip. "A month later I reported again. It was early afternoon. This time I was told to go home and wait for a telephone call at six o'clock as something was in the air." It was November 11, 1918—Armistice Day.[91] Ironically, the second wave of the influenza potentially saved him from the horrific slaughter of the Great War.[92]

CHAPTER 3

AFTER "THE REAL AMERICAN FOLK SONG," Ira and George were occasional—intermittently successful—collaborators. As "the tortoise to George's hare," Ira's early, fumbling attempts as a lyricist were subject to his brother's impatience.[1] George wanted his brother to work more quickly, as the endless melodies that flowed from George's fingertips could not wait while Ira struggled to find his own voice. This meant that many of George's tunes were given lyrics by competitors for George's attention, the most notable of whom was Irving Caesar, whose brash personality was the antithesis of Ira's reticence. (Ira had an uncredited hand in the lyrics to Caesar's "There's More to the Kiss Than the X-X-X.")[2] What Ira thought of "Swanee," the most successful of the duo's collaborations, remains unknown, but he acknowledged that the song's vast success transformed his view of his younger brother: "I began to look up to him then. He was a man of the world."[3]

INTO HIS EARLY TWENTIES, Ira pictured himself as "pretty much of a floating soul"; he could not "concentrate on anything. I haunted the movies; I read without plan or purpose. To tell the truth, I was at a complete loss, and I didn't care."[4] He was temporarily rescued from this ennui in June 1919 by his cousin Morris Lagowitz, who, under the pseudonym Colonel Maurice B. Lagg, ran a large traveling carnival, Lagg's Great Empire Shows—a "World's Fair on Wheels." But the "colonel" had recently lost his secretary-treasurer, who had run off with "Princess Fatima and the week's receipts" in Pittsburgh.[5] Lagg offered Ira $35 a week to take the job; only the firewalker earned more. Memories of boyhood days on Coney Island flashed before Ira's eyes, and he recalled mornings when he would lie in bed and dream with "gusto and anticipation" of how to "squander the munificent amount of 50¢" or a "stupendous fortune of $1.00" on rides, attractions, and food.[6] He felt lucky to be asked, and if it provided nothing else, the experience would surely be fodder for his writing.

By 1919, the name Gershwin was familiar enough that his new position merited a brief mention in the *New York Clipper*, although his first name was mangled as "Ezra."[7] George clipped the piece and sent it on, prompting Ira to jokingly lament that "I now belong, I see, to the ranks of Brothers of the Great." Although Lagg's carnival emphasized its suitability for men and women, boys and girls, it had its share of freaks and exotic female attractions. Ira's innocent relationships with young women were put to the test by these temptations: "Of course all the girls in the '49 show are just dying to fall into my arms, but Hell! as sec-treas of this outfit the bosses told me they expect a certain dignity of bearing, an external contempt for the charming vices of the Sirens, so demmit, the gals'll just have to swear and bear it. And there are GALS."[8]

He soon discovered that a familial relationship only went so far: "I had to put up my own tent, and that title, secretary-treasurer, is just a lot of hokum for ticket seller."[9] But his ear for interesting language meant that he soon grew "accustomed to the speech of the Punks (foreigners) in this part of the country." East Pittsburgh, Pennsylvania, was "quelque [French for "some"] helluva town. Here, it is Sunday, and the three movie palaces are closed as tightly as Frank Tinney's purse is reputed to be. Talk of a feller needing a friend!"[10]

The carnival band regularly played Walter Donaldson's current hit, "How 'Ya Gonna Keep 'Em Down on the Farm (After They've Seen Paree)," and one night, the bandleader let Ira bang on a drum, but his failure to keep time marked the end of his career as a musician.[11] The tour carried on into September, with Ira growing increasingly weary, his boredom only enlivened by a visit to Coshocton, Ohio, where "there was a small restaurant run by Negroes at the railroad station and among other dishes the menu offered at least a dozen different home-baked pies."[12]

Ira's months with the carnival were the longest he lived on his own, away from his family, during his entire adult life, but he opted to forgo the carnival's journey through the South. He returned to New York with only vague ideas about his future. George's success gave Ira thoughts of writing lyrics, but for the moment, the lure of readier money was hard to resist.[13] After hearing about two former classmates who had quickly doubled their money on Wall Street, Ira took out his savings and the $50 he had netted from the carnival tour to join the speculators. After his father offhandedly suggested an investment he had heard about at a pinochle game, Ira wrote a check that made him the "fully paid owner of a thousand Sinclair Oil rights—whatever they were" and marked the beginning of a lifetime of offhanded investments.[14]

UPON HIS RETURN HOME, Ira renewed his attendance at the Saturday night parties given by his friends Lou and Emily Paley at their Greenwich Village apartment. The affection and intellectual stimulation provided by the Paleys opened new worlds for a young man uncertain of his place in the world. The connection began in 1915, when George, while working at Remick's, had met Herman Paley, an older, successful staff composer; Herman invited him to meet his family, and George quickly became part of the attractive, entertaining clan. Two years later, Ira met Herman and his younger brother Lou at the opening night of Jerome Kern's musical comedy *Love O' Mike*.[15]

Lou Paley, an elementary school teacher at the time, immediately caught Ira's attention; Lou's erudition and humor drew Ira further into the Paley orbit. They shared a delight in light verse and an interest in writing lyrics for popular songs. In 1918, George left Remick's for a better-paying position at the publishing firm of T. B. Harms, and Ira noted that George and Lou completed ten "splendid numbers, which with the addition of say a half dozen more could score and lyricize a M.C. [musical comedy] book, as artistically and entertaining as any M.C. book I have seen."[16]

Ira also met another member of the Paley family, Lou's girlfriend Emily Strunsky, who was born in San Francisco in 1897, the oldest of Albert and Mascha Strunsky's three children. Shortly after the 1906 San Francisco earthquake and fire destroyed Albert's wholesale wine business, the family, which included a younger daughter Leonore, who was born in San Francisco in 1900, returned to New York City. Albert became a landlord, well loved for his benevolent rent policies; his business-minded wife operated restaurants in Greenwich Village and hotels in coastal New Jersey that became favorite spots for artistic New York Jews and their friends.

Over the years, this informal circle of artists, writers, and intellectuals included comedian and actor Groucho Marx, the publisher Richard Simon, songwriters Phil Charig, Lewis Gensler, Vincent Youmans, and Joseph Meyer, composer Marc Blitzstein, conductor William Daly, playwrights Sam Behrman and Morrie Ryskind, lyricists Irving Caesar, Buddy DeSylva, and Howard Dietz, the journalist Henrietta ("Henry") Malkiel, and actors Sam Jaffe and Edward G. Robinson, as well as the witty, if acerbic, pianist Oscar Levant. Also included were members of the extended Paley family, including Lou's niece and nephew, Mabel and Norman Pleshette, and his cousins, Max and George Abramson (later Pallay). The friendship and intellectual stimulation gave Ira the welcome opportunity to sharpen his mind as he closely observed his friends' actions and the words and phrases they used, storing them away as ideas that he could, perhaps, one day translate into lyrics.

THE NEXT FEW YEARS were spent learning his trade—one word, one line, one lyric, one song, at a time. An early break came with producer Edgar MacGregor's *The Sweetheart Shop*. George heard through the grapevine that MacGregor was looking for a new song. Ira was convinced that "in a period when the musical-comedy cycle called for at least one Pollyanna song in a show," he and his brother could write such a number.[17] But there was a problem. George, buoyed by the success of "Swanee," feared that MacGregor would not take the song seriously if he knew its lyrics were by his as-yet-unproven brother. George suggested to Ira that he invent a pseudonym.[18] When asked by MacGregor who the lyricist "Arthur Francis"—a combination of the names of the two youngest Gershwin siblings—was, George invented a not-so-inaccurate story: his collaborator was a "clever college boy with lots of talent."[19]

A $250 fee was agreed upon, and "Waiting for the Sun to Come Out" went into *The Sweetheart Shop* by the time it reached Rochester, New York. Ira earned his first songwriting royalty of $4.06 from the sale of 203 copies of the Harms-published sheet music. This involvement with George's publisher was a fait accompli: by the terms of George's contract, Ira was obliged to accept Harms as his publisher.[20] The show opened at New York's Knickerbocker Theatre in August 1920, and "Waiting for the Sun to Come Out" became a standout number, with sales of recordings and sheet music earning Ira over $1,100 (nearly $15,000 today) in the last quarter of 1920.[21]

IN FEBRUARY 1920, when George Gershwin was hired by the budding impresario George White as the composer for the second edition of his *Scandals* revue, Ira sensed that he had the opportunity to become his brother's regular lyricist; instead, George chose the more experienced—and, more important, faster—Arthur Jackson and Buddy DeSylva. Writing for the *Scandals* needed speed: White wanted snappy songs now; there was no time for the tortoise-like Ira to agonize over every syllable.

That summer, "Arthur Francis" instead began a brief partnership with a young composer who was an avowed admirer of George Gershwin. A budding theatrical producer named Alex Aarons—the son of Alfred Aarons, the producer of George's first full Broadway show, *La-La-Lucille!*—saw some of Ira's lyrics while he was working on that show in 1919 and told George that he would keep Ira in mind for a future production.[22] Aarons thought Vincent Youmans's melodies could be a good match for Ira's lyrics; George agreed and introduced the two men.[23]

The give-and-take struggle of the composer and lyricist to match words and music did not interest Youmans; instead he gave his lyricists a set of lead sheets and left them alone to find suitable words to fit his melodies.[24] The work of the Youmans/Gershwin combination was first heard in public in Atlantic City, New Jersey, in September 1920, where *Piccadilly to Broadway*, the revue for which they had been hired, was rehearsing under the watchful eye of its producer, E. Ray Goetz. After Youmans asked Goetz for "$15 a week (a lyricist for a successful show was paid approximately $25 per week)—Goetz replied that we were lucky to have anything in the show."[25] As the revue traveled along the East Coast and through the Midwest, most of Ira's contributions were discarded; the lone survivor was "Who's Who with You?" a sprightly number sung by Clifton Webb—who later appeared in the Gershwins' *Treasure Girl* before embarking on a successful career in Hollywood—and Anna Wheaton, best known for her role in the Jerome

Kern/Guy Bolton/P .G. Wodehouse musical *Oh, Boy!*.[26] By the time the revue had been retitled *Vogues and Vanities*, "Something Peculiar," a new George and Ira collaboration—with lyrics based on an earlier set by Lou Paley—was included. It did not amount to much, but it was a start.

ON DECEMBER 17, 1920, Ira Gershwin took his next significant step when publisher Max Dreyfus of Harms escorted a group of his songwriters to a small Manhattan office and watched as they, including Ira and his brother, became members of the nascent royalty collection organization, the American Society of Composers, Authors, and Publishers (ASCAP). By the middle of the decade, the quiet yet powerful Dreyfus (1874–1964) would come to dominate the world of popular music publishing, bringing under his umbrella nearly all the major American songwriters of the period.

THE MAN WHO gave Ira Gershwin his first opportunity to write the lyrics for a full Broadway score was, once again, the perspicacious Alex Aarons. Ira and Vincent Youmans continued to produce songs with an eye to further interpolations, and George, again acting on his brother's behalf, played some of the duo's work for Aarons, who sensed Ira's potential as a great light versifier, although the young lyricist was still working his way through a "June Moon" phase. Max Dreyfus failed to understand why Aarons wanted an unproven lyricist like Ira for his first Broadway production.[27] But Aarons, enthusiastic about Ira and Youmans producing a full score, approached them and the composer Paul Lannin with *All at Sea*, a book by the writer of *La-La-Lucille!* The trio signed an agreement that called for each man to receive 1 percent of the show's gross weekly box office. Although Ira admitted to being "scared stiff" at the prospect of writing his first Broadway show,[28] he was confident enough to want to abandon the Arthur Francis pseudonym and have the show's lyrics credited to "Isidor Gershwin."[29] But by the time details of the production were released to the press, Arthur Francis had returned.[30]

Paul Lannin was the son of the Canadian-born millionaire real estate tycoon Joseph John (J. J.) Lannin. With the looks of a "burly football player,"[31] the young Lannin studied concert music with Rubin Goldmark and was taught orchestration, conducting, and composition by Victor Herbert, who encouraged him to give up the world of classical music for Broadway. The first conference on the show was held at J. J. Lannin's luxurious Garden City Hotel on Long Island, where his son was working as a chef. The father had no time for his son's ambitions to be a composer; rather, he wanted him "to learn every phase of the hotel business." Ira recalled that Paul Lannin joined the conversations between Ira, Youmans, and the show's director, Ned Wayburn, still dressed in his chef's uniform.[32] Wayburn, who came to prominence as the choreographer for the *Ziegfeld Follies*, "had his own notion of an ideal musical setup." At one of their early conferences, Wayburn gave his lyricist and composers "slips of paper indicating what he thought the tentative musical spots in the script called for." Tempo was his only concern; Wayburn ignored "possible subject matter or type of melody or mood."[33]

Before rehearsals began, Aarons ran out of money and was forced out of the production; the show was taken over by its primary financier, the imperious producer A. L. Erlanger.[34] Ira, Youmans, and Lannin were "warned to stay away from rehearsals for a while. It was declared that if Mr. Erlanger saw how young they were he would think twice before entrusting [such an] investment to mere infants."[35] The possibility of being browbeaten by Erlanger added to Ira's insecurities, and to cover himself in case he got stuck, he paid lyricist Schuyler Greene, who had experience working with Jerome Kern, $200 to stick around to provide help if needed.

The retitled *Two Little Girls in Blue* opened before a packed house in Boston in April 1921 and grossed more money than any show in town.[36] When it debuted shortly thereafter at Erlanger's Geo. M. Cohan Theatre, the book had been tweaked and several songs—largely Lannin's—had been replaced or dropped. On opening night, nearly all the musical numbers received encores, leading one critic to say that "it was surprising that everybody was not sick of the show before it ended at a late hour."[37] Fred Jackson's plot revolved around young twin sisters stranded in New York City. To claim an inheritance in India, the penniless girls board a steamer as one passenger; since only one twin can appear at a time, romantic complications ensue when each girl falls in love with a different man. Further complications arise when a pair of thieves appear on board chased by a Scotland Yard detective.

Harms published seven numbers with the Arthur Francis moniker, and their sales added to Ira's bank balance. One song that he was not particularly proud of—"Oh Me! Oh My!"—became a commercial success. Written as a dummy title to remind Ira of Youmans's melody, the lyric needed work, but the composer loved it. Ira, who could not quickly arrive at a better set of words, relented.[38] Within weeks of its Broadway debut, piano rolls and disc recordings of the song boosted the show's popularity.[39] While the majority of Ira's lyrics for *Two Little Girls in Blue* were generic love songs or were driven by the necessities of the slim plot, he was able to devise a few playful lines. "I'm Tickled Silly" harkens back to Ira's love for silent movie comedians ("I'm a gent, and I'm a scholar, / Yet I'd part with my last dollar / Just to see a slapstick artist frolic"); while "Utopia" and "Wonderful U.S.A." include negative comments on Prohibition ("You can bet I'd make it my one mission / To prohibit Prohibition" and "I've taken a fancy to the U.S.A. / Despite the fact that the Volstead Act / Is driving me away"). "Utopia" also parodies genre songs like "Swanee"—the singer vowing that his dreamland will not have any "songs about that Mammy / Way down south in Alabammy"—and includes a reference to Erlanger stealing his show's "dollies" from the *Ziegfeld Follies*.[40]

Two Little Girls in Blue closed after 135 performances, a run that bested the 1921 edition of *George White's Scandals*—his brother's longest run to date—by one. Ira's share of the gross brought him a neat $125 per week, and the subsequent road tour kept the royalties flowing.

WHILE *TWO LITTLE GIRLS* was being developed, producer Edgar Mac-Gregor rehired the combination of George Gershwin and Arthur Francis to add songs to *A Dangerous Maid*, an adaptation of the 1918 comedy *The Dislocated Honeymoon*.[41] MacGregor was aware that the lyricist was George's older brother, but Ira's agreement with ASCAP maintained the ruse, and Arthur Francis remained on the published sheet music.[42] Although *A Dangerous Maid* closed in Pittsburgh, the songs were the first glimpse of the level of work that the brotherly collaboration could reach.[43] "Boy Wanted" is particularly notable, with a clever "advertisement / flirt is meant" rhyme in its verse and topical references to Nietzsche and Freud, while the catalog of girlish requirements for male partners—a love for musical shows, snappy clothes, and books—appears to come straight from Ira's own personality. The male refrain sung by soon-to-be theatrical producer Vinton Freedley in "Anything for You" charts sartorial territory as well, while "The Sirens" parodies Gilbert and Sullivan's "Three Little Maids Are We," although the quartet here are not Victorian-era schoolgirls but come-hither vamps whose methods of attracting men at the seashore include "something stronger than tea and knowing how to say yes."[44]

By the end of 1921, Ira had earned his first significant sum from songwriting: nearly $9,000 (equivalent to more than $100,000 today). The success of *Two Little Girls in Blue* was the catalyst he needed to pursue becoming George's primary lyricist.[45] Ira had no doubt that he was a superior wordsmith to Irving Caesar, whose lines came speedily but without much invention, but he needed a solid success to convince George of his worth.[46] That success was slow in coming, and Ira, like F. Scott Fitzgerald, could only lament that while his "friends were launching decently into life [he] had muscled [his] inadequate bark into midstream."[47] While George was furiously producing material for the *Scandals* at the family's new home on East 12th Street in Greenwich Village, Ira had to be content to practice his craft by placing numbers into any situation that came to hand. This included songs written with Louis Silvers to promote *Peacock Alley* and *Fascination*, two silent movies starring the popular actress Mae Murray; the success Silvers had with "April Showers" was not repeated here.

Alex Aarons's musical comedy *For Goodness Sake* contained two songs written with George—"Tra-La-La" and "Someone"—and "French Pastry Walk," a collaboration with lyricist Arthur Jackson and William Daly and Paul Lannin, the revue's primary composers. *For Goodness Sake* opened on Broadway in February 1922, and while its songs were negligible, it was George and Ira's first Broadway interaction with the brother and sister team of Fred and Adele Astaire, who dominated the show during its three-month run. It also brought the brothers into contact, once again, with Vinton Freedley, who had parlayed his inheritance into a producing collaboration with Alex Aarons.

THE FIRST OF Ira Gershwin's songs to successfully marry lyric, music, and performance began life in 1919 when Buddy DeSylva, George's lyricist for the 1922 edition of *George White's Scandals*, asked Ira whether "A New Step Every Day"—a set of rhymes without a home—was spoken for. DeSylva thought that the last line, "I'll build a staircase to Paradise, / With a new step ev'ry day," might have potential as a production number if he and Ira worked on it together. The following evening, after dinner with DeSylva at his apartment in Greenwich Village, "we started on the new song. About two a.m. it was completed, verse included." The result was pleasing, with a "complicated, for those days, twenty-four-bar verse, replete with sixteenth notes and thick chords, plus a refrain with key changes," but Ira was uncertain of its potential as a popular number.[48]

The fourth edition of the *Scandals* opened in August 1922, with "(I'll Build a) Stairway to Paradise" as the glittering finale to the first act. By the end of the year, the song had sold over thirty-five thousand copies of sheet music and nearly three hundred thousand discs.[49] Ira's one-third share of the royalties was enough to support him for a year.[50]

The work with the most potential for Ira at this point in his career was written with "one of the most erudite" men he had ever known: his brother's close friend, the composer and conductor William Daly (1887–1936).[51] The pair was approached by Edward Goldbeck, a former editorial writer for the *Chicago Tribune*, who had acquired the rights to a German-language play about the composer and pianist Frederick Chopin. Goldbeck, encouraged by the success of *Blossom Time*, a 1921 operetta about Franz Schubert, translated the original libretto into English; the result was a play entitled *Love Is All: An Episode from the Life of Genius*. Daly adapted pieces of Chopin's music and Ira added lyrics, four of which have survived. The most interesting is "Man, the Master" (set to Chopin's Prelude, Op. 28, No. 11), intended for a scene in which George Sand puts her publisher in his place. Ira was familiar with Sir William D'Avenant's seventeenth-century stage comedy *The Man's the Master*, as well as the use of the phrase in late nineteenth-century discussions of feminism in France.[52] Sand's declaration of rebellion ("Tyrant Man, / I've drawn the sword of battle. / Women's day is on the way") paralleled the idea of the New Woman and the passage of the Nineteenth Amendment in 1920 that gave American women the right to vote.[53] After a couple of months of making headway on the score, Goldbeck informed Ira and Daly that his option on the property had expired. A promising idea had reached a dead end.[54]

PART TWO

George the Music/ Ira the Words: The 1920s

CHAPTER 4

WITH THE CHOPIN ADAPTATION out of his grasp, Ira had time on his hands. On a late evening in January 1924, as he sat watching George and Buddy DeSylva play in a songwriters' tournament at a midtown Manhattan billiard parlor, he glanced through a copy of the *Tribune* and came across an article about George writing a new composition for Paul Whiteman to be featured in a concert at Manhattan's Aeolian Hall on Lincoln's Birthday. Ira showed the paper to his brother; George recalled having been asked to write the piece but had forgotten about the request.[1]

George immediately began work on a piece for piano and orchestra that, in its early form, was entirely rhythmic. Ira made a key suggestion: why not add a slow theme he had often heard his brother play from his notebooks as a contrast?[2] The final title was also Ira's suggestion. One night, while listening to George play his embryonic work at the Paleys' apartment, Ira—who had spent the afternoon at the Metropolitan Museum looking at James McNeill Whistler's innovative paintings *Nocturne* and *Harmony*—mused about colors. *Rhapsody in Blue* was a more evocative title than George's original *American Rhapsody*.[3]

On the snowy afternoon of February 12, 1924, *Rhapsody in Blue* was performed at the end of Paul Whiteman's *Experiment in Modern Music*, a lengthy program that had the capacity audience in airless Aeolian Hall sagging in their seats. As Ira nervously awaited his brother's appearance, he gripped the hand of Cecelia Ager, the wife of the songwriter Milton Ager, who sat next to him, or doodled on his souvenir program. Once

George sat down at the piano, Ira watched and listened to the explosive performance with amazement. Was this virtuoso the rapscallion he had known as a child?

RHAPSODY IN BLUE became the toast of the music world, and on the strength of its success, George was asked to come to London in June 1924 to write the score for *Primrose*, a new musical comedy produced by George Grossmith.[4] While George was away, Ira pondered his future as he sweated through a New York City heatwave. He and George had written several numbers that he hoped would make it into the *Primrose* score, so he was eager to hear details about the show from his brother: which lyrics were being used, who was "doing the others, what are you getting, what am I getting . . . how about second verses and extra choruses of the songs you have, what new songs do you want."[5] George, aware of his brother's proprietary interest in his artistic creations, tried to assuage his fears about the hiring of the Englishman Desmond Carter (1895–1939) to write new lyrics for *Primrose* but also to revise some of Ira's work. The numbers, George explained, had to be palatable to English audiences. He was also cognizant of Ira's focus on money; would Ira mind that George had "managed to give him [Carter] a cent a copy for writing new verses"? Carter had done a "very well written" lyric for "Wait a Bit, Susie," a number Ira had worked on without success, but George assured his older brother that he would still retain a half percent of the show's weekly gross.[6] Although Carter received sole credit for the lyrics when *Primrose* opened in London in September 1924, Ira had six numbers in this very English musical comedy, two—the Gilbert and Sullivan parody "Four Little Sirens" and the wistful "Boy Wanted"—borrowed from *A Dangerous Maid*.

THE ORIGINS OF Ira's first full collaboration with his brother lay in early 1923, when Alex Aarons had placed *For Goodness Sake* with producer Sir Alfred Butt for a British production with the show's original stars, Fred and Adele Astaire.[7] Largely rewritten and retitled *Stop Flirting!*, the show opened in London and turned the Astaires into stars. Aarons, convinced that he could duplicate their success at home, signed the siblings to a contract for a show that would open after *Stop Flirting!* finished its run. But who would write the songs? Aarons wanted George to compose the score. What about making it two sets of siblings? Aarons told Ira that "there is no one I should like so much for the lyrics as you. I feel this will be just the kind of thing we have been wanting for a long time to do."[8]

As he waited for word on the Astaire show, Ira took whatever opportunities came his way. "Imagine Me without My You," written with Lewis Gensler and the arranger/composer Robert Russell Bennett (1894–1981), was introduced in the pre-Broadway run of *Top Hole*, a musical comedy spoof on golf. Although the song was dropped before the show opened, it was published with the unique moniker of "Ira B. Gershwin" on the cover—B standing for Bruskin. This marked the end for Arthur Francis, as Ira acknowledged in the closing line of a letter that noted his string of identities:

Iz

Ira

Isid.

Arthur

Francis

Gershwin[9]

He explained how he arrived at his final first name: "I wanted to keep the 'I'—and I didn't like 'Irving'—there were so many Irvings. (The reason I wanted to change my name in the first place was that Isidore was too common.) And Ira seemed kind of uncommon. It was new then and distinct."[10] In Hebrew, "Ira" means—among other things—"watchful" and seems the perfect name, although Ira had scant knowledge of the language.[11] But in some countries, Ira is a woman's name, taken from Eirene, the Greek goddess of peace; this gender confusion was the occasional source of laughter through much of Ira's life.

DURING THE THREE months of George's absence, Ira worked on a few songs for *Be Yourself!*, an unlikely comedy about two feuding Southern families written by George S. Kaufman and Marc Connelly, two of the leading

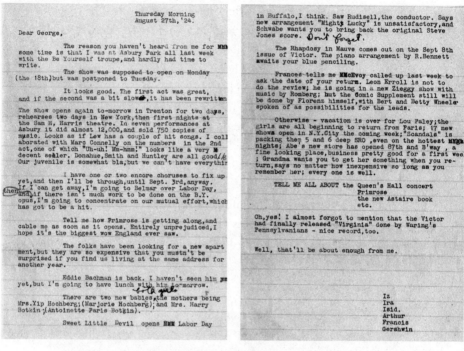

Thursday Morning
August 27th,'24.

Dear George,

The reason you haven't heard from me for MM some time is that I was at Asbury Park all last week with the Be Yourself troupe, and hardly had time to write.

The show was supposed to open on Monday (the 18th) but was postponed to Tuesday.

It looks good. The first act was great, and if the second was a bit slow, it has been rewritten

The show opens again to-morrow in Trenton for two days, rehearses two days in New York, then first nights at the Sam H, Harris theatre. In seven performances at Asbury it did almost 12,000, and sold 750 copies of music. Looks as if Lew has a couple of hit songs. I collaborated with Marc Connelly on the numbers in the 2nd act, one of which "Uh-uh! Mm-hmm!" looks like a very M decent seller. Donahue, Smith and Huntley are all good, Our juvenile is somewhat bla, but we can't have everythin

I have one or two encore choruses to fix up yet, and then I'll be through, until Sept. 3rd, anyway. If I can get away, I'm going to Belmar over Labor Day, and if there isn't much work to be done on the B.Y. opus, I'm going to concentrate on our mutual effort, which has got to be a hit.

Tell me how Primrose is getting along, and cable me as soon as it opens. Entirely unprejudiced, I hope it's the biggest wow England ever saw.

The folks have been looking for a new apartment, but they are so expensive that you mustn't be surprised if you find us living at the same address for another year.

Eddie Bachman is back. I haven't seen him ye yet, but I'm going to have lunch with him to-morrow.

There are two new babies, the mothers being Mrs. Yip Hochberg, (Marjorie Hochberg); and Mrs. Harry Botkin, (Antoinette Paris Botkin).

Sweet Little Devil opens MMM Labor Day

in Buffalo, I think. Saw Rudisell, the conductor. Says new arrangement "Mighty Lucky" is unsatisfactory, and Schwabe wants you to bring back the original Steve Jones score. Don't forget.

The Rhapsody in Mauve comes out on the Sept 8th issue of Victor. The piano arrangement by R.Bennett awaits your blue penciling.

Frances tells me MMcEvoy called up last week to ask the date of your return. Leon Erroll is not to do the review; he is going in a new Zieggy show with music by Romberg; but the Comic Supplement still will be done by Florenz himself, with Bert and Betty Wheeler spoken of as possibilities for the leads.

Otherwise - vacation is over for Lou Paley; the girls are all beginning to return from Paris; 17 new shows open in N.Y.City the coming week; "Scandals" is packing them 5 and 6 deep SRO, even on the hottest MMM nights; Abe's new store has opened 87th and B'way , a fine looking place, business pretty good for a first wee ; Grandma wants you to get her something when you return, says no matter how inexpensive so long as you remember her; every one is well.

TELL ME ALL ABOUT the Queen's Hall concert
Primrose
the new Astaire book
etc.

Oh, yes! I almost forgot to mention that the Victor had finally released "Virginia" done by Waring's Pennsylvanians - nice record, too.

Well, that'll be about enough from me.

Iz
Ira
Isid.
Arthur
Francis
Gershwin

Iz becomes Ira: a letter to his brother in London, August 27, 1924.

wits of the Algonquin Round Table. Ira's relationship to the members of the Round Table was artistic (Kaufman, Connelly) and casual (Dorothy Parker) rather than close; Ira's gentle temperament was ill paired with the acidic tones of the writers of the "Vicious Circle."

For *Be Yourself!*, Connelly, who had limited experience as a lyricist, asked Ira to work with him on the words to some melodies by Lewis Gensler and Milton Schwarzwald. Ira joined the company for the out-of-town opening in Asbury Park, New Jersey. The first seven performances "did almost 12,000 [dollars] and sold 750 copies of music,"[12] most of the sales coming from "Uh-Uh," which had a tune by Schwarzwald that reminded Ira of his carnival experience. It was the first time he had heard "the sound *Uh-uh* for *No*. In the East I'd always known and used *mm-hmmm* for yes or agreement, but hadn't known the antonymic sound, which naturally intrigued me."[13] *Be Yourself!* arrived on Broadway in September 1924, with Ira receiving credit for "extra lyrics"—a phrase that amounted to four numbers in the second act.[14] The show, which starred two actors who later appeared in Gershwin shows—Queenie Smith and Jack Donohue—received mixed reviews and headed for the road after a scant twelve weeks.[15] But it was a success for Ira: the weekly $50 added $1,100 to his bank account.[16]

STILL PREOCCUPIED with ideas for the Astaires, Ira wondered which of George's melodies were being saved for them and what book writer Guy Bolton had devised for a plot.[17] He was pleased that Fred and Adele were enthusiastic about "The Half of It, Dearie, Blues," a title based on a popular phrase: F. Scott Fitzgerald had used a similar line in his 1920 story "May Day," but Ira likely heard "Half of It, Dearie" sung as a catchphrase by the vaudevillian and female impersonator Bert Savoy.

Ira agreed with Alex Aarons that he and George needed to "concentrate on our mutual effort, which has got to be a hit."[18] The sporadic work Ira had turned out since *Two Little Girls in Blue* had not resulted in any theatrical success; even George, although he had blossomed as an attraction in the concert world, had yet to have a successful Broadway show that was not called the *Scandals*. With this new project, they hoped to be part of a show that was worthy of their talents, one that combined George's endlessly inventive melodies and rhythms with Ira's playful, slangy words in a musical comedy that would be of the moment and not beholden to outmoded routines.

When George returned to New York in late September, he was accompanied by Alex Aarons, Guy Bolton, and Felix Edwardes, the director of *Stop Flirting!* who had been hired to direct the new show, which had been given the title *Black-Eyed Susan*. The trio spent much of the journey across the Atlantic working on the book. The Astaires had arrived six days earlier,[19] and when the English writer Fred Thompson arrived from London to collaborate with Bolton, all the parts were in place. Ira's agreement with the producers gave him 1 percent of the show's weekly gross,[20] but his experience with having his lyrics altered during the production of *Primrose* prompted a secondary agreement that gave him the first opportunity to revise, rewrite, or replace any lyrics deemed necessary if the show were to receive an English production. Even if another writer were hired for the job, and the cost would be deducted from Ira's royalties, he would be assured of no less than two-thirds of what he was owed under the original agreement.[21]

For the next month George and Ira labored on their songs, several of which were already in existence in embryonic form or more fully developed; additional themes came from George's stay in London, including a tune called "Syncopated City" that would become "Fascinating Rhythm," the show's most famous number.[22] After George played the theme, Ira "mulled it over for a while,"[23] listening intently "until I [knew] it by heart," but George's extensive use of syncopation made "versifying more difficult because of the broken rhythms." The use of the word "quiver" led to a rare, lengthy argument:[24]

> The rhyme scheme was a, b, c, d,—a, b, c, d. When I got to the 8th line I showed the lyric to George. His comment was that the 4th and 8th lines should have a double (or two syllable) rhyme where I had rhymed them with single syllables. I protested and by singing showed him that the last note in both lines had, to me, the same strength as the note preceding. To me the last two notes in these lines formed a spondee, and as the best one can do with spondees are near-rhymes, the easiest way out was arbitrarily to put the accent on the last note. But this George couldn't see, and so, on and off, we argued for days. Finally I had to capitulate and write the lines as they are today: 4th line: I'm all a-*quiv*er. / 8th line: —Just like a *fliv*ver, after George proved to me that I had better use the double rhyme, because, whereas in singing, the notes might be considered even, in conducting the music the downbeat came on the penultimate note.[25]

As he pondered the tune, the situation, and the appropriate words, Ira tried to keep all distractions at bay: "Working incommunicado, trying to solve the riddle of a lyric for a tune, I sometimes didn't get to bed until after sunrise. Even then the tune could be so persistent that it could keep running on through sleep, and was still with me at breakfast. And later in the day when I was about to tackle some other problem, it was capable of capricious intrusion with the threat of 'Write me up! Work on me now or you'll never get through!' "[26] He borrowed some of his ideas for the tune from his lyrics to "Little Rhythm, Go 'Way," a song he had written with William Daly and Joseph Meyer in 1923. He was certain of one thing: "You must plant one idea in the song and it should be in the title. Usually the public does not hear anything else anyway, unless it is a comedy song."[27]

While not convinced of the brilliance of "Fascinating Rhythm" as a title, "A,—it *did* sing smoothly, and B,—I couldn't think of a better."[28]

BLACK-EYED SUSAN, now renamed *Lady, Be Good!*, opened in Philadelphia in November 1924 and was an almost immediate success with audiences, even if the pace of the show needed to be quickened and some of the songs had to be replaced. The simple book gave the Astaires ample opportunities to dance, and the addition of comedian Walter Catlett and the popular entertainer Cliff ("Ukulele Ike") Edwards provided a wealth of ideas for songs that matched their onstage personalities. Fred Astaire recalled that on opening night, Alex Aarons "came around between the acts to say, 'This thing is a cinch. I just made a deal for six months with the ticket brokers in New York. We're sold out already.' "[29]

For the first time, Ira's lyrics met with full-throated approval in the press; they had a "decidedly humorous poesy" that "stamp[ed] them as the most distinctive words-to-music we have listened to in the longest time."[30] But he was not initially convinced of the show's quality. While he expected his share of the gross to earn him $90 on Thanksgiving alone ("not so bad"), he lamented that he had to spend ten days after opening night writing new songs and rewriting the verses and choruses of existing material.[31]

One number that was cut had been sung in Philadelphia by Adele Astaire "charmingly and to an appreciative hand" in the opening scene,[32] but "seemed to slow up the show," which Ira admitted was "really a dancing show":[33]

In the spring of 1924 when I finished the lyric to the body of a song— the words and tune of which I now cannot recall—a verse was in order. My brother composed a possibility we both liked, but I never got around to writing it up as a verse. It was a definite and insistent melody—so much so that we soon felt it wasn't light and introductory enough, as it tended to overshadow the refrain and to demand individual attention. So this overweighty strain, not quite in tune as a verse, was, with slight modification, upped in importance to the status of a refrain. I gave it a simple set of words, then it had to acquire its own verse; and "The Man I Love" resulted.[34]

The song continued its poor theatrical record. Cut from *Strike Up the Band* in 1927 and considered for *Rosalie* the following year, "The Man I Love" unexpectedly succeeded on its own after Lady Edwina Mountbatten popularized it in London. The number became one of the Gershwins' greatest popular successes.

After weeks of rehearsals and rewrites, with George constantly at the piano and Ira patiently sitting or pacing behind him, a pen poised in one hand and a cigarette in the other, *Lady, Be Good!* had been tightened to perfection. Two weeks of sold-out performances in Philadelphia proved to all concerned that the show "was no hackneyed ordinary musical comedy. It was slick and tongue in cheek, a definite departure in concept and design."[35] Ira's worries were quelled after he heard the rapturous applause of the opening night audience in New York City. Even with the competition of the latest edition of Irving Berlin's star-studded *Music Box Revue, Lady, Be Good!* was turning away customers on its second night.[36]

The critics were nearly unanimous: the show was "just about the best musical comedy in town."[37] Ira had accomplished what he been striving to do for years: match George's jazzy tunes with slangy lyrics that mirrored the American zeitgeist of freedom and celebration; *Lady, Be Good!* was the Jazz Age musical personified. Although delighted with the $300 royalty he received every week, Ira was "still not completely satisfied with [his] contribution." Yes, he had "adequately fitted some sparkling tunes, and several singable love songs and rhythm numbers had resulted," but he remained "a bit bothered by there being no lyric [he] considered comic."[38]

IRA LOOKED TO *Lady, Be Good!* as a portent of future artistic and financial success. Not long after the opening, plans were already being developed to return the Astaires to their adoring fans by taking the show to London.[39] The combination of the Gershwins' infectious songs and the performances and personalities of the Astaires and Ukulele Ike kept seats filled on Broadway for ten months; the result was a steady stream of sizable royalties. *Lady, Be Good!* was so successful that after five weeks of performances, the top ticket price was raised and a second production in Los Angeles brought in income that Ira never imagined possible.[40] Money also flowed his way from the sales of sheet music and recordings of the most popular numbers in the show, "Fascinating Rhythm," "So Am I," and "Oh, Lady Be Good!"

As the show continued its run, Ira's name began to appear more frequently in the press; it was proof of his arrival on the Broadway scene as a talent worthy of mention in the same circles as his attention-seeking brother. In fact, it was George himself who gave the public its first hints at Ira's personality and the quality of his work. "His tastes have always been literary," George told a New York newspaper. "He devotes nearly all his time to reading and writing." George made a case for an appropriate balance in the type of songs he and Ira were now writing: "If I am writing a comedy song I write to the lyric, giving the lyric full scope, because the lyric is *the important thing* in a comedy song."[41]

Posing in plus-fours with his friend and brother-in-law, Lou Paley, Belmar, New Jersey, ca. 1924.

WHEN Aarons and Freedley were unable to quickly develop a successor to *Lady, Be Good!*, Aarons's father Alfred leaped in to offer George and Ira the chance to write a musical comedy score for the popular Yiddish vaudevillian Lou Holtz. The elder Aarons, concerned about Ira's ability to turn out lyrics quickly, hired the more experienced Buddy DeSylva to help complete the score to meet the intended opening in Atlantic City in early April 1925. It was a wise decision; not only was DeSylva a friend, but he was the "most efficient lyric writer" Ira ever knew: "When I worked with him, we'd decide the title of a song and then he'd get a yellow pad and carefully print the title on the top. Then we'd suggest lines, and he'd write them in, saying 'That sounds OK' or 'That's pretty good'—and then when there was a change, he'd rub out a line and revise it. I never got over it: We would write the whole lyric on one piece of paper!"[42]

To duplicate the magic of *Lady, Be Good!*, Fred Thompson was signed to write the book with William K. Wells, who had written material for Lou Holtz in the *Scandals* revues. The result, which ran out of town as *My Fair Lady* (later to be renamed *Tell Me More*), was "just another mistaken-identities story of the girl-loves-boy-but-almost-loses-him-pretending-to-be-someone-she's-not," but Holtz's role as Monty Sipkin, a Jewish tailor at a fancy Fifth Avenue millinery shop, gave Ira and DeSylva spots for ethnic humor that were lacking in *Lady, Be Good!*[43] "Mr. and Mrs. Sipkin" and "In Sardinia" are replete with playful references—both ethnic and popular ("I smoke the best of Cubans, / My meals are all by Reuben's" and "For the country's not dry, / And the bread's full of rye")—that Ira found irresistible. While one critic felt that the show's lyrics "out-Wodehoused Wodehouse with 'spiritual' and 'hear it you will'" (in "Kickin' the Clouds Away"),[44] there was one number that drew near-universal ire. "In Sardinia" was DeSylva's idea for a comedy number in the style of Jerome Kern and Clifford Grey's "(On the Banks of) the Schnitza Komisski" from the 1920 musical *Sally*.[45] The critic for the *New York Times* hoped that the weak copy of Kern's song had "crept into the show without the authors' knowledge."[46]

Tell Me More debuted on Broadway in April 1925, one of four musicals that opened over the Easter holiday, including two new productions of Gilbert and Sullivan operettas. While it was close to house capacity in its opening week, the show never filled the balcony, and over the next two months, it floundered as the book was revised, the producer considered moving to a smaller theater, and weekly performances were reduced. The show closed in July, after one hundred performances. Ira's weekly share of the anemic box office was a far cry from what he had pulled in from *Lady, Be Good!*, and none of the numbers received much public attention.[47] A longer London production opened in May 1925 with a largely intact score, although the much-maligned "In Sardinia" was dropped in favor of Desmond Carter's clever "Murderous Monty (and Light-Fingered Jane)."

THE CLEAREST INDICATION that Ira was moving out of the shadow of his brother was the publication in the *New York Herald Tribune* of his opinions on the state of musical comedy lyrics and the place of the lyricist in the world of contemporary musical theater. When asked if a lyricist was "to write independently of the musical score and make the composer conform to his model," he replied that each show had "its own problems. . . . Sometimes the music and the lyrics are separate problems in themselves. Sometimes I have a good song before I see the book. If the manager wants the song, the author has to make a place for it in the book, or write a scene leading into it. Otherwise, the book leads up to the song, and if the composer has a tune for that spot the lyricist has to fit the words to the music." Ira noted that W. S. Gilbert "wrote all his lyrics first and was unhampered. That was the ideal way."

To the question of whether "the writer of musical comedy lyrics [was] supposed to vie with Byron and Shelley," he concluded that "there is little literary value to our present lyric. A good lyric should be rhymed conversation. When people read poetry they see it printed before them and can take their time studying it. But lyrics in musical comedy songs are hurled at them and they have no chance to rehear or reread them." The "chief value" of lyrics "lies in the ingenuity of the lyric writer in twisting a musical phrase into words with meaning or in simply making the title stick in the memory. Thought is important in the first place, but is reduced to small importance afterward." He emphasized that songs should be a single, organic unit: "the combination of words and music, rather than the words and music as separate entities."[48]

DURING THE SPRING and summer of 1925, with George again in Europe and subsequently preoccupied with his Concerto in F, Ira relaxed: "A few days at Copake [a New York village near the Massachusetts state line], a week-end at Belmar, a show, papers, magazines, rides, the Stadium Concerts, anything to get away from work." He had yet to become the completely sedentary man of later years: he walked through "Manhattan cathedrals and art galleries" and played tennis and golf to varying degrees of proficiency. But he saved most of his energy for gambling, in this case losing "at craps to a group of songwriters while visiting the home of Max Dreyfus."[49] His only credits during this period—interpolations in two short-lived musical comedies—were nothing more than "doggerel."[50]

WHILE IRA RELAXED, George worked on his piano concerto. During its composition, the brothers signed a deal with Aarons and Freedley for *Tip-Toes*, a new musical comedy with a topical but lighthearted book by Guy Bolton and Fred Thompson about a vaudeville act and the Florida real estate boom. The writing of the songs for *Tip-Toes* ran side by side with the completion of the Concerto in F, which had its premiere at Carnegie Hall on December 3, 1925. "We worked best under deadlines," Ira recalled, "and we worked mostly at night. I might have been home reading a book, when George returned from a party, and, depending on where we lived at the time, he would call me up or say to me, 'Let's get to work.' But first we would go [to] the kitchen and have ice cream and figure out what we had to do. George's mind and his notebooks were full of tunes. There were times when melodies would pour out so quickly and naturally that he would have several ideas in a day."[51]

After a four-city tryout, *Tip-Toes* opened shortly after Christmas 1925. To Ira's delight, the show "contained longer openings, many of the songs had crisp lines, and the first-act finale carried plot action for four or five minutes."[52] His imagination ran wild, and he delivered a wealth of good lines, some of which he would later exploit in more popular songs than those in *Tip-Toes*. The phrase "come to Papa," used to great effect in "Embraceable You" and embraced by his father as a reference to himself, originally appeared in "Nice Baby," while "When Do We Dance?" previewed the tongue-twisting "Tschaikowsky" of *Lady in the Dark* with its reference to

Ira with his sister Frankie and his parents
Rose and Morris, ca. 1924.

being "fed up with discussions / About the music of Russians." "Harlem
River Chanty," a cut number, was "an attempt at irony in a Prohibition Era
when bathtub gin and flavored alcohol flooded the country, and pocket-
flask manufacture was at its peak."[53] With lines like "Yo, ho, ho, / And a
bottle of milk shake!" and "Yo, ho, ho, / And celery tonic!" Ira played with
the dreary alternatives to alcohol in one of his "happiest [sets] of guying
verses."[54] He was pleased when his portmanteau phrase "sweet and low-
down"—rescued from the line "He's the John McCormack of sweet and
low-down" in Cliff Edwards's discarded specialty number "Singin' Pete"
from *Lady, Be Good!*—was later included in a thesaurus of slang.[55] Decades

later, Babette Deutsch's *Poetry Handbook* revealed a rhyme classification in another *Tip-Toes* song of which Ira was unaware at the time: "apocopated rhyme, so called because the end of one rhyming word is cut off."[56] That he had rhymed "way" with "saying" in "Looking for a Boy" "titillated" him: "I now feel one with Moliere's M. Jourdain the day he learned he'd been speaking prose for over forty years."[57]

Tip-Toes stood out from the other holiday openings of the 1925 Christmas season and ran for 194 performances before closing in June; the London production, which opened the following summer, almost equaled that number.[58] It was a breakthrough that proved that Ira could support himself with the work of his pen; the two productions brought him a weekly royalty of nearly $250, which, along with the popularity of several of the show's songs and the continuing flow of money from *Lady, Be Good!*, boosted his income for 1925 to nearly $26,000 (approximately $375,000 today).[59]

The critics were kind to Ira's work; one visualized him as having been "born with a morocco rhyming dictionary" in his mouth,[60] while Alexander Woollcott, the often acerbic critic for the *New York World*, was pleased by Ira's "determination" to rhyme "enjoy it" with "Detroit" in "These Charming People."[61] As he grew as a lyricist, Ira considered that one good indication of success would be the creation of a successful comedy song in the style of P. G. Wodehouse's "Bongo in the Congo" (music by Jerome Kern) from the 1924 musical *Sitting Pretty.* "These Charming People" proved to be that number, as it "seemed to amuse the audience" as well as the critics.[62] No other lyric in *Tip-Toes* received more plaudits—its "cleverness" was "not superficial"—and Ira's work in sum invited comparisons to his idol as "the best disclosed in any musical comedy here since the Kern-Bolton-Wodehouse combination dissolved."[63]

It was a source of great pride for Ira to have his name mentioned in the same breath as that of Wodehouse, whom he had admired for many years; he said that "it was only when P. G. Wodehouse began writing for Kern and the Princess [Theatre] that the critics realized that here were lyrics worthy of attention."[64] Ira was particularly enamored of the original lyrics to Wodehouse's most famous song, "Bill," which had first appeared in the 1917 musical *Oh, Lady, Lady!!* George had brought home a copy of the sheet music, and Ira "remembered [the lyrics] by heart," including the couplet, "A motor car / He cannot steer / And it seems clear / Whenever he dances, / His partner takes chances," a line that the prolific Wodehouse did not recall having written.[65]

With *Tip-Toes*, Ira "chose to believe there had been some development in craftsmanship," but his modesty was belied by his growing reputation among his peers.[66] An expression of admiration came from one of his fellow practitioners, Lorenz Hart, who sent him a letter praising his *Tip-Toes* lyrics: "I have heard none so good this many a day. . . . Such delicacies as your jingles prove that songs can be both popular and intelligent."[67] Ira's typically muted response to Hart's encomium? It was "very decent of him."[68]

CHAPTER 5

I N FEBRUARY 1926, George was once again in London, and Ira sent him an update on what he was—and was not—missing. Money was "scarce since all those [road] companies closed on us." No producers were "sending around for contracts—in fact, if it weren't for Frances and Arthur incessantly pounding on the pianos, 316 [West 103rd Street—the new Gershwin family residence] would be as peaceful as a country house." Ira hoped that George was "preparing lots of stuff for the fall season" and that *Lady, Be Good!* would go over well in London. He was full of ideas for the show and concerned about the performances, asking George to be vigilant that William Kent—cast in the comedic role of the lawyer Watty Watkins—sing "Oh, Lady Be Good!" in its original lively but graceful tempo, rather than at the faster speed taken by Walter Catlett. (Kent's recording of the song indicates that he largely did.) He asked if "Something About Love"—an early song written by George and Lou Paley—had been added and recommended that if "Fred and Adele want a *very* peppy number instead of the Charleston," George should give them the rejected song "Life's Too Short to Be Blue."[1]

He went on to say that George's show *Song of the Flame* (lyrics by Otto Harbach and Oscar Hammerstein II) was "a little off, but so is everything else in town the reasons ascribed being, 1. Lent, 2. the recent break in the market, 3. income tax. One thing show business never lacks is reasons for poor business." Other than agreeing to meet with the writer Jack McGowan about a musicalized version of his play *Mama Loves Papa,* Ira had done little, "which I do so well when I haven't a contract." His primary focus upon

George's return was to find "good titles and ideas" for songs they could write together; the new house would "be a good place to work in this Summer. If you want to go away for a week or two, that'll be all right, but I'm sure if you cut out parties you will get more work done here than anywhere else."[2]

IN CONTRAST TO his attractive-to-the-opposite-sex brother, Ira Gershwin was a wallflower. Although he was always a natty dresser, he sported a less-than-imposing physique and manner: "The combination of a five-foot-six structure that weighs 175 pounds, wears glasses and is somewhat bald on top doesn't tend to bring out the wolf in women."[3] He was also not given to open displays of emotion and affection, traits he shared with his mother, who remained the predominant female figure in his life until he was nearly thirty years old.

Ira was a combination of the personalities of both of his parents, at times mirroring his father's casual, playful attitude to life, then sliding into his mother's emotional absence. The latter became more prevalent after George became a celebrity and their mother focused her love almost entirely on him, leaving Ira and his other siblings to grab what crumbs they could from her. Rose's coldness toward Ira influenced his withdrawal into the inner world of his mind.

Thus, Ira's announcement that he was stepping out with Emily Paley's sister Leonore Strunsky came as a surprise to his family and many of his friends, who thought Ira was, at best, indifferent to feminine charms. Although Ira had known her for more than five years, Lee (her preferred diminutive) had been a peripheral figure in the Gershwin/Paley ménage to this point, overshadowed by the love and admiration expressed for her older sister. Lee had a keen interest in fashion and art, studied at the Art Students League of New York after high school, and spent seven months on a grand tour of Europe in the early 1920s.[4]

On the surface, a woman who dated college men who were attracted to her flapper persona would not seem to be the type who would appeal to a man with intellectual pretensions. But if Rose Eisen was the type who appealed to Ira when he was struggling to find his voice as a writer, he now had a growing reputation as a Broadway lyricist and wit. And Lee Strunsky

Ira with Leonore (Lee) Strunsky and her sister Emily Paley, ca. 1925.

was a *different* woman, blessed with a personal flair that proved irresistible. Her intelligence—often concealed by a verbal cloak of "somewhat effusive and disarming colloquialisms" like "darling," "smashing," and "marvy"— acted as a barrier to some, while her penchant for saying exactly what was on her mind offended others.[5] Her "effective rhetoric" and the power of an "assertive woman" were traits she had learned at the feet of her mother, the formidable Mascha Strunsky.[6]

As Ira returned more often to the Atlantic Hotel, one of the Strunsky properties on the New Jersey shore, he and Lee became closer, even if he was oblivious to her thoughts regarding their potential future. In the summer of 1925, Lee was engaged to be married, but it has been suggested that she was left at the altar or had found her fiancé *in flagrante delicto* with another woman.[7] Whether this deception was the catalyst for Lee's turning toward Ira is uncertain, but it is clear that once she trained her sights on him, she became the pursuer, as evidenced by a calling card Ira kept in his papers until his death: "Miss Leonore Strunsky at home 12 to 12—always."[8] To Ira, Lee was a figure who had stepped out of an F. Scott Fitzgerald novel into his rather sheltered life. He was smitten, but she took the initiative and persuaded Ira to marry her.

THE DEVELOPMENT OF their relationship took place amid work on songs for the new Aarons and Freedley show that was to star the popular English actress Gertrude Lawrence. The story about bootleggers by Guy Bolton and P. G. Wodehouse went through a trio of titles before becoming *Oh, Kay!* to highlight the given name of Lawrence's character. The chorus of "Do, Do, Do," one of the first songs written after George's return from England, was completed in half an hour shortly before dinner one night at the Gershwin house on 103rd Street, while the family was awaiting Lee's arrival from her parents' home on Eighth Street. George liked how Ira had presented the "jingly possibilities" of the title phrase and "done, done, done."[9] Three decades later, in the midst of the civil rights movement and actress Pearl Bailey's insistence that actors in the film version of *Porgy and Bess* refrain from using the dialect of the opera's original lyrics, Ira hesitated to acknowledge that his inspiration for the "do, do, do / done, done, done" combination had come from his reading of Black performers and poets.[10]

Many of the new songs were tried out on friends and family during stays on the Jersey shore. Ira's lyrics to "Clap Yo' Hands" caused Irving Caesar's brother Arthur—himself a lyricist—to question the line "On the sands of time you are only a pebble." A dozen of Ira's friends grabbed hold of Caesar, "rushed across the street to the beach, and in a few seconds proved that there were pebbles on the sands, so the line did not have to be deleted."[11]

The score was well underway when, on an early morning in late July, Ira, suffering from severe abdominal pains, was rushed to Mount Sinai Hospital. A sizable down payment was demanded at the admitting desk; Ira, too distressed to write a check, was saved by Lee, who slapped her three-carat diamond engagement ring on the counter and said, "Take this!"[12] Acute appendicitis was diagnosed in the emergency room and Ira was quickly wheeled into the operating theater for a 2½-hour surgery to remove what turned out to be a gangrenous appendix.

After six weeks of frustrating hospital recuperation, he persuaded his doctors that he be discharged to finish his work on *Oh, Kay!* Once home, he remained weakened and struggled to get anything done before the afternoon. With rehearsals fast approaching and his ability to concentrate diminished by the incessant pain from what would eventually be six additional weeks of wound drainage, Ira realized that he needed assistance.[13] Another member of the Paley ménage, the promising lyricist Howard Dietz, appeared on the scene to offer his services. Dietz recalled a discussion about asking P. G. Wodehouse to help finish the work, but George thought that Dietz was a better choice: he was largely unknown as a lyricist and would not need to be paid as much as the Englishman.[14] Dietz's name appears on "Heaven on Earth" and the title song, although he was also responsible for the title of the biggest hit of the show, "Someone to Watch Over Me."[15]

WHILE WORKING ON *Oh, Kay!*, George and Ira received a request from producer Richard Herndon for numbers he could use for his new revue. The intimate *Americana*, by writer J. P. McEvoy, borrowed its title from H. L. Mencken's column in the *American Mercury*; like Mencken, McEvoy's sketches skewered American institutions: "the radio, Hollywood films, the tabloids and Rotarian after-dinner speakers."[16] Ira contributed three songs to *Americana*, including "That Lost Barber Shop Chord," a production number written with George, whose "portmanteau title" was derived from composer Arthur Sullivan's setting of the Adelaide Proctor poem "A Lost Chord" and the popular 1910 song "Play That Barber Shop Chord," a ragtime number often performed by Bert Williams, the African American star of the *Ziegfeld Follies*.[17] While it was called a "wonderfully beautiful" number by one critic, it "got lost pronto 11:15 p.m. closing night."[18]

The other two songs—"Sunny Disposish" and "Blowin' the Blues Away"—were written with Philip Charig (1902–1960) and appear to have been done while George was in London earlier in the year.[19] Charig, a regular at the Paley get-togethers and at the Strunsky hotel in Belmar, had been the rehearsal pianist for *Lady, Be Good!* "Sunny Disposish" is notable for Ira's first use of clipped final syllables in his lyrics, a device that he had heard the actor Walter Catlett use to humorous effect in his routines in *Lady, Be Good!*[20]:

> It's absolutely most ridic',
> Positively sil'.

The song made an impression on the writer John O'Hara, who has the protagonist of his 1934 novel *Appointment in Samarra* play bandleader Jean Goldkette's popular 1927 Victor recording, featuring the legendary cornetist Bix Beiderbecke, while drinking "his way to self-destruction."[21] Well-received by critics and audiences alike, *Americana* ran on Broadway through February 1927 before going on the road.[22]

IT WAS DURING this time, when Ira—distracted by pain and impending deadlines, and feeling so low that he wanted someone to look after him—agreed to set a date for his wedding. Since he could not leave the house for any extended period, his bride-to-be bought her own $12 gold wedding ring.[23] On September 14, 1926, in the midst of rehearsals for *Oh, Kay!*, Ira and Lee were married. George acted as Ira's best man during the ceremony, which was attended by a small group of family and friends who watched as the couple stood under the traditional Jewish marriage canopy.[24] With work still to be done on the show, and Ira still in recovery from his surgery, the newlyweds had no formal honeymoon and spent many of their first days in Philadelphia for the out-of-town opening in mid-October.

Ira's "intelligent and lilting" lyrics were an important reason for the success of *Oh, Kay!*, although as with any other show, the version Philadelphia audiences reacted enthusiastically to was not the same as that seen when the musical comedy debuted on Broadway.[25] *Oh, Kay!* was an immediate critical and financial success. The *Daily News* suggested that Ira's lyrics were "sustaining the family reputation,"[26] but it is unclear how audible they were to audiences, as "the big orchestra, with its two pianos, was inclined to throw up a wall which the voices of the singers found hard to clamber over."[27] The praise was not universal: in the *New Yorker*, Charles Brackett—whom Ira would later encounter in Hollywood—complained that all the lyrics in musicals sounded "as though they'd been put in so the singers could have something to use until somebody thought up what the real words should be."[28] But audiences loved the show and filled the house to capacity for five months, with the weekly gross lagging only behind Ziegfeld's lavish *Rio Rita* and the latest edition of *George White's Scandals*. When *Oh, Kay!* closed in June 1927, its 256 performances were the most of any production Ira had yet been involved in.[29] "Heaven on Earth," "Clap

Yo' Hands," "Do, Do, Do," "Maybe," and "Someone to Watch Over Me"
became popular through recordings and sheet music and helped Ira to earn
more than $30,000 during 1926.[30]

WHILE GEORGE SPENT the early months of 1927 vacationing and con-
certizing, Ira adjusted to being a married man. Having spent his first
three decades surrounded by family, and an innocent to many of the ways
of the world, would he change now that he was sharing his life with an
independent-minded wife? One easily resolved question was their residence, since for Lee moving into the sixteen-room white stone house on
103rd Street with Ira and the rest of the Gershwin family seemed entirely
natural.[31]

The year 1927 was "the height of Broadway's glory years—a time when
nightlife was at its gaudiest, materialism was running riot, the talkies
were just arriving, and skyscrapers were soaring ever upward in relentless
profusion—a time when the American theatre was at its most varied and
abundant."[32] Ira Gershwin played a part in that wonderful year, but his most
significant work was written for a show that died out of town. The previous
summer, producer Edgar Selwyn, who had promised to put together a show
for George if he could "find . . . a book that's entirely different from anything" he had seen before, stuck to his word.[33] The Gershwins and George
S. Kaufman conceived the idea for *Strike Up the Band*, a new style of show
that moved beyond standard musical comedy routines and boy-meets-girl,
boy-loses-girl plots; a book filled with barbed attacks on American political institutions and war profiteering accompanied by music and lyrics in
the style of Gilbert and Sullivan.[34] To Ira, the idea was thrilling; he could
parody his idol and explore lyrical forms and styles he had yet to try. Not
only would his words be on an equal footing to the music, but they could
move the plot along and enrich the personalities of the characters.

He eagerly got down to work, but the complicated book and score
delayed production until the spring of 1927, by which time George and Ira
had committed themselves to another Aarons and Freedley show. In search
of peace and quiet to concentrate on both projects, a summer retreat was
found at Chumleigh Farm in Ossining, New York, a bucolic getaway less
than an hour north of midtown Manhattan. But their plans for isolation

The married couple: Ira and Lee at Chumleigh Farm, Ossining, New York, during the writing of the first version of *Strike Up the Band*, spring 1927.

were shared by their friends, who also sought to escape from Manhattan. When they needed to get away from unexpected company, Ira retired to an upstairs suite in the main house, while George drove back to the city. Ira did not share his brother's enjoyment in driving; it did not take long for him to discover that the dangerous streets of New York City made him nervous. Fearing the continuation of the rude looks he received from other drivers for his lack of skill, he never sat behind the wheel again.[35]

The almost-daily demand to be in town for meetings and rehearsals caused them to give up the Ossining lease in early summer and return to the sweltering city.[36] By August, not only were they writing for the Selwyn and Aarons and Freedley shows, but they were marking their calendars to begin work on a Ziegfeld extravaganza to star Marilyn Miller.[37]

Strike Up the Band debuted in New Jersey in August 1927 to confused audiences and questions from critics about the show's viability. The authors had "attempted the impossible and got away with it. . . . That it will be a commercial success is doubtful, but it will unquestionably have a *succes d'estime*." Ira's lyrics were filled with "good-humored kidding" but were also "mordant, bitter, and stinging."[38] Kaufman, however, was horrified: after seeing Act I, he quickly returned to Manhattan to write a new second act.[39] A week later, the show moved to Philadelphia, still in need of work, but with critical unanimity about the lyrics: one critic said that "the versification . . . is clever and in intellectuality a grade or two above the average, yet not so elevated that none but the highbrows may enjoy it,"[40] while a second thought that Ira "exhibited a sensitiveness to the communal needs of words and music that is met with not too frequently."[41] His work was acclaimed as "a climax of very definite attainment" that began with *Lady, Be Good!*[42]

On Labor Day, Kaufman arrived for the first Philadelphia performance. Still unhappy, he "scurried back to New York without seeing" his worried producer.[43] One night toward the end of the run, Kaufman, George, and Ira—all three visibly disconsolate—stood outside the Shubert Theatre, watching a trickle of patrons enter the building. When they spotted two men, dressed as elegantly as any Edwardian Englishmen, Ira laughed sadly and remarked, "That must be Gilbert and Sullivan coming to fix the show," to which Kaufman acidly replied, "Why don't you put jokes like that in your lyrics?"[44] To an America enjoying the fruits of a wild decade and uninterested in recalling the war, *Strike Up the Band* struck too close to home; with audiences scarce and funds low, Selwyn pulled the plug after just two weeks.[45] Although the creators continued to tinker, hoping to bring the show back with a new cast, for now *Strike Up the Band* remained dormant.[46]

Harms, in anticipation of a hit, published five songs from the show under the New World Music imprint created earlier in the year by Max and Louis Dreyfus and George. But due to the out-of-town closure, few of the lyrics Ira had struggled mightily to make distinctive were ever heard. Despite the failure of *Strike Up the Band* to find an audience, Ira was certain that he had done his best work to date.

His lyrics combined an authentic American patriotism with an uncharacteristic cynicism sourced from Kaufman's dialogue, and the extended scenes that were crucial to the plot were filled with a playful combination of Gilbert comic opera, American slang, and topical and historical references. "Typical Self-Made American," a parody of Gilbert's "He Is an Englishman" from *H.M.S. Pinafore*, is given a patriotic, get-up-and-go twist via references to Horatio Alger and the Masons, Elks, and Woodmen. "Fletcher's American Cheese Choral Society," the impressive opening number, favorably compares the value the American public gets from Fletcher's product with that of "Listerine and Woolworth, / Lux and B.V.D.s" and parodies the health food fad already in vogue (George Gershwin being an early adoptee of then-odd eating habits), with "wheat cakes for breakfast, / cornflakes and lots of bran!"

If *STRIKE UP THE BAND* WAS new territory, then the reunion with the Astaires was a return to familiar ground. *Funny Face* began life as *Smarty*, a jokey book about jewel thieves by Fred Thompson and the Algonquin Round Table humorist Robert Benchley, who dropped out after the Philadelphia opening when his pride was wounded by a critic who pointed out the irony of Benchley, having taken potshots at the successful comedy *Abie's Irish Rose*, being credited with a clichéd plot about a stolen necklace. The final book (credited to Thompson and Paul Gerard Smith) was merely a prop for the score and the talented cast.[47] Through further stops in Washington, DC, and Atlantic City, the creators "worked day and night, recasting, rewriting, rehearsing, recriminating—of rejoicing, there was none."[48]

But the extensive work paid off, and when *Funny Face* debuted on Broadway on the day after Thanksgiving at the brand-new Alvin Theatre, everyone was pleased. Even in the face of stiff competition from Rodgers and Hart's *A Connecticut Yankee* and the long-running Vincent Youmans musical comedy *Hit the Deck*, *Funny Face* ran at capacity for nearly four months. Hints of an economic downturn brought an end after 244 performances, putting it just shy of *Oh, Kay!* A London production opened in the fall of 1928, with the Astaires reprising their starring roles, and continued until the following summer, giving Ira another steady source of income, even if he had to chuckle at yet another critic who referred to him as George's *sister*.[49]

Of the astonishing ten numbers from the show that were published, two stand out in Ira's oeuvre. In "'S Wonderful," Ira elongated the effect of the sound he had tentatively used in "Sunny Disposish":

Don't mind telling you
In my humble fash
That you thrill me through
With a tender pash.
When you said you care,
'Magine my emosh;
I swore, then and there,
Permanent devosh.

And by the deletion of the first two letters of "it's" and the "slurring [of] the leftover 's' with the first syllable of the following word,"[50] as in

'S wonderful! 'S marvelous!

and

'S awful nice! 'S paradise!

he created enduring catchphrases that Dorothy Parker used in her 1928 *New Yorker* short story "The Mantle of Whistler."[51] Ira felt so strongly about the proper singing of these lyrics that he condemned lazy vocalists who insisted that the line was "*It's* Wonderful" into "that inferno where singers go."[52]

The second number, the comedic duet "The Babbitt and the Bromide," went into the show during the run in Wilmington, Delaware, "when the audience," said Lee Gershwin, "consisted of no more than two hundred—mostly pretty and young and pregnant Du Pont matrons." The lyric was inspired by humorist Gelett Burgess's short book *Are You a Bromide?* (1906) and by hearing actor William Kent say "Heigh ho, that's life!"[53] "The Babbitt and the Bromide" made its first appearance late in the second act after Fred and Adele had exchanged platitudes as two "solid citizens" of the United States:

Hello! How are you?
Howza folks? What's new?'
I'm great! That's good!
Ha! Ha! Knock wood!

Well! Well! What say?
Howya been? Nice day!
How's tricks? What's new?
That's fine! How are you?

The number ended "to show-stopping applause" with the siblings chasing each other around the stage—their popular routine known as a "runaround."[54] A few years later, the lyric to "The Babbitt and the Bromide" was included in Louis Kronenberger's *An Anthology of Light Verse*, and Ira was amused to find his name in the index between those of John Gay and his idol W. S. Gilbert: "No kidding. . . ."[55]

CHAPTER 6

W HILE WORKING ON *ROSALIE*, a lavish musical for the impresario Florenz Ziegfeld, George pondered an extended trip to Europe in which he would absorb European musical influences as he developed a new concert work. Ira and Lee were eager to join him. But for the moment, the brothers continued to struggle to meet Ziegfeld's demands in the brief time allotted to them. So much material was needed for the show that in the end, two composers—George and Sigmund Romberg—were paired with two lyricists, Ira and P. G. Wodehouse.[1] Although most of their work was done individually—only three lyrics were credited to both men—Ira and Wodehouse enjoyed their exchange of ideas and having their meals together in a hotel suite.

Ira never forgot the Englishman's behavior on opening night in Boston. The first act finally ended at 10:40 p.m., and shortly after intermission, while Ira struggled to get any sense of the performance beyond the applause and the laughter, he felt Wodehouse's hand on his shoulder. Pulling out a large Ingersoll pocket watch, Plum (Wodehouse's nickname) pointed out that it was eleven o'clock and he had to go to bed. Nothing could keep him from being on the streets by 6 a.m. to check out the bookstalls.[2] On the final day of the out-of-town run, a grateful Wodehouse presented Ira with a copy of his collection of short stories, *Carry On, Jeeves*, to commemorate their work together. It was the beginning of a friendship that was conducted entirely in correspondence—overwhelmingly from Wodehouse, although Ira managed to send off a yearly bottle of champagne at Christmas.

Rosalie, Ziegfeld's third major musical of the season, following the latest edition of the *Ziegfeld Follies* and *Show Boat*, debuted in January 1928.

Although the lavish show ran for 335 performances, it was only at half capacity for much of its run, and Ziegfeld, unhappy with the quality of the Gershwins' efforts, pleaded with them—to no avail—to write a hit for him before their departure for Europe.[3] Harms, hoping for big sheet music sales from the combination of the Gershwins, Romberg, and Wodehouse, published nine Gershwin numbers from *Rosalie*, but the mediocrity of the score, including Ira's lyrics, is clear: the most popular song, "How Long Has This Been Going On?," was a reject from *Funny Face*.

WHILE GEORGE SPENT February in Florida, Ira prepared for Europe. In the process of applying for his first passport, he acquired a copy of his birth certificate and was surprised to discover that, contrary to family tradition and everything he had ever known or been told, his first name was not Isidore, but Israel. He later said that he might have kept that name had he known about it earlier.[4]

Ira was eager to see London and its many shops, filled with "the stylish clothes and accoutrements that he had spent his life fancying." There was little else to do, as "other than his interest in *That's a Good Girl*, a British musical starring Jack Buchanan to which he had contributed a number of lyrics, Ira was without a show to keep himself occupied." Perhaps feeling guilty about this inactivity, he purchased a journal to record the details of the journey.[5] The contents of this journal parallel his diary entries from a decade earlier; little had changed since he wrote, "How the world will benefit by this statement of various nourishing ingredients entering me this day, I know not."[6]

On March 10, 1928, George, Ira, Lee, and Frankie (a last-minute addition) left New York Harbor aboard the luxurious RMS *Majestic* of the White Star Line. Ira and Lee settled into their first-class B-deck stateroom for the six-day journey across the Atlantic. After a largely uneventful passage of dining, lounging on the deck, playing shuffleboard and card games, being entertained by George at the piano in the lounge, and having relaxing conversations with some of the one thousand passengers, they arrived in Southampton, England. After clearing customs, they boarded the boat train for the journey to London. Waiting for them at Waterloo Station was a chauffeured Daimler, which took the quartet to the elegant May Fair

Hotel. The first thing Ira noticed as they ventured out was the unexpected absence of fog.[7]

Over the next ten days, they journeyed about the city—collectively and individually—including a section that reminded Ira of the Lower East Side: "In Whitechapel saw an old Jew sitting on a pushcart being pulled by a young man, probably his grandson. But nowhere the crowded dirty Ghetto that is Orchard Street on a busy afternoon." There were drinks, food, and talk with people he knew—the Russian-born composer Vernon Duke and the writer Guy Bolton—as well as new acquaintances like lyricist Desmond Carter, with whom he was "quite tickled." A visit to the offices of Chappell, the English subsidiary of George and Ira's American publishers, where they met Jerome Kern, Vincent Youmans, and Robert Russell Bennett, became an unlikely London reunion of Max Dreyfus's notable roster of composers and lyricists.[8]

Ira spent much of his time writing copious notes about his consumption of food and alcohol, the latter providing a stark contrast to Prohibition-era Manhattan. He indulged his Beau Brummel side by purchasing several bespoke suits, as well as accoutrements from long-established tailors and haberdashers. To quote Noël Coward, he savored "to the full the sensation of being well-dressed for the first time."[9]

Naturally, he spent many nights at the theater, watching the "frivolous" comedy *Good Morning Bill!* by P. G. Wodehouse; the almost entirely rescored Rodgers and Hart musical *The Girl Friend* ("charm lacking"); Noël Coward's revue *This Year of Grace!* ("a great production for one man to do"); the thriller *A Man with Red Hair,* starring the "superb" Charles Laughton; and the final London performance of *Oh, Kay!,* where he sported his new white tie. Although told that the quality of the show had suffered, "it came as an agreeable surprise to find we rather liked it . . . although Gertie *did* clown too much."[10]

On March 19, the quartet plus the Pittsburgh-born lyricist Leo Robin— part of the Gershwin contingent on the *Majestic*—traveled to the London suburb of Lewisham for the opening night of what was intended to be the final pre-London run of *That's a Good Girl,* "a lively peppy show which is full of laughs." When the visiting group went backstage, Ira told the show's star and producer, the debonair Jack Buchanan, that he expected the show's success would mean that he would not see him in New York for two years.[11]

That's a Good Girl ran successfully in London until the spring of 1929, then toured through the provinces. Ira's participation was the result of the heavy schedules of Jerome Kern and Oscar Hammerstein II, who were far too busy with *Show Boat* to be bothered with this minor vehicle.[12] Max Dreyfus called in Ira, Phil Charig, and Joseph Meyer to provide songs for a book by English playwright and lyricist Douglas Furber about a female detective and the man she pursues and with whom she eventually falls in love. Meyer (1894–1987) had hits in the early 1920s with "California, Here I Come" and "If You Knew Susie," while Furber (1885–1961) had seen success with the songs "The Bells of St. Mary's" (1917) and "Limehouse Blues" (1924).

Four of Ira's six songs—"Let Yourself Go," "The One I'm Looking For," "Sweet So-and-So," and "Chirp-Chirp!"—were published in the United Kingdom, but the first three lyrics were modified by Furber as the show moved into rehearsals.[13] Furber also added "a line here and there," a fact that did not bother Ira because he knew he was not going to be available to make the changes himself.[14] But his attitude changed (his contemporaneous notes on the subject are less forgiving), when Ira was told that Furber had said, "Gershwin? Yes, clever boy and all that, but what a cinch, what a cinch!" in reference to Ira's receiving a 0.75 percent royalty[15] while "not having had to go through with rehearsals, etc." Although Ira acknowledged that Furber wrote as many lyrics for *That's a Good Girl* as he had, "he is a bit of a hog, Phil thinks, and I heartily concur, as he put his name (first) on three of my songs, and will collect on them, when all he did was change a few lines, not for the better either, and put in a couple of lousy rhymes like 'has been' and 'jazz queen.' Not that it really matters dear, dear, diary, as I never can raise any rancor against those who I think have done me dirt."[16]

GEORGE WAS EAGER to move on from London, and Ira—although he wanted to linger—as usual followed his brother's lead. A train took the group to the English port city of Dover, where they transferred to a cross-Channel steamer. Another train brought them from Calais through the French countryside to Paris, where they were met by friends who accompanied them to the Hotel Majestic before they wandered off to "see the whole world pass by" at the Café de la Paix.[17]

In the days to come, Ira strolled through the Champs-Élysées, gazed at the treasures in the Louvre, the Luxembourg Gardens, and Versailles, and noted his gastronomic exploits at both renowned and out-of-the-way places. He "alternately giggled and squirmed" through the "at times almost unbelievably bad" Paris prémiere of *Rhapsody in Blue*, but noted that "the middle theme couldn't be spoiled of course and came like a violet ray on a bald spot. And yet I realized that since probably ninety-five percent of the audience had never heard it before, they might take the occasional sour notes as a true reading and find it all interesting. Sure enough, at its conclusion that was real spontaneous applause all over the house and lots of cheers and bravos."[18]

A visit to the Eiffel Tower was a rare moment spent solely in the company of his brother:

> There was quite a line, but we joined it, and in fifteen minutes were in the elevator along with some fifty others, all French excepting for about a dozen Germans, and an English tutor with two boys. It was eight francs apiece to *le sommet*. At the second landing, we changed to another elevator, then a few hundred feet higher to a third, which took us to the top. I had never been so high up in a structure (twenty-two stories or so was my highest in New York) and it was terrific. I was afraid to walk the few feet to the railing, but finally did. George complained of peculiar sensations in his stomach and other portions. The view of course is magnificent. We walked around kidding one another, but really greatly impressed. After five minutes or so, we took it more casually and leaned over the railings. I must say the other visitors seemed to take it very naturally, one couple making love, the girl giving the man what we called as kids, 'feels.' George had a caricature made for twenty-five francs—not bad. Then down in the elevator to the second landing, from which we decided to walk. It was twenty-six flights down to the first landing, and twelve down from there—thirty-eight in all, and boy how my legs trembled when we finally got to the street. It took me three blocks' walking to get them straightened out.[19]

Time passed too quickly, and Ira regretted his departure from the "beautiful, deserted, mauve" city.[20] Frankie remained in Paris after unexpectedly being hired to appear in Cole Porter's *La Revue des Ambassadeurs*. During the next two weeks in Berlin and Vienna, the trio was joined by Lee's friend Henrietta Malkiel, a journalist for *Vanity Fair*. As in Paris, Ira's days were occupied by sightseeing while George entertained friends and colleagues between bouts of working on his new concert piece, which would become *An American in Paris*. The Hungarian composer Emmerich Kálmán acted as their host in Vienna and gave a lunch in George's honor at the celebrated Café Sacher, complete with a local jazz band that played *Rhapsody in Blue*.[21] Ira compared Kálmán's elaborate lifestyle to his own, estimating that it would cost three times as much money to live that way in Manhattan; he also noted with amusement the playwright Ferenc Molnár's explanation that the digestive pills he took after the meal aided in the process of "movement staccato and movement accelerando."[22] Evenings were spent at restaurants and the theater, including a performance of *Die Reise Benjamins des Dritten*, "a musical comedy in Yiddish, a show which is remarkably good, at times sensational in the direction, and all times in the acting."[23]

George, having heard a complaint to the management from a woman

Ira (*far left*) with Lee, George, composer Emmerich Kálmán,
and others, at the Café Sacher, Vienna, Austria, April 28, 1928.

whose suite was underneath his "that someone was continually at the piano
at most unearthly hours," and wanting to be on hand for Frankie's debut,
returned to Paris, while Ira, Lee, and Henrietta Malkiel opted for a leisurely
cruise down the Danube to Budapest, Hungary.[24] Lee was not as eager to
see Frankie as she was to see the sights, but to Ira, the scenic journey was
little more than a checklist of towns from the pages of his *Baedaker*. Upon
their arrival, the trio were transported to a riverside hotel in a horse-drawn
carriage. Albert Sirmay, a native Hungarian who was a music editor at the
New York office of the Gershwins' publisher, hoped to be their guide, but
the trip was cut short when Lee became ill, and the trio returned to Vienna
via train.[25] Since they could not get back to Paris in time for Frankie's
opening, Ira booked tickets on the Vienna-Cannes express, which traveled through the Alps, across an "architecturally and sartorially rather run
down" Italy, before arriving at the "much more substantial and lovely"
French Riviera, where they spent the next eleven days:

> The bathing. The sunning with coconut oil over all parts exposed.
> The chocolate for breakfast—the walk after breakfast to the beach
> or through the pines—the sunburn—lunch—the girls go to Juan
> Les Pins or Cannes to shop—the beach again in bathing suits if
> the weather is warm or in mufti if it isn't—dinner—coffee in the
> lounge—the sitting there for an hour or so after coffee—everybody
> rather reserved—a few small children seen in the daytime—no very
> young people in evidence—a few new faces every day furnish about
> all the interest required—to the room about ten-thirty. Hearts for an
> hour. To bed with a book or magazine.[26]

A small, chauffeured Renault took them along the Mediterranean coast,
then north through French towns and countryside back to Paris, where
they found that George had made progress on *An American in Paris*, but
that Frankie had departed from the Porter revue: the producers were more
interested in visuals and "practically nothing could be heard above the
dishes." Ira was glad to settle down again, and while George continued
his "usual round of parties," Ira enjoyed "the *Times*, *Life*, *Judge*, the *New
Yorker*, the *Boulevardier*, and two issues of *Variety*" that were waiting for
him at the American Express office. The second go-round in Paris was

much like the first: three weeks of eating, drinking, entertainment, and seeing friends. The Paris premiere of the Concerto in F was an "enormous success," but Ira felt that the Russian-born pianist Dimitri Tiomkin "might have been better. Of course having heard George play it so often, Tiomkin suffers greatly by comparison." Two days after the concert, the brothers were the guests of honor at an elaborate event that was "a mixture of Mayfair, the Rialto, and Left Bank." Among the two hundred people George and Ira hobnobbed with were actress Beatrice Lillie, composer Deems Taylor, architect Ernő Goldfinger, composer and teacher Nadia Boulanger, composer and arranger Robert Russell Bennett, the artist Man Ray, Sylvia Beach (the owner of the famed Shakespeare & Co. bookstore), the famous hostess Elsa Maxwell, as well as, in Ira's phrase, "some counts and barons [and] a couple of guys with monocles and dirty shirts." The party lasted until four in the morning, Ira having consumed "lots of champagne" without ill effects.[27]

The final ten days of the trip were spent without George, who was in London. Ira's journal entries during this period—more sightseeing and museum going—become shorter and more labored. His friend, Arthur Kober, a journalist for the *Paris Comet* who was married to the tempestuous playwright Lillian Hellman, persuaded the reluctant lyricist to be interviewed. "I told him whatever I could about the shows I had seen, not feeling at all that I had anything worth writing about, but Kober seemed satisfied and maybe he'll get a story out of it."[28] Besides being Jewish, Ira and Kober shared a common wit, with a playful knack for finding the right words (while struggling to do so). They were both charming and shy, with wives who were their diametric opposites emotionally.

On June 13, Ira, Lee, and Frankie took a train from Paris to Cherbourg, journeyed across the Channel to meet George, and once again boarded the *Majestic*. The ennui Ira felt during their return is captured by his final sentence: "The food is to be sneezed at."[29] He would not return to Europe until 1950.

IRA SOON BEGAN work on yet another show for Aarons and Freedley to again star Gertrude Lawrence. He and George completed a few numbers within a couple of months, but the book by Fred Thompson and Vincent Lawrence was, typically, delayed. When *Treasure Girl* began its tryout in October 1928 in Philadelphia, it was clear that even if Lawrence was "never shown to better advantage" in an American show, the book—about a hunt for buried pirates' treasure—was seriously flawed. New writers were brought in, but the run at the Alvin Theatre was short-lived. Noël Coward's *This Year of Grace* had opened the night before *Treasure Girl*; the Gershwin show, with a "canned, made-to-order quality" about it, paled by comparison.[30] A talented cast and a fine score were wasted, as the doors closed in January after sixty-eight performances, taking "us all to Cain's Warehouse."[31]

Robert Benchley was on the mark when he stated that *Treasure Girl* was "a grand conspiracy by the librettists to nullify what should otherwise be an unqualifiedly successful class musical show."[32] The *Treasure Girl* score is filled with numbers that should have been popular but remain obscure because of the show's brief run. Notable among these are "I Don't Think I'll Fall in Love Today," a comedic duet for Gertrude Lawrence and her leading man. The refrain—ironically—was derived from G. K. Chesterton's poem "A Ballade of Suicide," with its refrain of "I think I will not hang myself to-day."[33] But Ira's lyrics showcase the divergent attitudes of the song's protagonists toward love with humor rather than tragedy:

> *Ann*: When evening shadows creep,
> I like dancing—
> *Neil*: I like sleep.

and

> *Ann*: Still it might be fun to bring
> Your carpet slippers;
> When the dinner bell would ring,
> I'd serve a can of kippers.
> *Neil*: Don't you know how to cook?
> *Ann*: I could look in a book.

The other notable song in *Treasure Girl* was, in its original form, a "pleasant enough" ballad called "I've Got a Crush on You," which was given a faster tempo for the 1930 revision of *Strike Up the Band*.[34] In the 1940s, a recording by the vocalist Lee Wiley brought the original ballad

version back, and the number, now one of Ira's most popular, has remained
a ballad ever since.

> I've got a crush on you,
> Sweetie Pie.
> All the day and nighttime
> Hear me sigh.
> I never had the least notion
> That I could fall with so much emotion.
>
> Could you coo,
> Could you care
> For a cunning cottage we could share?
> The world will pardon my mush
> 'Cause I've got a crush,
> My baby, on you.

IRA'S INCOME for 1928 jumped by 40 percent, due to royalties from six shows
and from his new status as a Double A-rated member of ASCAP, a mark
that put him into the earning calculation ratio of his brother, Jerome Kern,
and Irving Berlin.[35] This financial security came with a restlessness for a
home of his own; George agreed that it was time to leave, and at the end
of November 1928, they rented adjacent penthouses at 33 Riverside Drive,
an elegant seventeen-story Italian Renaissance-style building on the Upper
West Side. Ira had spent more than thirty years living in the "simultaneous
stamping ground of the other members of the family and the numberless
relatives and visitors who would lounge through, lean on the piano, chat,
tell stories, and do their setting-up exercises."[36] Would he miss the chaos?

Ira's east-facing penthouse looked out at the busyness of West End Avenue and Broadway and wrapped around the corner for a southern view
of the Hudson River. He and Lee moved into their new residence in the
late winter of 1929. The rent was $300 per month ($4,500 today), while
George paid one-third more for his direct view of the Hudson River and
the New Jersey Palisades—as well as the industrial detritus of the pre-
Robert Moses West Side Improvement redevelopment of Riverside Park.

While Ira arranged his library and workroom, he likely recalled his youthful dreams of how he might decorate a room in his family's apartment. As George hired a man to run his apartment, so Ira hired Ingrid Berggreen, a Norwegian woman from Oslo, as a maid to perform a similar role.[37] The first spring at 33 Riverside Drive was glorious, filled with sunshine and long afternoons spent lazing in hammocks on the wrap-around terrace that connected the brothers' apartments. The penthouses impressed at least one visitor with a "quietude all but monastic,"[38] but the silence was rare, as family and friends constantly rode up the elevator to Ira and Lee's Sunday "frankfurter parties."[39]

A close circle of friends—the Paleys, Arthur Kober, Sam Behrman, Vernon Duke, Lillian Hellman, Howard Dietz, Milton Ager, Kay Swift, Moss Hart, Morrie Ryskind, Irving Caesar, Harold Arlen, Yip Harburg, Jay Gorney, Harry Warren, and Oscar Levant, among many others—lingered "long past midnight, vitalizing the air with wit and wisdom, criticism and vitriol, shop talk and violent discussions." As the night progressed, people would drift over to George's apartment to be entertained with excerpts from the brothers' latest work in progress.[40] But writer Carl Hovey observed that Ira, once the party had broken up, had an advantage that he previously lacked: the lyricist could retreat to the privacy of his own apartment, where he could muse about the evening's events.[41]

IRA'S INVOLVEMENT WITH *East Is West*, a long-gestating musical comedy adaptation of the 1918 play *Ming Toy*, went back to the spring of 1927, when the play's original producer, William Harris Jr., hired the Gershwins to write the score.[42] Due to an overabundance of musicals, Harris postponed the production, telling George and Ira that they would meet again upon their return from Europe.[43] Thus, it came as a surprise when Vincent Youmans said he was going to do the score.[44] But when Flo Ziegfeld bought the rights in May 1928, George and Ira were back in business.[45]

Although a few songs were complete, and casting had begun, by late January 1929, William Anthony McGuire (the author of the book for *Rosalie*) had failed to deliver a plot outline.[46] Ziegfeld, in the meantime, turned his attention to J. P. McEvoy's popular novel *Show Girl*, whose heroine was a Ziegfeld dancer; the "hypnotically persuasive" producer, with his "great charm until a contract was signed," turned on a dime and told George and Ira that McEvoy's "snappy" novel would be his summer show.[47] This meant turning out a completely new score in two weeks. Ziegfeld asked Ira if he would agree to have the lyricist Gus Kahn (1886–1941), to whom the producer owed a new assignment, work with him. Ira was happy to have Kahn's assistance.[48] The German-born Kahn, Ira's equal in diminutive stature and chubby figure, was a consistent purveyor of popular songs ("My Buddy," "It Had to Be You," and "Makin' Whoopee"), and by late April, the trio were at work on Riverside Drive.[49]

Many of the twenty-seven completed numbers "were for imagined spots," as rehearsals got underway with only the opening scene of the book complete. Adapting McEvoy's novel was as difficult for McGuire as *East Is West* had been. *Show Girl*, Ira later remarked, probably "set a record for

Ira with George and fellow lyricist Gus Kahn, on the patio of 33 Riverside Drive during the writing of *Show Girl*, spring 1929.

sparseness of dialogue in a musical."[50] Performances began in Boston in June, with the last scene rehearsed on the train from New York.[51] Surprisingly, the haste with which the show was put together was of little concern to audiences, who greeted it with applause, much of it due to the personality of eighteen-year-old Ruby Keeler as the showgirl and to the memory of the moment on opening night when Keeler's husband Al Jolson stepped out of his seat into the aisle and sang a chorus of "Liza" while she danced.[52] *Show Girl* was number one at the box office for the first three weeks of its run in New York City—it had little competition during the typically hot summer—but enthusiasm ran dry after Keeler left the cast.[53] The comedy of Jimmy Durante and the power of Duke Ellington's orchestra kept the doors open until October, when it closed after just 111 performances.

The critics agreed that the main problem was the score, a confirmation of Ziegfeld's disappointment with the songs. Of the six published numbers, only "Liza," which fulfilled Ziegfeld's request for a minstrel number with "one hundred beautiful girls seated on steps that cover the entire stage," made an impression.[54]

Ira's verdict? *Show Girl* "wasn't much—it cost much and lost much" but *East Is West* "would have cost much more."[55] The *East Is West* score was salvageable, but "the plot would have to take new twists as the day of the story of the girl who turns out to be what you expected all along saw its twilight when Romberg had to become president of S. P. A. [the Songwriters Protective Association, founded in 1931, now the Songwriters Guild of America] because the public finally got on to that type of operetta."[56] Some of the *East Is West* material was reshaped for songs that made their way into later shows, but "In the Mandarin's Orchid Garden"—written to accompany a Chinese ballet—was published in the hope that the artsy number might appeal to recitalists. It never found a place in the classical repertoire, but it did have a subsequent life: during George and Ira's first visit to Hollywood, Ira heard their hostess at a swank party recite the lyrics. When he asked how she learned such an obscure song, the woman replied that she was taking "elocution lessons and my teacher gave me the words to learn."[57]

BY THE LATE 1920s Ira had put the royalties from several successful shows into a series of margin accounts.[58] He also became an investor in shows.

Although he kept a vigilant eye on these investments, he was aware of his haphazard "methods" and his propensity to choose incorrectly.[59] In the summer of 1929, Ira and his comedian friend Groucho Marx were in Bridgeport, Connecticut, looking at a possible site for a housing development in which they hoped to invest. Groucho seemed to sense a stock market plunge in the offing.[60] Just over three weeks after *Show Girl* closed, both men saw their accounts largely wiped out as the markets sank, an outcome that Groucho had joked about a few months earlier in a *New Yorker* essay.[61]

PART THREE

George the Music/ Ira the Words: The 1930s

CHAPTER 7

A s THE NEW DECADE BEGAN, Ira was both pleased and concerned about a revival of *Strike Up the Band*. While he welcomed the opportunity to reshape his rhymes and couplets, as it "was less troublesome to write a new number than to defend a number that was in doubt," he worried that the country's financial crisis would put a damper on even a well-received musical comedy.[1] While one of his peers had said that Ira's lyrics in the original production had brought the lyricist "closer to the mountain top" that was W. S. Gilbert "than anyone else" in the United States, the 1927 attempt had been a box office failure.[2] To correct the earlier deficiencies, producer Edgar Selwyn, stung by the criticism that the original show was too harsh, hired Morrie Ryskind to tone down George S. Kaufman's book, a task Ryskind compared to rewriting "*War and Peace* for the Three Stooges."[3] Ryskind's new idea defanged Kaufman's satire by turning the entire war—the hinge of the plot—into a dream. Selwyn also brought in the comedy duo of Bobby Clark and Paul McCullough, hoping that their popularity would draw audiences.

These changes meant extensive revisions to the existing score as well as new songs, and after stops in Boston and New Haven to get the show into running form, the new *Strike Up the Band* made its long-awaited Broadway debut in January. It was greeted with continuous applause for the Gershwin score and uproarious laughter for the antics of Clark and McCullough.[4] For seven weeks it was standing-room only, then a warm May forced a closure the following month after 191 performances, as audiences dwindled in the unexpected heat that drove New Yorkers out of the city.[5] Although the abrupt end meant that Ira did not earn as much as he had hoped from the deal that gave him an extra half percent per week of any gross over $10,000,[6] the critics acknowledged his contribution. Robert Benchley noted Ira's "consistently literate, correct, and amusing" work,[7] and the artist Ralph Barton praised the lyrics for being "as intelligent and bitingly satirical as the book, but so nimbly and deftly fashioned that their serious import sinks in without hurting."[8] With *Strike Up the Band*, Ira could take his "place among the world's humorists."[9]

The new numbers—the ballads "Soon" and "I've Got a Crush on You" (the latter brought in from the *Treasure Girl* score)—were more in tune with the show's romantic spots, and the satire was gentler; the bitter denunciation of war profiteers was replaced with songs like "If I Became the President," a humorous duet in which Bobby Clark's Colonel Holmes is wooed by Mrs. Draper, a wealthy widow, with visions of how they would run the White House if he were elected:

> *Holmes*: If I became the President—
> *Draper*: And I were the President's wife
>   You'd flood the Senate with your orat'ry.
> *Holmes*: I'd make each politish-i-on
>   Prohibit Prohibish-i-on—
> *Both*: A hundred million drinkers would be free.
> *Holmes*: I'd grow a beard I'm thinkin'.
> *Draper*: You'd be as great as Lincoln,
>   And Mister Hearst would surely print your life.
> *Holmes*: But I'd never go so far afield
>   As Tyler, Polk, or Gar-a-field—
>   If I became the president—
> *Draper*: And I were the President's wife.

In Boston, Clark, hoping to extend the number, "came up with four pen-ciled pages of new lyrics . . . he himself had written for possible encores." Ira shuddered: "No actor had ventured to change or add to my lyrics before this; besides, these were pretty terrible." But Clark was a great comedian, and "management asked me to go along with him as far as possible. I was able to make some corrections and to cut the encores down to two." Unhappily, "his lines received as many chuckles as did mine."[10]

GEORGE'S ENTHUSIASM for work was a mountain that Ira often found hard to climb; the phlegmatic pace of his output could never equal the constant stream of melodies that came from his brother's mind and fingers. But when they were deep into a new score, Ira mustered his energy and could be found standing beside George's piano, gazing "ceilingward out of closed eyes" as he worked his way through a new lyric. He sang self-deprecatingly but surprised himself and anyone within earshot with the occasional "quasi-operatic outburst."[11]

Once a show was finished, "I always felt as if I'd earned a year off."[12] Although he was little more than a dabbler, returning to his paint brushes was a way to unwind, and two canvases from this period show Ira's range

"I never thought much of myself as a looker": Ira's 1930s
revealing self-portrait known as *My Body*.

of interest and his humor. The first, *Charlie's Lawn*, is a bird's-eye view from Ira's penthouse of "Riverside," the seventy-five-room mansion of the steel magnate Charles M. Schwab. It was a long way from the Lower East Side to living so close to—and *above*—such a structure. Ira's sense of himself is revealed in *My Body*, a self-portrait of the artist in a yellow sleeveless undershirt and a matching pair of boxers, both items dyed in his bathtub, a quirky hobby he indulged in for many years. It made him "quite a character, I."[13] The painting, a response to his brother's formal *Self-Portrait in Evening Clothes* of the same period, shows Ira unkempt, cigar gripped between his teeth. "I never thought much of myself as a looker," he told a reporter thirty years after the painting's creation.[14]

THE RELAXATION WAS always short-lived, and in the summer of 1930, the brothers began work on *Girl Crazy*, another musical comedy for the producing team of Aarons and Freedley. The pun-filled book by Guy Bolton and John McGowan about a New York playboy banished by his father to an Arizona dude ranch offered plenty of spots for romance and comedy. Allan Kearns, in his third Gershwin show (following *Tip-Toes* and *Funny Face*) played the fish-out-of-water city slicker who meets and falls in love with the local postmistress, played by nineteen-year-old Ginger Rogers in her second Broadway role. William Kent (also in his third Gershwin show on Broadway) and the powerfully voiced Ethel Merman, an unknown secretary from Queens, played the comedic supporting roles of Slick Fothergill and his brassy wife Frisco Kate.

Girl Crazy had a well-regarded two-week run in Philadelphia before opening in October at the Alvin Theatre. For the first two months, the show was as big a hit as anything on Broadway, and it remained popular through the end of the year. But no musicals could escape the drastic downturn in ticket sales that began in early 1931; still, when *Girl Crazy* closed in June, after 272 performances, it became the longest-running Gershwin show since *Rosalie*, spawning sizable sales of sheet music and recordings.

"But Not for Me," "Embraceable You," "I Got Rhythm." No other Gershwin musical comedy for the stage contains so many songs that have become standards; George's distinctive melodies remain in the repertoire of jazz musicians, while Ira's alternately romantic or humorous lyrics have continued to catch the attention of singers in many styles. Ira's friend, the light versifier Newman Levy, observed that the "deftness and . . . wit" of Ira's work on this show and *Strike Up the Band* "demonstrated that he is the most skillful versifier writing for the American stage."[15]

The ballad "But Not for Me" contains some of Ira's most poignant lyrics:

> With Love to Lead the Way,
> I've found more Clouds of Gray
> Than any Russian play
> Could guarantee.

And ends with one of his cleverest twists:

> When ev'ry happy plot
> Ends with the marriage knot—
> And there's no knot for me.

The song's phrase "a feller needs a friend" was intended as a "tangential tribute" to the recently deceased comic strip artist Clare Briggs, whose "When a Feller Needs a Friend" was a popular cartoon of Ira's boyhood.[16]

The show's second ballad, "Embraceable You," includes a set of four-syllable rhymes—"embraceable / replaceable" and "tipsy in me / gypsy in me"—that were rare for a lyric in most love songs, which rarely strayed from the standard "moon—June—croon" set. The song was a favorite of Ira's father, who believed his eldest son had written the lyric about him; when he heard someone sing the line "Come to papa—come to papa do!" Morris "would thump his chest, look around the room, and beam."[17] Ira felt that he had reached a peak; when a cast recording of *Girl Crazy* was proposed in 1951, he suggested the use of the song's second chorus, asking producer Goddard Lieberson if he could "deny that, say, in the second refrain of, say, 'Embraceable' a rhyme like, say / glorify / more if I / isn't worth the price of, say, the entire album?"[18]

But he found that joining lyrics to George's tricky melody for "I Got Rhythm" was an extended task. For more than two weeks, he played "with various titles and with sets of double rhymes" in dummy lyrics (temporary words that are meant to help the lyricist remember a rhythm scheme), including "Roly-Poly, / Eating solely / Ravioli, / Better watch your diet or bust. / Lunch or dinner, / You're a sinner. / Please get thinner. / Losing all that fat is a must." But the words "seemed at best to give a pleasant and jingly Mother Goose quality to a tune which should throw its weight around more." He experimented with nonrhyming dummy lines: "Just go forward; / Don't look backward; / And you'll soon be / Winding up ahead of the game." He was struck by the repetition of the phrase "who could ask for anything more?" and thought that such an emphasis meant that it should be the song's title, but since "I Got Rhythm" felt more "arresting and provocative," it remained, and launched Ethel Merman's career.[19]

Yet it was the lyric to "Bidin' My Time," one of the show's lesser-known—but highly praised—numbers, that combined Ira's wit and his own personality. It came from a quatrain he wrote that was published in a 1917 issue of *Cap and Bells*:

> A desperate deed to do I crave,
>   Beyond all reason and rhyme:
> Some day when I'm feeling especially brave,
>   I'm going to Bide My Time.[20]

Contemporary critics described the lyric as "a philosophic poem"[21] or as "a philosophy of life which goes back to the Hindu for chronic relaxation."[22] But when asked if his words were meant to have such an effect, Ira demurred; they were "escapist," not an incitement to become another Ilya Ilyich Oblomov, the title character of the Russian writer Ivan Goncharov's 1859 novel about a young man who could not make any important decisions or take any significant actions.[23] The well-regarded critic Brooks Atkinson was charmed, writing that any lyricist who could start "a cowboy spiritual with—'I'm bidin' my time, / That's the kinda guy I'm'—may look forward with confidence to a comfortable and jovial old age."[24]

THE MOVIE RIGHTS to *Girl Crazy* were sold to RKO while the show was still on Broadway, with the $33,000 fee divided between the songwriters (George and Ira getting one-quarter of the total), the book writers, and the producers.[25] The brothers received a separate $2,000—divided equally, in a rare moment of monetary equality, as Ira typically received only 40 percent—for a new song for the picture.[26] "You've Got What Gets Me" was shaped from the release of "Your Eyes! Your Smile!," a number dropped from *Funny Face* before it reached Broadway.[27]

With *Girl Crazy* a definite hit, Hollywood came calling, and George and Ira were invited to join the ranks of musical comedy songwriters who had fled the flagging stages of Manhattan for the sunshine and money of the movie colony. In the spring of 1930, the brothers signed a $100,000 deal with the Fox Film Corporation to write material for what became *Delicious*, their first movie musical.[28] On November 5, George, Ira, and Lee were joined in their private rail car by Guy Bolton, who had been hired to write the screenplay, and producer Edgar Selwyn for a party-and-poker-filled journey across the continent.[29] After a few days at the luxurious Beverly Wilshire Hotel, the Gershwin trio moved into a house on Chevy Chase Drive that had once been occupied by Greta Garbo. Although some numbers were in embryonic form when George and Ira left for California, it was in this house that most of the score was written.

Scores of movie stars and studio executives attended the Gershwins' lavish parties, but Ira quickly saw behind the glitzy facade: "You get used to measuring a man's stature by hundreds (weekly) and grands (for a single job)."[30] His Manhattan friends facetiously expressed their concern about the effect of sunshine on the lethargic lyricist.

WHEN IRA ARRIVED in Hollywood, an interview in which he expressed his opinions on the art of lyric writing and his working partnership with his brother was published in the *New York Times*. He confessed that being a lyric writer was a precarious existence; it required a combination of "a certain dexterity with words and a feeling for music . . . the infinite patience of the gemsetter, compatibility with the composer and an understanding of the various personalities in a cast." Although not every member of an audience was conscious of lyrics during a performance, a lifetime of theatergoing encouraged him to hope that "there are enough listening with a critical ear to make the lyric writer strive to get away from the banal and hackneyed."

After six years of continuous work together, he and George had developed a routine. They found little point in writing too many songs between shows, although three numbers of this sort were complete before the *Girl Crazy* contract was signed; he told the *Times* that each, "with a line changed here and there . . . were easily cued in the story." George's melodies and Ira's lyrics were developed after the plot outline had been received, which was usually all they had to base their songs on. "We are both pretty critical and outspoken, George about my lyrics and I about his music. . . . Occasionally I suggest that a note or a 'middle' (the seventeenth to twenty-fourth bar of the chorus) be changed, while now and then a line is thrown me." Once agreed upon, Ira pondered; while he could not read music, he had an instinctual ability to recall melodies. Then, working alone, alongside his carefully selected collection of pens (preferably Parker 51s) and pencils, and with a ready supply of reference books and cigars at hand, he painstakingly studied the moods of the melody and the plot.

Theoretically, his years of experience would make lyrics "flow easily . . . but instead of becoming easier, there is so much one cannot repeat, so much snow of yesterday that is slush today, so many trick rhymes that have become second hand, so many titles that creak, and so few new angles on Jack and Jill, the Pied Piper and Little Goody Two-Shoes that working on a score and trying to set reasonable ideas to unreasonable rhythms becomes four months of intensive criss-cross word puzzling." Even the maid was puzzled by his methods; when she came across Ira singing to himself at his desk, she asked Lee, " 'Don't Mr. Gershwin never go to work?' "[31]

SHORTLY AFTER Christmas 1930, Ira finished his work on *Delicious*, leaving him with "nothing to do but get up at noon, read the papers, see pictures, and dine in or out. A pleasure!"[32] When it came to gambling, he followed in his father's footsteps, and Ira was often found among a loose-knit collection of New York–based poker players known as the Hoyle Club, who, by the time Ira arrived in Hollywood, also gathered there. Largely made up of songwriters, playwrights, actors, and producers—Jerome Kern, Russell Crouse, Howard Lindsay, Arthur Kober, and Morrie Ryskind among them—the men met once a week at 9 p.m. to play six hours of alternate rounds of stud and draw. There were no kibitzers, but a few "rules": when a player bought a second stack of chips, all the others rose from their chairs to sing "Happy Birthday," and once in a while, they would wear "red beards which cannot be removed until a player uncovers a full house."[33] Ira's party trick was to balance poker chips on his forehead.[34] So, it was no surprise that a successful 1930 would be capped by a New Year's trip to Agua Caliente, Mexico, where Ira lost $800 at the gambling tables. His friends at home wondered if he would "be satisfied with New York and its simple pleasures (gambling losses never more than $200.00) . . . after the opulence of Hollywood."[35]

One person Ira became acquainted with in Hollywood failed to make a good impression. The publisher Horace Liveright had recently come west to work for Pathé Studios, and in an alcohol-fueled moment at one of the Gershwins' parties, flirted with Lee. Although Liveright called it a harmless incident, Ira—in a rare moment of pique—described the publisher as "that dope."[36]

WITH THEIR WORK on *Delicious* in the hands of the movie makers, George and Ira returned to New York in late February 1931, where two potential projects were waiting for them. Another show for Aarons and Freedley eventually collapsed when no suitable book could be found, and it seemed likely there would be no show from the Gershwins' longtime producers in the new season at all.[37] Ira suspected that the second show, with a book by Kaufman and Ryskind, was more likely. While they waited, George, who had considered a return to California to watch the filming of *Delicious*, completed the scoring of his *Second Rhapsody*, an "underrated" work that Ira considered "overshadowed" by the *Rhapsody in Blue*.[38]

THROUGHOUT HIS CAREER, Ira was content to leave ideas for potential shows or movies to his collaborators, but in the money-scarce summer of 1931, he found a "very funny idea" in the "just finished . . . proofs" of *Turnabout*, a new book by the novelist and short story writer Thorne Smith, best-known for his *Topper* novels of the 1920s. Ira enjoyed the plot about a "husband and wife [who] retain their own minds but change bodies," and he and George pursued Smith to write a libretto "in the vague future." Ira was aware that his life at the moment "consist[ed] of a nervous lolling—lolling because there is nothing to do and nervous because there should be something to do."[39]

In June 1931, newspaper columnist Heywood Broun announced that the Gershwins were to contribute a song to his new revue, *Shoot the Works*. "We would like to help," Ira was quoted as saying, "and if you could use a straight love song (Situation 3, Type 17A, 72) please get in touch with us and we'll try to find something you'd like."[40] But by the time *Shoot the Works* opened in late July, the only Gershwin song to be heard was Ira's "Chirp-Chirp," recycled from *That's a Good Girl*.

Ira spent many of his weekends during the hot summer of 1931 at the Strunsky hotel in Belmar, and when he returned home, it was to face the task of proofreading the pages of Isaac Goldberg's forthcoming biography of his brother. George acknowledged Ira's importance to this book, and told the author that he would look favorably on seeing more about his brother—and samples of his lyrics—in the volume.[41] *George Gershwin: A Study in American Music* was published by Simon & Schuster on George's thirty-third birthday and was dedicated to Ira and Lee, but Goldberg's chapter on Ira—"Ira Gershwin: Tricks of the Words-and-Music Trade"—is hardly devoted solely to the lyricist.

When Sam Behrman suggested that Ira accompany him to California to work on a screenplay, Ira responded with a vague "who knows?"[42] George encouraged his brother to think about it; being a Hollywood writer "would be a great thing," particularly if he could gain the assistance of their experienced screenwriter friend Sonya Levien.[43] A few months later, Fox producer Sol Wurtzel proposed that Ira work at his studio, but as Lee Gershwin told a friend, "you know Ira"—such a drastic change was not in the cards.[44]

CHAPTER 8

I RA'S NEXT SHOW, *Of Thee I Sing*, was the result of George S. Kaufman's reaction to how *Strike Up the Band* was "doctored for the supposed public taste" (although he seemed not to hold a grudge against Morrie Ryskind for doing the doctoring). Kaufman "wanted to write one show that would make no concessions to anyone." The new, biting satire on American politics and the presidency again gave Ira the opportunity to work with a cohesive narrative, with the standard verse-and-chorus songs of musical comedy replaced by "a sort of recitative running along and lots of finales and fina-lettos" that allowed for extended lyrical ideas.[1]

Everyone agreed that little material needed to be cut before *Of Thee I Sing* made its Broadway debut on the day after Christmas 1931. It was an immediate artistic and financial success, was in the black by April, when it was the only capacity show on Broadway, and stayed strong through the typically weak summer months. The show's popularity earned a transfer to a larger theater, where it continued drawing crowds until closing in early January 1933 after a run of fifty-five weeks.

For a show that relied on lengthy musical material to push the plot along, *Of Thee I Sing* includes some of Ira's most recognizable and popular songs, including its rousing title number, which was worked out in California between hours spent on the songs for *Delicious*:

> Of thee I sing, baby—
> Summer, autumn, winter, spring, baby.
> You're my silver lining,

> You're my sky of blue;
> There's a lovelight shining
> Just because of you.

"There were one or two strong objectors who thought that juxtaposing the dignified 'of thee I sing' with a slangy 'baby' was going too far," but Ira disagreed: "Opening night, and even weeks later, one could hear a continuous 'Of thee I sing, *Baby!*' when friends and acquaintances greeted one another in the lobby at intermission time."[2]

The second song was based on a plot twist that takes place during Wintergreen's search for a first lady: his choice of the all-American Mary Turner because she can bake corn muffins is met with vehement objection by the French Ambassador to the United States, who claims that his country was slighted by Wintergreen's failure to choose another woman, who was half-French. In fact:

> She's the illegitimate daughter
> Of an illegitimate son
> Of an illegitimate nephew
> Of Napoleon.

The economic depression, and its effect on Ira's bank balance, clearly had an influence on some of the lyrics in the otherwise lighthearted romantic duet "Who Cares?":

> Who cares
> If the sky cares to fall in the sea?
> Who cares what banks fail in Yonkers
> Long as you've got a kiss that conquers?
> Why should I care?
> Life is one long jubilee
> So long as I care for you—
> And you care for me.

Ira had never invested in one of his own shows, but after the first Boston performances were rapturously received, Kaufman took him aside and suggested that he could get Ira 5 percent of the show for $2,500. Ira lacked ready cash, having lost or spent all the money he had received from his movie contract, but George came to the rescue with a loan. *Of Thee I Sing*'s quick success allowed Ira to pay off his debt to George and make a tidy profit of $11,000.[3]

When it was later pointed out that Lorenz Hart had used the same "Yonkers / conquers" rhyme in "Manhattan," Hart's popular song of 1925 written with Richard Rodgers, Ira admitted that while he "generally eschews using an unusual rhyme that he knows has been sung or printed before him," he would not have changed his lyric, since it would be impossible to "trace all the way back to Chaucer . . . to check on some unusual rhyme, whether it is a 'mosaic' or 'trick' rhyme, or one derived from eponymy or jargon or dialect or whatever."[4]

OF THEE I SING showed that Ira Gershwin's lyrics were as valuable to the success of a Broadway show as his brother's music. His work stood for itself, and he took pleasure in being talked about: "he'll sit back smoking that big cigar, looking out from behind big glasses and thinking it's about time people realized there was more than one Gershwin."[5]

With that fame came a willingness to make a stand for songwriters and their right to be fairly compensated. In the early 1930s, Ira began attending meetings of the Songwriters Protective Association, of which he later became a vice president. The group, he said, was "trying to get a minimum basic contract such as the Dramatists Guild has, for the popular songwriter. But it's tough going because of a couple of publishers who think they buy a birthright when they pay an advance of 50 or 100 dollars."[6]

DELICIOUS, THE GERSHWINS first attempt at writing for the movies, premiered at New York's lavish Roxy Theatre on the same night *Of Thee I Sing* took the stage at the Music Box. Unfortunately, audiences had lost interest in movie musicals by the end of 1931, and that, combined with the effects of the poor economy on Hollywood, ended the brothers' immediate hopes for a second picture. Although a few of the songs were published, none were commercial successes. The standout lyrics are "Blah, Blah, Blah," a spoof on the typically trite lyrics of movie theme songs:

> Blah, blah, blah, your hair,
>   Blah, blah, blah, your eyes;
> Blah, blah, blah, blah, care,
>   Blah, blah, blah, blah, skies.
> Tra la la la, tra la la la la, cottage for two—
> Blah, blah, blah, blah, blah, darling with you!

and the title number, with the adjective drawn out in an imitation of Ira's father-in-law:

> You're so delishious
> And so caprishious;
> I grow ambishious
> To have you care for me.[7]

THE 1931–32 BROADWAY SEASON had many hits: Eugene O'Neill's *Mourning Becomes Electra*; Philip Barry's *The Animal Kingdom*; Paul Green's *The House of Connelly*; Maxwell Anderson's *Night over Taos*; Sam Behrman's *Brief Moment*; Robert Sherwood's *Reunion in Vienna*; and Elmer Rice's *Counsellor-in-Law.* "Yet not one of these American dramas was as devastatingly complete a revelation of the American scene" as was the acerbic, comedic, melodious hit by Kaufman, Ryskind, and George and Ira Gershwin.[8]

Ira was on a golfing weekend with George at the estate of the publisher Bennett Cerf when Lee telephoned with the news that *Of Thee I Sing* was rumored to be the winner of the Pulitzer Prize for Drama, but when she congratulated Kaufman, he said nothing about either Gershwin being a recipient.[9] Kaufman's silence was to be expected: neither George nor Ira was included in the letters he and Ryskind had received, informing them of the award; and the news was to be kept from the public until May 3.[10] On that morning, Ira was greeted at the breakfast table by a headline on the front page of the *New York Times* that he had been awarded the Pulitzer; when he turned inside the newspaper to continue reading, he found his photograph alongside that of Kaufman, Ryskind, and seven other Pulitzer recipients.[11]

Pulitzer Prize winner was a long way from the publication of "The

Shrine," but the fact that George was not a recipient—there was no Pulitzer for music at the time—left Ira conflicted.[12] He was honored to be recognized but was equally perturbed by the ignorance of the committee that discounted the inventiveness of the music, which allowed his words to spring to life. To ignore George was to ignore what made *Of Thee I Sing* unique. Reminded of the engraving on the lighter his brother had given him—"George the Music; Ira the Words"—he thought he might decline the award, even though George urged him to accept.[13]

The inclusion of Ira's name was the work of producer Sam H. Harris's press agent, who telephoned Ira after the letters to Kaufman and Ryskind had been received and told him that the three-man jury that made the original selection had not given any thought to including the lyricist in the award—none had ever won the prize before—but that they were happy to add Ira's name.[14] Friends sent their congratulations. Carl Hovey thought that it was only proper that Ira's talent be matched by such an honor.[15] Ira was delighted by the pair of colorful "braces (suspenders to you)" that Hovey and his wife Sonya Levien gave him; they "made an exhibitionist of me. On the slightest (and usually with no) provocation off goes my coat in the most public places because I can't resist giving the world a thrill. Strong men

The creators of the Pulitzer Prize–winning *Of Thee I Sing*: Ira and George with book writers George S. Kaufman and Morrie Ryskind.

swoon and passionate women leap."[16] He jokingly told Sam Behrman that he "really did it for P.S. 20" and that he intended to "take a trip to Stockholm this summer, just in case" he was to be awarded the Nobel Prize.[17]

WHAT MOST DAMPENED Ira's pleasure at receiving the Pulitzer Prize was the condition of his father. Morris Gershwin had been diagnosed with lymphatic leukemia, and no treatments could relieve his suffering. On the morning of May 14, 1932—just eleven days after the announcement of the award—Morris died of cardiac failure in his bed at the Hotel Broadmoor. He was fifty-nine-years-old.[18] After the body was laid to rest at the Westchester Hills Cemetery in Mount Hope, the family sat shiva for a week, but as none of the Gershwin children were familiar with the prayers to be read during the ceremony, they did it because it was the tradition, not through any sense of devotion to Judaism.[19] The lack of familial warmth was brought home to Ira a year later, when the family gathered for the traditional unveiling of the departed's tombstone. Casting sidelong glances at his mother, seemingly unaffected by the solemnity of the event, Ira mourned his father's passing and regretted how Rose had treated her mild-mannered husband.[20]

SHORTLY AFTER receiving notice of the awarding of the Pulitzer, Ira was handed a summons at the office of producer Sam H. Harris.[21] Ira had heard rumors that a lawsuit regarding the origins of *Of Thee I Sing* was to be filed, but he thought the plaintiff was unlikely to get a verdict in his favor.[22] The complaint was filed in New York Federal Court in August 1932 on behalf of the left-wing poet Walter Lowenfels, who was "living in the Latin Quarter of Paris in an atmosphere of starvation." His attorneys charged that Kaufman, Ryskind, the Gershwins, and Harris, as well as George Jean Nathan, Irving Berlin, Alfred Knopf, and the Gershwins' publishers, had plagiarized Lowenfels's 1929 "operatic tragedy" *U.S.A. with Music*, which he had written with composer George Antheil, who was not a party to the lawsuit. It was alleged that Ryskind had a copy of the text before it was copyrighted, and forty similarities between the two plays were detailed, including a lyric with the lines "America, we love you best of all. / In the spring and summer, winter and fall," which are echoed in Ira's lines to *Of Thee I Sing*'s rousing title number.[23] Four months later, the lawsuit was rejected by US District Judge John Munro Woolsey, who declared that "in this cause, as is usual in plagiarism causes, obscurity is taking a long shot at success."[24]

BY THE MIDSUMMER OF 1932, Ira had been creatively inactive for six months but expressed no concern about his lack of production. Even if no new show appeared, *Of Thee I Sing* remained profitable. Ira joined George and Oscar Levant on a journey to Chicago to see the opening of the second company in September, and the royalties continued when the show returned to Broadway for a month of performances.[25]

The New York theater was not immune from the weak economy, and the number of new musical comedies on Broadway had drastically declined as the decade progressed. In the spring of 1932, Aarons and Freedley had the playwright Robert Sherwood working on an idea for a show with a Gershwin score,[26] but when nothing usable was produced, Jack Buchanan, the star of *That's a Good Girl*, agreed to lead the cast of a different show.[27] As usual, problems with the book—originally the work of Herbert Fields and Morrie Ryskind, who later dropped out—impeded the progress of the score.[28] By the time Buchanan arrived in New York City, the final title had been agreed upon: *Pardon My English*.[29]

IN NOVEMBER 1932, New York Governor Franklin Delano Roosevelt was elected president of the United States in a landslide, giving hope to a weary nation and to the staunchly Democratic-voting Ira Gershwin. Less than a month later, those dreams for a Broadway success to equal Roosevelt's were dashed by the reaction to *Pardon My English* after it opened in Philadelphia. The raggedy book about an English nobleman who becomes the proprietor of a speakeasy due to a case of amnesia failed to cohere, and while opening night was stopped on four occasions by vocal approval for the stars, the show was not in good shape. Any good songs were obscured by the suave Buchanan's unsuitability as a tough guy and by a plot that stumbled between slapstick and the ethnic joking of the supporting players, Jack Pearl and Lyda Roberti.

If *Pardon My English* had been promising, the word of mouth from the crowds that packed the theater for the first three performances would have carried over to New York.[30] Instead, "two trying try-out weeks" were spent in Philadelphia, during which Ira and George staggered back to their hotel rooms each night as songs were thrown out, revised, and added as the cast and book were changed. The flagging lyricist returned home shortly before Christmas.[31] Buchanan, unhappy in his role, bought himself out of his contract and left the show in Boston.[32] George Givot, another ethnic comedian (Greek), who lacked the Englishman's natural appeal, was brought in, only to be replaced himself during the Broadway run.[33]

Pardon My English staggered into New York in January 1933, with Pearl and Roberti now in the leading roles and with Herbert Fields—"the only one brave enough to allow himself to be billed"—receiving credit for the book. Ira, one of the few standees on opening night, saw that it was hopeless after twenty minutes: "a bad cold and a lukewarm audience had me home by nine thirty."[34] Hoots of derision issued from the critics, with only a few cheers for Ira's lyrics. Most telling—and clearly true after all the problems Aarons and Freedley had put the Gershwins through since 1924—was the critic who noted the frequency with which George and Ira had wasted "their musical and lyrical wit" on a string of "mediocre musical comedy books."[35]

To go from the triumph of *Of Thee I Sing* to the "headache from start to finish" of *Pardon My English* was a severe blow. Ira had an enormous dislike for "the central notion" of the Aarons and Freedley debacle: "duo-personality or schizophrenia or whatever the protagonist's aberration was supposed to be," but Aarons, in financial straits, pleaded that his "potential backers would back out" if the score was not from the Gershwins. Only their long-standing friendship with the producer convinced the brothers to "toil and moil for six months" on a show they did not want or need to do. The critical pans were succeeded by the worst storm New York City had seen in four years, which caused *Pardon My English* to sink without a trace after forty-six increasingly dire performances played to increasingly empty houses.[36]

It was the worst showing ever for a Broadway run of a Gershwin musical, and the songs shared the show's fate, although the comedic "The Lorelei" and "My Cousin in Milwaukee" and the romantic "Isn't It a Pity?" received the lyricist's own stamp of approval. Both Jerome Kern (with lyricist Anne Caldwell) and Noël Coward had written popular songs about the deadly Rhine maiden known as the Lorelei before George and Ira took their turn. (They had heard both: the former in 1920's *Sally* and the latter when it was performed in *This Year of Grace* in London eight years later.)

> I'm treacherous—ja, ja!
> Oh, I just can't hold myself in check.
> I'm lecherous—ja, ja!
> I want to bite my initials on a sailor's neck.

The number was originally sung by Warsaw-born Lyda Roberti in her heavily accented voice. Three decades later, when Ira heard an early acetate of "The Lorelei" sung by Ella Fitzgerald for her multi-record Gershwin songbook, he observed that she had rendered the German exclamation as "jaw, jaw!" Producer Norman Granz agreed to take Ella back to Capitol Studios to rerecord the entire number.

Roberti brought down the house with "My Cousin in Milwaukee" as she told the tale of her Midwest cousin who "got boyfriends by the dozen / When she sang in a low-down way":

> So if you like the way I sing songs—
> If you think that I'm a wow,
> You can thank my squawky cousin from Milwaukee—
> Because she taught me how!

The one song from *Pardon My Eng*lish that has continued to attract attention is the duet "Isn't It a Pity?," in which the character of Michael blames their having never met on the time they had wasted:

> *Michael*: You, reading Heine,
> I, somewhere in China.

Ilse: My nights were sour
Spent with Schopenhauer.

THANKFULLY, by the time Ira returned from a trip to Havana in the winter of 1933, *Pardon My English* was just a bad memory, but the show did put an end to the Gershwins' professional relationship with Alex Aarons and Vinton Freedley, who fled to Hollywood and foreign parts, respectively. At this time, still feeling flush from their *Of Thee I Sing* royalties, the brothers moved out of their penthouse apartments to residences on East 72nd Street. Ira leased a ten-room, three-bath apartment on the eleventh floor of a fourteen-story building at the corner of Lexington Avenue in the Lenox Hill neighborhood of the Upper East Side, while George ensconced himself in a two-level duplex across the street.[37]

In early 1932, while *Of Thee I Sing* was still packing them in, Morrie Ryskind wrote a comedic novel called *Diary of an Ex-President*, which purported to be John P. Wintergreen's description of his first four months in the White House, with George Gershwin making an appearance as the

On vacation with Lee, George, and Ellin and
Irving Berlin, in Nassau, Bahamas, 1933.

forever-piano-playing guest who could not be kept away from the keyboard, even by a fire in the East Wing. The lightweight book lacked the humor brought to *Of Thee I Sing* by the character of Vice President Alexander Throttlebottom, but its publication enticed Sam H. Harris to consider bringing the popular characters of the original back to the stage.

The larger ingredient in what became *Let 'Em Eat Cake* was the world political situation: Adolf Hitler had come to power in Germany in January 1933, years after Benito Mussolini had established his own fascist state in Italy, and right-wing elements in the United States promoted an agenda they were eager to expound upon. Kaufman and Ryskind's "satire on Practically Everything" was, in Ira's words, "at times wonderfully witty—at other times unrelentingly realistic in its criticism of the then American scene."[38] To match the plot about a fascist takeover of the American government, Ira added more political content to his lyrics, but some of his more pointed ideas remained as scribbles in his notebooks: "Song for Nazi musical comedy," "Hitler Puts Ban on 'Negro' Music and Calls for the Return of the Waltz," and a chilling couplet that portends the Nazis' Final Solution:

> Opponents we griddle
> We cut up the Yiddle
> In ¾ time[39]

His focus on the Nazi leader was publicly expressed two days after *Let 'Em Eat Cake* opened, in a short verse contribution that was published in F.P.A.'s column in the *Herald Tribune*:

> BOOK REVIEW:
> "MY BATTLE" [Mein Kampf]

> Of Germany
> And her many
> —Well—minds,
> None's littler
> Than Hitler
> One finds.[40]

Even with the show's original stars, William Gaxton, Lois Moran, and Victor Moore, returning to reprise their roles as Wintergreen, Mary, and Throttlebottom, the sequel to *Of Thee I Sing* was unbalanced. Two of the original female roles were eliminated; the one replacement had only one song—"First Lady and First Gent"—and that was cut before the Boston opening. This left Moran's lightweight voice to carry the burden of the individual numbers for women.[41] Philip Loeb was the most important new member of the cast, as Kruger, the political rabble-rouser who represents the musical's more nihilistic elements. Kaufman was enthusiastic about what he heard of the score during its composition; the ensemble numbers went beyond those in the original show, but George—on the lookout for a hit—felt the show needed songs that could stand on their own without being connected to the story.[42]

Let 'Em Eat Cake played to a packed house for its opening night in Boston in October 1933. The city's mayor took to the stage to praise the show's four creators after the curtain fell, and Ira's "play of words, rhyme and humor," said the *New York Times* critic, gave "an edge to the lyrics."[43] By the time the highly anticipated sequel debuted in New York a few weeks later, it had lost forty-five minutes.[44] The smart, wealthy crowd that filled the opening night seats departed in a generally unhappy mood; they did not care for the attacks on Fascism or for Ira's exposure of the members of the Union League:

> Cloistered from the noisy city,
> Standing pat and sitting pretty,
> We are they who represent
> Safety First and 5%.

Even so, *Let 'Em Eat Cake* was the number one attraction at the box office for its first two weeks, but the critics were divided: some thought it worthy of the original and properly in keeping with the times but the majority gave it a thumbs down.

Ring Lardner opined that "You can count on the fingers of one thumb the present-day writers of song words who could wear becomingly the mantle of W. S. Gilbert, or even the squirrel neckpiece of Ira Gershwin,"[45] a sentiment echoed by critics who felt that the lyrics were the best part of the sequel. Whitney Bolton, in the *Morning Telegraph*, wrote that Ira had "accomplished miracles this time, forging couplets and rhymes which never let down the satiric implications of the story,"[46] while Brooks Atkinson, after seeing the show a second time, said that there was "more skill and versatility than the rhymes" in *Of Thee I Sing*, being "suave, idiomatic and droll, and . . . lively with the enthusiasm" that Ira had for his work.[47]

Ira again relished the opportunity to move beyond standard love songs and write integrated-to-the-plot sequences, including Kruger's call to the masses, "Union Square," which begins with

> Down with one and one make two,
> Down with ev'rything in view!
> Down with all majorities;
> Likewise all minorities!
> Down with you, and you, and you!

and ends with a free-for-all among the protestors as they turn on each other:

> So down with this, and down with that!
> And down with ev'rything in view!
> The hell with this, the hell with that!
> The hell with you, and you, and you!

As with the impeachment proceedings that concluded *Of Thee I Sing*, the finale of *Let 'Em Eat Cake* is an extended farce. It begins innocently enough, with a baseball game between teams of the Americans and the League of Nations to decide the resolution of the war debt, then darkens into the mordent tones of the trials of John P. Wintergreen and Alexander Throttlebottom, and ends with the bleak Fascism of "Hanging Throttlebottom in the Morning," in which "seven beheadings" provide the celebration for a new dictatorship.

Two months after the show opened, Prohibition was repealed, and ticket sales began a precipitous slide; audiences seemed more interested in going back to the bar than being pummeled by descriptions of political situations they had yet to understand. *Let 'Em Eat Cake* expired in early January 1934 after only ninety performances. Ira, eager to invest in the sequel, lost his 5 percent share of the venture.[48] Ira loved the "exciting contrapuntal accomplishment" of the show's opening sequence of opposing campaign cheers for Wintergreen and his opponent, Tweedledee, but he was disappointed that it "was mostly lost on a sabled and diamond-glittering first-night audience that kept trooping to its seats for minutes after the campaign marches began."[49]

CHAPTER 9

J UST DAYS AFTER the Broadway opening of *Let 'Em Eat Cake* in October 1933, George Gershwin signed an agreement with the prestigious
Theatre Guild to adapt *Porgy*, DuBose Heyward's 1925 best-selling
novel about life in Catfish Row, a Black tenement in segregated Charleston,
South Carolina, and the subsequent dramatic adaptation by Heyward and
his wife Dorothy. It was the culmination of George's years of contemplation
about the composition of an opera based on American themes.

George assumed that Ira would be available to work on the project
and had his name added to the agreement, presumably as a fallback if
DuBose Heyward was unable to write the lyrics or needed assistance. After
Heyward's visit to Manhattan in the fall of 1933, a division of labors was
agreed upon that played to the strengths of George's collaborators: Heyward would write the libretto and the adaptation (that is, the operatic
recitative), while Ira would be responsible for the lyrics to the stand-alone
songs.[1] The royalties were split between George (5 percent), Heyward and
his wife (4 percent), and Ira (1 percent).

In December, George traveled to Charleston to visit Heyward before
heading to Florida, where, in addition to composing "Summertime," he
completed a new work for piano and orchestra that was to debut during
a forthcoming tour celebrating the tenth anniversary of *Rhapsody in Blue*.
This short piece, the *"I Got Rhythm" Variations*, was dedicated to Ira and
was first heard at Symphony Hall in Boston in January 1934.

COMPOSING THE OPERA was a lengthy process, which left Ira free, and eager, to consider other work, and he agreed to collaborate with Yip Harburg on the lyrics for *Life Begins at 8:40*, a new revue with music by Harold Arlen. Harburg, who had just finished the score for the revival of the *Ziegfeld Follies* with Vernon Duke, sensed that after two poorly received shows, Ira needed an emotional pick-me-up and money.[2] The contract for the revue gave Ira a $500 advance and 2 percent of the gross, both certainly fair recompense, but he balked when he read the clause, prepared by Harburg's attorney, that gave his client top billing for the lyrics; in a rare instance of Ira claiming what was his due, he forced a change—after all, he was the more experienced writer.[3]

Life Begins at 8:40 was the first significant work Ira would do without his brother in a decade. For Harold Arlen, it was the first step away from the ballads and torch songs he had written for the Cotton Club. Arlen was an open admirer of George Gershwin, yet he was not an imitator; the peculiar construction of his melodies left Ira never knowing where Arlen would go next. Ira surmised that it was the "Hebraic influence" on Arlen that made him different from George; there was "no Jewish religious music" in the Gershwin family.[4]

During the writing of the score, Arlen and Harburg arrived at Ira's apartment late in the evenings and happily spent six or seven hours with Arlen at the piano and the lyricists trading lines as if they were working on a crossword puzzle. Although Ira and Harburg were temperamental opposites—the former serene, the latter prone to outbursts—they shared an urge to satirize love songs and to hone their phrases and words to a perfect sharpness that retained a "certain elusiveness."[5] The combination jelled; the skits for the revue were satires of Broadway, Tin Pan Alley, and Hollywood, and the lyrics were fashioned to stick a comedic fork into New York politics and its celebrity mayors, Jimmy Walker and Fiorello La Guardia. The actors who had been cast, including slapstick specialist Bert Lahr and the nimble song-and-dance man Ray Bolger, were given numbers fashioned for their strengths.

Ira had a keen sense of individual responsibility when it came to work. He balked at interference with his lyrics and was cautious about making suggestions regarding other parts of a show.[6] But for the first time in his career, he became actively engaged with something other than his lyrics.

While the sketches for the new revue were credited to gag writer extraordinaire and fellow CCNY alum David Freedman, Ira and Harburg wrote the dialogue for the extended opening and closing numbers.[7]

The opening number, "Life Begins (at Exactly 8:40 or Thereabouts)," set the stage with the character types who feature in the revue—the sister act, the crooner, the hoofer, the husband, the lover, the wife, the ingenue, the comedian, the dancing girls, and the torch singer—emerging from a giant clock. The finale, "Life Begins at City Hall," was a satire on New York City's current mayor, Fiorello La Guardia (the Little Flower), whom the authors, via Bert Lahr, portrayed as a Caesar-like dictator. La Guardia's official greeter, Grover Whalen, proclaims that the "mighty Latin" has made the city classy by introducing Picasso "to the boys at City Hall" and by cleaning up the slums with "chromium-plated showers." With cameos by a well-traveled Eleanor Roosevelt, who skips her job of christening "the first gondola to ply between Manhattan and Staten" in favor of launching one that will take her from Puerto Rico to Havana; and the former mayor of New York, Jimmy Walker, and his girlfriend, the actress Betty Compton, acting as stowaways looking to return from their two-year European exile, *Life Begins at 8:40* brought down the curtain with Walker being named Commissioner of Reprises and leading the entire ensemble through their paces.

THE STANDING-ROOM-ONLY AUDIENCE at the first performance of *Life Begins at 8:40* in Boston in August 1934 greeted the three-hour revue with "joyous acclaim and rapt admiration."[8] Although cuts were made to bring the evening to an earlier close, no songs were dropped prior to the Broadway opening at the end of the month. One critic judged that the lyricists "came out on top of the melee" with words that were "spangled with bright rhymes [and] affectionate phrases."[9] The season's first success, *Life Begins at 8:40* packed the house for the first three months of its run, quickly earning back its cost, and went on to an equally profitable tour after 237 performances at the Winter Garden.[10]

While a few of the songs from the revue had limited contemporary popular success, the lyrics, credited jointly to Ira and Yip, display the playfulness and word play that the two old friends had mastered by the mid-1930s.

In the ribald "Quartet Erotica," the once-scandalous authors François Rabelais (James MacColl), Guy de Maupassant (Brian Donlevy), Giovanni Boccaccio (Bolger), and Honoré de Balzac (Lahr) lament:

> We once stopped all the traffic
> With stories pornographic–
> But we can see the handwriting on the fence.

Now, after the publication of James Joyce's *Ulysses* and D. H. Lawrence's *Lady Chatterley's Lover*:

> Babes in the wood are we.
> For even with the censors
> And Mr. Hays,
> The kids know all the enswers
> Nowadays.
> We'll go back to our rockers
> For we're just four *alter kockers!*

In "C'est La Vie," Bolger, Lahr, and Luella Gear act out a parody of Noël Coward's sophisticated characters in the movie version of his play *Design for Living*. Ira and Yip wrote the sketch as well as the lyrics, in which two Frenchmen contemplate jumping into the Seine over having been betrayed by the same woman, who suggests a ménage à trois before the men realize they were more interested in each other than "la femme":

> Breakfast will be set
> Tête à tête à tête,
> We'll awake and we'll have crèpes Suzettes.
> C'est l'amour!
> C'est la guerre!
> C'est la vie!

The love song "Let's Take a Walk around the Block" tells the story of a young couple who dream of foreign lands while they toil away in a drab New York City travel agency helping others fulfill their fantasies:

I've never traveled further north
Than old Van Cortlandt Park,
And never further south than the Aquarium.

As they take their daily journeys around their neighborhood, they see what they hope will be their future:

In winter, at Christmas,
We'll visit the Isthmus
To see how they lock up a lock;
And then in Caracas,
On a jackass,
We'll sit and ride around the block.

EVEN WHILE WORKING with Arlen and Harburg, Ira always made himself available to assist his brother as he constructed his opera. DuBose Heyward's work was, in most cases, done elsewhere; Heyward sent his libretto and lyrics to George in New York City, where the brothers massaged the poet's beautiful but sometimes hard-to-sing lyrics "to conform to the rhythm of ordinary speech."[11] Heyward later wrote that it was an extraordinary visual and aural experience to watch George and Ira "pound, wrangle, swear, burst into weird snatches of song, and eventually emerge with a polished lyric."[12]

When Heyward completed a draft of the powerful fourth scene of Act II—set in Serena's room during the hurricane—he admitted that he was not capable of providing the lyrics for this "greatest musical opportunity" of the opera. Only Ira could write them, as it was "a job calling for the closest form of collaboration."[13] During the impressive sequence, the members of the Catfish Row community intone a sequence of prayers for delivery from the storm, but other than "a shrieked 'Doctor Jesus' or 'Heav'nly Father' one couldn't catch a word of the prayers but one wasn't supposed to. What was striven for came off: an effect with almost shock-treatment impact." Unfortunately, only a select audience at Carnegie Hall, gathered prior to the first performance of the opera in Boston, heard the entire set of prayers, which Ira described as a "hi-fi recording, full volume, of musical bedlam at the Tower of Babel (set to music) in one of the most exciting musical moments anyone ever heard."[14]

FROM FOLLY BEACH, South Carolina, where George made an extended visit in June 1934 in search of local atmosphere, Ira received some unexpected news. A "rather embarrassed" DuBose Heyward had spoken to George "about the fact that he was writing most of the lyrics" for the opera, and "wondered if it would be all right with" Ira that Heyward be credited as the author of the book and lyrics, while Ira would receive an "additional lyrics" credit. George took it upon himself to tell Heyward that Ira would not mind, "in view of the fact that it was true [Heyward] was doing most of the work." George seemed to think that this "might relieve [Ira] a little of the responsibility," but tried to douse the flames by assuring his brother that the change would have no effect on the "royalty arrangement" that gave Ira 25 percent of the publishing rights.[15] Although Ira's response to the question of credits is not extant, since there is no reference to "additional lyrics" in the program for the first performances, one can conclude that he succeeded in making his feelings known about the vital part he played in the creation of the opera.

Between George's work on episodes of *Music by Gershwin*, the weekly radio series that provided him with a steady flow of income during the lengthy process of composing the opera, the brothers pored through the score, matching melodies to words "with an amazing rapidity and seemingly without effort," but "those close to them knew how often they would struggle over a single phrase."[16] As the end of the year neared, George was eager to set a date for rehearsals and to begin casting.[17] During Christmas week, the baritone Todd Duncan made a second visit to George's apartment, where, after he finished singing for George and the entire board of the Theatre Guild, those in attendance saw George sit down at the piano, and for two hours heard him and Ira—"with their awful, rotten, bad voices"—sing through the entire score.[18]

Rouben Mamoulian, the Russian-born director of the 1927 staging of *Porgy*, reprised his role for the opera and was treated to a similar performance. Mamoulian watched Ira stand over his brother "like a guardian angel." The pair "blissfully closed their eyes" before they performed "Summertime," and while George played with "the most beatific smile on his face," Ira threw "his head back with abandon, his eyes closed, and sang like a nightingale!" George acted as "the orchestra and sang half of the parts, Ira sang the other half. Ira was also frequently the 'audience,'" Mamoulian continued, noting how "touching" it was "to see how he, while singing, would become so overwhelmed with admiration for his brother, that he would look from him to me with half-open eyes and pantomime with a soft gesture of his hand, as if saying, '*He* did it. Isn't it wonderful? Isn't *he* wonderful?'"[19]

BUT STILL there was more work to be done, and George received a postponement of the premiere until the following season of 1935.[20] Since Ira's "job as collaborator" on the opera was not "continuous," he was free to accept an offer to write the lyrics and contribute to the sketches for the next edition of the *Ziegfeld Follies*, which had been revived by the Shubert brothers after the death of Flo Ziegfeld in 1931.[21] Although concerned about taking on such a large job so soon after *Life Begins at 8:40*, Ira was relieved to hear the suggestion that he again collaborate with Yip Harburg, who at the time was in Hollywood to produce a movie of *Show Boat* for Universal.[22] Finding someone to write the music was more difficult, and Ira joked that "every composer in town" was approached, including "my brother Arthur." When Harold Arlen was unavailable due to a commitment to an Eddie Cantor movie, Arthur Schwartz was suggested, but Ira held out for his preference: Vernon Duke.[23]

Ira and the tempestuous composer Vladimir Dukelsky—who wrote popular songs under the pseudonym Vernon Duke—had met in the early 1920s, not long after the composer arrived in New York as an already devoted acolyte of George Gershwin. Duke's personality, and his background as a member of the Russian upper classes, was a stark contrast to the lower-middle-class Gershwins. Ira's first work with Duke occurred in 1930, with "I Am Only Human after All," a number sung in the third, and final, edition of the Theatre Guild's intimate *Garrick Gaieties* revue. With lyrics cowritten by Yip Harburg, the song did not become the hit Duke had predicted.[24]

The *Follies* agreement gave Ira 2½ percent of the weekly gross, which, he told George, was only right:

Of course they're paying me more than they usually do on a revue but I'm to do more than the lyrics—I've got to keep on Freedman's tail about the skits (talk over ideas and if they need pointing, suggest notions, etc.), discuss cast, get ideas for production etc. Anyway, I've started with Duke, and he already has 7 or 8 very good tunes, 3 or 4 of which I have tentative ideas for. Now the contract I'm signing calls for rehearsals late in August, but it will probably go into rehearsal in September which of course is ample time.

Having originally turned down work on the Cantor picture with Arlen because he did not want to overcommit himself, Ira now hoped to head to Hollywood for six weeks and to convince Universal to allow Yip to come back to New York to assist with the revue. This "naturally would take some of the responsibility off me and make the job somewhat easier." If Ira believed he could "do justice to the 'Follies' and get in some extra money at the same time," he had the Shuberts' blessing.[25]

IRA AND DUKE spent a weekend together at Red Oaks, a hotel in Atlantic Highlands, New Jersey, run by his mother-in-law, "and when we weren't belly-whopping down a long, steep road we were playing ping-pong, so, all in all, a good time was had even if Duke *didn't* make a girl he guaranteed me he would." Duke introduced Ira to Igor Stravinsky during the intermission of a performance of Dmitri Shostokovich's new opera *Lady Macbeth of the Mtsensk District*.[26] The treatment of *Mtsensk* reminded Ira in spots of *Of Thee I Sing* and *Porgy*, and he hoped that Shostakovich would "return the compliment" and see George's opera when it opened in Moscow.[27]

To better understand what David Freedman had in mind for the revue sketches, Ira visited the writer in his tower penthouse at the Beresford building on the Upper West Side. "Boy, what a place!" Freedman occupied "four floors [with] sunrooms, ping pong rooms and a room about fifty-feet long for the jokes which are continually being added to by three assistants," two of whom had just graduated from Columbia University, where they had edited the university's humor magazine, *The Jester*.[28]

Progress on the *Follies* came to a halt when Duke became preoccupied with the debut of his ballet *Public Gardens* [*Jardin Public*].[29] What progress *was* made came "slowly but vaguely." A series of "mostly straight or cute" songs were begun, but since the comedian Fanny Brice was still the only contracted performer, no one knew who these songs might be for. "After a few more of these, I'll get around to the special stuff for Fanny. But there's plenty of time and I don't expect to worry until about 7.30 P.M. July 8th when Billy [Rose—Bruce's husband] will call up to say he doesn't think Fanny has quite the right material."[30]

Duke described Ira's working method as "slow and soothing"—a pleasant change from Yip Harburg's "strident screams and wild pacing of the floor." But the pace did not suit Duke for long:

After a long and copious meal, the company [Ira and Lee and their guests] would repair to the drawing room, which housed the piano, and hectic conversation would ensue. . . . I would shoot expressive glances at ever-placid Ira, who affected not to catch their meaning and willingly joined in the conversation. After an hour or so of this, I, totally exasperated, would invade the piano determinedly and strike a few challenging chords. This time Ira would heed my desperate call, stretch himself, emit a series of protracted sighs, say something to the effect that "one had to work *so-o-o* hard for a living" and more in that vein, then interrupt himself to intone the magic word: "However . . ." This "however" meant that the eleventh hour had struck and the period of delicious procrastination was over. Ira, sighing pathetically, would then produce a small bridge table, various writing and erasing gadgets, a typewriter and four or five books, which he seldom consulted—Roget's *Thesaurus*, Webster's dictionary, rhyming dictionary and the like—wipe and adjust his glasses, all these preparations at a *molto adagio* pace, and finally say in a resigned voice; "O.K., Dukie . . . play that chorus you had last night." After wrestling with last night's chorus for a half hour, Ira would embark on an ice-box-raiding expedition, with me, fearful of too long an interruption, in pursuit. There we'd stand in the kitchen, munching cheese and pickles, Ira obviously delighted with this escapist stratagem, I dutifully pretending to enjoy it too. Another sigh, another "however," then back to the piano. At 2 or 3 a.m. Ira would put away his working utensils and victoriously announce to Lee that he had completed four lines for the new chorus.[31]

Ira found Duke's version of these events "fairly amusing," but because Duke was so musically prolific, the pair completed "an enormous amount of work" in a year.[32]

IRA LEFT CROWDED Manhattan to spend the summer of 1935 with Lee, George, Moss Hart, and Vernon Duke in a large rented house on Fire Island's Ocean Beach. There were "no telephones, no automobiles, but I'm not so sure about sand flies." Friends like Fanny Brice and Arthur Kober lived nearby, "so, it ought to be fun."[33] Ira confessed that he was not in a "Work Rhythm":

> *Not that I've been doing nothing. . . . I've played golf, I've been inter-viewed, I've been to the tailor seven times for fittings. . . . I've watched the market like a hawk, I've listened to Moss' recital of his trip around the world, I've had consultations with Harry* [Kaufman—a Shubert executive] *. . . I've had sessions with Freedman, I've read sketches by other hands . . . but the fact remains that on the "Follies" I've written only two songs in the last two months and therefore I feel I haven't been working.*[34]

CHAPTER 10

I F IRA WAS, IN HIS MIND, inactive, George was at the height of his cre-
ativity. Having finished the composition of his opera in April 1935, he
dove straight into months of orchestration, casting, and rehearsals. In
May, after the hitherto unknown Anne Brown was chosen to play Bess,
the opera's title was changed to differentiate it from the play and the novel.[1]
While DuBose Heyward publicly stated that *Porgy and Bess*, a title in the
well-trodden path of *Pelleas and Melisande, Samson and Delilah*, and *Tristan
and Isolde*, was his idea,[2] it seems he had forgotten that Ira had referred to
it as such for a year.[3]

The curtain rose on *Porgy and Bess* at Boston's Colonial Theatre on September 30, 1935. Isaac Goldberg recalled Ira's "quiet ardor," as he absorbed
what his younger brother had accomplished.[4] As in 1924, when George
debuted the *Rhapsody in Blue*, Ira looked on with a mixture of pride and
wonder—who could have foreseen this?

With the plaudits of Boston's theater critics, but the "lukewarm" response
of the city's music critics, still on everyone's mind, George agreed to cut his
opera from its original four-hour length.[5] On the evening of October 10,
1935, following the triumphant New York debut, the audience rose to its
feet after the curtain went down at 11:20 p.m. George, DuBose Heyward,
and Rouben Mamoulian headed for the stage to take their bows. Each
man took his moment to bask in the spotlight and receive a curtain call
as photographs were taken. Ira was nowhere to be found; it was not in his
nature to appear onstage or take a bow, but this night would be different:
"I was in sort of a daze," he recalled. "I was standing in the wings with
my hat and coat."[6] As Mamoulian took the final bow, someone—Ira never

Porgy and Bess, fall 1935: posing with George and
DuBose Heyward prior to the premiere of the opera.

knew who—unexpectedly shoved him onstage to upstage the director. He
forgot the exact details of what happened next but was assured that his
"appearance got quite a hand."[7]

As in Boston, most of the audience for the first few weeks of performances at the Alvin was made up of Theatre Guild subscribers, whose
discounted tickets kept the gross steady. A price reduction gave the box
office a brief boost but failed to prevent a steady decline in ticket sales.[8]
Ira agreed to waive his weekly royalty and George took a 50 percent cut,
but it had no effect and the opera closed in late January 1936.[9] George had
accomplished what he set out to do artistically, but the brothers' financial investment—George's 10 percent and Ira's 5 percent of the cost of the
production—was lost.[10]

THE CREDITS FOR the lyrics in *Porgy and Bess* have been a puzzle since
its creation. The confusion began with a clause in the original agreement

that included a proposal to make DuBose Heyward a member of ASCAP; to do so, he needed a certain number of published song credits in the opera. Ira admitted that he did "something pretty silly" by adding Heyward's name to "It Ain't Necessarily So," but always remembered Heyward's response: "Ira, you're very sweet, but no one will ever believe I had anything to do with that song."[11] Ira later realized that his generosity was unnecessary; Heyward's credit for the opera itself gave him an entry into ASCAP.[12] Ira wrote "I Loves You, Porgy" alone, but was happy to share the credit.[13] His friends were not as sanguine; Kay Swift told Ira that she would "never get over the way you gave DuBose, bless him, first billing in the lyric writing. . . . All of us who were around know the way it really was."[14]

Sixteen years after the debut of *Porgy and Bess*, Ira tried to clarify the issue for DuBose Heyward's first biographer:

In all honesty, I don't recall having had much to do with polishing any of DuBose's lyrics. True, if a scene was too long or a substitute line was required here and there in the text, I was always available and if DuBose wasn't around I would help my brother cut, edit or change—but so far as "Summertime," "A Woman Is a Sometime Thing," "Buzzard Song," "It Take a Long Pull to Get There," and many others are concerned they are all the work of DuBose and a lovely job too. . . .

DuBose sent me a version [of "I Got Plenty o' Nuttin'"] that had many useable lines; many, however, looked good on paper but were awkward when sung. This is no reflection on DuBose's ability. It takes years and years of experience to know that such a note cannot take such a syllable, that many a poetic line can be unsingable, that many an ordinary line fitted into the proper musical phrase can sound like a million. So on this song I did have to do a bit of "polishing." All in all, I'd consider this a 50–50 collaborative effort. . . .

Although DuBose wasn't in New York when George and I did "Bess, You Is My Woman Now" it was only fair that his name was on it along with mine as I took the title from one of the lines in the text and probably used three or four other lines from the libretto in the body of the song.[15]

THE SONGS IN *Porgy and Bess* for which Ira is best remembered—and for which he was solely responsible—were those written for the citified pimp Sportin' Life, portrayed by the great vaudevillian John Bubbles. The first number was developed from a short melody, and Ira wrote down the first phrase he could think of to help "remember the rhythm" that "accented the second, fifth, and eighth syllables" of the tune. After a two-day struggle to find a better title than "It Ain't Necessarily So," he realized that this dummy phrase fit the character's "cynical and irreligious" response to the "group of religious Sons-and-Daughters-of-Repent-Ye-Saith-the-Lord picnickers":[16]

> De t'ings dat yo' li'ble
> To read in de Bible—
> It ain't necessarily so.
>
> . . .
>
> Methus'lah lived nine hunderd years—
> But who calls dat livin'
> When no gal'll give in
> To no man what's nine hunderd years?

In "There's a Boat Dat's Leavin' Soon for New York," Sportin' Life tempts the susceptible Bess with liquor and "happy dust" and the future of a fabulous life in the big city, away from the disapproving glances of the residents of Catfish Row:

> I'll buy you de swellest mansion
> Up on upper Fifth Avenue,
> An' through Harlem we'll go struttin',
> We'll go a-struttin',
> An' dere'll be nuttin'
> Too good for you.
> I'll dress you in silks and satins
> In de latest Paris styles.
> All de blues you'll be forgettin',
> You'll be forgettin',
> There'll be no frettin'—
> Jes' nothin' but smiles.

As *PORGY AND BESS* WAS being readied for the stage, Ira and Vernon Duke prepared for the end-of-year opening of the *Ziegfeld Follies of 1936* in Boston. They spent much of the pre-Broadway run trimming or deleting songs. The most elaborate of the deleted numbers was "The Ballad of Baby Face McGinty," a "combination hillbilly-gangster-T-Man song ballet" that was seen only by those in the theater on the first night in Boston. Performed in four episodes set in the first four decades of the twentieth century, the lengthy piece was sung "by Judy Canova, as Maw, to her three bearded sons in a Kentucky cabin":

> "Get Baby Face McGinty!"
> Said Mr. Morgenthau.
> "He cheated on taxes, di'n't he?
> That's one thing we can't allow!"
> They got, they shot McGinty;
> They never gave a damn.
> For you're up against true ma-ni-acs,
> When you don't pay up your income tax.
> The moral of McGinty
> Is: Don't cheat your Uncle Sam.

Those who did see the piece "thought it a stunner," but "unless you are Richard Wagner or Eugene O'Neill, overlength has to be considered. The Show Must Go On—but not too long after eleven p.m."[17]

The *Ziegfeld Follies of 1936* made its Broadway debut at the Winter Garden Theatre during the coldest January Manhattan had seen in eleven years. The revue contained the widest range of Ira's work than any show in his entire career, from love songs to satires, and gave him another opportunity to write connecting sketch material. From the age of twenty, he had seen most of the annual productions of the *Follies*, so his parody of the revue's penchant for glorifying undraped showgirls in the opening number, "Time Marches On," strikes true:[18]

> We say, A pox on girls who are
> merely pulchritudinous,

> Who keep arousing only the animal
>   or the lewd in us.
> Away with those undulating Amazons
>   whose voices are like static,
> Who clutter up the witty, the
>   humorous, the epigramatic.
>   . . .
>
> So, on with the ultra in *Follies*—
> The sex-ridden angle is gone!
> Gangway, ye platinum dollies—
> Time marches on!

But the new tone was half-hearted: in the face of a bevy of lovely show-girls, the revue continued apace, with an assortment of unrelated songs and sketches. Although the star, Fanny Brice, was supported by a cast of soon-to-be-famous actors (including Bob Hope and Eve Arden) and the legendary Josephine Baker, making her return to the United States after years spent in Paris, the new *Follies*, wrote one critic, gave "the impression of having been staged by tired producers with material furnished by tired brains."[19] Any momentum that was gathered by Brice's appearance came crashing down when she developed laryngitis, causing the cancellation of a number of performances. A brief recovery in ticket sales was followed by a steady decline, and the show closed after a mere 115 performances.[20] Ira's conclusion? Brice was "better than she had ever been . . . but some of the others! What temperaments, what tonsils, what Josephine Baker, what not!"[21]

Only one number from the *Follies* made a name for itself, but "I Can't Get Started"—a comedic duet for Bob Hope and Eve Arden—did not find that audience until trumpeter Bunny Berigan's swing recording became a hit in 1937:

> I'm a glum one; it's explainable:
> I met someone unattainable.
>   Life's a bore,
> The world is my oyster no more.
> All the papers, where I led the news
> With my capers, now will spread the news:

"Superman
Turns Out to Be Flash in the Pan."

The melody continues to be a popular vessel for jazz musicians, but Ira gave the refrains a myriad of revisions over the following decades at the request of singers, including an updated duet for Bing Crosby and Rosemary Clooney written in collaboration with lyricist Sammy Cahn and in versions for female (Nancy Walker) and male (Frank Sinatra) performers:

I've flown around the world in a plane;
Designed the latest IBM brain.

and

In Cincinnati or in Rangoon
I simply smile and all the gals swoon.
Their whims I've more than just charted,
But I can't get started with you.

Brice returned when the revue came back to Broadway as *The New Ziegfeld Follies of 1936–37,* with Bobby Clark replacing Bob Hope. Several of Ira's songs were replaced with interpolations by other writers, but as the revue played through the end of the year, Ira felt he had no cause for complaint. "So long as it continues to do over 28,000 it's the best revue ANYBODY ever saw."[22]

VINCENTE MINNELLI, a key member of the *Follies* team, was introduced to the "never-closing open houses" on 72nd Street by Yip Harburg and was soon taken in by Ira and Lee as a lifelong friend.[23] After the revue opened, he joined the couple on a cruise to the West Indies, but the intended three-week journey around the islands soon became a "fiasco."[24] Minnelli recalled that after an excellent week in the Virgin Islands, Martinique, and Barbados, they ran into trouble upon disembarking in Port of Spain, Trinidad. It was the beginning of Lent, and "merry-making was on forty-day leave." They tried to set a schedule to get through the days, but rain often washed out their plans, and Ira and Minnelli spent their afternoons being fitted for a half dozen suits each at a "handsome British establishment." But when they got home, the ill-fitting garments were given away. Every evening, the trio stood in line to get tickets at the island's only movie theater. On four consecutive nights, they were reduced to watching the RKO movie *I Dream Too Much*, with songs by Jerome Kern and Dorothy Fields. "I didn't like it in the States," Ira said, "but it looks pretty good here."[25] The MV *Georgic* arrived in Port of Spain on March 6, and the trio happily entered New York Harbor twelve days later.[26]

BEFORE *PORGY AND BESS* made its debut, Yip Harburg predicted that he and Ira would soon see each other on Hollywood's Cahuenga Boulevard.[27] Ira was sanguine about the prospects: "It seems to me there have *always* been deals." He and George had received a dozen offers to write the score for a new Broadway show, but "revues we no want and libretti offered are, at best, fair. Boy, what pix have done to the legit!"[28] The attitude in Hollywood toward George in the post-*Porgy* period was initially cool, which forced him to assure the nervous studio heads that the rumors of his being a "highbrow" were false; he was "out to write hits."[29]

Arthur Lyons, owner of one of the largest talent agencies in the United States, was chosen to make the Gershwins' Hollywood deal. RKO and Universal expressed interest in adapting *Strike Up the Band* for either Fred Astaire or Harold Lloyd; RKO producer Pandro Berman suggested a musical based on P. G. Wodehouse's comedic novel *A Damsel in Distress*. The third idea, a vehicle for Astaire and Ginger Rogers, proved the winner, and Berman offered twenty weeks of work on the movie, then entitled *Watch Your Step*, for $60,000; Lyons countered with $75,000, although the original figure was acceptable if the length of the contract was reduced. The nonexclusive compromise gave George and Ira a total of $55,000 for sixteen weeks on the first picture, with a studio option for another sixteen weeks on a second picture at $75,000 that would begin six months after the exercise of the option. George and Ira could negotiate for a third movie with another studio, but they could not start work until the songs for picture number two were complete.[30]

On August 7, 1936, Ira, George, and Lee headed for Newark Airport to board a TWA transcontinental sleeper for the West Coast. As Ira posed for photographs with his brother on the steps that led into the passenger compartment, he "seemed somewhat disappointed" about the size of the airplane, George's friend William Daly observed: "Maybe he'd been looking at pictures of the China Clipper" that flew across the Pacific Ocean.[31] The fifteen-hour, overnight flight on the twin-engine Douglas DC-3 Skyliner was a luxurious experience, however: the air-conditioned cabins, with room for only fourteen passengers, had one revolving sleeper-lounge chair per row on either side of the center aisle, with a single hostess on board to serve complementary meals. The windows were draped with curtains, while luggage was stowed above the seats in hammock-like compartments.

The pictures coming out of the Hollywood studios had changed since the clunky black-and-white musicals of six years earlier; movies were now as streamlined as air travel, and RKO was the acknowledged master of this technologically superior product. Ira was lucky to be in Hollywood at this time and lucky to have experienced hands on the job, even if incomplete scripts plagued the movies as much as they did the stage. The preliminary script for *Watch Your Step* was unimpressive and gave little sense of the scenario, but after a piano was brought into George's suite at the Beverly Wilshire Hotel, he and Ira began to develop ideas they had started before the journey to California.[32]

Oddly, Ira initially found that he was uncomfortable with George's style; having spent much of the previous year working with Vernon Duke, "listening to *his* rich playing and lush harmonies, I wondered what had happened to my brother (or to me)."[33] When George began to play through the melody for "the eether-eyether notion" in "Let's Call the Whole Thing Off," Ira "nodded approval at the time and rhythm he favored. Inwardly, though, I was bothered. The tune seemed thin and unimportant, and for a day or two I felt I was being fed a sparser musical diet than with Duke. Then, gradually, notes began to fill out and rhythms sparkle."[34]

For the next two and a half weeks, between working on ideas that might fit the still-amorphous script, they almost went crazy looking at houses that

would suit their living and working needs. In mid-August, Lee discovered a
lovely spot that made everyone happy.[35] A Spanish-style house at 1019 North
Roxbury Drive in Beverly Hills was leased for six months, with a six-month
option to take them through the end of August 1937. Located two blocks
north of Sunset Boulevard, it had once been the home of the late crooner
Russ Columbo. Sigmund Romberg was their immediate neighbor, and as
Ira sat at his desk, he could often hear Romberg at the piano; Eddie Cantor
lived across the street. But a celebrity-filled neighborhood meant little to Ira,
who commented on his neighbors with a line from W. S. Gilbert's lyrics to
The Gondoliers: "When everyone is somebodee, / Then no one's anybody!"[36]

They had a tennis court, where Ira faced off against Harold Arlen.
George volleyed balls across the net with the modernist composer Arnold
Schoenberg, but Ira, not a particular fan of modern classical music, once
compared his laryngitis to the "peculiar sounds [of] Schoenberg's latest."[37]
An orange tree in the garden produced a small amount of usable fruit—
"by February we should get at least two glasses from it." The brothers spent
their days and nights with friends from New York who welcomed them
as the latest members of the Broadway-in-exile brigade. At one party, Ira
encountered "every song writer I had ever met and some I had never seen."
Not all of them were successful, "but even those who haven't contracts refuse
to go back [to Broadway] and meantime get along on [ASCAP] money."[38]

The leisurely summer was briefly interrupted by a request to write a
new college fight song for UCLA; instead, Ira made some adjustments to
his "Strike Up the Band" lyrics, and he and George presented the revised
number to the student body. Their reward was honorary student membership and season passes to the home games of UCLA's football team.[39]

By early October, the songs for the Astaire picture had moved along:

*We have 4 songs set, possibly 5, and, at the most, the picture can only use
2 more. Of course, we haven't done the verses yet nor 2nd chorus lyrics
but that I can do in the last two weeks of our contract. They seem pleased
with what we've written and I am pleased with what we've written so
I'm writing you that it's all god-damned pleasing.*[40]

A few weeks later, George and Ira performed six of these remarkable
songs—"(I've Got) Beginner's Luck," "Let's Call the Whole Thing Off,"

"Slap That Bass," "They All Laughed," "They Can't Take That Away from Me," and "Hi-Ho!"—to the delight of Astaire, Rogers, and director Mark Sandrich.[41]

IT TOOK LESS THAN a month away from the hustle and bustle and the depressed economy of Manhattan for Ira—and his wife and brother—to recognize that Southern California suited his indolent nature. As George had separated from his lover Kay Swift, he could now—thanks to his sessions with the psychiatrist Gregory Zilboorg—allow his older brother,

With Fred Astaire and George, RKO Studios, late 1936/early 1937.

whom he had driven to try to produce lyrics at the frantic pace he composed music, to live his own life. Analysis had changed George; he learned that "he got more pleasure out of giving than receiving."[42] By October, Ira was considering the purchase of a property in the nearby San Fernando Valley.[43] "Life is charming," he wrote, "one has so many friends, there are so many diversions."[44] And life *was* charming—after a brief taste of the rainy season, Ira found himself sitting bare-chested by the pool, basking in the rays of the warm California sun.[45]

As the songs for the Astaire/Rogers movie took shape, they awaited news about a possible deal with Samuel Goldwyn. A few weeks later, RKO informed them that they wanted to take up their option.[46] Ira and George would start on the second Astaire picture for RKO in mid-January 1937 and be finished by May; they would then move on to the Goldwyn movie, which they expected would take until October.[47] The Goldwyn deal was worth $75,000 for another sixteen weeks of work, with an option for a second movie at $85,000.[48] But Ira rightly suspected that after writing songs for three motion pictures in fourteen months, he and George would "probably be fed up."[49]

JUST BEFORE CHRISTMAS 1936, Rose Gershwin, along with her daughter and son-in-law, arrived in Beverly Hills to get away from the harsh New York winter. Rose reluctantly agreed to come out only after George explained that he and Ira would be staying in California much longer than they had originally intended. (When she had seen her sons off at the airport in August, George had told her that there was no guarantee that RKO would pick up their option, so the California stay could be a short one.)[50] The family enjoyed a New Year's Eve dinner at the posh Clover Club on Sunset Boulevard.[51] Ira—after miraculously winning $700 at the illegal gambling tables at the Dunes, a plush hot spot conveniently located outside the reach of the law in an unincorporated area just outside the city limits of Palm Springs—was also a patron of the Clover Club's illegal, and often raided, backroom casino, which was guarded by "machine gun-toting goons."[52] He hoped for a "killing" on New Year's Eve. But his luck ran out, and he proceeded to lose much of what he had made at the Dunes and the Clover Club. Yet even the fact that he was still "ahead, however little," amazed him.[53]

Playing poker was a regular part of Ira's weekly schedule. On any given Saturday night, "Black Heart Ira (The Killer)"[54] competed—largely without success—against fellow songwriters (Kern, Arlen), actors (Charles Coburn, John Garfield), writers (Clifford Odets, Morrie Ryskind, Russell Crouse, Marc Connelly, Charles Lederer), directors (William Wyler), movie studio executives, and the likes of *Hollywood Reporter* owner Billy Wilkerson. Some of the games were played at a rental unit at the El Cabrillo, an apartment complex in the heart of Hollywood that was a popular hangout for those in the entertainment business.

Even if he held a bad hand and faced horrible odds, Ira played through to the end.[55] His losses were notable: in 1937, he dropped over $12,000 (more than $220,000 today), nearly 20 percent of his entire income for the previous year.[56] But neither his poor luck at cards nor the coldest winter in Los Angeles in fifteen years got him down: "If I can't have Miami or Havana, I'll take Southern Cal. for the Winter."[57]

CHAPTER 11

IRA BEGAN WORK on *A Damsel in Distress*, the second Astaire movie for RKO, without the benefit of anything usable from George's tune books. But by this time in the brothers' partnership, the method of their collaboration had changed; where it once had been the norm that the lyrics were written to a generally completed tune, they now "had come to a working arrangement whereby the words and music were written almost simultaneously." They sat side by side—George at the piano and Ira at a small table next to him—with George penciling Ira's lyrics into his piano score as they went along.[1] Each man played his part in the synthesis of words and music that Ira defined as songwriting; while Ira never tried to write the music, George "did not try to write lyrics." But they always made suggestions, George's typically asking his brother to "Make it simpler, much simpler."[2]

PRIOR TO A SERIES of performances with the San Francisco Symphony in January 1937, George spent a weekend with his friends Sidney and Olga Fish at their Palo Corona Ranch in Carmel.[3] Ira, at the urging of producer Pan Berman, joined him and director George Stevens on a train ride to Santa Barbara to attend a sneak preview of Berman and Stevens's forthcoming movie, *Quality Street*. The trio and screenwriter Pinky Wolfson then caught the midnight train to Salinas to meet George in Carmel to discuss *A Damsel in Distress*. The ranch was "lovely," Ira said, "even though it rained all day."[4] On January 11, George and Ira drove up the coast to San Francisco, where they lunched with the symphony's conductor, Pierre

Monteux.[5] Ira—plus his wife and mother, who also arrived to attend the concerts—returned to Beverly Hills on January 16, while George flew to Detroit for another concert.

IN EARLY FEBRUARY, at an afternoon rehearsal for an all-Gershwin concert in Los Angeles, George nearly toppled off the stage while conducting the orchestra in a section of *Porgy and Bess*. He shrugged it off, saying he had merely lost his balance, but during the evening performance, he briefly blacked out at the piano during the Concerto in F and stumbled over some of the notes.[6] Ira saw nothing amiss at the lavish after-party at the Café Trocadero on the Sunset Strip, but George agreed that he was tired and submitted himself to a medical exam. George's choice—and it likely *was* his choice, given his fondness for dieting, psychotherapy, and exercise—was Philip M. Lovell, who lacked a medical degree but who had fashioned himself into a celebrated Southern California homeopathist. Lovell's report indicated that George's blood pressure and other numbers were within normal ranges, and the diagnosed sinusitis, intestinal problems, and gradual baldness were consistent with his patient's prior complaints.[7] Everyone relaxed; any symptoms George displayed were only further manifestations of the "composer's stomach," which he had talked about for many years. Why would this time, at least to Ira and Lee—the latter with a well-known aversion to sickness—be any different?

BETWEEN POKER GAMES, desultory work on *A Damsel in Distress*, and attending George's concerts and parties, Ira considered his future; for the first time in his life, he saw possibilities that excluded his brother. The warm weather and the relaxed lifestyle of Southern California had become increasingly attractive. He had commitments with George, but after that, who knew what the future might bring? George recognized that Beverly Hills was a "good place" for his brother, but George needed the faster pace of Manhattan.[8] In the end, they agreed on a compromise: Ira would try to buy a house in Beverly Hills with space for "a small studio for George's use whenever he came to Hollywood to work or visit."[9]

After eight weeks, there was little to show on *A Damsel in Distress* beyond "a couple of promising beginnings."[10] In mid-April 1937—after a nearly

Beverly Hills, ca. 1936–37: in typically
relaxed mode. Photo by George Gershwin.

four-month visit—Rose Gershwin returned to New York. The house was
now free of long-term guests (Frankie and her husband having departed
after only a month in California), but there were only four weeks left to
complete the songs before their obligations to Samuel Goldwyn began. Ira
knew that his brother was anxious to return to New York. Writing songs for
the movies was a frustrating experience for George; while Ira was content to
leave the final product of a motion picture to those who were experienced
in the ins and outs of production, George was restless. His mood began
to darken, and his feelings of being trapped in the enervating sunshine of
Southern California became heavier.

SHALL WE DANCE, the first product of Ira's second stint in Hollywood,
was released in May 1937. Audiences loved Astaire and Rogers, two of
RKO's biggest stars, as sparring lovebirds, but Ira was disappointed by the
treatment of the songs: "Either enough wasn't done with the singing—or
the score was cut." He was mollified by early reports of box office success,
however, and if Shall We Dance were to equal the grosses of Top Hat, an

earlier Astaire/Rogers picture that contained one of Irving Berlin's greatest collections of hits, Ira agreed that it would add to the popularity of the Gershwins' score with bands.[11]

Shall We Dance proved that George and Ira could still write hit songs, and the score contained at least three that rank among the greatest of their storied careers.

The idea for the lyric of "They All Laughed" came from the 1920s boom in the business of self-improvement, with an extremely popular correspondence school advertisement for the US School of Music: "They laughed when I sat down to play the piano but when I started to play!"[12] One of the lines—"They laughed at Fulton and his steamboat"—may have been borrowed from Ira's friend Groucho Marx, who reportedly made that quip to George S. Kaufman.[13]

> They all laughed at Christopher Columbus
> When he said the world was round;
> They all laughed when Edison recorded sound.
>
> They all laughed at Wilbur and his brother
> When they said that man could fly;
> They told Marconi
> Wireless was a phony—
> It's the same old cry!
>
> They laughed at me wanting you,
> Said I was reaching for the moon;
> But oh, you came through—
> Now they'll have to change their tune.
>
> They all said we never could be happy,
> They laughed at us—and how!
> But ho, ho, ho—
> Who's got the last laugh now?

One of the cleverer ideas in "Let's Call the Whole Thing Off" was inspired by Lee Gershwin's youthful—and retained in adulthood—pronunciation:

You say eether and I say eyether,
You say neether and I say nyther;
Eether, eyether, neether, nyther—
Let's call the whole thing off!

You like potato and I like po-tah-to,
You like tomato and I like to-mah-to;
Potato, po-tah-to, tomato, to-mah-to—
Let's call the whole thing off!

For Ira, the key ingredient in "They Can't Take That Away from Me"
was the lovely, raised note that his brother gave him to accompany the
buildup to the emotion of the word "life" at the end of the song:[14]

The way you wear your hat,
The way you sip your tea,
The mem'ry of all that—
No, no! They can't take that away from me!

The way your smile just beams,
The way you sing off key,
The way you haunt my dreams—
No, no! They can't take that away from me!

We may never, never meet again
On the bumpy road to love,
Still I'll always, always keep
The mem'ry of—

The way you hold your knife,
The way we danced till three,
The way you've changed my life—
No, no! They can't take that away from me!
No! They can't take that away from me!

WITH A FINAL PUSH, the songs for *A Damsel in Distress* were finished by the first week of May. It was an "interesting score," yet Ira remained uncertain about "what it will finally turn out to be when they start shooting in a couple of months without our being present to nurse our offspring."[15]

Their longed-for week of rest before having to produce new songs for "the Great Goldwyn" was reduced to a single day. Ira fervently hoped to be done with this "chore" in October.[16] By the end of the month, ensconced in a studio on the Goldwyn lot, five numbers—"I Love to Rhyme," "Love Walked In," "I Was Doing All Right," "Just Another Rhumba," and "Love Is Here to Stay"—had been "completed, or mapped out substantially."[17]

Ira's plans when he returned to New York were to "look over the site for the [World's Fair] Exposition, have a snail at the Brevoort [Hotel], take a trip to Albania, or Mexico or Staten Island for a couple of months, and then do a show or return [to Hollywood] for another pic. But I'll never do three pictures in one year again."[18]

AFTER A BRIEF TRIP to Agua Caliente in June that failed to help him recover his health, George consulted the German-born psychoanalyst Ernst Simmel, who diagnosed George's condition as "physical not mental." Simmel recommended an examination by the internist Gabriel Segall, who found nothing to be concerned about.[19] Segall, in a letter more than a year later to George's psychiatrist, Gregory Zilboorg, reported the details of his examination: The patient's occasional dizzy spells had occurred over the course of the past three months and had been accompanied, for the past three weeks, by headaches. This "momentary giddiness" lasted for thirty seconds and was accompanied by an "olfactory sensation, a very fould [*sic*] odor." The spells occurred "at least once a day and were usually present in the morning when the patient first wakened and have recurred during times of emotional tension, such as during a concert performance or even while he was playing tennis." George complained of pain in his left shoulder and arm but displayed no visual symptoms and no vomiting. "Insomnia was present four months ago, when the patient was in love. He stated that he is a nervous individual, attributing this to his creative work and pressure in the studios." No abnormalities appeared in the physical examination and no heart damage was revealed by an electrocardiogram; George's blood pressure of 110/80 and pulse of 60 to 65 were normal, as were his urinalysis and blood count.[20]

IN LATE JUNE, George seemed listless at a lunch with his friend George Pallay and the actresses Paulette Goddard and Constance Collier.[21] Lee, recalling that George had told her that his first blinding headache had occurred after a party at Irving Berlin's house,[22] called Dr. Segall, who insisted on a full neurological exam, which "failed to reveal any clear-cut evidence of intracranial diseases." Segall, in consultation with Simmel and a third doctor, recommended that George be hospitalized for X-rays of his head and sinuses.[23]

On June 23, George was admitted to the Cedars of Lebanon Hospital in Los Angeles.[24] An ophthalmological examination was "entirely negative," according to Segall. "We discussed the advisability of a spinal puncture and we decided against it," as George was "anxious to leave the hospital."[25] George remained overnight for observation, and although his first nausea happened on the following morning, "no symptom of any organic or physical illness" could be found during his four-day stay, leading the doctors to conclude that George's nerves were to blame, "perhaps self-induced by worry, overwork or general emotional geographic unhappiness or something."[26] When George returned home on June 26, his final discharge notes indicated "most likely hysteria."[27] The following day, Paul Levy, a nurse trained in psychiatric care who worked for Dr. Simmel, was brought in.[28]

The theory that George's condition was entirely mental was common among George's family and friends. P. G. Wodehouse, who lived near the Gershwins, said that Lee Gershwin had told him that George's condition was "simply something psychological."[29]

Although the external displays of George's changing health seemed to pass by Ira without comment, it was clear that his brother needed peace and quiet. On June 28, Ira asked their agent, Arthur Lyons, to arrange for a two-week leave from the Goldwyn contract.[30] An unpaid leave effective until July 12 was agreed to, by which time "Mr. Gershwin will be fully recovered."[31] George's signature on the document was little more than a scrawl.

During dinner on July 2, George listened to a radio broadcast of his tunes with Ira and Lee. No one could know that it would be the final time George and Ira would, together, hear the songs they had jointly written.[32] That evening, Sam Behrman called, and Ira told him that George was suffering from "some nervous ailment." On Saturday, Behrman, Oscar Levant, and Sonya Levien visited the Roxbury Drive house. "George was upstairs," Behrman later wrote. "We waited in the living room. George came downstairs accompanied by a male nurse. I stared at him. It was not the George we all knew." When asked, George twice repeated that he felt pain behind his eyes. He refused to play the piano and mused that he "had to live for this, that Sam Goldwyn should say to me: 'Why don't you write hits like Irving Berlin?'" The nurse got George up from the couch and took him back upstairs. Lee told Behrman that George seemed "worse tonight. Maybe it's seeing you—reminds him of the past." She also told him that she had had to cut her brother-in-law's food for him. Everyone sat in silence, wondering what it all meant. Ira seemed almost numb with concern and disbelief. Behrman later told Levant and Levien that he thought George was "*very* sick."[33]

Lee saw George's unusual and increasingly depressed comments as signs of his illness.[34] She was reportedly disgusted by "George's behavior at the table—dribbling as he drank, dropping his knife, leaving food on his chin. In one temper tantrum, she ordered him away from the table. Ira accompanied George up the stairs to his bedroom." Years later, Ira told Mabel Schirmer that "he would never forget the look in his brother's eyes as he entered the room."[35]

Everyone hoped that the impending visit of Lou and Emily Paley would improve George's health and outlook, but on July 4, he was taken by car to Yip Harburg's nearby vacant house, where Ira visited him on the following day.[36] Simmel and Zilboorg had "decided it would be wise to separate George from his family," and "Ira was relieved by the fact that the two analysts had conferred and come to a conclusion."[37]

Dr. Zilboorg, kept abreast of George's illness, urged his former patient to obey Simmel's orders.[38] After his discharge from the hospital, George was seen by Simmel every day, and although he was incapable of work, George seemed more at ease.[39] (This narrative contrasts with that of another observer of the situation—presumably George's manservant Paul Mueller—who indicated that his employer thought that Simmel "was doing him no good.")[40]

On the afternoon of July 5, Mueller told Behrman that George "was all right" until they got to Harburg's house, when he asked to have the shades pulled down and asked for a towel to put over his eyes. Behrman told Ira and Lee that he thought George was "gravely ill," and they agreed when Behrman asked if he could telephone Abraham Flexner, a New York authority on medical conditions, for his advice. Flexner was reached at his summer place in Canada, and he recommended that Behrman get hold of the renowned neurosurgeon Walter Dandy at Johns Hopkins University. Unfortunately, Dandy was on Chesapeake Bay. "By this time," Behrman wrote, "Lee and Ira were a bit scared." He told them to "concentrate on trying to get adequate medical help for George."[41]

Ira continued to keep up the facade that his brother was "improving."[42] On July 8, Ira visited George to discuss the Goldwyn songs, and George signed a notarized document giving Ira power of attorney.[43] That same day, George attempted to play the piano for a visiting Dr. Simmel, but lost his coordination.[44] Frankie, thousands of miles away, and increasingly worried about her brother's condition, urgently wired from Vienna.[45]

At 4 p.m. on July 9, Ira and George Pallay drove over to the Harburg house, where they found George asleep, for the first time "without pills to relieve headache." Pallay's account is unclear: did they *see* George or were they merely *told* about his condition? Three hours passed. George began to shake and tremble when the nurse escorted him to the bathroom. Upon being returned to bed, George's eyes began to swell. In Vernon Duke's narration of events—based on his 1950 discussions with Lee Gershwin—she and Ira returned to Harburg's house "to decide on the action to be taken. Lee remembers seeing six doctors testing George's reflexes as she entered the bedroom." George had fallen into a coma.[46] (The nurse presumably had notified them, as well as the doctors, of the change in George's condition.) But another version of this event indicates that Lee and Ira arrived at the house "just as George was being carried out on a stretcher" to the ambulance, where a stunned Ira heard George mumble "Astaire" as the stretcher was loaded into the back of the vehicle,[47] a moment that Astaire confirmed having heard from Ira himself.[48]

The ambulance returned George to Cedars of Lebanon, where he was readmitted at 11 p.m. Dr. Segall consulted with local neurosurgeon Carl Rand; the patient was in a "rather deep coma."[49] The doctors were now certain that George's ailment was not mental. X-rays failed to disclose a tumor, so air was to be pumped into George's brain to allow the X-ray to "take."[50] Ira and Lee arrived and were joined by their friends.

In the early morning of July 10, attempts were made to reach Dr. Dandy, and the US Navy was ordered out to find him.[51] At 11 a.m., Ira, Lou Paley (he and Emily had arrived days earlier), and Arthur Lyons went to the bank with Ira's power-of-attorney document; Lee headed for the hospital an hour later, Ira and Lou arriving thirty minutes after her. By 2 p.m., Ira and Lee were back home, and numerous attempts were made to find his mother, who was located at 4:30 p.m. in Long Branch, New Jersey. She "was asked to fly [to California] as soon as possible. Mrs. Gershwin notified her immediate return to New York."[52] In the meantime, Dr. Rand judged that George must have a tumor in one of his temporal lobes. Segall had consulted Howard Naffziger, chairman of the Department of Surgery at the University of California, San Francisco, and at 9:15 p.m., Ira and Lee, with Henry Botkin and Arthur Lyons, returned to Cedars of Lebanon to meet Naffziger, who arrived around 10 p.m. from Lake Tahoe, Paul Mueller having flown north to bring him back. By 10:30 p.m., George's pulse had dropped to 53; surgery was imperative. Dr. Rand was chosen to wield the scalpel, as Naffziger was without his personal equipment or operating room assistant.[53] A ventricle study was completed under a local anesthetic, revealing a tumor in the right temporal lobe; "immediate and energetic action" was necessary.[54] At 10:45 p.m., Ira and the others returned home while George was prepped with the injection of a spinal anesthetic.[55]

At 12:30 a.m. on July 11, George was wheeled into a seventh-floor operating theater. Pallay monitored the situation from a nearby office, while family and friends—Ira and Lee, the Paleys, Oscar Levant, Moss Hart, Vincente Minnelli, the screenwriters Gene Solow and Elizabeth Meyer Lorentz, conductor Alexander Steinert, and Henry Botkin—gathered three floors below. Arthur Lyons later joined Pallay; they were the only nonmedical people to view the procedure.[56] By 1:30 a.m., the first part of the operation—pumping air into the brain—was complete and George was taken for X-rays of his skull. Returned to the operating room, the removal of the tumor began at 3 a.m.[57] At 4:01 a.m., Pallay told the worried people on the fourth floor of the "nature" of the growth.[58] By 4:30 a.m., a cyst was revealed; it was, in the desperate circumstances, a cause for great cheerfulness. The tumor was then, horribly, discovered to be embedded deep in George's brain.[59] The doctors removed as much cancerous material as possible; they concluded that no further surgery was possible "at this time."[60] George's postoperative condition was "poor and he was given a blood-transfusion which was followed by 5% glucose intravenously."[61]

The doctors told Pallay that the patient was in "grave" condition. George's chances for survival, said Dr. Rand, were "very small." At 6 a.m., Pallay suggested that the family leave the hospital; orderlies were taking George to a fourth-floor room, and it was "inadvisable for friends and family to see patient on operating table." Pallay did not reveal the seriousness of the situation, only that the last remaining threat was "post-operative."[62]

When Ira, Lee, and the others returned home at 6:15 a.m. on that "dank, gray morning" of July 11, 1937,[63] Ira had been convinced by his wife, who had no heart to tell her disbelieving husband the truth she had heard from Pallay, that the lengthy operation had been successful and that his brother was recovering.[64] At 6:30 a.m., in that moment of relief, Ira called his mother, who was about to leave for the airport, and "advised her not to fly out."[65] He relaxed; his hopes—and prayers, if he had them—had come true.

What Pallay had revealed to Lee on their ride home—*but had not revealed to Ira*, who was driven home separately by Paul Mueller and whom everyone suspected was too emotionally and physically fragile, teetering on the edge of a nervous breakdown—was that, were George to live, the best outcome would be that his entire left side—from face to leg—"would be forever paralyzed."[66] At 6:15 a.m., George was wheeled back to his room, where his "pulse and respiration rallied."[67] But hyperthermia quickly developed and could not be controlled.[68] George's temperature reached 107 degrees Fahrenheit, and at 10:25 a.m., he died of "paralysis of his respiratory organs" at the age of thirty-eight.[69]

PART FOUR

Words with New Music I

CHAPTER 12

O N THAT SAME MORNING of July 11, 1937, an exhausted Ira, believing that the operation had been carried out successfully, picked up the ringing telephone and told Max Dreyfus that there was no need to worry about George.[1]

When that same telephone rang again later that day, the voice from the hospital at the other end of the line delivered a crushing, soul-destroying blow. George Gershwin, the Jazz Age meteor, was dead, and Ira, because of a well-meaning, if tragically misguided, decision, was not at his side during his brother's final moments. Although he would continue to state that "everything known to science that could be done, was done," Ira Gershwin was plunged into the depths of despair.[2]

There was no time for public grief. In a daze, he mustered the energy to act on the matters at hand. He sent a cable to his worried sister, who was still in Vienna, but kept the news of George's death from his younger brother and his physically and emotionally fragile mother for as long as possible.[3] But when he called them on the morning of July 12, he discovered, to his surprise, that Rose already knew the fate of her beloved Georgie from her attorney, Emanuel Alexandre, who had been with her and Arthur for some hours after he himself had learned of George's passing.[4]

Within hours of George's death, Ira consulted attorneys from the Los Angeles firm of O'Melveny, Tuller & Myers. He told them that George had died without a will; this fact, combined with George's having declared himself a California resident for tax purposes and the need for immediate action to secure the estate, led the attorneys to conclude that under California law, the special administrator of the estate should be located in California. Since Ira was George's "nearest living relative in the state," it was clear that he should be appointed.[5] On July 12, 1937, after a brief hearing in a Los Angeles courtroom, the order of administration was issued.[6] George's California estate was valued at more than $10,000 and Ira's bond was placed at $208,000.[7] The reaction from the East Coast to Ira's appointment was swift and, to Ira, once again, surprising; in his grief and confusion, he had given little thought to how his family and their hangers-on would respond.

A MAN AS internationally beloved as George Gershwin deserved a funeral befitting his stature. Rose Gershwin was adamant that her son receive a proper Jewish service and that it should happen in New York; Ira had no objections, but there was no one in the family currently capable of attending to the many details that had to be decided upon. With Frankie and her husband still in Europe, songwriter L. Wolfe Gilbert was put in charge of arranging for George's body to be transported to New York and for a Hollywood memorial service; Gene Buck of ASCAP in New York attended to the arrival of the body and the funeral service to be held at the vast Temple Emanu-El on the east side of Central Park.[8]

On July 13, Ira and Lee boarded an American Airlines transcontinental Douglas DC-3 for Newark, New Jersey. As Ira climbed the stairs to enter the aircraft, his mind returned to the day, eleven months earlier, when he and his youthful, athletic brother had arrived in California with high hopes for their future. As the cabin door was closed and the twin propellers began to roar, Ira looked down at the blanket that covered his lap and legs and vaguely registered the air sickness bag in his hands. He pulled back the curtain of his window and peered out to watch the steps being wheeled away from the airplane; all he could see was his own reflection. His haggard visage was the last thing he wanted to see; it was a reminder of the reality he could not face—he was alive while his brother was dead. George was the "stupor mundi"—the wonder of the world. What was he in comparison?

Memories began to flood his mind: childhood, friendship, partnership. All gone now, in the blink of an eye, in a breath of wind. Not even sleeping pills could help him relax or could ease the nightmare of the twenty-hour flight. He dozed fitfully, then was awakened with a start—not by the turbulence, but by a dream: George, hands outstretched, pleading, asking

why Ira had not believed him. Lee, under the influence of the same medi-
cation, roused from her own dreams and took Ira's arm to wake him from
his nightmare. He shook his head to clear away the visions, stared out the
window at the clouds, and asked his nameless God why he had not been
chosen instead of his brother. Surely no one would miss *him*?

They arrived in Newark on the afternoon of July 14 to find a city that
was enjoying a welcome respite from six days of near-record heat. Ira hastily gathered his papers and, with Lee, headed for the exit of the airplane.
As he made his way down the stairs—slightly slippery from a light, misty
rain—he stumbled and nearly fell, with only his hand, as he reached out
to grip the rail, and another hand from Lee, keeping him from tumbling
headlong to the tarmac. When he reached the ground, his knees began to
give way, but he steadied himself and slowly moved toward the terminal.
Waiting for them was Vernon Duke, aghast at the ashen complexion and
sunken eyes of his erstwhile lyricist.[9] As Duke escorted them to a car, Ira
shook his head in sorrow at the reporters who crowded around asking
for comments.[10]

When he stepped into his mother's apartment on East 72nd Street, he
was lethargically greeted by his younger brother, who was too stunned to
comprehend the situation. Also there were his mother's attorneys, Emanuel
Alexandre and former New York Deputy Attorney General Abe Rosenthal, both eager to persuade Ira that he had been wrong to obtain powers
of administration in California; George was, in their opinion, a resident of
New York, and his estate should be handled there.[11] Ira sheepishly replied
that he had only heeded the advice of his lawyers but agreed to waive his
rights to the administrator's role.[12]

THE CASKET containing George Gershwin's body traveled by rail across
the continental United States in a freight car of the Twentieth Century
Limited and arrived at Grand Central Station at 9:15 a.m. on July 15,[13]
where Gene Buck and a group of George's friends escorted the casket to
a waiting hearse.[14] The funeral home of Samuel Berliner and Charles N.
Pollak on East 65th Street prepared the body for the memorial service
that afternoon at the Temple Emanu-El,[15] the Romanesque-style house of
worship for the Reform branch of Judaism, located on the former site of

the John Jacob Astor mansion at the corner of Fifth Avenue and East 65th Street. It was a humid, rainy day in Manhattan, and the weather mirrored the tears and the grief-stricken faces of the mourners as they passed through the heavy bronze doors of the temple. A phalanx of policemen in raincoats held back the umbrella-wielding throng of nearly a thousand who stood outside, eager to catch a glimpse of the casket or of one of the celebrity attendees.[16] Reporters with press passes stuck in their hatbands, also unable to get inside, eagerly sought out an angle for their stories.

Of the thirty-five hundred mourners who jammed inside, those seated in the pews were arranged into categories: family and friends; society figures; special guests; and the press. But even in less segregated New York City, the cast of *Porgy and Bess* was isolated in its own pew. Less exalted mourners were assigned to the rear balcony or quietly stood where they could find space. Family members in attendance included Ira's father-in-law, Albert Strunsky; his brother-in-law, English, with his wife, Lucy; and his aunt, Kate Wolpin.[17] Also paying their respects were politicians—New York City mayor Fiorello La Guardia and his predecessor, Jimmy Walker, and New York governor Herbert Lehman among them—and George's many friends and colleagues: Kay Swift, Mabel Schirmer, Vernon Duke, Al Jolson, Irving Caesar, Todd Duncan, George S. Kaufman, Walter Damrosch, George M. Cohan, Max Dreyfus, Vinton Freedley, Ferde Grofé, W. C. Handy, Otto Harbach, Alexander Smallens, Leopold Godowsky, Ruby Elzy, Deems Taylor, Harry Warren, Paul Whiteman, Bennett Cerf, Franklin P. Adams, Frank Crowninshield, Alfred and Dick Simon, and Herbert Bayard Swope.

At 2 p.m. East Coast time, Dr. Stephen Wise, the rabbi of the Free Synagogue, began to speak. His words, about how the United States—in stark contrast to Central Europe—had welcomed this "gifted young Jew," were a reflection of a question Wise had asked Ira before the service: had George Gershwin been "a good Jew"? Ira was puzzled. The rabbi explained that he wanted to know if Ira's younger brother hated Hitler. To Ira, it was a strange way to define belief, but since he was eager to get the service underway, he mumbled yes before making his way to his family.[18]

Ira sat, staring at George's casket, which rested "between clusters of white lilies, and before the Ark of the Covenant . . . blanketed with pink roses and purple orchids." He barely registered the psalms that were read and what Dr. Wise said. Although it had been suggested that *Rhapsody in*

Blue be performed, none of George's music was heard during the service. The processional music by J. S. Bach—the "Air on the G String"—was played by Gottfried H. Federlein, the veteran organist at the temple; cellist Ossip Giskin gave a solo rendition of Robert Schumann's *Träumerei*; and the Perolé Quartet played a portion of one of Beethoven's string quartets. As the mourners filed out, the strains of Handel's "Largo" could be heard from the organ and the quartet.[19]

As the casket was carried out past the rows of honorary pallbearers, a black hearse waited at the main entrance of the temple on Fifth Avenue. The crowds pushed forward to get a glimpse and the police again held them back, while the family discreetly exited from a side door on 65th Street. As Ira stepped down onto the sidewalk with Arthur, their mother—her face covered in a black veil with polka dots—was visibly weighed down by grief and in a state of physical collapse. Arthur took her left arm, but Ira, a step behind them, with eyes closed and head bowed, seemed unable to recognize her fragility, so wracked was he by guilt and despair.

Fifteen limousines followed the hearse for the twenty-mile journey to the Mount Hope Cemetery in Hastings-on-Hudson.[20] It was a procession fit for a king: traffic was stopped by the police along Fifth Avenue and on the route to the cemetery.[21] Kaddish was said over the casket before it was lowered into the ground next to the grave of George's father.[22] Although "badly shaken," Ira and his mother showed little emotion during the service.[23] His mind drifted back to an entry he had made in his diary twenty years earlier, as he witnessed the funeral of his grandfather Gershon Bruskin: "A hole. Box lowered. Shovelfuls of dirt."[24]

IRA WAS EAGER to return to California after the wearying funeral, but family matters and legal issues weighed him down and forced him to remain in New York City for another two weeks. His strained relationships with his mother and younger brother, further deteriorated by his decision to delay informing them of George's death, were thrown further out of kilter. Rose appeared unconcerned about mourning, throwing open her closets and jewelry box to don her furs and diamonds,[25] while Arthur, attempting to find his own voice as a songwriter, was brash enough to think that he could convince Ira that he could replace George as Ira's musical collaborator.[26] The day after the funeral, he prodded Ira to listen to some of his tunes. Arthur could not understand the symbiotic relationship that Ira and George had developed over more than a decade, and Ira retreated, mumbling that this was not the time to discuss the matter.[27]

That same day, a New York surrogate court appointed Rose Gershwin as the administratrix of her son's estate; Ira was named as a special administrator in California.[28] The estate was estimated at between $500,000 and $800,000, largely in cash and securities; George's compositions were deemed to have little monetary value. Rose received George's ASCAP income and his share of the publishing rights in New World Music and Gershwin Publishing Corporation. The papers Ira had so hastily filed in California would be revoked.[29]

THE STRESS WAS becoming too much, and now Samuel Goldwyn added more. With shooting soon to begin on the *Follies*, the producer pressed Ira to quickly complete the songs he and George had begun.[30] In addition, there was the verbal commitment George had given to Goldwyn to sell him the rights to use *An American in Paris* for a ballet sequence in the movie. These negotiations were among the first steps in Ira's decades-long, often contentious relationship with Emanuel Alexandre, a "very slippery character" who had insinuated himself into Rose Gershwin's life.[31] The Russian-born attorney was unfamiliar with negotiating entertainment deals, yet never failed to push himself into every contract, usually underestimating the value of George's work in the process.[32]

As Ira finally prepared to leave Manhattan, he was given another reminder of his brother. Exhausted, he was "just about knocked . . . out" by a condolence letter from a family who asked where George was buried. "Someday they expected to be in New York and wanted to visit his grave." Ira confessed that it would "be a long, long time before we get over it, if ever."[33]

THE RETURN FLIGHT to California was calm compared with the journey that took him to New York City. "I actually slept for five hours."[34] Awaiting him was the question of who he would collaborate with to complete the score for *The Goldwyn Follies*. His agent, Arthur Lyons, suggested someone intimately familiar with George's music: Vernon Duke.[35] Ira agreed that Duke was a good choice, but thought it would take more than sitting down at the piano and writing a set of new numbers. Unfortunately, while Ira expected to take six weeks to mine "possible tunes from those George left behind," Goldwyn wanted the job done quickly and was unwilling to provide Ira with even a two-week guaranteed contract. The producer's "attitude is that I ought to be able to finish it in a week—if it takes longer[,] if there is any other work to be done, *he* wants to be the judge." Ira thought that Goldwyn was "not ready with his book, also that the actors' salaries start in a week or so and the picture is going to cost him much more than he bargained for, and he has come to a realization that he may not need any new songs because after all most pictures do not have more than five songs (which he already has)." Ira conceded that he had no choice but to comply with Goldwyn's wishes, although "frankly I've found him a great disappointment to put it mildly, and personally I don't care if I go on with it at all."[36]

IRA LEARNED one thing from the painful weeks in New York: Beverly Hills was clearly now his home. The majority of his friends and colleagues were in Southern California, good-paying work was more readily available, and, most important, the three thousand miles from coast to coast meant that his troublesome family could more easily be held at bay. For the moment, however, there was little time to relax; his mail was filled with requests for physical reminders of George, including from the women who asked for the return or the destruction of their correspondence with George. Kay Swift's letters were particularly sensitive; even if Ira was unaware of the full scope of her relationship with George, he knew that these letters might be embarrassing, particularly to Swift's three young daughters. Ira, torn between his obligations to protect his brother's name from scandal and his instinct to preserve whatever he could of his papers, obliged, and at Swift's request destroyed the items that were in his possession.[37]

HIS "DAYS AND NIGHTS passed in a blur" accompanied by a "deep and unshakeable sense of despondency," until the afternoon came when he sat down to listen to Fred Astaire's recordings of songs from *Shall We Dance*. "In a few moments, the room was filled with gaiety and rhythm, and I felt that George, smiling and approving, was there listening with me—and grief vanished."[38] Only when he was able to believe that his brother was gone physically, yet remained with him in a way others might describe as spiritual (even if Ira would quibble with the term), did he know that he and George would never be separated. Ira was comforted by the belief that his beloved brother "never knew there was anything physically wrong with him but up to the last thought it was just a mental breakdown."[39]

VERNON DUKE's never-ending stream of amusing stories about his love life was a welcome distraction for Ira and they kept him from dwelling on his sorrows as the songs for *The Goldwyn Follies* were completed. But when it came to credits, the pair diverged: Duke claimed that he arranged and harmonized George's melody for "Love Walked In" and supplied the verses to "I Was Doing All Right" and "Love Is Here to Stay."[40] Ira stated that the "musical end of short verses" was typically "governed by a melodic line" he himself had suggested, once he knew "where [he wanted] to go lyrically."[41] For example, George added the "*and* notes" to the refrain of "Love Is Here to Stay" at his suggestion; the lyricist felt "they were to be the song's trick."[42] Duke's authorship claim is also disputed by Oscar Levant, who heard George play melodies that might have fit the verses to these songs.

Ira explained that "if, once in a great while in deliberations with the composer, a short musical phrase came to me as a possibility and was found acceptable to my collaborator, that didn't make me a composer." Typically, the "suggestion arose from some musical phrase of the composer's own, which he had overlooked or whose potentiality he was unaware of." A "musically inclined" lyricist "can sometimes be of help to the composer. (Not that the composer can't be of help with suggestions to the lyricist, but, in my experience, alas, rarely. Really.)"[43] In fact, the ever-self-effacing Ira said that it was obvious that he was responsible for the music to the verse to "Love Is Here to Stay"; the tune's lack of distinction easily distinguished it from anything his brother had composed.[44]

Staged publicity photographs taken of Ira and Duke posed at George's

piano show the deteriorated lyricist desultorily playing along with the photographer's instructions that he pretend that all was fine and that he was
happy to be back at work. The pain of knowing that he had only recently
sat next to his brother at the same instrument was excruciating.

It took twelve days to finish the work on *The Goldwyn Follies*; Ira's
compensation ended when the lyrics were submitted. "Legally there's nothing to do," he complained. "Morally, Goldwyn proved himself lacking." But
there was no use in worrying. "I'm quite run down and maybe it's better
that I didn't continue." Life was hard to bear surrounded by reminders of
George: "For the past two weeks the loss has hit me harder than ever. I'm
still getting letters from people like [Emmerich] Kálmán in Vienna and
John Alden Carpenter in Paris. An hour doesn't go by but that some memory doesn't suddenly hit me." He knew his mother was suffering, too, but
"we've just got to be brave about it. Maybe time will smooth off the edges
of our pain. Let's hope so."[45]

Although their relationship was difficult, Ira recognized his mother's
concern about his physical and mental health; she worried that he was
alone too much, his head filled with dark thoughts.[46] Ira's mood and that
of everyone around him was, he admitted, "quite gloomy at times," but he
reassured her that he would soon be fine: "All I need is a good night's sleep
and that shouldn't be very far off. Don't worry."[47]

While his movie contracts and songwriting royalties had recently
brought Ira to a new level of income, there was no work on the horizon to
pay the endless bills. He had burned up the long-distance telephone lines
since July 11, and he needed to cut the size of the household staff by two-
thirds.[48] One of the first to be terminated was George's valet, Paul Mueller;
although Mueller later expressed resentment at his abrupt departure, at the
time he happily presented Ira with a trove of doodles that George had idly
drawn on telephone pads, then tossed into the wastepaper basket. (Ira gave
many of these sketches to his brother's friends and fans.) Ira retained Carol
Stevens, a secretary on loan from RKO, to handle his business correspondence and urged that George's New York secretary, Zena Hanenfeldt, be

continued on salary to access George's files at the Chappell offices and his manuscripts in storage.[49]

As he arranged for the organization of his brother's papers, Ira pondered his future, including where he would live. The owners of the house at 1019 North Roxbury Drive offered the property to him, but $55,000 was too much to pay in his current financial circumstances.[50] Encouraged by rumors that the movie studios were interested in him, he sought a suitable rental property.[51]

Ira and Lee departed for Manhattan again just before Halloween, this time on the luxurious new Super Chief of the Atchison, Topeka and Santa Fe Railroad, which ended its route at Chicago's Dearborn Station, where the couple's Pullman passenger car was shuttled onto a second train for the rest of the journey.[52] Ira installed himself at the Gotham Hotel at West 55th Street and Fifth Avenue for the next five months (Lee went back to California earlier), where he saw to the details of George's estate and tried to make some sense out of his brother's jumble of papers. One of his first steps to solidify his brother's legacy was to ask Chappell music editor Albert Sirmay about the possibility of publishing a badly needed conductor's score for *Rhapsody in Blue*.[53]

AT THE END OF 1937, Ira attended an exhibition at a Manhattan gallery of some of the paintings George had done: "It looked quite professional. What the critics will say during the week I've no idea, but the worst they can say is 'talented amateur.'"[54] Ira was unsure if he had the legal authority to take the paintings out of California before the estate was settled without "eventually getting into hot water," but his action had no consequences.[55] The division of George's art collection was more complex: many of the works remained with Ira in California, but in a gesture of good will, he sent several paintings to his mother,[56] although he knew that "it was sworn to in New York" that the only possession that his brother had in California at his death "was a bank account."[57]

Ira's time in Manhattan was spent in "conferences with the family—renewing old acquaintances which ne'er should be forgot—listening to various tune writers who insist they were destined to work with me and who won't take no for an answer because they got the message from heaven—

seeing shows—being interviewed—ordering clothes—conferring with my
publisher—reading proofs on 'Follies' songs—discussing my future with
various future discussers—writing letters to people who write me about G.
G.—going to a couple of parties a week, those which I can't get out of—
keeping away from the poker game here after one not so much costly as
dull evening which lasted until 7 a.m.—kibitzing with song writers at my
publishers where I can be found practically every afternoon from 3 to 6."[58]

And so it went. His Christmas holidays were spent in the rural luxury
of Fairview Farm, Moss Hart's eighty-seven-acre retreat in Bucks County,
Pennsylvania, where Ira hoped "to find the pool fur-lined, and the pastures
steam heated as it's starting to get pretty cold Down East."[59]

IRA WAS PLEASED with the songs that he and George had produced for
Shall We Dance, but he sensed that they were "a little sophisticated. Maybe
that was a mistake, to put so many smart songs in one picture." *A Damsel
in Distress*, released in the late fall of 1937, had "some sentimental songs as
well as the smart ones. It's probably a better-rounded score, with a little bit
of everything."[60]

"A Foggy Day," one of Ira's favorite songs, was created in the early hours
of the morning, after George returned home from one of his frequent parties. Always thinking of music, and finding Ira still up reading, George
"took off his dinner jacket, sat down at the piano [and said] 'How about
some work? Got any ideas?'" Ira thought of a scene in the script that took
place in the fog and wondered if "*foggy day in London* or maybe *foggy day
in London Town?*" would work. George thought that the idea was a good
one, "and he was off immediately on the melody. We finished the refrain,
words and music, in less than an hour."[61]

The physical and emotional gloom of the first lines of the verse and the
refrain give way to hopefulness and joy:

> A foggy day in London Town
> Had me low and had me down.
> I viewed the morning with alarm.
> The British Museum had lost its charm.
> How long, I wondered, could this thing last?

But the age of miracles hadn't passed.
For, suddenly, I saw you there—
And through foggy London Town
The sun was shining ev'rywhere.

"In lyric-writing," Ira wrote, "it's nice work when you get hold of a seemly title, for that's half the battle. But what follows must follow through in the verse and refrain, whether the development is direct or indirect. In brief: A title / Is vital. / Once you've it—/ *Prove* it." There are few songs in Ira Gershwin's catalog that meet that objective better than "Nice Work If You Can Get It":

Just imagine someone
    Waiting at the cottage door,
    Where two hearts become one . . .
    Who could ask for anything more?

Loving one who loves you,
    And then taking that vow . . .
    Nice work if you can get it,
    And if you get it—Won't You Tell Me How?

IRA WAS SOON ENGAGED in one of the most important tasks of his life: the preservation of the physical legacy of his brother's life and career. By gathering George's papers, books, and scrapbooks, he attempted to ensure that they were safe from harm. Even George's collection of bound printed music was retained, and he purchased "two large cabinets to hold the collection which will be locked and kept at Chappell's against a shrine or some sort of memorial room in the future."[62]

The first revival of *Porgy and Bess* took place in California while Ira was in New York; he wrote additional lyrics to "It Ain't Necessarily So" and made "quite lengthy" cuts to the opening scene with the assistance of Alexander Steinert that "really helped the pace."[63] The production played to enthusiastic audiences in Pasadena, Los Angeles, and San Francisco, but the effects of flooding in Los Angeles prevented further bookings. Merle Armitage, the producer of the revival, planned an elaborate volume of tributes to George, to which Ira was asked to contribute, but writing about his brother so soon after his death was difficult: "I'm afraid I can't go through with it. I started one while in the Hotel Gotham one night and couldn't do two lines."[64] Ira's contribution, "My Brother," was a prominent feature of the book when it was published in the fall of 1938, and although the volume was dedicated to Ira—and Armitage presented him with the first copy—"My Brother" was little more than perfunctory.[65]

THE "FROSTY AIR" of a late January in New York City brought on the "grippe," and the powerful medicine Ira took affected his memory of having attended a screening of *The Goldwyn Follies* prior to its nationwide release.[66] Other than the songs he wrote with George, it was not a movie that provoked happy memories.

Beyond the prediction that "Love Walked In"—a number for which Ira felt he had wallowed "in a swamp of vague generalities"[67]—would become a hit, the Gershwins' songs in *The Goldwyn Follies* were rarely mentioned in contemporary reports.[68] Ira's misgivings were compounded when the song reached the top of the charts during a weekend automobile tour he and Lee took of California and Nevada in May 1938:

> Saturday at twilight we were rounding the top of nine-thousand-foot-high Donner Pass when we were sideswiped by an oncoming car whose driver was higher than the Pass. Fortunately, no one was hurt, and another car offered to send us help from Truckee, a matter of waiting a couple of hours for a tow truck. We had overcoats on, but it was getting very chilly, so I said to my wife: "Let's get in the car, where it'll be warmer." We got in, turned on the radio, listened to a local commercial for a few seconds, then tried for some music and happened to get the Hit Parade. "Love Walked In" had been one of ten songs on the show for some weeks; however, since the program had just a few minutes left to go, I supposed we had missed finding out if the song was still on the list or not.

But they were in luck: the announcement that "Love Walked In" was now the number one song in the United States "more than made up for a badly-busted fender."[69]

IRA REMAINED in Manhattan into the spring of 1938, huddling with Kay Swift to collate material from George's tune books and enduring ten weeks of expensive and painful ("drilling, drilling, drilling") daily visits to a dentist who had promised to solve Ira's two decades of problems with his teeth. By week nine, neuralgia had settled in his gums, and he was "doped up" around the clock to get through the intense pain.[70] Although his mother helped to pay the $3,500 bill,[71] the cost and the trauma was for naught; by late April he had broken the bridge.[72]

On March 10, 1938, Ira listened on a small radio in his New York hotel room as the Academy Awards were broadcast from the Biltmore Hotel in Los Angeles. It was 2 a.m. as the orchestra played the nominated tunes, and the conductor introduced "They Can't Take That Away from Me" as the likely recipient of the prize for Best Song. Moments later, "Sweet Leilani" by Harry Owens, sung by Bing Crosby in Paramount's *Waikiki Wedding*, took home the award. Ira was disappointed "for George's sake."[73] Later that month, after five months in New York—"fed up with dull hotel life . . . and with estate matters and what not"—Ira "scurried" back to Beverly Hills.[74]

The most important result of his stay was a four-year legal agreement that defined his services to his mother as executrix of George's estate. He was to receive a minimum of 60 percent of the gross amount paid for the use of any of his brother's unpublished work for which he wrote the lyrics and did "research and editing and rewriting of the music." The agreement also dealt with a proposed Hollywood biopic of his brother: if his mother made a deal with a studio that used any of George's concert works and Ira made a separate deal to work on the same movie, the proceeds from the deal itself would be Rose's; if any of George's concert works were used in any other type of movie, Ira would receive 20 percent of the gross.[75]

Ira was the logical choice to write the screenplay for the biopic, even if he had no screenwriting experience. He never seriously considered the suggestion, but did prepare an outline of his reasons for such a project:

A film based on the life and work of George Gershwin offers a story peculiarly American but since music speaks an international language, the portrayal of this magnetic personality who broke many musical traditions should be of interest to audiences the world over. From Gershwin emanated a new American music not written with the ruthlessness of one who strives to demolish established rules but based on a new native gusto and wit and awareness. His was a modernity that reflected the civilization we live in as excitingly as the headlines in today's newspapers.[76]

The key to George's story was not that he was Jewish, but that he was a member of the melting pot that Ira defined as the key to being an American. By the fall of 1938, however, it was clear that the studios, with the threat of a European war on the horizon, were not interested in such a movie, particularly "one like this which would necessarily, because of the amount of music to record in it, be more expensive than most."[77] After a year of negotiations, Ira resigned himself to "giving up the idea for a long time to come."[78]

UPON HIS RETURN from New York, Ira decided that what he had told Yip Harburg in 1935—if he returned to California, he would "probably love the place and never want to go East"—was true.[79] Lee Gershwin—who never stopped believing that Southern California lacked the artistic and emotional stimulation of Manhattan and lobbied for a permanent return there—reluctantly located another Beverly Hills house. Although 817 North Bedford Drive was far from perfect—"stinky furniture but the pictures will take care of that"—it had three bedrooms, a workroom for Ira, a library, and a pool. Lee noted her husband's jitters upon his return but was pleased that he "recovered almost immediately—and is enjoying being a country squire—but I do wish he could get to work."[80] Ira signed a six months' lease and hoped to enjoy the summer, "at least physically,"[81] relieved "to get away from drab hotel life to a home, even if temporary, of my own."[82]

MOST GERSHWIN HISTORIANS have concluded that had George Gershwin lived, the brothers' partnership would have continued but with changes. Ira would likely have created a domicile in California, making occasional journeys East, while George would have returned to Manhattan, making occasional journeys West. "Whatever George did . . . Ira was going to do some of them with George," said Broadway historian Robert Kimball. Ira could not "imagine a life that didn't include collaborating with his brother."[83] But Ira's sister-in-law, Emily Paley, disagreed: "Ira wanted to stay there [California] and if Ira wanted to stay there so much, he [George] would have stayed because of Ira."[84]

Lee Gershwin preferred that her husband keep busy and not dwell too much in the past. Most of all, she wanted him to "take his place" on his own merits.[85] Ira had always relied on George's drive to push him to create, but now—without any work on the horizon—his innate inertia settled in, and he began to wonder whether his career as a lyricist was over.

IRA SPENT much of early 1938 at the Rockefeller Plaza offices of his publishers, where—with the invaluable assistance of Kay Swift and Albert Sirmay—he organized his brother's musical notebooks and stray sketches, hoping to find items that might stand on their own or to which he could add lyrics. Ira's mother, his siblings, and their attorneys knew that Ira was the only person who could successfully exploit this material, and his diligence led to the collection of "thirty to forty possibilities for tunes, opening choruses and verses" that had the potential to create new sources of income for the estate and himself.[86]

The first of these possibilities to reach the public came through Kay Swift when she was working on the entertainment slate for the upcoming New York World's Fair. She demonstrated one of George's unpublished tunes to the organizers, who suggested that Ira should write a lyric to it.[87] The agreed-upon fee was $3,500, with two-thirds of the proceeds going to the lyricist. The music to the verse of what Ira entitled "Dawn of a New Day" was based on part of "Come, Come, Come to Jesus," a number written around 1930 from an abandoned show with the writer Ben Hecht and the producer Billy Rose; the music of the refrain was a blend of two other tunes.[88]

IT WAS NOW Summer 1938, and the first anniversary of George's death, money worries, and concerns about his wife's health had Ira feeling "rather low." To continually prod the managers of the World's Fair to pay him his fee for "Dawn of a New Day" was "most humiliating."[89] In addition, an uncooperative landlord had forced him to find yet another house. Their new dwelling at 718 North Beverly Drive lacked a "pool or tennis court but is quite comfortable and the important thing is that we finally managed to get a decent house for reasonable rent." Ira and Lee would remain at this address for the next two years.[90]

Without money from a biopic of his brother or from the score for a movie or stage musical, Ira began to suffer financially. Lee desperately wanted him to take one of the Broadway offers being dangled so he could again enjoy the act of creation,[91] but Ira was reluctant to return to New York: "Frankly in this day and age unless I were crazy about the libretto, I doubt whether it's worthwhile. Eight-or-ten weeks' work and a month in rehearsal and a month on the road would mean at least a three months' stay in the East which would mean my expenses would eat up half the royalties even if the show was a hit."[92]

He was as doubtful about the biopic as he was of the rumor that producer Arthur Freed wanted him and Jerome Kern to write the songs for an MGM musical adaptation of L. Frank Baum's children's novel *The Wizard of Oz*.[93] But after Harold Arlen and Yip Harburg were hired for the job, Ira played a small, uncredited role in the creation of the movie's most famous song, "Over the Rainbow." Harburg only agreed to write up Arlen's tune after getting Ira's opinion of its merits; when the duo came by with the finished number, Ira felt it needed a coda and immediately supplied the line "If happy little bluebirds fly / beyond the rainbow / why, oh why, can't I?"[94]

The summer of 1938 also saw the death of his brother's first biographer, Isaac Goldberg; "no passing," Ira told Goldberg's widow, "outside of George, has affected me so."[95] Three years earlier, Goldberg had discussed with George a revised version of his book; less than two weeks after George's death, Goldberg suggested to Ira that he be its coauthor.[96] He insisted that Ira had more to offer than just writing lyrics.[97] Ira was interested; they would have "a pretty complete set of records to work from" once Ira regained possession of his papers from the Manhattan facility where they were stored, but he thought it was too early to think about a life-spanning biography of his brother. "Without being sentimental, I don't feel that G.G.'s creative career is over yet."[98]

BY 1938, the political situation in Europe had turned dire, and it became apparent that war was on the horizon. Ira's early flirtation with Socialism had been an act of his dilettantish youth; now, under the influence of Lee Gershwin, who had grown up in the boiling pot of New York left-wing politics and who, by the fall of 1936, had become "the uncrowned queen of the [Hollywood] intelligentsia," Ira began to ever-so-gently dip his toe into liberal causes.[99] Lee organized a fundraiser for the jailed labor leader Tom Mooney and an elaborate circus-themed party for the "progressive, anti-Fascist" Motion Picture Artists' Committee, with all proceeds going to the Spanish Loyalists fighting against the forces of Generalissimo Francisco Franco.[100] Ira contributed financial and other support to pro-Loyalist organizations such as the Medical Bureau to Aid Spanish Democracy and the Friends of the Abraham Lincoln Brigade.[101] He donated money to the recently formed Hollywood Anti-Nazi League, and his name was added to the list of the welcoming committee for a speech by Secretary of the Interior Harold Ickes in Los Angeles.[102] By the late fall, after the promise of Neville Chamberlain's "Peace for Our Time" deal with Adolf Hitler in Munich had proven false, Ira exclaimed, "Thank God the last couple of weeks seem to show a realization on the parts of people in England and America that it's got to be stopped at any cost, short of actual war."[103]

In early December, at the home of Edward G. Robinson, Ira and George's old friend from the Lower East Side, Ira was one of fifty members of the motion picture industry who met to discuss how to support democracy and fight Fascism. The group signed a "Declaration of Independence" asking President Franklin D. Roosevelt to sever economic relations with Nazi Germany in the wake of Kristallnacht, the burning and destruction of Jewish homes, businesses, and synagogues that had taken place a month earlier.[104] The activities of these members of the Hollywood community were, at the time, deemed patriotic; in the anti-Communist postwar years, they would be used to damage—or in some cases destroy—many careers.

YET AMID THIS worldwide tension, Ira spent much of his time watching UCLA play football or visiting "a certain roadhouse on a certain Strip where a certain gang convenes once a week" to deplete his checkbook at the poker table. Reluctantly, he decided it was time to refill the coffers. In the fall of

1938, Ira and Jerome Kern began to collaborate on "some songs against a possible future assignment."[105] Always fond of Kern's distinctive, original, and charming melodies,[106] "after a year of inactivity it feels good to get to work again."[107] He was initially encouraged, yet without a libretto or a concept, Ira strained to develop his lyrical muscles, and the results were not encouraging. The only numbers to see the light of day—the paired songs "Once There Were Two of Us" and "Now That We Are One," based on Ira's memories of Kern's 1921 musical comedy *Good Morning Dearie*, in which the second song was dependent on the thoughts of the first[108]—were published in 1968 but disappeared as quietly as they had arrived.[109] A few songs written with Harold Arlen during the same period remain similarly obscure.

Ira's only published song during this period was "Baby, You're News," written with Yip Harburg and the composer Johnny Green, which was heard in *Sticks & Stones*, a political revue presented by the Motion Picture Artists' Committee in the early 1940s. The lyrics were oddly self-referential, with "Who Cares?" and "Love Walked In" making an appearance. It was the type of song that was being bought "for a few hundred dollars apiece from writers who used to get $750 a week and more."[110]

This inactivity worried Ira's friends. Vernon Duke prodded him about possible projects, but Ira was reluctant to resume work with the lively but temperamental composer, whose ingrained habit of moaning over "some supposed grievance" disturbed Ira's quietude.[111] When Duke proposed *The Carousel*, an adaptation of Robert Nathan's 1931 novel *The Orchid*,[112] Ira begged off, citing commitments to "Metro, Warner's, Goldwyn, Twentieth Century, Grand National, Major, Republic and Little Productions, Inc." for a biopic of his brother. "First one, then the other, but at no time none. At Metro contracts were prepared, money no object, when the war scare jumbled things up and suddenly the studios went cautious and presto! musicals disappeared from the face of the earthy [*sic*]. So here I was stuck with a two-year lease in this artificial, paper-moonish spot, of which, by the way, I'm very fond."[113]

IRA'S MAIN CONCERN was to get his brother's estate in order and to protect George's musical reputation. His most important idea—one that he would pursue for decades—was the merger of the publishing of his and George's songs, now under three separate imprints, as well as any material Ira created from his brother's melodies, into one company: "With television around the corner these combined catalogs could make a mighty strong house."[114] By the spring of 1939, the veteran music publisher Herman Starr was running Warner Bros.' publishing interests—Max Dreyfus had sold Harms and its related companies to them a decade earlier—and Ira told his mother that if she approved, he would give Starr his ideas for the "project which if it can be carried through would excite me not only for your sake and mine, not only for commercial considerations, but for the great tribute it would bring to George."[115]

Ira was convinced that his publishers were indifferent to the Gershwin catalog, writing that "with practically no campaigning," five numbers—"I Got Rhythm," "I Got Plenty o' Nuttin'," "Summertime," "The Man I Love," and "Liza"—were consistently heard on records and on the radio. It would take little work to make a hit out of any of the eighty-five George Gershwin songs currently registered with ASCAP, and "a merger of all our songs and major works with a small but efficient organization" could nearly double the "potentially active" songs; "at least fifty" more could come from the melodies in George's tune books, and a series of short orchestral novelties could be made from others. He also suggested diversifying the portfolio of the new company by purchasing the work of other composers and lyricists. His financial bait for the merger was the estate's one-third share of New World Music, its 40 percent of Gershwin Publishing Corporation, and their copyright renewals.[116] Three years later, as Ira noted with gratification the increase in the number and variety of Gershwin songs that he heard on the radio, he regretted "that Starr, Dreyfus and myself couldn't even get to the discussion stage about pooling all the Gershwin works into one publishing firm as it would have made a unit we could all have been proud of."[117]

THESE EFFORTS on behalf of the entire Gershwin family did not protect Ira from the treatment he received from his mother at the behest of her attorneys. Rose Gershwin tried to direct the way George's estate should be run, and she reacted poorly when her children made alternative suggestions. Ira's sister wished that he were not so far away; she and Arthur could not manage the situation the way Ira could.[118] He sympathized; they should be getting some money from George's estate. But Ira painfully concluded that because his mother consistently failed to understand the nature of his collaboration with George, Rose would hold on to as much of the estate as possible, regardless of Ira's financial circumstances and his unspoken need to be part of the family.[119]

In January 1939, when he was told that George's estate had been resolved and that all its assets had been transferred to their mother, it was suggested that a $3,000 New World Music dividend be split equally between Rose, Ira, and Arthur.[120] Although he tried to avoid arguments—fearing the anger of others as much as he wanted to have his own way—Ira released some of his buried frustrations. "I don't understand why the dividend should be split up three ways," he said to Emanuel Alexandre. "I trust neither my mother nor you nor Arthur misunderstands my attitude. It isn't that I wouldn't like to see Arthur get a few dollars—my giving him and my sister two thirds of the $8,000 I received [from George's estate] shows that."[121]

But the New World publishing situation was "a very different thing. Here is a company whose catalog is comprised entirely of Gershwin songs of which over 90% have lyrics by me and from which I receive nothing in the way of royalties—royalties which my mother and the estate do receive and which I hope for my mother's sake keep growing larger and larger each year. It is a company in which, although at the present moment I officially own no stock, George always recognized my right and interest by giving me part of the dividend from the very first year it began to function." His long-simmering bitterness bubbled up: he "never got a penny from New World" after "publishers began paying royalties on dance arrangements," even though, to his knowledge, "every lyric writer in the business" received an equal share with the composer; "George's contract with New World was such that the publishers felt they couldn't pay me anything in addition to what he received." If the estate did not recognize the injustice of Ira's receiving only a third of the dividends, now was the time to take a stand.[122]

His argument about the New World dividend, and his feeling that his sister—notably absent from the proposed division—should be a recipient of the income from George's estate as well, was successful, but it hinged on Ira's relinquishing his right to take back the copyright renewals from the songs he had written—"not only those with George but with Youmans and others." This meant that when each song's original twenty-eight-year term of copyright expired, Ira was unable to have the rights revert to himself from the song's first publisher, a process that could have allowed him to sell his publishing rights to another firm for more money than he was getting from Harms.[123]

IN THE YEARS FOLLOWING his death, George Gershwin's reputation grew by leaps and bounds, and museums and libraries began to request donations of his original manuscripts. One of the earliest requests came in the spring of 1939 from Harold Spivacke, the head of the Music Division of the Library of Congress. Ira was justifiably proud that a national institution such as the Library of Congress considered George's papers worthy of being added to their collections, and he sent Spivacke George's handwritten sketch of "The Crap Shooter's Song" from *Porgy and Bess*. It was the first donation of what is now the largest collection of George—and eventually Ira—Gershwin manuscripts in the world. Ira's later donations included his brother's custom-made desk and his handwritten score for the *"I Got Rhythm" Variations*, as well as Ferde Grofé's original score for his symphonic orchestration of *Rhapsody in Blue*. But Ira was never entirely convinced that the Library of Congress should be the repository of *every* manuscript, and at one point he suggested that the full score of *Porgy and Bess* might be given to the New York Public Library.[124]

AUGUST 1939: "I've been having more teeth pulled out so that I haven't been quite myself physically the past month or so."[125] He ruefully joked that most of his teeth were "probably being used in billiard balls."[126] The physical pain was not alleviated by an increase in his income, but Ira was not alone in feeling this financial discomfort: none of the prominent songwriters in Hollywood were currently under contract to a studio; instead, the trend was to hire songwriters en masse for a movie and not commit the score to a single writer or an established team.[127]

The trauma of the past two and a half years hung over Ira like a shadow. He was being pulled in all directions, and it seemed as if his career as a lyricist was now running a distant second to the incessant demands on his time, the endless minutiae of contracts and royalties, and the competing forces that threatened to tear his family further apart. The flood of paper created by his brother's death was akin to that torrent so vividly described in Charles Dickens's classic novel *Bleak House*; to Ira, it began to seem as if lawyers and accountants would become as important as the creators of the songs that provided those lawyers and accountants with their livelihoods.

CHAPTER 13

I
RA'S CREATIVE REVIVAL came as a complete surprise to him, since he admitted that after the events of July 11, 1937, there had "been absolutely no form or pattern" to his life.[1] It had been four years since the *Ziegfeld Follies of 1936*, and it seemed increasingly unlikely that he would ever work in the theater again. So when, in early 1940, playwright Moss Hart asked Ira to collaborate with him and the German émigré composer Kurt Weill on a new show, he was eager to listen, particularly when he understood that his lyrics would play a significant role in the motivation of the characters. When Hart arrived in Hollywood in February, he elaborated on his plot about a successful woman, the editor of a popular fashion magazine, who was widely adored and envied, yet who was also unhappy and alone.[2]

Ira found the idea, based on Hart's preoccupation with psychoanalysis, intriguing, even if he was not enamored of psychological character studies.[3] The parallel to George's final months was uncomfortable, but after more than two years of inactivity, with an income that had yet to recover from the precipitous drop it had taken in 1938 and having recently made a deposit on the purchase of a house on Roxbury Drive next door to the one he and George had lived in, he needed a successful show. With all that in mind, Ira agreed to become part of what Hart originally called *I Am Listening*, but which was soon to become *Lady in the Dark*.[4]

Ira and Weill barely knew each other (they first met when Weill had attended a rehearsal of *Porgy and Bess* in September 1935), but Ira was well aware of the German's celebrated career in Europe as the composer of such seminal works as *Die Dreigroschenoper* (*The Threepenny Opera*). Although Ira expressed uncertainty about working with someone other than his brother—perhaps with a sense that he was being unfaithful to George's memory—Lee Gershwin was "delighted" with the idea of her husband's finally getting back to work. It was "no competition to George to work with Kurt," whose intriguing European style and sensibilities were so markedly different from those of George.[5]

IN EARLY MAY, Ira boarded a sleeper train for Manhattan, finding "little conviviality among the passengers because France had just been invaded by Germany and the world looked a mess."[6] Still, he could not resist a wager on the Kentucky Derby: "From a hat, the horse I picked was Gallahadion who turned out to win . . . but all I received was $15 for my $5 and after tipping the steward $5 all I had was $10—which made even money and that's how I won the Kentucky Derby."[7]

Word quickly spread about Ira's return to Broadway and resulted in a number of other offers for stage and screen musicals; while he liked some of the ideas (*The Funnies*, an adaptation of a comedy written by the cartoonist John Held Jr., had, he thought, a chance to become something unique), he felt that resuming his career with the assistance of Hart and Weill was more than enough for the time being.[8]

For the next thirteen weeks—"during the hottest summer I've ever known (and no air-conditioning either)"—Ira spent nearly every day working in his suite at the Hotel Essex with Weill. The duo often stayed "at the piano after dinner until 11 or 12, when he would leave for the country while I then would go on working until 4 or 5 in the morning."[9] This was followed by an attempt "to sleep in a half-filled bathtub for a few hours" before going "back to the grind again to find a new rhyme."[10]

Ira initially found it hard to adjust to Weill's methods; unlike George or Harold Arlen, who played a brief theme or melody at the piano that Ira could react to with suggestions that led to a development of the words and music as one, Weill preferred to have the lyrics in front of him before he could compose.[11] By late June, most of Ira's time was spent in conferences rather than working on the score.[12] Gertrude Lawrence was interested in taking the leading role of Liza Elliott, and after Hart read the script to Lawrence and her agent, with Kurt and Ira "playing and singing" what they had written, the three men "happily congratulated each other" that their hoped-for star seemed to like what she heard of the score and of how it would be integrated into a series of elaborate dream sequences that punctuated the dramatic or comedic plot situations.[13]

Although his work on *Lady in the Dark* kept him busy that summer, Ira did find time to pursue several other activities, including attending the Third Annual Gershwin Memorial Concert at Lewisohn Stadium with the writer Dashiell Hammett to hear performances by Oscar Levant and Todd Duncan, whose singing of excerpts from *Porgy and Bess* recalled to Ira's mind the passing, a month earlier, of DuBose Heyward.[14] Less than five years after *Porgy and Bess* had premiered, Ira was now the only survivor of the trio who had so happily worked together on his brother's pride and joy. There was also a visit to his publisher Max Dreyfus's farm, although Ira joked that it "nearly ruined" him.[15] A few years later, he told Dreyfus that he missed "jumping those fences and bending over to pick those strawberries—but it's probably just as well—I doubt that I have the agility I had in 1940. And I was no acrobat even in those days."[16]

THE SCORE FOR *Lady in the Dark* was not yet complete when Ira returned to California via an airplane from LaGuardia Field on August 8, 1940, but he was pleased with what he and Weill had done, particularly "the new and novel treatment we have given to the dreams musically. If the show isn't a hit it won't be because a great amount of thought and industry wasn't given it."[17]

Ira blamed his poor physical condition after returning from New York on the "crazy existence" he had "led there what with lack of sleep and the heat and what not," but awaiting him at home was a different sort of pressure. It was time to move into the house he had purchased at 1021 North Roxbury Drive, even if, "because of more and more improvements [it was] not nearly finished."[18] Ira had asked his mother for financial assistance with the purchase, but she rebuffed his request, claiming that her bank balance was too low to help. Ira's suggestion that she use some of the funds from George's life insurance policy was met with a shrug.[19] Eventually, Rose relented, but the $7,500 she gave Ira was much less than the $25,000 she had told everyone she would be providing. Ira later lamented that he had put himself "through the agony and belittling of myself to argue for this reduced gift."[20]

The spacious five-bedroom, six-bathroom, two-story house was built in 1928 in the Spanish style so prevalent in Southern California and combined elegant living space with comfortable furniture, game rooms for billiards and poker, and Ira's archive. The interior design, described as an unlikely juxtaposition of "cabbage roses and Brussels lace curtains" for the winner of a Pulitzer Prize, was Lee's purview.[21] The windows of Ira's study and office looked across to his neighbors at 1023 North Roxbury Drive: initially Sigmund Romberg and subsequently actress Agnes Moorehead. Over his desk was a large oil painting of Lee done by George, and a long table given to him by Vincente Minnelli stood in the center of the room and held a mass of unsorted papers and manuscripts. The study walls were lined with bookcases, while on the walls of his bedroom hung paintings and lithographs owned by his brother.[22]

Ira and Lee were surrounded by memories and physical reminders of the man who had lived his final months in the house at 1019 North Roxbury. George's bound scores were preserved here, and the Steinway piano from George's New York apartment, on which he and Ira had written their last songs, soon became the source of new songs with new composers and was the centerpiece of evenings with their legion of friends and colleagues. Ira vowed that he would never "move again,"[23] and other than a seven-month period in 1956–57 when the property was extensively—and expensively— remodeled, he kept that promise.

IN NOVEMBER 1940, it was back to Manhattan to resume work on *Lady in the Dark*. Songs needed to be eliminated or severely cut, and the demands of Gertrude Lawrence for funnier material would have to be met.[24] Given the expense to stage them, the lengthy dream sequences Ira was so proud of were ripe for change. The third sequence, which began as a "mixture of Court Trial and Minstrel Show," was "practically completed when it was decided that minstrel costume and background weren't novel enough. Agreeing that a circus setting seemed preferable—there could be more riotous color and regalia—we changed the opening, the jury patters, and most of the recitatives, from an environment of burnt cork and sanded floor to putty nose and tanbark."[25]

One element of the sequence never changed: Liza Elliott's defense of her behavior, although its initial form as a "pseudo-metaphysical dissertation based on the signs of the Zodiac and their influences, all pretty fatalistic; in short, she'd done what she did because she couldn't help doing whatever she did do," was altered after producer Sam H. Harris delivered the bad news that "something lighter and perhaps gayer was required."[26] A fourth dream sequence, lasting twenty minutes, "in which Liza envisions her possible Hollywood life: an enormous ranch in the San Fernando Valley with a palatial home furnished from the Hearst Collection, butlers galore, private golf course, Chinese cooks, [and] fifty-thousand barrel gushers on the property," also became a victim of the need to trim an already lengthy evening.[27]

Although Ira was upset at the elimination of the "Song of the Zodiac," its replacement—from a suggestion by Moss Hart for something "about a woman who couldn't make up her mind"—had possibilities, and after "experimenting with style, format, and complete change of melodic mood," Liza's new defense, entitled "The Saga of Jenny," was ready for Gertrude Lawrence.[28]

EVERYTHING LOOKED GOOD as rehearsals began; although it still ran long, the complicated production was coming together. Lawrence was in great form, particularly in "My Ship," the number that was to be the leitmotiv of the score and her outstanding ballad. For the first two weeks, Ira later recalled with a tinge of embarrassment, Lawrence sang the song's original release, "I can wait for years / Till it appears, / One fine day one spring," until one afternoon she stopped and fixed her eyes on the lyricist, sitting not far from the front of the stage. She demanded to know: "Why *four* years, why not five or six?" Ira had been caught in a rare error; his lyric had given equal "musical value" to the preposition "for" as it did to "wait" and "years." Chagrined, "for years" became "the years."[29]

The cast and crew headed to Boston on Christmas Eve 1940. "The score is down now to practically bare essentials," Ira said before his departure, "so I'm hoping Moss finds cuts in his play. There's no entire scene he can cut so it's a question of cutting lines here and there and that's quite a thing when the author is also director and it's his first important play away from" George S. Kaufman.[30] When *Lady in the Dark* opened at the end of December, Ira was not convinced that "The Saga of Jenny" would work as well as his preferred Zodiac number, but the audience reaction on opening night convinced him otherwise.

AMONG THE ITEMS that Ira had brought with him to Manhattan—"a dictionary, a thesaurus, and Clement Wood's *Rhyming Dictionary*"—was a folder of possible titles and lines of light verse that he had composed years earlier. One of the pieces Weill particularly liked was "The Music Hour," published under Ira's Arthur Francis nom de plume in the humor magazine *Life* in the early 1920s, for which the budding writer received $12.[31] It consisted of a series of rhymed names of Russian composers that Ira had found on the backs of sheet music in George's collection.[32] Weill's mad tempo transformed Ira's barely changed innocuous versifying into Danny Kaye's career-making tour de force, "Tschaikowsky (and Other Russians)":

> There's Malichevsky, Rubinstein, Arensky and Tschaikowsky,
> Sapelnikoff, Dimitrieff, Tscherepnin, Kryjanowsky,
> Godowsky, Arteiboucheff, Moniuszko, Akimenko,
> Solovieff, Prokofieff, Tiomkin, Korestchenko.

This went on at an incredible pace, with Kaye rattling off the names of thirty-three other composers, famous as well as obscure—including Dukelsky (aka Vernon Duke)—until he realizes that he has mentioned Rachmaninoff twice and declares a stop, as "the subject has been dwelt upon enough!"

Danny Kaye had just finished his tongue-twisting performance in the elaborate Circus Dream and was basking in raucous cheers and applause, a reaction not granted to Gertrude Lawrence to this point in the evening. Standing in the back of the house, a member of the producer's staff grabbed Ira by the arm and, *sotto voce*, said, "Christ, we've lost our star!" "The next few lines of dialogue weren't heard because of the continuing applause," Ira recalled. "Then, as Danny deferred to Miss Lawrence, [the applause] ended; and 'Jenny' began. She hadn't been singing more than a few lines when I realized an interpretation we'd never seen at rehearsal was materializing. Not only were there new nuances and approaches, but on top of this she 'bumped' it and 'ground' it, to the complete devastation of the audience. At the conclusion, there was an ovation which lasted twice as long as that for 'Tschaikowsky.'" Lawrence's performance revealed "that we didn't have to worry about losing our brighter-than-ever star."[33]

> Jenny made her mind up when she was twelve
> That into foreign languages she would delve;
> But at seventeen to Vassar it was quite a blow
> That in twenty-seven languages she couldn't say no.
>
> Jenny made her mind up at twenty-two
> To get herself a husband was the thing to do.
> She got herself all dolled up in her satins and furs
> And she got herself a husband—but he wasn't hers.
>
> Jenny made her mind up at thirty-nine
> She would take a trip to the Argentine.
> She was only on vacation but the Latins agree
> Jenny was the one who started the Good Neighbor Policy.

To which the jury judging Liza's case responded with this refrain:

> Poor Jenny! Bright as a penny!
> Her equal would be hard to find.
>   Oh, passion doesn't vanish
>   In Portuguese or Spanish—
> But she would make up her mind.

LADY IN THE DARK smashed the house record during its two weeks in Boston. Broadway was next. The "musical play" opened at the Alvin Theatre in late January 1941 with a portent of the show's future that came while Ira was standing at the urinal during the first act intermission. A man came into the restroom and stood at the urinal next to Ira. When asked if he was Gershwin, Ira replied in the affirmative and was told that the show would run forever.[34] If that prediction was not entirely accurate, *Lady in the Dark* did become the longest-running and most successful Broadway show

of Ira Gershwin's career and quickly earned him so much money that by
the summer of 1941—when the movie rights were sold to Paramount for
a then-record price of $285,000—he was immediately able to pay off the
mortgage on his Beverly Hills house.

Ira's return to Broadway was hailed as a long-awaited triumph. His
lyrics for *Lady in the Dark* were, according to the esteemed critic Brooks
Atkinson, those of a "thoroughbred. Uproariously witty when the time is
right, he also writes in impeccable taste for the meditative sequences."[35]
"The Princess of Pure Delight," one of Ira's favorite numbers for the show,
had its origin at Moss Hart's Bucks County property:

> The food was excellent, the guestrooms cozy; there were a large
> swimming pool and thousands of trees and any amount of huge and
> overwhelmingly friendly, woolly dogs; there was even that rarity for
> those days . . . , a TV set; but the show was ever on our minds and
> mostly we were at it, discussing the score in progress and what lay
> ahead. Dinner, though, usually brought additional guests; and one
> Sunday night Richard Rodgers, who had been weekending at nearby
> George S. Kaufman's, offered us a ride back to the city . . . a conve-
> nience gladly accepted. We were to leave about nine p.m., but it was
> decided to wait until city-bound traffic died down a bit. To pass the
> time, Dick picked an old quiz-and-conundrum book of the Twenties
> from Moss's shelves; and all present spent an hour or so answering
> quiz questions, correcting twisted quotations, solving riddles, &c.

A few weeks later, Ira and Weill were at work on the second dream
sequence:

> We came to a spot where Liza and some children were alone on the
> stage. I suggested—and Kurt liked the notion—that here a sung
> fairy tale might be incorporated. So next day I got hold of some
> Andersen and the Brothers Grimm, and leafed through for some-
> thing not too well known to base a narrative on—any short one that
> could be transformed into a song. In my anxiousness to find some-
> thing quickly, probably much possible was overlooked; my hurried
> impressions pictured mainly young princes turning into frogs and

vice versa. Which form of corporeal alchemy seemed too complicated and farfetched. Metamorphosis out, I began thinking of other
legendary magical gimmicks and concluded that the kind used so
frequently in *The Arabian Nights' Entertainments* might do the trick:
one where an in-a-spot young man answers brilliantly one or several
loaded questions, and reaps, from an amazed and delighted poten-
tate, rewards of non-decapitation, bushels of diamonds and rubies, a
harem, and other desiderata. It was then that I remembered the Sunday night mentioned above and *my* brilliant answer to a conundrum
Dick put: "What word of five letters is never spelled right?" This
seemed short, sweet, and possible for a device; so, having something
to head for, I started.

> "I'll answer that riddle," cried the Singer of Song.
> "What's never spelled 'right' in five letters is 'wrong,'
> And it's right to spell 'wrong'–w-r-o-n-g!
> Your Highness, the Princess belongeth to me.
> And I love her, anyway!"

The gag line of the song, delivered by the King's Dean of Sorcerers—
"That will be twenty gulden, please!"—was inspired by the fee several
of Ira's friends, including Moss Hart, paid for their psychiatric sessions.[36]

AS THE SHOW CONTINUED through the spring of 1941, Gertrude Lawrence
repeatedly asked that one of her numbers, "One Life to Live," be replaced.
Weill "was willing to oblige," Ira wrote years later, "but collaboration by
mail would have been unsatisfactory; and I didn't fancy going to New York
for three weeks or more to work on replacing a number which was doing
all right, and which perhaps we couldn't better." The time off in the summer cooled everyone's heels.[37] But the success of *Lady in the Dark* was, no
matter the brilliance of Weill's music and Ira's lyrics, in many ways due to
Lawrence, a supremely talented, yet temperamental, star, who became the
subject of an event Ira dubbed "Gertie Refused to Sign!"

In January 1941, Bennett Cerf, of Random House, suggested a limited
edition of the *Lady in the Dark* vocal score: three hundred copies bound in

full leather to match the style of *George Gershwin's Song-Book* of 1932, with a separate page signed by Lawrence and the three creators of the show. Ira supported the prestige project—even though there would be no royalties—and persuaded his fellow authors to agree. Ira was convinced that Lawrence was happy with the idea.[38] The publishers announced the edition and Ira put his signature to the blank sheets he was sent and mailed them back. A few weeks later, he received a telegram: Lawrence had refused to sign. Ira could not understand why, since everything had appeared settled when he had last seen her in New York.[39] By the time Lawrence had returned to England, it was clear that the edition would never be published, and Ira expressed his frustration with a rare use of Yiddish: the whole thing was a "megillah."[40]

The conclusion of this saga of Gertie took place two years later, when *Lady in the Dark* reached Los Angeles for the final dates of its tour. Ira found Gertrude Lawrence "as enchanting as ever" in her performance, but when his appearance backstage met with "so reluctant and lukewarm a response . . . about a minute and a half later I found myself taxiing back to Beverly Hills."[41] Ira discovered the reason for her inaction a decade later, while working on *A Star Is Born* with Moss Hart, who thought Ira already knew: "It was just that she suddenly got mad because Hildegarde's album of *Lady in the Dark* was released before hers. Simple as that." Ira turned the saga into verse:

CODA (TO THE TUNE OF "JENNY")

Gertie made her mind up in '41
That because of Hildegarde she'd been undone.
She got even by the autographing she forebore;
So—no limited edition of the vocal score.[42]

IN THE WARMTH OF California, Ira basked in his new house and in the success of *Lady in the Dark*: "I get a big kick having my library with me again and not having it languish in the warehouse" after five years. "It's a very lovely house. So what? So yesterday termites appeared in a wall, and it'll cost me $700 to get rid of them. The house has cost me over $10,000 more than I expected so it's a damned good thing 'LITD' [*Lady in the Dark*] came along."[43] When he was asked about the possibility of working on another revue, he begged off; there was "pretty good money (if I may be that practi cal)" in other possibilities: movie work, a new show with Jerome Kern, and the plan by Weill and Hart "to keep me away from the tennis court . . . by getting me to work with them on a follow-up" to *Lady in the Dark*.[44]

Sheet music and recordings of the songs from *Lady in the Dark* jumped off the racks, with only one blemish: the refusal of some small radio stations to play "The Saga of Jenny" because of the references to gin and "the husband who wasn't hers" in the lyrics.[45] But what really hurt the songs' popularity was the fight between ASCAP and the broadcast networks that led to an extended period of no ASCAP songs being played on the air.[46] Gertrude Lawrence's insistence on returning to England to support her country by doing war work meant the show's future was uncertain; would she be able to return?[47] Moss Hart thought that Ira was lucky being three thousand miles away from the action; Hart knew that his friend was more interested in perusing the *Oxford English Dictionary* than in dealing with the details of keeping their show running successfully.[48]

THE DARKENING PICTURE in Europe arrived on Ira's doorstep in early 1941 via a letter from a Belgian Jew named Felix Manskleid, who had been a prisoner of war in Germany. Freed in October 1940 to join his family in Marseilles as a refugee, he asked for Ira's help to acquire an emergency visa to allow him into the United States. Ira had donated money to organizations assisting European refugees, so he agreed to write the requested affidavit and sent it off to the American Consul in Marseilles. Yip Harburg agreed to write the second affidavit.[49] But the wartime chaos, exacerbated by the entry of the United States into the conflict following the attack on Pearl Harbor, caused Ira to caution Manskleid that it was "probably silly to be too optimistic about the successful completion of this matter but let us keep hoping."[50] The Exiled Writers Committee in New York told Ira that no visas were being granted in Europe after the United States had declared war on Nazi Germany.[51] Although Ira's efforts went awry, Manskleid eventually made his way via Lisbon, Portugal, to the Belgian Congo, and expressed his gratitude for Ira's work on his behalf.[52]

Ira's patriotism became more evident as the world plunged further into war. When he heard about possible Gershwin shows that might be done in England—hoping "for the sake of morale" that they would be—he was unconcerned about royalties.[53] His first work influenced by the war crisis came in May of 1941, when he and Yip Harburg wrote the lyrics to an Arthur Schwartz melody for a United China Relief Drive fundraiser. The title of "Honorable Moon" was Ira's and was derived from a Japanese-influenced lyric he had written with Buddy DeSylva to music by William Daly in 1923.[54] "Hope it does something in the way of sales," Ira wrote a friend.[55] Madame Chiang Kai-shek honored the three writers with a scroll for their work.[56] Two years later, with the war still raging in Europe and Asia, the number was used in the Warner Bros. movie *Princess O'Rourke*, and the songwriters donated what they received for its use to the same cause.[57] A second number for political/humanitarian purposes came along in the fall of 1941, after Nazi Germany invaded the Soviet Union, break-ing the two countries' nonaggression pact of 1939. The theatrical producer Gilbert Miller asked Ira and Harold Arlen for something to be sung at a Russian War Relief benefit at Madison Square Garden.[58] "If That's Propa-ganda" was quickly completed and was off to director Joseph Losey, who oversaw the production, in early October. Sung by Vaughn Monroe before a crowd of twenty thousand, Ira called it "quite a militant" number.[59]

Ira desperately wanted to celebrate the demise of the Axis trio: "What a day *that* would be! What a day that *will* be!"[60] But he was unwilling to match Lee Gershwin's more active commitments to liberal causes, includ-ing in June 1941, when she was listed as one of the petitioners seeking the release from prison of labor leader Harry Bridges. During the McCarthy era, some of these signatories would lose their careers, and others would serve prison terms, because of their political beliefs.[61]

NOT LONG AFTER the *Lady in the Dark* movie deal was completed, months of negotiations for a George Gershwin biopic came to an end with a "ten-tative and optional" agreement with Warner Bros. "The studio feels that it does not know that there is a definite picture in the life of George (although they hope there is)," Ira told Kay Swift, "and have the right in ten weeks to decide whether they will take up their option or whether they will take up the option calling for the use of Gershwin music in any story where the

music could be used as a so called cavalcade" in the style of the successful
Irving Berlin movie musical *Alexander's Ragtime Band*.[62] The studio paid
$125,000 for the rights to make the biopic ($25,000 less if the cavalcade were
green-lighted), with 40 percent going to Ira and 60 percent to his mother.[63]
Beyond the rights to George's story, Ira negotiated eight weeks of his "special services" to the producers for an additional $15,000.[64]

Warner Bros. gave the project to the German-born producer Henry
Blanke and assigned screenwriter Robert Rossen to work with Ira on a
basic outline. Rossen had been in Hollywood since the late 1930s and was
a well-known liberal who was later blacklisted after testifying before the
House Un-American Activities Committee. As Ira remarked in a letter to
Kay Swift, "Rossen's first statement to me (and he told me Blanke agreed)
was that if Warners were thinking of merely the cavalcade type of picture . . . he, for one, was not interested." Ira concurred. "The important
thing was to get an approach or a device," and by the third week of discussions, Ira felt that they had an idea to begin the picture "with either the
Hollywood Bowl Memorial Concert or one of the Lewisohn Concerts. In
such a concert we can have, say, Oscar Levant playing the Concerto, Ethel
Merman singing 'I Got Rhythm,' Paul Whiteman conducting 'Rhapsody
in Blue' etc., etc. From the platform during a musical piece or at the end
of one we will pan to various people in the audience at various times and
show that person's connection with George at a certain period in George's
life."[65] The proposed concept was rejected by the studio as "too depressing
theatrically," as it would indicate "that the protagonist had already passed
away and all subsequent sequences would therefore suffer."[66]

Rossen wanted more than just the surface story Ira had told in his essay for
the Merle Armitage volume or the facts he could get from Ira's scrapbooks. A
movie needed conflict, and what better conflict than love versus career? Rossen asked Ira about George and the women in his life. Ira revealed that his
brother "wanted terribly to have a wife and kids," but "felt he wasn't getting
anywhere. He had a great admiration for family. The results of [George's]
analysis showed he had a 'Don Juan' complex, a naïve sort of thing. He was
constantly seeking the ideal woman. He always had a great admiration for
school-teachers. What he actually wanted was a girl who was beautiful, who
would be a good mother, who came from a good family, who was a good
musician, who was educated, one who would help him with his career, etc.

He put women on too high a pedestal regarding marriage." When Rossen asked what quality would be missing in the character of such a woman, if he were to invent one, Ira said that from his brother's point of view, she would be "selfish . . . because she had a career of her own that was important to her, and therefore she couldn't cater to his own career," a comment that echoed George's feelings about Kay Swift. Ira concluded that his brother "was never completely happy. He was always looking for something."[67]

Rossen, after complaining that the real story of George's life would make a dull film, but that invented material would distort the picture, produced his outline.[68] After six weeks of meetings and discussions, Rossen, who "felt he wasn't quite up to the musical background the film would require," quit, leaving Ira relieved that the story would be about George's music and not "a psychological study."[69] The project was turned over to Kathryn Scola, who met with Ira to lay the groundwork for a second outline that would help the studio executives decide on making a biopic, a cavalcade, or whether they would "call the whole thing off."[70] The idea of Ira doing the screenplay was rejected "because my specialty was lyrics and because even if I had had screen playwright credits they felt the subject was too close to me and I would be too sensitive and tentative wherever liberties had to be taken."[71] For the moment, his job was complete; "the time that I can really be of service to them will be after the writers get an adequate story line and begin to think about how the songs and the music are to be introduced."[72]

"I'M AFRAID YOU'RE not going to see me this fall," Ira told his sister-in-law in August 1941. "No show has come along worthwhile doing." He expected good royalties from the Broadway return of *Lady in the Dark* and concluded that "there's no sense in just doing a show hoping to make some money."[73] When his show reopened at the Alvin in September, Gertrude Lawrence was the only member of the original cast to reprise her role, and she continued to make her feelings known to Ira and Weill about the quality of her songs. Ira, as usual, played the waiting game, telling Weill that "I figured the longer I took answering you or rather, not answering you—the more louse I would be and the more you could blame me for what Gertie wants and hasn't as yet received. Of all the thankless jobs in show business it is to be asked to write a new song for a hit which is in its second season."[74]

The waiting paid off: Lawrence eventually ceased complaining, and when *Lady in the Dark* finally closed in May 1942, after a stupendous run of 467 performances, Ira had more than doubled in royalties what he had earned from *Of Thee I Sing*, his most successful show to date.

PORGY AND BESS had languished since the original production closed, but by 1941, hopes for a revival were improving via the independent producer Cheryl Crawford, a founder of the influential Group Theatre, who was now running a successful stock theater in New Jersey. Ira found the majority of her ideas interesting, and her plan to hire most of the opera's original cast convinced him of her good faith, but when she suggested a reduction in the size of George's original orchestration, Ira bristled, arguing that while this might be fine in Maplewood, "it would sound pretty awful in New York."[75]

The Crawford revival opened in October 1941, with Todd Duncan (Porgy), Anne Brown (Bess), Georgette Harvey (Maria), Warren Coleman (Crown), and Edward Matthews (Jake) returning from the original production, and Avon Long replacing John W. Bubbles as Sportin' Life. The initial advertising referred to the opera as "George Gershwin's *Porgy and Bess*," although Dorothy Heyward insisted on the addition of her husband's name; Ira's name was found only inside the program, as he had agreed to the placement of newspaper advertisements without his credit if there was only space for George and DuBose.[76] His major contribution to the revival was a set of extra verses for the encore of "It Ain't Necessarily So."[77] He recommended that since the audience had never heard the words, the encore "should be taken a shade slower than the song itself." After the loose interpretation of his lyrics by Bubbles in 1935, Ira wanted to be sure that Avon Long sang " 'sench-ree' for 'century' and 'penitench-ree' for 'penitentiary.' "[78] He also spent a few days writing a limerick for Long to recite in the same number:

> 'Way back in five thousand B.C.
> Ole Adam an' Eve had to flee.
> Sure, dey did dat deed in
> De Garden of Eden—
> But why chasterize you an' me?

Alexander Smallens, who reprised his role as the opera's conductor, thought the lines were well worn, but Ira defended them: "When you tell me a gag about Adam and Eve has been used in every musical on Broadway and Timbucktoo you are talking about gags and not 'It Ain't Necessarily So' which, believe it or not is about the Bible and, believe it or not in which Adam and Eve figure quite prominently."[79]

The revival opened in New York City in January and ran for 286 performances, followed by a lengthy tour and two return engagements on Broadway, but Ira had mixed feelings, bemoaning the fact that "a great deal has been lost to make way for speed."[80] The cuts to the opera left Ira and others feeling "that this particular version has lost some of the musical subtleties. . . . Still, as it seems to have reached an entirely new and enthusiastic audience, we can't complain."[81]

FOLLOWING THE devastating December 7, 1941, air assault by the Japanese military on the US naval facility at Pearl Harbor, the West Coast of the United States went onto a wartime footing. Ira elaborated on the situation in Southern California to Kurt Weill:

Yes, it was quite exciting for a while—what with black-outs, sirens, last minute rushes to get black-out materials, search lights and soldiers suddenly appearing all over the place. The last few weeks this particular kind of excitment [sic] has been less apparent but one has a feeling that everyone out here is aware of the emergency and is taking it quite seriously.

You gather this not only from your friends and acquaintances but from visits to the shops where it seems the sons of the owners are all off to the wars and the proprietors are wondering whether they will be able to replenish this or that stock in the near future. Two of Hollywood's most exclusive night clubs announced last night they would be closed for quite a while. The point is that although people are still going to movies, shows and concerts as formerly, night clubbing seems frivolous to say the least. All the women are studying and taking courses in first aid and airplane spotting and relief work. People think twice before undertaking any kind of long trip in thier [sic] cars and so Palm Springs and Death Valley aren't doing much business because of a very practical reason—the wear and

tear on automobile tires. But I am telling you nothing that probably
isn't happening out your way also and you personally are very lucky to
be working on those short wave broadcasts because so many of us out
here would like to do something to aid directly but everything seems to
be well taken care of already so far as personel [sic] goes.[82]

The wartime issues were compounded by Lee's health; she had been in
the hospital on four recent occasions—"quite a series of journeys"—and
money was again on Ira's mind. There would be "very little left of the
income I've had this year after the new taxes, the thousands (far too many)
I've had to spend on the house this year in addition to those already spent,
the hospitals and what not. But even if I only broke even it isn't bad living
in a country like this when the rest of the world's gone crazy. Let's thank
whatever God there is for Roosevelt."[83] The death of his father-in-law on
the last day of 1941 struck another somber note, somewhat relieved by the
knowledge that Ira had, for the first time, earned over $100,000 in a single
year for the fruits of his labor.[84]

His thoughts about his future on Broadway as the United States mobi-
lized for war were similar to those of "ten years ago when we were in
the midst of the worst depression the country had ever known and at
the same time George and I had the biggest hit we ever had—'Of Thee
I Sing.' I felt then that it was a tough period for any new show unless it
was so extraordinary that it could overcome the prevailing gloom. I was
proved right." *Pardon My English*, "which we felt at best could only be
fair," turned out to be a disaster. "It's ten years later now and there's a
war instead of an economic depression and we have a hit." He told Weill
that the time was not right for a new show "unless we feel it's something
that *has* to be done."[85]

OFFERS TO PURCHASE the film rights to *Porgy and Bess* multiplied in the
wake of Cheryl Crawford's successful revival, including one by Crawford
herself that the opera's owners rejected before the first performance in New
Jersey.[86] When Crawford was preparing her production, Ira recalled that the
Theatre Guild, "believing *Porgy and Bess* a dead property, were prepared
to give in" to her offer; Ira was adamant that anything Crawford and her

producing partner had regarding *Porgy* was "simply a nuisance value and any talk of *their* version (simply a cut version) being the basis of a possible movie is just nonsense." Just because Alexander Steinert and Ira cut the version that Merle Armitage did in Los Angeles in 1938 did not "make it Steinert's version." Ira was determined, and tried to influence the other rights holders, that there was no need to quickly agree to a deal for the movie rights "so long as the stage performances continued," but he would "not stand in the way of any deal once both estates and the Guild feel they have a proper offer."[87]

Ira knew that the major studios were reluctant "to tackle this work but that does not mean that we should let the first independent have it at his own terms."[88] A successful bid to purchase the movie rights required the unanimous approval of Ira, his mother, Dorothy Heyward, and the Theatre Guild, with each party bringing their own interests to the table. Playwright Clifford Odets told Ira that if *Lady in the Dark* was worth $285,000 to a studio, *Porgy* should garner $500,000. Ira was content to hold out for at least $200,000.[89] Any proposal "should be carefully studied in the light of potential revival possibilities which might be jeopardized by such a sale."[90]

IN 1942, the George Gershwin biopic was revived when producer Jerry Wald hired Clifford Odets to write a new script. Ira thought Odets might be a good choice, but since Odets "was far more interested generally in plays about the class struggle," he wondered what his take on George's story might be.[91] Ira gave Odets a chronology of the events surrounding George's final illness and death, but their time together was "devoted mostly to playing records of Gershwin music so he could acquaint himself with all the musical possibilities." Ira read the first draft and Odets's full script, noting that other than "immediate family and an occasional character like Oscar Levant, the rest of the cast is entirely fictional as is the love story." Arguments among the family about some of what the playwright was doing were natural, and the studio would listen to "reasonable protests, but in the last analysis they have absolute final say on story, cast and choice of music." Regardless, "Odets seems to have caught the spirit of George and his work very well and I have my fingers crossed hoping they turn out not only a good picture but an important one."[92]

The movie would be a long time coming. When Jerry Wald went into the army, Jesse L. Lasky took over the seemingly endless production, and Odets's lengthy script was handed over to be halved by George and Ira's old friend Sonya Levien.[93] Howard Koch's final script was based on Levien's and Odets's attempts, with the merry-go-round only ending after Elliot Paul, the author of the widely acclaimed book *The Last Time I Saw Paris*, was called in to provide a final polish. Ira liked Paul but the "script was a secondary consideration" during their meetings: "Mostly he talked about baseball."[94]

CHAPTER 14

THE WAR YEARS WERE the busiest years of Ira Gershwin's life, on both the home and professional fronts, since the death of his brother in 1937. In April 1942, Ira registered with the Selective Service as part of the "Old Man's Registration," the expanded draft for males between the ages of forty-five and sixty-four. Although unlikely to see active service, Ira was a patriotic American and was happy to play whatever part he could to fight Fascism and ensure the future of democracy around the world.

During this time, he served on the editorial committee of the Los Angeles branch of the *Lunch Time Follies*, an American Theatre Wing–sponsored organization that brought entertainment to factory and shipyard workers; appeared on a panel with fellow lyricists Leo Robin and Oscar Hammerstein II to discuss "Song Writing in War"; hosted a star-studded reception for Brigadier General Benjamin O. Davis, who was touring the country to promote the War Department's Frank Capra–produced documentary *The Negro Soldier*; and wrote, at the behest of the author Rex Stout, an American-style chorus for Noël Coward's satirical song "Don't Let's Be Beastly to the Germans" for a Writers' War Board event.

Lee Gershwin's wartime activities included volunteering for the Office of Price Administration and planting a victory garden to offset local meat and fish rationing, but her most symbolic act—a sign of the respect that the country now held for her late brother-in-law—was her sponsorship of the launch of the Liberty ship SS *George Gershwin* in San Pedro Harbor, where she "managed to break the champagne bottle at first swing."[1]

THESE MORALE-BOOSTING EFFORTS merged with Ira's career when Samuel Goldwyn hired him to work on a series of Russian-style folk songs for *The North Star*, a picture that was one of a number of movies made by the major studios at the request of the federal government to promote the allied cause.[2] With the bitter memories of how he was treated by the producer after George's death still in his mind, Ira balked at writing propaganda for Goldwyn, but relented when Lillian Hellman said she would be more comfortable writing the screenplay if she knew that Ira was on board. He then tried to back out of the project by suggesting that Goldwyn hire an experienced film music composer like Shostakovich, Prokofiev, or Stravinsky, thinking that he would not be needed if one of these giants of classical music were chosen.[3] When that ruse failed, Ira, asked to come up with another name, suggested Aaron Copland but asked Goldwyn for $15,000, reasoning that Copland—with little experience of songwriting—would need more assistance than if Ira had been working with Harold Arlen or Harry Warren. Although Goldwyn accepted Copland as the composer, he felt that Ira wanted too much money for too little work; Ira, fed up with arguing the subject, settled for $7,500.[4]

Although some of his lines in *The North Star* were overtly political—"Song of the Guerrillas" originally contained the phrase "The Red Star will shine as before"—Ira generally took a more universal tone: praising the Russians who were defending their homes while not being held in fealty to a particular political doctrine.[5] The film, which "seemed a little dated," received generally poor reviews and a disappointing box office.[6] But the "gay spirit" of Ira's verses to "Younger Generation," a gentle reminder to parents that they were once scamps and rebels themselves, broke through the propaganda.[7] Ira was not surprised to hear that the songs from *The North Star* failed to make the hit parade; "it may be as in the case of Harburg and Kern's 'And Russia Is Her Name'" that the songs he and Copland wrote "would be considered 'controversial' by the advertising agencies, which, frequently, control the policy of music on their programs."[8]

A PROJECT WITH more promise arrived via the composer Arthur Schwartz; now producing movies for Columbia Pictures, Schwartz turned the aimless partnership of Ira and Jerome Kern in the late 1930s into a reality by signing them to write the songs for *Cover Girl*, an elaborate Technicolor musical starring Gene Kelly and Rita Hayworth. The earlier numbers Ira and Kern had written were largely discarded and a new set was put together from scratch at Kern's house a block and a half from Ira's residence.[9] Although the lethargic lyricist was unhappy about working in unfamiliar surroundings, without his reference books to provide an excuse to step away from his writing whenever he felt the urge, the collaborators completed most of their work by the due date of mid-May 1943, although delays in casting and production kept them sporadically active on the film through the late summer.

Cover Girl, released in the spring of 1944, was a gigantic hit and caused Ira to extol its virtues in more enthusiastic-than-usual language: "I take the long, historical, objective, comparative, un-affiliated-with-studio-superlative viewpoint and say it's *one* of the *best musicals* in *years*."[10] The comment is a reflection of the winning gamble he had made in agreeing to a smaller up-front payment of $16,000 in exchange for 7.5 percent of the gross receipts after the picture's cost had been recouped. This unexpected windfall, plus the popularity of "Long Ago (and Far Away)" with wartime listeners, who heard their pining for their loved ones in the lyrics, finally brought Ira's accounts with his publisher into the black. The royalties from sheet music sales of over six hundred thousand copies and numerous recordings represented the biggest hit of any single year in Ira's career.[11]

It came as a surprise that "Long Ago (and Far Away)," with a lyric that Ira felt was no more than "an adequate job," had struck paydirt.[12] Its success was "one of the minor casualties of war," as the "utter demolishment of previously romantic places (on the map)" resulted in a blacklist of "practically every dot in the atlas."[13] It had been difficult to write a lyric that suited Kern's melody, and the experimentations ("Midnight Music" and "Midnight Madness" were both rejected) went on too long for everyone except Ira. He filled a "dozen crowded worksheets" with ideas on how to "embed the title" in the "smooth, meditative, melodic line." There were many good notions, "but no this-is-it enthusiasm was engendered. I seem to remember that the only advice I received at conferences was 'Keep it simple, keep it simple.'" The problem continued to confound him until the day Arthur Schwartz rang up and said that the number "had to be recorded in a couple of days. Did I have anything? I mentioned the latest I'd been wrestling with: 'Long Ago and Far Away.' 'Fine. Let's have it.' 'Now? On

Checking out his latest losers at Santa Anita racetrack with
his friend, writer Robert "Doc" McGunigle, January 20, 1940.
Photograph by Leonore S. Gershwin.

the telephone?' 'Sure.' So I read it to him; he wrote it down, and that was
that. I heaved an enormous sigh of relief at not having to go down to the
studio to face anyone with this lyric."[14]

The racetrack terminology of "Sure Thing" allowed Ira to conflate a
romantic relationship with one of his favorite activities. "At Hollywood Park
once I bet on all twelve horses in a race and won a few dollars when $2 on
a long shot paid over $50. On the other hand—and more typical—I bet
on seven horses in an eleven-horse race, mostly $2 each and $2 across on
a couple. . . . My horses ran fifth to eleventh—I didn't even get fourth."[15]
Kern wrote the tune during the period he and Ira had worked together after
George's death. Ira hummed a bit of it to jog the composer's memory, "but
he had never put it on paper, and couldn't recall it. I told him his daughter
Betty had been very fond of this melody, so he called her in and between
us and our snatches, it came back to him. 'Good tune,' he said. 'What about
it?' I told him it had begun haunting me that morning, and if he could split
the opening note into two notes, I had a two-word on-the-nose title for the
flashback number in the film."[16]

THERE HAD BEEN numerous attempts—largely on the part of Kurt Weill—to capitalize on the success of *Lady in the Dark*, but Ira remained vague, saying only that "if we both agree the right show is clamoring to be born I can be one of the papas."[17] The playwright Edwin Justus Mayer presented them with an idea about "Cinderella after she married her prince, and in which she turns out to be a termagant."[18] Weill was interested, and *Around the Cape to Matrimony* was announced as a Jed Harris production for a Christmas 1943 opening.[19] But Ira and Mayer concluded that the story "might do for a one-acter but was too much of a one-joke notion to carry a full Broadway production." The same fate met Mayer's idea for a show about the seventeenth-century actress Nell Gwyn.[20] Weill thought he had Ira's agreement to work with him and producer Cheryl Crawford on a musical version of F. Anstey's 1885 novella *The Tinted Venus*,[21] but Ira could not see himself as a contributor to this somewhat farcical story of a statue of the goddess Venus coming to life.[22] (Weill and lyricist Ogden Nash would have a nearly eighteen-month run with the retitled *One Touch of Venus* in 1943 and a major commercial success with its hit song "Speak Low.")

But Ira and Weill agreed that if they failed to identify a stage vehicle, a movie musical would do for the moment, and in late 1943, the pair signed a deal with 20th Century Fox to write the score for a wartime-themed fantasy called *Where Do We Go from Here?* for producer William Perlberg. Ira settled for a lower-than-usual $40,000 fee because the studio had a lyricist under contract who "wanted this particular job so Perlberg couldn't go overboard with outside writers."[23] The work was complete by the end of January, and Ira, who loved the score, agreed to record the numbers with Weill as reference material before the composer returned to the East Coast. Ira admitted that he was "not a singer but in addition had a bad cold that night, [and] that Kurt and I hadn't had time to rehearse."[24] But he told everyone to listen to the discs if they could; it was "one of the best scores in years. In fact, delightful. No kidding, it's refreshing. Yes, if I may venture the opinion, *quite* refreshing."[25]

Ira had high hopes for *Where Do We Go from Here?*, calling it "the first movie musical I know that has some of the flavor of 'Of Thee I Sing' in the writing and music."[26] Everyone had put "a lot of effort and imagination" into the work, and he hoped that the "results warrant it."[27] But extensive production delays and cost overruns brought the budget to $2.5 million, and by the time the Technicolor time-shifting spectacle reached theaters in the summer of 1945, audiences had had their fill of stories with wartime themes. Although Ira's lyrics were praised for their literacy and their enhancement of the plot, the movie quickly disappeared, and none of the songs made the Hit Parade.[28]

The showpiece of the movie, a Columbus-discovers-America parody entitled "The Nina, the Pinta, the Santa Maria," was, at ten minutes, the "longest musical sequence in the history of film" at the time of its release,[29] with the studio spending $250,000 on this sequence alone.[30] Fred MacMurray, as the time-leaping GI, forestalls a mutiny by Columbus's men with promises of what they would find when they spotted land:

> And oh, my hearties,
> What fun and what parties:
> The Democratic party and the
>   G.O.P.,
> The Prohibition party and the
>   Boston Tea. . . .
> What a wonderful land in which to
>   be living—
> Where you celebrate the Fourth of
>   July, Saint Patrick's Day, and
>   Thanksgiving.
> And if you want an extra day off,
> What you're doing to Columbus is
>   away off.
> For the man you want to betray
> Can give you not only Columbus
>   Circle and Columbus, Ohio, but
>   also Columbus Day!

In 1954, Ira agreed to the publication of "The Nina, the Pinta, the Santa Maria" after his publishers received many requests from discerning listeners following the commercial release of Ira's demo recording with Kurt Weill. "Even though eleven pages are only one third of the Columbus sequence, they do make an entity and I'm delighted the piece is being published."[31]

THE FIRST HALF of the 1940s saw big-screen adaptations of four of Ira's Broadway musicals—MGM's versions of *Strike Up the Band*, *Lady, Be Good!*, and *Girl Crazy* and Paramount's *Lady in the Dark*—with varied results. Judy Garland and Mickey Rooney starred in both *Strike Up the Band* and *Girl Crazy*; both were big hits. Ira changed a few lines in his lyrics at the request of the studio, but his friend, composer Roger Edens, made additional changes to the verse of "Treat Me Rough" that Ira was unaware of for many years until André Previn brought him a copy of the sheet music that had been issued to promote the movie.[32] This almost happened again when Ira's publishers capitalized on the success of Frank Sinatra's 1947 Columbia recording of "I've Got a Crush on You" by issuing new sheet music with the singer's photograph on it; when they also suggested a replacement line that Ira disapproved of, he wagged his finger at them and said, "You wouldn't want me, after 28 years of song writing, to be accused of a bad rhyme, would you?"[33]

Paramount's movie version of *Lady in the Dark* failed to reach the heights of the groundbreaking musical. What puzzled Ira the most was the omission, "for some unfathomable reason," of "My Ship," even though "the script necessarily had many references" to the show's key song: "I hold a brief for Hollywood, having been more or less a movie-goer since I was nine; but there are times."[34] These movie deals sharpened Ira's hopes of leveraging *Of Thee I Sing* to Hollywood, but its cynical book was not a good fit for the patriotic tone of the United States during the war years. Another roadblock was the changing political beliefs of the once-liberal Morrie Ryskind.[35] Those differences aside, Ira happily continued his Saturday night poker games with Ryskind and his other friends—Arthur Kober, Russell Crouse, Marc Connolly, Clifford Odets, and the actor John Garfield—who "used to kitty out somewhere between $125–150" for the monthly rental of an apartment on Sunset Strip, plus "$50 to a young Filipino who prepared the midnight meal for us [and] for expensive Cuban cigars." There was also the exciting "night we were 'raided' by two detectives from the D.A.'s office" and the hilarity that ensued when actor Charles Coburn (who played Max Dreyfus in the George Gershwin biopic, *Rhapsody in Blue*) arrived late for the game, "excusing himself by saying he had been appearing for a Jewish charity and when asked which he said 'The Bonnie Brae' when he meant the B'nai B'rith."[36]

ALTHOUGH IRA HAD little interest in doing another Broadway musical,[37] he agreed to a second show—"of all things a costume piece"—with Kurt Weill in the spring of 1944.[38] The idea was a musical adaptation of *The Firebrand*, Edwin Justus Mayer's 1924 hit play about the Florentine sculptor Benvenuto Cellini. This was not the first attempt at putting music to Mayer's play. Horace Liveright, who produced the original 1924 staging, attempted the feat four years later; directed by a young George Cukor, it never got past Atlantic City. In 1934, the play was successfully adapted for the movies as *The Affairs of Cellini*, with Fredric March and Frank Morgan.[39]

Weill's eagerness for the project rubbed off on Ira, who enthused that this was a chance to create the "international operetta" George had often spoken about, one "whose background would be understandable to audiences in any country."[40] For three months, he and Weill worked together on the songs for *The Firebrand of Florence* at Ira's house, the composer sitting at George's piano while the lyricist sat nearby with his pens and pads of paper or paced around the room, trying to distract himself from the work at hand, to Weill's frequent frustration.[41]

One of Ira's excuses for not wanting to work quickly was Mayer's absence; the playwright was busy finishing a screenplay for Ernst Lubitsch's movie *A Royal Scandal*.[42] Weill was exasperated and told Ira that he had to begin writing *now*. Ira reluctantly agreed but pushed back on his being in New York in what he was sure would be a repeat of the unbearably hot summer he spent working on *Lady in the Dark*.[43] Since he had come East to work on that show, surely it would be fair that the second one be written in California?[44]

Weill dubbed Mayer and Ira the "two tired old men," even though he was only four years younger, and Ira tried "every single trick to keep from working," even pleading illness and taking medicine that made him "dopey."[45] But after days of "complaining and kicking," the words began to flow.[46] Weill was pleased by Ira's technique and his love for lyrical novelty, qualities that made the composer happy to be working with the only man who had the skills and the mind to accomplish what Weill was thinking about for this show.[47]

Weill pushed his collaborators forward, knowing that he had Lee Gershwin backing him up in his urge to get Ira working again.[48] But Ira's confidence ebbed and flowed; one moment he wondered whether the comedy in the book was "a little dated,"[49] then enthusiastically told the show's producer,

Max Gordon, that what he and Weill were creating was "better than" *Porgy and Bess* and *Of Thee I Sing* "combined."[50]

BELIEVING THAT most of the *Firebrand* score was complete when Weill departed for New York in October 1944, Ira sensed a "comparative creative cinch" when he himself arrived in December. Disappointment quickly set in.[51] They had lost Moss Hart as director, and difficult work was ahead. Did the show lack the "impact" of the original play?[52] After much trial and error, *The Firebrand of Florence*, under its original title *Much Ado about Love,* opened in New Haven on Washington's birthday before moving to Boston. In both cities, it was well received by the local writers, but the national critics were puzzled: was it an operetta or a musical comedy? The show *looked* wonderful, but the "book, cast, dances, lyrics and music, in that order of necessity," needed an overhaul.[53]

The revue specialist John Murray Anderson turned out to be the wrong choice to replace Hart, since he "distained any members of the company whose function it was merely to speak lines." Ira predicted that they would find "the chorus rehearsing on the stage and the principals rehearsing in the toilets."[54] George S. Kaufman was quickly brought on to tinker with the script before the New York opening.[55] After a "tough session with the elements in Boston,"[56] Ira—dosed with antibiotics—made his way in body, if not in spirit, to the Alvin Theatre for the opening in late March. The reviews were not good: Mayer and Ira had "managed to extract an extremely tiresome script" out of the play, while the "lyrics range from second to third, fourth and even fifth rate W. S. Gilbert." The entire "production has a clumsy air about it that is hardly to be associated with a professional Broadway musical attraction these days."[57]

Many of the reviews touched on the casting, which had been a divisive issue from the start. Ira was ambivalent about Weill wanting to cast his wife, Lotte Lenya, as the duchess, and his argument that casting friends and relatives made for difficulties held no weight with the composer, who bullied him into backing down.[58] In the end, the principal performers—Earl Wrightson as Cellini, the ingenue Beverly Tyler as Angela, Neville Cooper as the duke, and Lenya—seemed to be in different shows, and the book problems were amplified by the varied concepts of Anderson, Kaufman, and choreographer Catherine Littlefield, who wound up directing much of the show without credit.[59]

Wartime brownouts and curfews negatively affected all of Broadway, but the downfall of *The Firebrand of Florence* was easily accounted for: lack of a star name, negative reviews, and competition from long-running shows (*Bloomer Girl, Harvey, Life with Father, Oklahoma!*, and *On the Town*) and star vehicles for Fredric March, Tallulah Bankhead, Beatrice Lillie, and Bert Lahr. The death of President Franklin Delano Roosevelt on April 12, 1945, and the cancellation of all matinees on the following Saturday, was no help to an already battered show. The stake in Ira's heart was delivered by George Jean Nathan in a long attack in the *New York Journal-American*: he complained that Ira's "passion for puns, spoonerisms, and other wordplay" had become tiresome.[60] *Firebrand* closed on April 28, after only forty-three performances. Ira failed to recoup his investment, as did his family members and the friends he had encouraged to back the show. The wounded lyricist departed for California to lick his wounds. As Ira remarked to his sister-in-law, "it looks as if nine months of hard work has been shot to hell."[61]

Much of Ira's energy was spent on the eighteen-minute sequence that opened the show. Set in a public square in Florence in the sixteenth century, as a gallows is being erected, "the plot is explained solely with words and music":[62]

> *Hangman*: When the bell of doom is clanging
> For the man awaiting hanging,
> Let's face the fact with no misgiving:
> One man's death is another man's living!

> *Gallows*
> *builders*: One man's death is another man's living
> Under the gallows tree.
> With union pay,
> We sing all day,
> The while our hammers bang.
> If the world doesn't like it
> The world can go hang!
> Under the gallows tree!

Oh, riddle dee diddle dee dee!
Oh, under the gallows tree!

The gallows are for Cellini, who steadfastly awaits his fate:

And so, unflinching I face the shadows,
And if the future sings this glad refrain:
"He lived life, he loved love, he laughed laughter"—
I've not lived or loved or laughed in vain.

The tune for "Sing Me Not a Ballad," a solo feature for Lotte Lenya's
duchess, was developed by Weill, at Ira's suggestion, from the first six
ascending notes of her young page's singsong entrance:[63]

Sing me not a ballad,
Send me not a sonnet.
I require no ballad:
Rhyme and time are wasted on it.

Save your books and flowers;
They're not necessaries.
Oh, the precious hours
Lost in grim preliminaries!

Deck me not in jewels;
Sigh me not your sighs;
Duel me no duels;
And—please don't vocalize!

Romance me no romances;
Treasure not my glove.
Spare me your advances—
Just, oh just, make love!

An exercise in the use of spoonerisms for comedic effect, "The Cozy
Nook Trio" was an idea that Ira had tried to accomplish in *Lady, Be*

Good![64] Here, the lecherous Duke Alessandro tries to seduce Angela, with humorous consequences:

> *Duke*: I know where there's a nosy cook—
> *Angela*: My lord, you mean a cozy nook?
> *Duke*: Yes, yes, of course. A cozy nook for two.
>   And there we two can kill and boo.
> *Angela*: My lord, you mean we'll bill and coo?
> *Duke*: I cannot promise bedding wells.
> *Angela*: My thoughts were not on wedding bells.
> *Duke*: Whatever I do is for the fatherland;
>   And so I love your sturgeon vile.
> *Angela*: My lord, you mean my virgin style?
> *Duke*: It's wonderful how love can understand!

AFTER YEARS OF DELAYS, Warner Bros.' black-and-white biopic *Rhapsody in Blue* was finally released in the summer of 1945. Ira expected criticism, but understood that a movie version of his brother's life had to take liberties with the facts: "A great deal of telescoping" of time and the introduction of "a romantic note or two which would point to no special individuals" were necessary evils.[65] At the time of its release, he "was too emotionally involved to enjoy the film,"[66] but he felt that Robert Alda captured "a good deal of the spirit" of his brother.[67]

Ira was portrayed as a teen by Darryl Hickman and as an adult (with much more hair than reality) by the character actor Herbert Rudley, who received little assistance from Ira about how to play him. Rudley "guessed the characterization would be a lot of Rudley and very little Gershwin, and [Ira] said that was all right."[68] The biopic was promoted as saying "something important about the democracy which gave Gershwin a chance to prove his genius."[69] To that end, the Manhattan opening supported a "George Gershwin Jubilee," a theme the critics duly ignored. Capturing George Gershwin's "complex nature," wrote the critic for the *New York Times*, was beyond the ability of "the craftsmen who made the picture."[70]

IN LATE 1945, Ira received a wire from George S. Kaufman about *Park Avenue*, a new musical he was planning with producer Max Gordon, composer Arthur Schwartz, and the writer Nunnally Johnson, based on Nunnally's 1933 *Saturday Evening Post* story "Holy Matrimony."[71] Although Schwartz was excited to work with Ira after his positive, and profitable, experience as the producer of *Cover Girl*, Ira did not "relish" the idea of another Broadway show.[72] But he agreed to join, hoping for a better result than he had had with *The Firebrand of Florence*: "As I see it, it's a farce with music rather than a musical comedy. It offers many problems but we hope we can lick them."[73] Ira and Schwartz planned to head East at the end of July 1946, where they would stay at Kaufman's Bucks County farm to put the "final polish" on the songs and their placement in the book, "then return to New York for rehearsals."[74]

As spring turned to summer, Ira's positive attitude dimmed. If he could make it through the creation of *Park Avenue*, he vowed to be done with Broadway, since "instead of getting easier it gets tougher because you keep competing with everything you've done in the past. Yesterday, for instance

With Jerome Kern and producer Arthur Schwartz
(*center*), at Kern's house during the writing of the songs
for *Cover Girl*, 1943.

I worked with Schwartz from 2 to 6 in the afternoon. Then I worked by myself from 8:30 last night until 4 a.m. this morning and what was the sum total? Six lines that I liked. I repeat, it's a tough life if you're conscientious."[75]

BY AUGUST, Ira was ensconced in his Manhattan hotel suite, where friends paid him visits, eager to hear him sing the new songs through the haze of smoke that drifted up from his ever-present cigars.[76] *Park Avenue* opened in New Haven in mid-September, then moved to Boston, where the *Billboard* critic blasted it as "a musical without a singable tune."[77] Although ticket sales were good during the first week in Boston, Ira was unhappy; leading lady Leonora Corbett provided the "elegance we hoped for. But the constant strain on a voice unused to the demands of musical comedy proved too taxing."[78] Corbett had "great charm and is excellent in the part but we never should have entrusted four numbers to her."[79] Although the vocal trouble extended to much of the cast, Ira sensed that the show, with a few comedy numbers and some amusing plot twists that seemed to please the out-of-town audiences, still might just make it after the New York opening.[80]

The show's fate was quickly determined. While some of Ira's "insistent lyrics" were "off the laugh shelf," the New York critics followed their Boston colleagues and picked up on the show's "vocal malnutrition."[81] *Park Avenue* opened well opposite *Annie Get Your Gun, Carousel, Oklahoma!*, and a revival of *Show Boat*, but managed just seventy-two performances before closing shortly after New Year's Day 1947. Ira's $5,000 investment in the show disappeared with it: "Heigh ho—guess I can't afford to do any more flops—two in a row is about six too many."[82]

The authors mistakenly thought that *Park Avenue* had a novel quality that would make it successful, since "it pertained to the upper-bracket-income-and-black-tie set as against four or five years of nothing but costume and period operettas"—including *The Firebrand of Florence*—but in the end, the reasons for its failure were clear: "(A) charm wasn't enough to sustain the second act; (B) evidently divorce is a ticklish subject to be funny about for an entire show."[83] Ira's disappointment was evident. Even if "a couple of the critics liked the show most of them didn't and another ten months' work was shot."[84]

THE SHOW may have failed, but Ira was pleased with his work on it and chose to include five *Park Avenue* lyrics in his 1959 book, *Lyrics on Several Occasions*, including the protofeminist number "Don't Be a Woman If You Can," in which a trio of women lament what a man's world forces them to do and to put up with. The title paraphrased a remark by the lyricist Dave Clark, who, when asked about a new Broadway show, said, "Don't miss it if you can." Ira often encountered Clark in the 1920s. The older lyricist was "always neatly dressed, clean-shaven, and soft-spoken, even though over the years the poor chap's brain had become disordered. He was supported by contributions from the boys and a publisher or two, but he had his dignity and definite notions on quotas, so wouldn't accept more than what he considered correct. Once when I tried offering him a dollar—others gave him more—he shook his head and took only the usual quarter. (I like to think this sum was not his measure of me as a songwriter, but that either I was a newcomer or wasn't doing too well financially.)"[85]

"The Land of Opportunitee" was written for a male quartet of respectable Park Avenue types, who sing of some of Ira's favorite pastimes—the stock market, the racetrack, and puzzles—in an "improvised calypso," which "with its odd syllabic stress and loose rhyme, can narrate, advise, philosophize, fulminate, use this morning's headlines—and any theme goes, including the political and sexual."[86] But for all his pleasure in devising clever rhymes for the show, Ira could not help thinking that there was one number from *Park Avenue* that summed up his feelings about his recent experiences—and his future—on Broadway: "Good-bye to All That."

CHAPTER 15

I N JUNE 1945, Ira had met with producer William Perlberg about a second movie musical for 20th Century Fox; although he had enjoyed working with Perlberg on *Where Do We Go from Here?* and the two had become friends, Ira was doubtful: "How I dread it! Work! Work!"[1] But he agreed to discuss the possibilities of the "Technicolor-Boston-1870-Betty Grable-women's rights, etc." entertainment that Perlberg described to him.[2] When MGM refused to release Harry Warren from his contract and Harold Arlen elected to move forward with Johnny Mercer to work on *St. Louis Woman*, a new Broadway show, Ira suggested to Perlberg that an entirely new George Gershwin score could be created out of some of his unused melodies.[3]

This was not a new idea: Vernon Duke thought of an adaptation of Sam Behrman's play *Serena Blandish* using material from George's tune books in 1938.[4] Four years later, producer Cheryl Crawford and the librettists Sam and Bella Spewack brought Ira the concept for a show called *Birds of a Feather*.[5] Neither project met with his approval. Ira had thought to hold back George's tunes for a movie about the "life of a modern composer," but when Perlberg said he liked the concept, Ira agreed to take the plunge into the depths of his brother's musical trunk.[6]

To accomplish the difficult task of combing through George's tunes and fitting them into cohesive melodies that met the needs of the movie's plot, he needed the assistance of a composer who was intimately familiar with his brother's music but also one who would defer to Ira's wishes. The person who most desperately wanted to work with Ira in the years following George's death was Kay Swift, but he had avoided her since the creation of

"Dawn of a New Day" in 1938. Ira was fond of Kay, but she was a constant reminder of George; more crucially, Kay and Lee Gershwin did not get along. Was Ira willing to disturb the equanimity of his relationship with his wife by bringing his brother's former lover to collaborate with him at their house for ten weeks? Weighing the costs, he decided it was worth a try and agreed to pay Kay an 11 percent share of the $90,000 he received from Fox under his contract.[7]

The two scrutinized every page of George's notebooks and manuscripts, searching for suitable material, with Kay seated at George's piano and Ira nearby, scribbling down his ideas. At times, she watched as Ira sang while doing "a little turn around with his eyes shut. Entirely beguiling."[8] She compared his work as a lyricist to that of a jeweler, painstakingly fitting stones into a setting and polishing the result until it shone with a brilliance it did not have in its original form.[9] When the job was finished, Kay had created lead sheets for dozens of potential numbers—some with lyrics that Ira had begun during George's lifetime—along with verses and openings. Ira diligently took an additional two months to find "eight bars from here and eight from there to round out a tune" before settling down to polish his final lyrics.[10]

IRA'S VERDICT on *The Shocking Miss Pilgrim* upon its release in January 1947 was that while it was "not a terribly exciting film," it did "have some charm and intelligence."[11] One thing the score lacked was a result of the period setting: George's "more rhythmic and modern" tunes had to be discarded in favor of those with a romantic bent.[12]

"Aren't You Kind of Glad We Did?" a duet for Betty Grable and Dick Haymes, began as one of the few numbers that George and Ira wrote between shows in the 1930s; for the movie, Ira adjusted his original lyrics from what he described as an "Epithalamium of the Depression to a Mid-Victorian Colloquy."[13] The result was innocuous, but Ira soon realized that there were some listeners who heard a different meaning in his words: if the lyric was experienced without seeing Grable and Haymes on the screen innocently enjoying a carriage ride around Boston without a chaperone, what Ira thought was tame became risqué, a turn of events that led to the song being "banned from the air by the networks."[14]

Honestly, I thought you wouldn't;
Naturally, you thought you couldn't.
And probably we shouldn't—
   But aren't you kind of glad we did?
Actually, it all was blameless;
Nevertheless, they'll call it shameless.
So the lady shall be nameless,
   But aren't you kind of glad we did?

EVEN AS THE United States settled into the early years of the postwar period in which the country briefly found itself as the world's sole remaining superpower, there were Americans who wondered about the horrors that human beings had wrought on each other since 1939 and whether the future could be different. Ira kept his thoughts about these matters to himself. He remained on the sidelines of the vital issues that came to the forefront during this period—Communism versus democracy, and civil rights among them—continuing his monetary support for liberal organizations and joining a group of writers who refused to allow their shows to be performed in Jim Crow–era Washington, DC, but always balancing a theoretical commitment to change with a deep reluctance to support drastic action.[15]

He lent his name and gave his money to public discussions on "The Challenge of the Post-War World to the Liberal Movement" and to organizations such as the Progressive Citizens of America (cited by the House Un-American Activities Committee as a Communist front group) and the Emergency Committee of Atomic Scientists (an anti-bomb group founded by Albert Einstein). But one event put him into the spotlight, although the circumstances—as always—were not of his making.

The Committee for the First Amendment (CFA) was founded in September 1947 by screenwriter Philip Dunne and the directors William Wyler and John Huston to protest congressional hearings into alleged Communist activity in the United States, and Hollywood in particular. Although Ira did not lend his name to the group's full-page advertisement in the *Hollywood Reporter* on October 24, he did allow the first organizing meeting of the group to be held at his home on the following evening. This was not a sign of Ira's growing political involvement but rather a matter of convenience; Lee was in Palm Springs, and when Ira was asked if he would host, he felt he could not refuse.[16]

The day after the meeting, Ira joined a large group of CFA members on a chartered flight to Washington, DC, to attend the hearings of the House Committee on Un-American Activities (HUAC) on October 27.[17] Ira was a friend of many of his "fellow travelers"—Huston, Humphrey Bogart, Lauren Bacall, John Garfield, Edward G. Robinson, Richard Conte, Danny Kaye, Larry Adler, Gene Kelly, Arthur Kober—and an acquaintance of others, but he was no Communist sympathizer. Unfortunately, the consequences of what were, to Ira, straightforward actions in defense of democracy at home soon became clear.

Hollywood, he said, was "in a turmoil over the movie investigation and everyone is concerned over the harm it has done." HUAC had "discovered a publicity gold mine," but Ira was adamant that he had never "see[n] anything subversive about any American movie" he had viewed.[18]

The anti-Communist legislators saw Reds everywhere and tried to slow or prevent what they were convinced was the infiltration of Communists into Hollywood by pressuring individuals in the industry to name names: did they know if Mr. or Mrs. X was a Communist? Less than four months after the first CFA meetings, the California State Senate Committee on Un-American Activities—chaired by the former songwriter (now state senator) Jack Tenney ("Mexicali Rose")—issued subpoenas to Ira and five actors, including Morris Carnovsky, who had played Morris Gershwin in the *Rhapsody in Blue* biopic.[19]

Ira could not comprehend what such a committee could possibly want to know from him unless it was to find out whether the music or the lyrics came first.[20] But on February 19, 1948, he took his seat at the witness table in the Assembly Chambers of the State Building in Los Angeles and "promptly declared, in response to the question, that he had never been a member of the Communist Party" but remained silent about his brief membership in the Socialist Party when he was twenty-one. He readily admitted that he was one of the less than seven hundred members of the CFA and acknowledged that the first meeting of the organization had been held at his house. When a list of names, prepared by the committee, was placed in front of him, he without hesitation confirmed the identities of the attendees at the meeting.[21] Senator Tenney "complimented" him for such a "ready answer."[22]

A month later, he summed up his testimony as having "turned out to be nothing, but it's pretty bad that these committees have the power to drag you to them just because someone's uncle said he thought you were wearing what seemed to him a red tie at a football game one day last fall."[23]

Although Ira's naming of names caused boos among some members of the Hollywood community, his career was not affected.[24] But Lee Gershwin, with her long-standing involvement in organizations alleged to be Communist fronts, became frightened and vowed that she was not going to let Ira's fate become that of Yip Harburg, whose outspoken liberal views made him anathema in Hollywood. She steered away from overt political activity and urged Ira to do the same.[25]

SEVERAL PROPOSALS for shows and movies crossed his desk in the late 1940s, but returning to Broadway was impossible "unless it's the last word in the way of a new idea or something. If a movie offer comes along I'm their boy but the studios aren't taking on new expensive musicals other than those already contracted for, so it looks as if I'll spend quite a number of additional months golfing, reading, gabbing and wasting time pleasantly."[26]

Less pleasant moments were occupied by avoiding writers who wanted access to Ira's papers and his imprimatur to write a new biography of George: "I have had numerous offers either for me to write or collaborate on such a work, but somehow I have felt that I would like to assist rather than officially collaborate on what I would regard as *the* biography."[27]

One of the first writers to approach Ira was Moses Smith, a music critic for the *Boston Evening Transcript* and the author of a controversial biography of the Russian composer Serge Koussevitzky. Ira told Smith he could certainly proceed but that a biography of George would not be "geographically feasible just now," since he and Smith were on opposite coasts.[28]

The most persistent man on the biographical scene was David Ewen, who had written a biography of George Gershwin for younger readers in 1945 and was now looking to turn his attention to an adult audience. Ira, unaware of the earlier book until he saw an advertisement for it, was not impressed; he hesitated to recommend it if the child's "mentality seems to be over 14 or 15."[29] To put Ewen off the scent, Ira repeated that "a definitive life" of his brother was surely needed, but that he was unable to cooperate "just now or in the near future."[30]

AFTER THE FAILURE OF *Park Avenue* at the end of 1946, Arthur Schwartz apologized for involving Ira in the show when he would have been more pleasantly occupied writing songs for Judy Garland in Hollywood with Harry Warren.[31] Thirteen months after that declaration, Ira received a call from producer Arthur Freed at MGM about *The Barkleys of Broadway*, a new picture for Garland and Fred Astaire.[32]

By 1948, Harry Warren had become the most successful songwriter in Hollywood, having won three Academy Awards for Best Song, with five additional nominations as well as numerous number one hits. Ira and Warren had first worked together in 1930, when "Cheerful Little Earful," one of Ira's more popular numbers not written with his brother, was included in producer Billy Rose's revue *Sweet and Low*. A second Warren-composed number, "The Merry Month of Maybe," did not survive the tryouts for *Sweet and Low* but became popular after Warren's publisher successfully promoted it, which encouraged Rose to add it to the score of another of his revues, 1931's *Crazy Quilt*, starring his wife, Fanny Brice.[33]

The Barkleys of Broadway was Ira's first opportunity to write for Judy Garland, although there had been a moment in 1937 when he thought he had. It was during an evening at the Trocadero nightclub, when "a little thirteen-year-old-girl singer from MGM, accompanied at the piano by her bespectacled mother, was cheered by the professional audience after each of three songs." When the announcer stated that the next song would be "Slap That Bass," Ira "turned to producer Pandro Berman with a look that could mean only: 'What's *this*? Where'd she get *that*?'" only to discover that the song Garland sang was not the one he had written with George.[34] Eight years later, Ira functioned as the best man at Garland's Beverly Hills wedding to Vincente Minnelli, and in 1946, he became the godfather of the couple's first daughter, Liza.

Ira and Warren quickly produced a dozen songs for Garland, Astaire, and their costar Oscar Levant, but after only a month of rehearsals, Garland was suspended by the studio due to her constant illnesses. Ginger Rogers was quickly hired as her replacement, which created an unexpected reunion with Fred Astaire.[35] For the songwriters, the biggest problem was that "Rogers isn't quite the vocalist Garland is," which meant replacing all the latter's solo numbers.[36] So back to work they went, the duo eventually creating nearly two full sets of songs, many of which remain in the dusty corners of both songwriters' catalogs.

IRA'S MOTHER HAD suffered from a number of ailments—longtime treatment for asthma and an emergency appendectomy among them—so Ira was not immediately concerned about her health complaints, including those during her visit to Beverly Hills in early 1948. But when she took a turn for the worse that November, Ira made his way to New York. He found his mother weak, but on the mend, so he returned home, only to hear of a serious relapse, and hurried back, arriving a few days before Rose Gershwin passed away in her bed on the evening of December 15, Ira, his siblings, and their aunt Kate by her side. Following the service at Riverside Memorial Chapel, Rose was interred near George and Morris in the elaborate, blue-glassed mausoleum that she had directed to be built at Westchester Hills Cemetery.

Since July 11, 1937, Rose Gershwin's apartment had become a shrine to her late son. Ira was disappointed to see how she had spent George's money but was shocked to discover that her will showed little regard for her eldest son.[37] Rose had made numerous changes to her will in the last year of her life. She initially left most of her estate to charities,[38] but the final document left 40 percent of her estate to Arthur Gershwin, 40 percent to Frankie, and just 20 percent to Ira, based on her estimate of the "relative financial circumstances" of her children.[39]

Since a significant amount of the estate's income was derived from songs Ira had written with his brother, he was naturally angry at this insulting distribution and how his mother seemed oblivious to what Ira had done to keep her financially afloat since George's death. The money that came to Rose from the sales of sheet music and recordings of songs from *The Shocking Miss Pilgrim* alone was a case in point. Ira "could

have worked with any composer" to write those songs; "the responsibility that I would make good on leftovers and things that had never been
put down on paper but which I more or less remembered" was beyond
Rose's comprehension.[40]

IRA VOWED THAT going forward, he would not leave his and Lee's financial
future at the mercy of Rose's ignorant legal representatives. He immediately
contacted Leonard Saxe, an experienced, Harvard-educated attorney. Saxe
came with significant credentials as an authority on the law of New York
State, an associate law professor at New York University, and a former
executive secretary of the New York State Judicial Council. He was also
the cousin of Ira's brother-in-law, Leo Godowsky.

Ira informed Saxe that he had spoken to his siblings about modifying
the will into equal thirds and asked Saxe if he would represent his interests
in the probate proceedings and in subsequent estate administration. Before
agreeing, the principled and unlawyerly Saxe spoke with his cousin to avoid
any conflict of interest.[41] On December 19, 1948, Saxe, Frankie, and Leo
Godowsky joined Ira in his hotel suite. Frankie did not object to the new
division of the estate, but Godowsky asked for a time limit on the modification in the event of any future financial difficulties resulting from the
change. Ira agreed, and the following morning, the three Gershwin siblings
and Godowsky arrived at the offices of Rose's attorneys, Hugo Pollack and
David Berger, for the reading of the will. Ira told the assembly of the new
split, which was confirmed by his sister and brother. The financial division
would be effective until the death of any of the three parties or December
31, 1953, whichever came first, subject to renewal.[42]

IRA WAS "completely exhausted and depleted" upon his return to California, but the hiring of Leonard Saxe as his legal representative was a balm
to Ira's psyche.[43] For more than a decade, he had put up with Emanuel
Alexandre and his bogus claims of entertainment industry expertise, but
Ira confidently wagered that his work to promote George's music would
stand against Alexandre's "any time at any stakes." He took pleasure in the
knowledge that Alexandre had discovered, to his displeasure, that the man-

agement of Rose Gershwin's estate was not a simple matter and certainly not as easy as exerting control over the woman herself.[44]

Many issues arose in the immediate aftermath of his mother's death, but lingering bronchitis and treatments for bursitis in his right arm left Ira with little energy to deal with them. The first of these was settling the rights to his brother's music for a proposed movie at MGM, a project that had its gestation during producer Arthur Freed's visits to Ira's house to play billiards. Ira suggested $50,000 for *An American in Paris*, with an equal amount for any unpublished tunes with his lyrics, and a further $50,000 for his supervisory activities. The executors of Rose's will argued that this was double-dealing, but Saxe countered that Ira had always been transparent in matters where his interests and those of his brother's estate were in potential conflict.[45] "After ten long months," following his publisher's determined argument that they had the right to "stymie" such a project, the negotiations finally came to an end.[46] MGM agreed to the $50,000 for the concert work and paid Ira $56,250 for eighteen weeks of exclusive work, followed by ten additional weeks in which he could be occupied elsewhere, as well as nearly $20,000 for his grand rights in the songs to be considered for the film.[47]

As THE TERMS OF Rose Gershwin's will were examined by the affected parties, the distribution of artworks from George Gershwin's collection— particularly Pablo Picasso's 1901 masterpiece *The Absinthe Drinker*—became a bone of contention. Ira's cousin Henry Botkin had persuaded him that it would be a "nice gesture (or words to that effect)" if he sent the painting, which had been in California at George's death, to their mother. "Through a legal technicality," Ira felt that he still owned the painting; now that it was going to be offered for sale, he planned to place a bid on it.[48] His sister argued that this was unfair; because she had acquiesced in Ira's request to redistribute their mother's estate, he should stay out of the bidding. Ira thought that who bid on the painting was irrelevant, "but to be perfectly frank, this is wrong of you: you imply that I oughtn't make a bid because, as you put it, you have demonstrated your sense of fairness to me in two instances. Certainly, you've been fair but then have I been unfair?"[49]

Did she find it "unfair, when by California law I became executor of

George's estate that I stepped out immediately on learning that Mom and Alexandre wanted him declared a New York resident so that Mom could control everything herself [?]" Did she think it was unfair that he helped Rose's attorney Abe Rosenthal "to attain that result even though the local bank advised me that I was silly to give up the fees that I would get as executor?"[50]

Frankie said that her brother failed to recognize what had been done on his—and more important, on Lee's—behalf.[51] Ira's response was twelve years in the making. He began by reassuring his sister that he had "nothing but your best interests at heart and expect to feel that way the rest of my life"; what followed was a rare, unbridled statement about the way he had been treated:

> *Ask Aunt Mary, ask Kate and Abe* [Wolpin, Kate's husband], *you might even ask Arthur (if his memory can go back to the twenties and the financial jams George and I rescued him from). . . . The lack of understanding of creative relationships was appalling. But that's all water under the bridge. . . . I had ever since "Lady in the Dark" resigned myself to understanding that Mom was that kind of woman and I loved her just the same. . . . If all this is beginning to sound like a stream of consciousness with the typewriter as my couch, I'm sorry—but, unfortunately, one little phrase of yours "a sense of fairness" started it.*

He acknowledged that his sister *had* been fair:

> *As regards the readjustment of the will (about which there's no question you influenced Arthur also to give up 6⅔%) the moment you showed some concern about what it might mean to you economically didn't I immediately say, "Look, let's make it for only a few years" and on top of that didn't I sign an agreement to indemnify you should there be any tax liability?*

She was not the only person who had been fair:

When I inherited something over $9,000 from George (and that gift, tax-exempt, meant a lot of money to me at the time) the moment I heard of it from Alexandre I said, "Split it four ways." When he told me it was very nice of me, but he didn't think Mom would want a share didn't I then divide it three ways and give you and Arthur each a third? As for the New World stock, believe me again, it wasn't Alexandre's idea that you and Arthur each participate—it was my idea. I remember writing him about it. And the deal couldn't have been made without my throwing in all my renewals of songs published by Warner firms including not only those with George but with Youmans and others. But enough of this. And enough of probably the longest letter I've ever written.[52]

THE BARKLEYS OF BROADWAY, released in May 1949, was not, in Ira's opinion, "the most robust musical ever made, but it has enough novelty and charm to make it entertaining."[53] The critics pointed out that the decision to interpolate "They Can't Take That Away from Me" into the movie "serves to point up the inadequacy of the rest of the score."[54] It certainly indicated an unhappiness at MGM with the songs Ira and Harry Warren had produced.

"It's tough to get a title for a song about a dance," Ira said about "Shoes with Wings On," Fred Astaire's "one-man ballet" set in a shoe shop. In search of ideas, Ira found an illustration of the Greek god Mercury in his copy of *Bulfinch's Mythology* and thought it had possibilities: "But leaden rather than mercurial were the time and effort spent on the lyric to fit Warren's tricky tune. There was much juggling and switching and throwing out of line and phrase and rhyme—maybe ten days' worth—before the words made some singable sort of sense."[55]

> When I've got shoes with wings on—
> The Winter's gone, the Spring's on.
> When I've got shoes with wings on—
> The town is full of rhythm and the world's in rhyme.
>
> The Neon City glows up;
> My pretty Pretty shows up.

We'll dance until they close up—
(Got my Guardian Angel working overtime.)

In the initial meeting about the songs, Arthur Freed suggested a Scottish-style number for Astaire. Afterward, "on our way to inspect the work-cottage the studio had assigned us, I thought of the title with its play on the word 'fling.' We spent only half an hour in the cottage—it was merely a perfunctory visit because both Warren and I preferred working at home. But while we were there Harry made several tentative attempts at a main theme, one of which we felt good about." A search through the Los Angeles telephone book and his copy of *Who's Who* provided Ira with the Scottish surnames used in "My One and Only Highland Fling," but to avoid rhyming "McTavish" and "lavish" because this pairing belonged to Ogden Nash (in his 1931 poem "Genealogical Reflection"), Ira opted for "MacDougal" and "frugal."[56]

This careful work proved fruitless, as the Scottish dialect was mysteriously removed from the prepublication copies of the sheet music. Ira complained to the publishers that "when practically every English-speaking child in the world sings 'Where early fa's the dew' and 'Gie'd me her promise true' in 'Annie Laurie' I cannot see—even for commercial reasons—why our song had to be emasculated. . . . How in the world idiomatic Brooklynese like 'spoke real soft' got into the song where 'spoke me soft' was indicated is something I'll never understand." Ira got his way: the chagrined publisher destroyed the original plates, and the original text was restored for public consumption.[57]

When I went romancin'
I gied no thought to any weddin' ring;
Ev'ry bonny lassie was my highland fling.
    No chance was I chancin';
I'm not the mon you dangle on a string.
I was canny, waitin' for the real, real thing.
        Though I danced each girl
        In the twist and twirl
    Nae one would do.
        An' I went my way

Till the fatal day
In the fling I was flung with you.

THE LITTLE new work that Ira did at the end of the 1940s was overshadowed by the possibilities of theatrical revivals. In the fall of 1949, Ira
began discussions with George S. Kaufman about bringing *Of Thee I Sing*
back to the stage, but their opinions of the Pulitzer Prize–winning musical diverged: Ira felt that few changes were needed for a successful revival,
while Kaufman argued that it had to be fresh and contemporary.[58] And
who could replace the unreplaceable—but physically frail—comedian Victor Moore as the fumbling Vice President Alexander Throttlebottom? But
all these questions were moot without the cooperation of Morrie Ryskind,
who steadfastly stood in the way of any revival of a show that he now found
offensive to his political ideology.

PRODUCERS WERE once again thinking of *Porgy and Bess*, too, now that
the field was clear after Cheryl Crawford's proposed prolongation of her
production had been rejected. The Theatre Guild's Lawrence Langner indicated a plan to revive the opera in 1950 and send the company to Europe.[59]
Langner also raised the issue of a movie adaptation; Ira responded that he
and the estate "would not consider any movie offers until after the Guild
had revived the piece on Broadway." He told Langner that Columbia's
Harry Cohn had once approached him with the idea of casting Al Jolson
as Porgy; Ira had replied that "although Jolson was a great artist and could
undoubtedly do a sincere job, a storm of protest would be raised not only
by the Negro press but many music lovers who would want the integrity
of the piece to be unimpaired."[60]

IRA WAS STUNNED, and thought that "someone must be kidding," when he
heard that the New York probate court had valued his mother's estate at $1.2
million.[61] The provision that Arthur Gershwin receive $25,000 off the top
before the estate was settled hung over the entire process. It was suggested
that Ira and Frankie give up their share of the estate's ASCAP income "so
that it can go into the common pool thus unquestionably assuring Arthur

of his $25,000 a year." His sister—"generously"—and his younger brother—
"somewhat reluctantly"—had conceded to increasing Ira's share of the residuary portion of the estate, but "at the time I looked at this as a friendly
family correction of a will that otherwise would have seemed scandalously
unfair to the music world. Believe me, even in my muddled condition at the
time I felt (and I still feel) that this extra 13% of the residuary or whatever
it's called couldn't mean very much financially but that I could say that
Arthur was very well taken care of and after that the three children shared
equally." What was most concerning to Ira was whether he had the "moral
right" to sign off on the ASCAP agreement if it were true that if Arthur
died, Lee would "never see a cent of the share" Ira was "giving up." He
was reluctant to discuss the matter with his wife, as any mention of Rose's
will made Lee "miserable and humiliated—not for herself—but for me."
He knew that if he signed, and if Lee found out—"as find out eventually
she must"—he would not be able to explain himself.[62]

Yet even as these concerns weighed on his mind, Ira was mollified: the
1940s had been the most financially successful decade of his career, during
which he had earned more than $1 million in "the greatest [years for sales]
the music business ever knew."[63]

CHAPTER 16

T HE 1950s BEGAN with three major projects—the MGM musical *An American in Paris* and stage revivals of *Porgy and Bess* and *Of Thee I Sing*—all in need of Ira's attention; but in what had become an annual event, he was ill during the first weeks of the new year, this time with a "Virus X" that he treated with pills that "must have been made of platinum (by the bill)."[1]

After his recovery, work on *An American in Paris* began with preliminary discussions with the lyricist Alan Jay Lerner, who had been signed to write the screenplay, and musical director Saul Chaplin. Any definite decisions about which of George's songs would be used, and how much would need to be done to them to fit the plot, awaited decisions about casting. Gene Kelly was to play Jerry Mulligan, an American GI who stayed in Paris after the Second World War to pursue a career as a painter, but the supporting role of the older Frenchman had yet to be cast. Ira preferred Maurice Chevalier, but "Freed tells me (confidentially) that Metro upstairs may prefer a certain terrific star now playing in the smash of the decade [*South Pacific*'s Ezio Pinza] who has a contract with Metro in June but Lerner and I feel that wonderful as this star is, he hasn't the Gershwinesque jauntiness required."[2]

BRINGING ALL THE PARTS together for stage revivals—particularly *Porgy and Bess*—was an infinitely more complicated process, and Ira was committed, no matter what else might happen, to protecting his brother's original concept. A series of offers came along in the winter and spring of 1950 for a new production of the opera, including one via Rouben Mamoulian, its original director; the team of Herman Levin (*Gentlemen Prefer Blondes*) and Robert Lewis (one of the founders of the Actors Studio); Arthur Freed, who conceived of a film of George's opera as a worthy successor to *An American in Paris*; and John Wildberg, Cheryl Crawford's erstwhile producing partner, who dangled a London staging.

To Ira, none looked promising, and he quickly became "passive about the whole thing."[3] It was time for new blood. Robert Breen, a former actor from Hibbing, Minnesota, ran the nonprofit American National Theatre and Academy (ANTA) and had successfully toured a production of *Hamlet* through Europe in 1949. Breen promised financial backing for a new staging of *Porgy and Bess* from ANTA's millionaire board member Blevins Davis, but any deal to revive the opera was complicated by the continued involvement of the Theatre Guild, whose leaders were reluctant to bring *Porgy and Bess* back during the 1950–51 Broadway season.[4]

The situation surrounding a movie adaptation of *Porgy and Bess* became more puzzling in May 1950, when, during a meeting of the estate trustees, Ira's attorney became suspicious of Emanuel Alexandre and asked him point blank if he was representing the Theatre Guild—who were making a new proposal on the property—as well as Rose Gershwin's estate. Alexandre admitted his role on behalf of the Guild but explained that he was under the impression that everyone, including Rose Gershwin and Ira, had been aware of the agreement and had no objection. Ira denied any such knowledge.[5] When he found out that Rose had indeed signed the 1946 agreement, Ira noted that it was "unethical if not actually criminal" behavior by Alexandre and that it was "stupid" of the Guild to have done it. His mother "had a right to sign whatever she wanted to with the Guild but if the signatures of Mrs. DuBose Heyward, the Heyward Estate and my own aren't there, along with hers what good was it and what good is it?"[6]

LEE GERSHWIN desperately wanted to do something special to celebrate her fiftieth birthday, but Ira, ever reluctant to leave his comfort zone, was uncertain about her request to return to Europe in October 1950. Her entreaties, plus the added attraction of being in Paris during the brief location filming for *An American in Paris*, eventually changed his mind.[7] But any travel plans were temporarily put aside by Ira's emergency hospital stay in July:

I got a terrifically painful attack in the stomach, and thought maybe I had developed another upstarty appendix, or something. An hour later I was rushed by ambulance to the hospital, given three hypos before the pain subsided. By Sat. aft. I was able to take all kinds of X-rays and other exams and probings. Turned out it was a kidney stone.

Did his mind flash back to Samuel Pepys's infamous kidney stones?

Haven't passed it yet but since there's no pain and the doctors don't want to operate until it's absolutely necessary I've been sent home. Tomorrow I've got to go to doctors' offices in different parts of town for further searchings. But the worst is over so far as I'm concerned and after tomorrow to hell with kidneys, stones and allied matters.[8]

Ira and Lee left California on August 22 for a week of meetings in New York, with a brief stop at his sister's sixty-acre property in Westport, Connecticut, before boarding their flight to Paris, where they settled into a suite at the Prince de Galles, an art deco hotel on Avenue George V.[9] The next two weeks were filled much as they had been in 1928 when they stayed at the Majestic: sightseeing, gambling, concerts and ballets, movies, and reading novels, ranging from an innocuous Agatha Christie mystery to Henry Miller's *Tropic of Capricorn*, at the time banned in the United States. Ira's journal also details encounters with friends old and new: his agent Swifty Lazar; writer Harry Kurnitz; composers Leonard Bernstein, Burton Lane, and Franz Waxman; director Jules Dassin; photographer Robert Capa; directors Jean Negulesco, Gregory Ratoff, and John Brahm; actress Barbara Stanwyck; and journalists Art Buchwald (whose recommended Paris restaurant "wasn't so hot") and Truman Capote.[10]

Meals—and their expense—were also a continued topic of fascination. In the first three days of their stay in Paris, Ira and Lee "lunched or dined in five or six restaurants . . . all good but (outside of La Tour d'Argent) not better than La Rue [West Hollywood] or Romanoff's [Beverly Hills]."[11]

On September 10, Harry Kurnitz and his lady friend joined the couple on a four-day trip around Normandy in a hired car: "Deauville-Trouville, Caën, Mont. St. Michel and . . . dozens of tiny towns. Also we visited Omaha Beach (the D-Day one). It was a fascinating trip and we had pretty good weather, too."[12] Then it was off, via TWA, to the Hotel Excelsior in Rome on September 23 and another hired car for the "most sight-seeingest day" Ira had "ever seen or known": the Forum, the Colosseum, the Jewish ghetto, the Appian Way, the Catacombs, and watching the "many processions [and the] thousands of people" who were visiting the city during Holy Year.[13]

They left for Venice on September 27, with Ira, Lee, Irving Lazar, and Kurnitz speeding off from the airport in a motorboat to the Hotel Danieli on the lagoon, a former doge's palace of the fourteenth century. Then it was Harry's Bar for dinner with John Brahm. The damp of the Catacombs gave Ira a bad cold; soon Lee was also sick, but they made their way up the Grand Canal via gondola to the Rialto Bridge and to have their photographs taken with the pigeons in St. Mark's Square.[14]

October 3 was Lee Gershwin's fiftieth birthday, and although the Gershwins rarely celebrated these dates, Lee was justifiably depressed that her husband had failed to remember this significant one.[15] It was just another sign of the nature of the couple's relationship, and it was only after Lee informed Ira that birthdays "are usually celebrated" that he even entertained the idea of how important they were to some people.[16] Although Lee held this omission against Ira for nearly twenty years, his diary indicates that the medicine he had been prescribed made him sleepier than usual; the document also indicates that he had lunch with Lee and Brahm's girlfriend and her mother on October 3 and took Lee out for dinner and a long walk in the evening.[17] Four days later, Ira was diagnosed with arthritis in his back and visited a large Catholic hospital in a former church or monastery for a series of electric treatments.[18]

The sightseeing continued through Padua, Verona, and Tortona, where Ira ate a bad lunch but refused the recommendation of their hired driver to remain overnight in Imperia.[19] "The Italian driver was charming," Ira later recalled, "and the car was a large limousine, but at least twenty years old. We started off in splendor but soon felt that the springs weren't very springy. I got so carsick on Mussolini's auto-strada that by the time we reached Genoa I was on the floor of the car. At midnight, when we got to the French border, I was still lying there, and I was probably the first tourist to cross the border in that fashion."[20]

Upon arrival at the Hotel Martinez, he vowed to "never try again Como to Cannes in one day."[21] After twelve days of relaxation during the day and gambling at the casino at night, another hired car took them to an airport in Nice for a smooth three-hour flight back to Paris, where they once again checked in at the Prince de Galles.[22] Sightseeing, horse races, and meals with friends took up the final two weeks in a Paris that was "almost exactly as it was 22 years ago—food wonderful, museums still tops, city beautiful as ever if a bit run down."[23]

The boat train took Ira and Lee from the Gare St. Lazare to Le Havre, where they boarded the SS *Liberté*, "a grand ship with wonderful food and tres gai atmosphere."[24] It was smooth sailing across the Atlantic, the voyage enlivened by a gala concert during which he "drank oodles of champagne" and found himself taking bows with some of his fellow passengers, including Harry Kurnitz, Salvador Dalí, the actor Ray Milland, and the violinist Nathan Milstein.[25]

He left Europe with one major regret: that "fate played us a lousy trick" when the planned location filming for *An American in Paris* was canceled. "But what a time we'd have had ourselves."[26] After eleven interesting weeks in Europe, the ten days in New York before returning to California were mundane: visiting his siblings and attending more meetings regarding *Porgy and Bess*. Ira hoped that a decision had been reached regarding the revival and forlornly expressed the wish that he could check any proposed agreement "in five minutes and say 'O.K.'"[27]

As the lengthy discussions about *Porgy and Bess* continued without a resolution, Ira became concerned about the nonprofit status of ANTA, which pushed him toward supporting the Theatre Guild or producer Herman Levin.[28] But "with everyone pulling in opposite directions," he was "inclined to agree" with his sister that it was best to wait until the Alexandre/Theatre Guild agreement was "a thing of the past."[29]

He became increasingly "numb" about the subject until Goddard Lieberson, of Columbia Records, proposed a new cast recording.[30] Ira's status as the sole living lyricist of the opera provided him with the opportunity to find "substitutes for that these-days-objectionable-six-letter-word-which-I-thought-was-too-freely-used-even-in-those-days."[31] Each of the offending twenty-six words or phrases had to maintain the idiom of the original and its original sense. "I eliminated every one of them, not an easy job."[32] In late July 1951, Lieberson arrived with the acetates of the recording, and Ira invited thirty friends over for a listen.[33] The success of the Columbia discs prompted a new spurt of activity for the opera, with multiple parties clamoring for attention from the rights holders for a potential revival.

THE EARLY PART of the 1950s saw another renewal of interest in a new biography of George Gershwin, yet Ira continued to hesitate, declining to put his weight fully behind any of the authors who staked a claim for the project, other than his preferred choice, his and George's longtime friend, Sam Behrman. A new candidate had arrived in the person of Edward Jablonski, of Bay City, Michigan, who had peppered Ira with letters ("several times I had to write him to lay off a bit") since the last day of December 1940 and had visited Beverly Hills with Milt Cohen, a friend of Jablonski's who had written his thesis on Ira's lyrics.[34] The two young men told Ira that they had received some preliminary interest from Simon & Schuster and hoped to collaborate on a Gershwin biography.[35] Ira was, as ever, unwilling to say a definitive "no" to anyone, knowing that if he did, the author might choose to turn a straightforward biography into an embarrassing exposé by touching on areas of George's life that Ira was loathe to see on the printed page.

To get the type of biography Ira wanted, he would need to push Behrman, which would not be an easy task. He assured Behrman that he was not "going to consider anyone but you even if you can't get around to it" for some time. "I'm not one to pin you (or anyone) down," but Ira thought that the job should not take more than eighteen months, even if Behrman only worked on it part-time. As for Jablonski and Cohen, or any other authors who might be interested in writing the book, Ira told Behrman, "I'm sure any intimation to that firm [Simon & Schuster] that you are in any way interested will be of paramount moment to them." All the material Behrman needed was in Beverly Hills. "You've got *me* and I'm no slouch—and I hope to be your #1 boy all along the way." It was not a "job where you'll have to go to Venice or castles in Kent for material."[36]

AFTER AN EXTENDED PERIOD of inactivity as a lyricist, during which Ira was preoccupied with more pressing concerns, he agreed to Burton Lane's suggestion that they collaborate on a new musical for MGM. Lane, in need of a lyricist after the departure of Alan Jay Lerner, was surprised at Ira's reaction, having assumed that he would give his usual excuse of being too busy to work.[37] Although Lane and Ira were well acquainted, their only previous professional interaction had come in 1939, when the composer was forced to pay Ira and his publishers for inadvertently plagiarizing the melody of "Tell Me More" for his and Frank Loesser's hit song "Says My Heart."[38] Lane was nervous when he arrived at Ira's house to begin work on the movie that would eventually be released as *Give a Girl a Break*. He told Ira that he had taken a pill to relax; Ira smiled and showed him his own box of pills. He had taken one too, remembered Lane: "whether it was true or not—it made me feel comfortable."[39]

Since the 1940s, the popping of pills—whether uppers to lift his mood during the day or barbiturates to calm him down or help him sleep— had become a commonplace event for both Ira and his wife. Prescribed for them by Dr. Eliot Corday, the Canadian-born chief of cardiology at Cedars of Lebanon Hospital, it was a standard Hollywood practice by the early 1950s. Ira claimed Dexedrine made him feel "chipper,"[40] and he and Lee were known to give out pills to their friends to help them get through their work after a long night of partying and drinking.[41] Into the 1960s, Ira and Lee steadily worked their way through a pharmacological wasteland of heavily advertised medications—Seconal (Jacqueline Susann's "dolls"), Nembutal ("yellow jackets"), Tuinal, Dexamil, and Miltown, the wildly popular "Mother's Little Helper"—without seeming to know or care what the intake of such powerful narcotics was doing to them, physically or emotionally.[42]

Although he had a "tops for lyrics alone" deal for *Give a Girl a Break*, the movie was a headache from the start. The B-level production, which starred Debbie Reynolds as one of a trio of young Broadway hopefuls, failed to secure an audience-attracting leading man, which made it difficult for Ira and Lane to complete their work, and the project would be returned to, in fits and starts, for many months.[43]

YET ANOTHER Emanuel Alexandre–created crisis forced Ira into an unwanted confrontation. In their contract with the Theatre Guild, Ira and trustee Hugo Pollack had not agreed to pay Alexandre a fee. In a moment of spite, Alexandre informed the special guardian, appointed under the terms of Rose Gershwin's will to look after the interests of the minor children, of Ira's side agreement with MGM to provide services to the production of *An American in Paris*. Ira was incensed: any suspicion "that the interests of the Estate and mine might, at times, be at variance could come only from an ignorant and jealous mind. Maybe I'll add slimy."[44]

He was puzzled: because he was not an executor of his brother's estate, there could be no conflict over any deal he made *before* his mother's death. But since he had become an executor, he had made $70,000 for the estate by creating the songs for *The Barkleys of Broadway*; other songwriters' estates had been unsuccessful in getting *their* unpublished tunes used, so if the special guardian "wants to do a really good job and cares about future income for the grandchildren he should encourage rather than question any activity of mine where my brother's music and my lyrics are concerned." The work Ira did with George meant far more to him "past, present or future" than any songs he had written with other composers, yet he had made more money from *Lady in the Dark* and "Long Ago (and Far Away)."[45]

The special guardian's report was issued in January 1952, and despite Ira's explanation of the circumstances surrounding the birth of the project and Arthur Freed's insistence that it would never have happened without the lyricist's involvement, Ira was accused of using his role as an executor to pad his bank account.[46] Ira's attorney submitted a lengthy rebuttal on his client's behalf, as Ira sighed, "It's all so silly—this questioning of my importance in the enterprise, but alas and alack! I suppose the world has some sort of need for surrogates and special guardians."[47] The report was unnecessary: by late May 1952, the special guardian had withdrawn his objections to Ira's actions, leading Ira to wonder, in jest, whether he should have his agent provide a copy of the document to the movie studios "for a screenplay to be called 'Objection Overruled.'"[48]

IRA'S REFUSAL to commit to a producer for the revival of *Porgy and Bess* exasperated Dorothy Heyward, whose income was heavily dependent on royalties from the opera. What made the situation more frustrating for her was that she knew that Ira's opinion carried more weight than that of any of the other executors or stakeholders. Her constant pressure did, eventually, cause him to concede and to agree to her preference for Blevins Davis and Robert Breen.[49] The five-year agreement for the stage revival of *Porgy and Bess* gave the rights holders a $10,000 advance and 10 percent of the gross in the United States (12 percent in European cities with a population over six hundred thousand, or 10 percent if under). The share of the pot mirrored that of the original production: 50 percent to Rose Gershwin's (that is, George Gershwin's) estate; 40 percent to the Heywards; and 10 percent for Ira—although Ira would now receive his one-third share of his mother's estate. All four authors—George, Ira, DuBose, and Dorothy—were to be credited with the creation of the opera, but if advertising space were limited, Ira and Dorothy agreed that only George and DuBose's names would be printed. The two living authors were also given an "absolute right of approval" of director. The movie rights were excluded, a clause that quickly became a bone of contention.[50]

Finding the director caused more headaches. Dorothy Heyward was desperate to know what Ira thought and said she would go along with his choice.[51] Did he like Rouben Mamoulian or Robert Ross, the director of the Cheryl Crawford–produced revival? What about actor Burgess Meredith or Robert Lewis? Ira was confident that he had persuaded Blevins Davis to revert to the original conception of the opera, but he worried that the failure to find a director might jeopardize the entire production.[52] Robert Breen told Ira and Dorothy that he had been unsuccessful in hiring any of several prominent directors, but since he "knew the piece practically by heart," was there any reason not to give him a chance? They agreed: Breen would be "most capable."[53]

MARCH 20, 1952: a red-letter day. That evening, Ira settled down in front of his television set to watch the Academy Awards. *An American in Paris*, which had opened to terrific box office returns and critical acclaim in the fall of 1951, had garnered eight nominations, and Ira was "a long-shot optimist" that it would be the first musical to win Best Picture since the 1930s.[54]

Ira was heavily involved with the production, attending meetings and consulting about casting, the script, and the overall feel of the movie, as well as suggesting songs from George's catalog. The latter task resulted in the inclusion of "By Strauss," a rarely heard waltz, written at Vincente Minnelli's request for his 1936 revue *The Show Is On*. The song's original verse included references to fellow songwriters Irving Berlin, Cole Porter, and Jerome Kern, but to use their names in *An American in Paris* would have required clearances and payments; for Ira, it was "less bothersome to write new lines" that retained the image of Broadway composers "pounding on tin" but removed the offending proper nouns.[55]

As the awards evening progressed, five statuettes were handed out for the movie's technical prowess, followed by Alan Jay Lerner's win for Best Story and Screenplay. At 1:40 a.m., New York time, the elated lyricist awakened his attorney from his sleep to inform him that the big prize was theirs.[56] *An American in Paris* was "as tasty a musical as has ever been turned out in this town," Ira told his publisher. "George would have loved the ballet . . . it has everything—charm, excitement, suspense, humor."[57]

Director Vincente Minnelli, Ira, Gene Kelly, and producer
Arthur Freed, on the "Stairway to Paradise" set of
An American in Paris at MGM, August 1950.

OF THEE I SING was the only property other than *Porgy and Bess* that Ira felt had any potential of a stage revival or that could be sold to the movies, but the war years had not been an ideal time for the acerbic show, and it remained in limbo.[58] In early 1951, Ira had hired Irving Paul Lazar as his new agent, and the lyricist joined a client list that was a who's who of stage and screen (Humphrey Bogart, Moss Hart, Cole Porter, Gene Kelly, Noël Coward). Lazar's dealmaking abilities earned him the nickname "Swifty," and he proved the accuracy of the appellation by an immediate attempt to sell *Of Thee I Sing* to Paramount, but the studio, convinced that there was no overseas market for this American-centric subject, offered only $100,000 for the rights, a figure that was unacceptable to the show's creators.[59]

Instead, they turned their attention to a new stage production, and that same spring a tentative deal was reached with producer Herman Levin, but Levin quickly dropped out after actor Robert Cummings demanded too much money to play John P. Wintergreen.[60] A month later, a new agreement was signed with Chandler Cowles, a young producer who had recently staged a Broadway adaptation of Herman Melville's novel *Billy Budd*. The deal gave Ira 2 percent of the gross, with Kaufman, Ryskind, and Rose Gershwin's estate each receiving 2.5 percent.[61]

Other potential male leads for the revival came and went, and when George S. Kaufman suffered a stroke in October 1951, the entire project seemed doomed.[62] But the writer/director's health improved, and after Jack Carson was cast as Wintergreen and Victor Moore agreed to return as Throttlebottom, Ira was confident that the revival was "off to a flying start."[63] But another jolt was felt soon after, when illness forced the popular, seemingly irreplaceable Moore to withdraw in favor of Paul Hartman, the actor/dancer who had been the choice to play the Vice President before Moore came out of semiretirement.

Of Thee I Sing opened in New Haven, Connecticut, in April 1952 and was in trouble from the start: the original choreographer withdrew; Lenore Lonergan, who played the scheming Diana Devereaux, wavered over her plans to leave the production; and Ira battled a virus that he picked up the day after the opening. The bug, and the antibiotics, left him without a sense of smell and taste for the next two years: "If I smelled anything at all, it all was like smoke."[64] The show moved on to Philadelphia, but Ira returned to his hotel suite to conduct the majority of his work over the telephone

next to his bed. Most of his efforts were centered around changing the
original show's topical references: "moratorium" became "foreign policy,"
"Depression" became "Taxation," and all talk of breach of promise suits and
Herbert Hoover was removed.[65] Although most of these decisions were his
own choice, the alteration of Diana Devereaux's eyes from Prussian (Hitler-
esque) blue to baby blue was requested by George S. Kaufman. "But, alas,
Ira's iris modification didn't seem to help the revival one whit."[66] But he
knew that some of his own work was just as inane: the "mild joke on Bis-
marck herring" in "A Kiss for Cinderella" was not going to help a "show
which twenty years earlier had won the Pulitzer Prize."[67]

Ira bought dozens of tickets for the Broadway opening for his family
and friends, but when loud applause greeted "Love Is Sweeping the Country," he joked that he did not think he had *that* many relatives."[68] As he
looked at the competition from the powerhouse musicals currently playing
on Broadway—*Gigi, Guys and Dolls, The King and I, Pal Joey, Paint Your
Wagon*, and *South Pacific*—he became pessimistic. There was good word of
mouth for *Of Thee I Sing*, "but without much of an advance, it'll be tough."[69]
The words of Gilbert Gabriel summed up the critical reaction: while he
wanted to "maintain that it was just as grand a show as ever," the revival
was actually "pretty middling-poor."[70]

Similar reviews quickly put a damper on ticket sales, and although the
principals and crew took pay cuts, and the authors had waived payment of
their royalties before the show even reached Broadway, the revival collapsed
after only seventy-two performances.[71] Ira looked back a few months after
the closure and said that while "the first act had as many laughs and received
as much applause" as the original, the second act, with "the 'Illegitimate
Daughter'—the threat of war with France, the possible impeachment of
the President—all probably seemed small potatoes to audiences that were
able to live through and withstand the headlines and havoc of the past
twenty years."[72]

New editions of songs from the original show, plus "Wintergreen for
President" and "Mine" (the latter interpolated into the score from *Let 'Em
Eat Cake*), held no interest for the public; a similar fate met the Capitol
Records cast album, which came as no surprise to Ira, who remarked that
"as for the singers, many of them aren't."[73] The artistic failure was com-
pounded by the loss of his entire financial investment.

A MONTH AFTER the less-than-stellar *Of Thee I Sing* opening, Ira and Lee traveled to Dallas, Texas, to attend the premiere of the Robert Breen and Blevins Davis production of *Porgy and Bess*, which, Ira was happy to say, looked like a "very big success."[74] Breen did "a fine job on the whole; the production is exciting." The opera was "in good hands. If Cab Calloway turns out to be a great Sportin' Life, this will be (if it isn't already) a better show than it was in 1935."[75]

The revival of *Porgy and Bess* played several cities in the United States to "wonderful notices everywhere." The federal government, eager to show that the United States was a free and open society in the middle of the Cold War, put up the money for a European tour. Robert Breen wanted Ira to be with the company when the production opened in Vienna in September,[76] but he begged off: *Give a Girl a Break* needed his attention.[77] While there *were* a few lyrics to be completed on what he ironically referred to as *Give a Girl Something or Other*, there was nothing that would have prevented him from making the journey had he really wanted to.[78] "Work" was—as his friends knew—just one of many excuses he used to get himself out of uncomfortable situations.

But whether he went to Europe or not, Ira was overjoyed about the revival: not only was it an artistic success and proved that his brother's opera was ahead of its time, but it became "a bull's-eye for the Gershwin estate which after four years will now be able to pay the inheritance taxes."[79] The production was "lavish and meticulous," and Ira had nothing but praise for producer Blevins Davis; it was due to Davis that "we have an extra year's income" and a higher royalty rate than anyone else would have been willing to pay.[80]

PART FIVE

Words with New Music II

CHAPTER 17

B Y THE FALL OF 1952, Ira was casting aside all stage offers, unwilling to commit, based on the failures of *The Firebrand of Florence* and *Park Avenue*, to the "grind and responsibility" of setting aside a year of his time on a Broadway show that was unlikely to become a hit.[1] But in early December, when Harold Arlen alerted him to an attractive movie offer, he sharpened his pencils and got ready to start work again.[2]

The project, to be produced by Judy Garland's third husband, Sid Luft, was a remake of the 1937 musical *A Star Is Born*. Luft's troubled wife had attempted suicide shortly after giving birth to her second daughter, Lorna, in November 1952, and had seen her mother die of cancer two months later. Garland needed to be reminded of her power and presence as a performer. Luft thought that *A Star Is Born*, with its ultimately uplifting story of success overcoming misfortune and with songs by her old friends Harold Arlen and Yip Harburg, was the answer to their prayers. When Harburg was rejected by Warner Bros. for his liberal politics, Ira was brought into the project.[3] He agreed to a $35,000 fee with Luft and Garland's production company, Transcona Enterprises, with a deferred $7,500 to be paid if the movie made back its money.[4]

In early January, Ira, Arlen, and screenwriter Moss Hart began a series of conferences during which Hart outlined his conception of the story of a girl singer who makes it from drive-in carhop to the big screen, highlighting the changes he had made from the 1937 script by Dorothy Parker, Alan Campbell, and Robert Carson. The seven spots for songs—all to be sung by Garland—were discussed "in terms of their place in the story as well as their psychological motivation in respect to the characters and the plot." Ira devised an outline: Garland would do a song with a band at Los Angeles' Shrine Auditorium; a second would be sung in a dive bar; a lively number would be seen in a rehearsal and in a full version; one would be filmed on a sound stage as Esther Blodgett (Garland) received a marriage proposal; number five would be done in a motel room; number six would be a Garland "tour de force" of vocal imitations with props; the final number would likely be a reprise of the motel room song.[5]

"Gotta Have Me Go with You," the up-tempo number for the Shrine Auditorium scene, was the first to be completed. The dive number came next and provided a key moment in the plot. With this song, the audience and James Mason—playing Norman Maine, the washed-up, older, alcoholic actor—sees, for the first time, the potential of Esther as an actress and singer. Arlen presented Ira with an eight-bar phrase; the lyricist liked "the insistent movement of the rhythm" and, in turn, presented the composer with the "The Man That Got Away" as a title. "I like," said Arlen.[6] Unbeknownst to Ira, Arlen's tune had already been written up by Johnny Mercer as "I Can't Believe My Eyes," and although Ira may have been unhappy had he learned this fact, it was not the first time a composer had given him a melody that another lyricist had worked on; Ira himself often borrowed from his unused lyrics for new melodies.

During the writing, Arlen took a weekend off to go to Palm Springs for his health. Ira made him promise not to reveal what they had written so far, since Ira was aware that Garland and Hart would also be in the desert at that time. But when Arlen saw Garland and Luft teeing off at the Tamarisk Country Club, he walked with them as they played their round and teased Garland by whistling the tune to "The Man That Got Away." When the group got to the clubhouse, Garland persuaded Arlen to play it for her on the piano. "Ira, Smira," Garland said, "he'll be happy about it." Hart and his wife, Kitty Carlisle, were delighted too, and when they called Ira, he, too, expressed delight. When Arlen returned to Beverly Hills, Ira beamed at him and never mentioned the composer's "broken promise."[7]

Ira was a digger for lyrical nuggets and constantly edited his work, even to the point of making last-minute changes to a word or a phrase as deadlines approached. Arlen found Ira's attempts to free himself from work amusing, even amid the creation of a song. Ira would suddenly get up from the piano, and when asked where he was going, say, "Upstairs to get typewriter ribbon; it's the only way I get exercise."[8]

Half of the numbers for *A Star Is Born* were complete by the middle of February 1953; although the work was slowed by the death of Arlen's father in early March, Ira felt that they "had such a good start it didn't matter about the delay."[9] Five weeks later, they were done. Arlen said that he did not know "any lyric writer who studies his work line for line, progressively for the ideas and for the rhymes, as Ira does. And I don't know any lyric writer who gets as much of a kick out of a song as Ira does when it's finished."[10] Garland came by to hear the results of what Ira considered okay but happily uncomplicated numbers.[11] He certainly expected that Garland would give his and Arlen's songs "better treatment" than he and Burton Lane had received with *Give a Girl a Break*.[12]

W ITH THE SONGS FOR *A Star Is Born* complete—or so he assumed—Ira traveled to New York City for the Broadway opening of the Breen/Davis production of *Porgy and Bess* and to confer with his attorney Leonard Saxe

Ira and his publisher, Max Dreyfus, at Dreyfus's
office in New York City, 1946.

before a lengthy executors' meeting. On a whim, he again kept a small diary of his travels, but as before, it largely consisted of lists of people met, money spent, and food eaten, although there were a few brief reviews of the shows he saw, including Arthur Laurents's play *Time of the Cuckoo* with Shirley Booth ("liked only fairly well"); the musical *Wish You Were Here*, based on his friend Arthur Kober's 1937 play *Having Wonderful Time* ("lively and interesting"); *Wonderful Town* by Leonard Bernstein, Betty Comden, and Adolph Green (a "good lively show"); Cole Porter's *Can-Can* ("not the greatest musical and Porter's score not up to par but dancing and some comedy made it entertaining"); and George Bernard Shaw's *Misalliance* ("generally delighted with it").

In an effort to exploit his brother's catalog to the financial benefit of all concerned, Ira suggested to his publishers the creation of an overture consisting of tunes from the Gershwins' movies, as well as the publication of the *Girl Crazy* and *Of Thee I Sing* overtures and a piano transcription of the *Cuban Overture*. Max Dreyfus agreed these were good ideas and set music editor Albert Sirmay and arranger Robert Russell Bennett to work on them based on Ira's thoughts.[13] *Gershwin in Hollywood*, the largely forgotten result of the first idea, was recorded by the conductor Morton Gould in 1954. Ira thought that Bennett would have written "more impressive arrangements" but admitted that it was, in part, his own fault for giving Bennett too many songs to work with.[14] Although Ira's suggestion that "giving the piano many of the passages . . . would be not only a challenge to pianists but also point up more fully some of the rhythms and melodic lines" of the *Cuban Overture* was a sound one, this project never made it past a conceptual stage.[15]

Another successful creation—with the assistance of Ira's brother-in-law, Leo Godowsky Jr.—was the Gershwin Concert Orchestra, a touring concern that would perform Gershwin music in venues throughout the United States. Ira did not want the group to be "too long-haired, 'cause we got rhythm too."[16] The orchestra of twenty-five musicians and five singers, under the baton of conductor Lorin Maazel, made its first of two successful tours in the spring of 1953. Ira suggested much of the program, including an overture of his brother's well-known melodies, followed by *An American in Paris*, *Rhapsody in Blue*, various songs and piano transcriptions, selections from *Porgy and Bess*, and the finale of the Concerto in F.[17]

OF MORE long-term interest was the settlement of Rose Gershwin's estate—valued at nearly $1.1 million—in the fall of 1953:[18] "Thank heaven . . . —it's taken about ten years of my life keeping in touch with what was going on. Hardly anything left in the Estate as of now, but praise be! all the taxes are paid."[19] He was equally relieved by his younger siblings' agreement to continue the division of the estate that had been in effect since their mother's death.[20]

Progress had been made regarding the future of Ira's finances, but another matter remained unsettled when he returned to Beverly Hills. Rumors had begun to float through town that Sid Luft and executives at Warner Bros. were unhappy with some of the songs for *A Star Is Born*. Ira and Arlen heard that "Green Light Ahead" was considered a weak number, not nearly powerful enough to accompany the transformation of Esther Blodgett, carhop, into Vicki Lester, star; but instead of asking Hart to write a new scene and Ira and Arlen to write a new song, Luft first went behind their backs and approached composer Roger Edens, in the mistaken belief that neither Arlen nor Ira were writers of revue-style material.[21] Garland, initially enthusiastic about "Green Light Ahead," wanted a more striking replacement; annoyed, Ira suggested that what she needed was something like "The Star-Spangled Banner," but without its range. The new number he and Arlen reluctantly came up with, "I'm Off the Downbeat," again at first met with Garland's approval, but Luft thought that it, too, was second-rate. The songwriters found themselves in a funk; Luft meant well, but he clearly had no concept of what type of musical material was required.[22] While Ira enjoyed the rushes of *A Star Is Born*, he became concerned that the entire structure of the picture rested on the shoulders of its shaky star, who, he was convinced, would eventually fall apart.

WITH *A STAR IS BORN* in a state of flux, other projects and issues took up Ira's time. Producer William Perlberg dangled another movie, an adaptation of Clifford Odets's play *The Country Girl*, to star Bing Crosby as a has-been singer, Jennifer Jones (replaced by Grace Kelly) as his wife, and William Holden as the director who backs Crosby's comeback. Only a few musical numbers were necessary, but Ira dawdled, uncertain whether to take on another job so soon and equally puzzled about which composer he would be working with.[23] A week later, after Harold Arlen agreed to continue their partnership, Ira signed on to work on the new movie for $35,000.[24] Even with three decades of writing for stage and screen, Ira admitted that he "approach[ed] any oncoming job with plenty of trepidation."[25]

BY THE EARLY 1950s, one-fourth of Ira's annual income was derived from his ASCAP royalties, so it was with close attention that he read the news in November 1953 about the filing of the first briefs in a $150 million lawsuit against the rival performing rights society Broadcast Music, Inc. (BMI) that accused its executives of creating a monopoly on New Year's Day 1940, when radio broadcasters began to boycott material by ASCAP writers.[26] In April 1954, Ira was deposed over the course of two days at the Garden of Allah apartments in Hollywood in sessions filled with lawyerly acrimony, and he returned home exhausted after "being asked many questions I had no answers for."[27] As one of the original complainants in the case he not-so-laughingly referred to as "Brother, Can You Spare a Million?,"[28] Ira contributed $4,500 over the next three years toward the attorneys' hefty fees.[29]

IN THE FALL OF 1952, Walden Records—"a very small (but obviously smart) young outfit" cofounded by would-be Gershwin biographer Edward Jablonski—released *Lyrics by Ira Gershwin*, the first long-playing record devoted solely to the lyricist's work.[30] Ira played a significant role in the creation of the LP, attending the New York rehearsals, answering questions regarding lyrical interpretation, and suggesting, rejecting, or adjusting songs.[31] Actress Nancy Walker, the album's best-known performer, sang a revised version of "I Can't Get Started," while her husband, David Craig, did "Put Me to the Test," and the lesser-known Louise Carlyle was chosen for "Sing Me Not a Ballad" from *The Firebrand of Florence*. The lyricist was a silent partner in the little company, with a $3,000 investment in his wife's name that entitled him to 20 percent of any profits.[32] He advised Jablonski to record as many "non-commercial (unknown) songs" as possible. "It gives both critic and buyer a sense of discovery" and, he hoped, would turn the albums into commercial successes.[33] This advice led to two volumes of

Gershwin Rarities, for which Ira—as "a sucker for minutiae"—added "extra lines for [these] obscure and hitherto unrecorded songs."[34]

Jablonski also wanted to put out a series of cast albums of the Gershwins' most popular musicals; Ira, in favor of digging harder, countered with the "better rounded score" of *Tip-Toes* and with *Park Avenue*, which had the "raciness" of *Pal Joey*.[35] He also suggested—before succumbing to fear or "good taste"—releasing some of the recordings he and Burton Lane had made for *Give a Girl a Break*.[36] But the company, as many small record labels were wont to do, sank into a "hole of red ink" that never turned into a "nice, clean pool of black."[37] Ira loaned Walden $1,000 to fund the recording of a collection of Harold Arlen numbers, but by 1960, the enterprise was floundering, and Ira's attorney extricated him from the money-losing partnership.[38]

A YEAR AFTER the first *Gershwin Rarities* LP, another small New York–based record company, Heritage Productions, released *"Tryout,"* a selection of demo recordings by Kurt Weill. (Ira suggested the title *Behind the Scenes*, as he felt that the chosen title suggested that the "recordings were made for auditions.")[39] The disc included the numbers that Weill and Ira had made for *Where Do We Go from Here?* Although Ira was "proud of the stuff" and thought that the records "weren't too bad considering we hadn't rehearsed," he did not "see eye to eye (and especially ear to ear) with" releasing it to an unsuspecting public.[40] But Weill's widow, Lotte Lenya, convinced Ira otherwise, and Ira agreed—and even wrote the liner notes to explain how the "bizarre" disc "was foisted on a small and defenseless public."[41]

The record was an example of how Ira's voice and manner was eminently suited to his lyrics. As he stood by the piano and closed his eyes, he held his glasses by the stem and twirled them between his thumb and forefinger, waving them slightly in time with the music, or pushed them up onto his forehead while moving his finger back and forth in the air to punctuate some of the words.[42] "Heaven help the phonograph business," he joked.[43] But he was in for a shock. Instead of "the panning the singing would get critically,"[44] the disc was greeted with applause, with one critic noting that it was "surprising—and pleasant—to discover how effective these presentations are." The most entertaining number was judged to be the lengthy "The Nina, the Pinta, the Santa Maria," for which Ira provided

all the voices and sang "in clarion tones and [with] a sure comic style."[45] He
could only conclude that it was a "funny world, funny critics."[46]

THE LONG GESTATION of *Give a Girl a Break* finally ended with its release
in late 1953. When the movie about three actresses competing for a role in
a Broadway show went before the cameras a year earlier, Ira knew it was
not an award winner, but "we do have some bright young kids and Stanley
Donen" as director, "so we won't be too bad."[47] But, in the end, not even the
popularity of Debbie Reynolds, just off her winning performance in Donen
and Gene Kelly's magnificent *Singin' in the Rain*, and the presence of Bob
Fosse in one of his early acting roles could save the movie from being a
"stinker."[48] Even Ira's wife knew it; upon leaving a "studio projection room
after seeing a rough cut," Lee asked Ira if he owned stock in MGM's parent
company. When he told her that he had "bought several hundred shares the
previous year," she bluntly told him to sell them immediately.[49]

   Ira had little to say about the songs for this movie, indicating that his initial positive feelings about them did not last.[50] Repeating what he had done
with Kurt Weill in the 1940s, Ira and Burton Lane made a set of demon-
stration recordings of the numbers from *Give a Girl a Break*. Released on
LP in 1975 as part of the two-record set *Ira Gershwin Loves to Rhyme*, the
songs come off far better than they do in the movie, with Ira's nonsinger's
voice bringing out the humor in the patter verse of "Applause, Applause":

> Whether you're a Swiss bell ringer
>   Or a crooner or a singer
> Or monologist, ventriloquist or what—
>   Or a dog act or magician
>   Or a musical saw musician
> Or an ingenue or pianist who is hot—
>   Whether you play Punchinello,
>   Little Eva or Othello—
> Having heard the call, you've given all you've got.
>   And what better reward for a trouper
>   Than the sound we consider super?

The lyric to "In Our United State" was based on "State of the Union," a love song using political speech that was written up during Ira's work on *Park Avenue* in 1946.[51] The number was charmingly sung and danced by Bob Fosse in the movie but was totally ignored otherwise, although it was one of Ira's favorite items from the score.[52]

> The state of our union,
>   Hearts in communion
> Never will know any foreign entanglements;
>   Outsiders will not rate
>   In our united state!
>
>   We'll make the altar
>   As strong as Gibraltar—
> Fooling around will be unconstitutional.
>   Great will be our united state!

The fate of another song from the movie pointed toward future trouble. Burton Lane's publishers, Leo Feist, issued the ballad "It Happens Ev'ry Time" on two pages because Ira was not given the opportunity to write a verse that would have brought the sheet music to the standard four to five pages. This had never happened to him before.[53] Was it, he wondered, an indication that his songs no longer had a cachet and were no longer worthy of publication or promotion? The situation, quite naturally, soured his feelings about further work in Hollywood.[54]

CHAPTER 18

A s 1954 DAWNED, Ira and Harold Arlen were two tired songwriters. After the struggles of *A Star Is Born*, writing four numbers for *The Country Girl*, "only one of which has any production values and those are very simple," looked to be an easy job.[1] Yet, with both men suffering from illnesses and keeping late hours at the piano with the deadline approaching, they were uncertain if the results of their efforts were worthwhile. The introductory patter of "It's Mine, It's Yours" suggested the transformation of the song into a more optimistic one than originally intended. Ira wanted to scrap the entire number, but Arlen liked it, so a new set of lyrics was required. Ira was also bothered by "The Land around Us," its title an allusion to Rachel Carson's 1951 book *The Sea around Us*, as Ira could not get past the feeling that the final lines—"The land around us / Will grow and grow"—were grammatically incorrect.[2] But director George Seaton liked it and so it stayed.[3] When "Liebermeyer Beer," the final, short piece was complete for a sequence in which Crosby records a radio jingle, Arlen returned to New York to begin work on *House of Flowers*, a new musical with Truman Capote as lyricist.[4]

PAINFULLY AWARE that the failure of *Give a Girl a Break* had put his reputation "somewhat already in jeopardy,"[5] Ira took heart in columnist Walter Winchell's prediction that "The Man That Got Away" would sell a million copies.[6] He was also encouraged when Frank Sinatra asked him to write a male version of the song.[7] But all was not well with *A Star Is Born*; to Ira's surprise, the movie's choreographer was unable to develop a good dance routine for "I'm Off the Downbeat," another number Ira thought was well liked. "Don't know what to do about it," he lamented.[8]

In addition, Sid Luft was unhappy with the songs for the big production number that was to come before the intermission of the now three-hour movie. Keeping to his motto that it was better to write a new song than argue the merits of something a singer had taken a dislike to,[9] Ira hoped that Arlen might be able to take time away from his work on *House of Flowers* to try to "give them what they think they want."[10] But when Arlen was hospitalized—and near death—with a bleeding ulcer, there was nothing Ira could do. He refused to lose any sleep after learning that Luft was considering interpolating songs by other writers into the movie: "there's too little sleep left as is."[11] The "messy situation" was out of his hands; "with probably the most talented girl in pictures starred (but addicted to truancy) [and] with retakes in the offing,"[12] he knew that "lost is the hope of the producer that the film would be released by now."[13]

Luft bluntly said that one of the problems with the film was that it did not have enough music. Trying to hold back his exasperation, Ira reminded Luft that his contract called for songs for a *two-hour* picture, not a *three-and-a-half-hour* one.[14] When Luft responded that he had commissioned a medley for Garland that included a series of songs without Ira's lyrics, as well as "Swanee," all Ira could say was that "if what they had would help the film I could make no protest especially since Harold wasn't available to work on the spot in question."[15]

Even at three hours plus, *A Star Is Born* was an impressive movie, and "Judy is, of course, a remarkable performer." James Mason was "great too. The money spent shows. The story and acting make the tears fall. It's slow in spots and needs lots of cutting," although the new sequence was still to be filmed. "Generally the songs come off O.K. or better."[16] A second sneak preview "went bigger than any I ever attended. Judy could do no wrong and applause exploded 20 or 25 times during the showing." Cuts were still needed but Ira was confident; *A Star Is Born* was going to be a "big hit [and] undoubtedly will gross more than any musical ever did."[17] The interpolated special material "was excellent for its original purpose . . . but it added fifteen minutes to a three-hour film, held up the show, and cost $300,000." It was, he concluded, all a "big mistake (but all none of my business)."[18]

IN THE SPRING OF 1954, with David Ewen hard at work on a biography
of George Gershwin, Ira again tried to pin down Sam Behrman. He was
willing to let him "off the hook." He had "encouraged no one" to write
George's biography, let alone a biography that included Ira as well. There
could not "be anything definitive on me," he joked. "I have yet to be ahead
on a Santa Anita meet."[19] Behrman finally relented; the time had come to
relinquish the idea.[20]

Ewen wanted to visit Ira in California to interview him and to exam-
ine his voluminous scrapbooks. Ira sought the advice of producer Arthur
Freed and Oscar Levant; he also consulted Lawrence D. Stewart, a young
professor of English at UCLA, who had entered Ira's life in the fall of
1952 as yet another prospective biographer of George. Stewart—"trained in
Seventeenth-and-Eighteenth-century English history and literature as well
as archival research"—proved an ideal companion for Ira, who soon asked
Stewart to organize his jumble of loose papers.[21] Stewart, still thinking of
his own book about George and protective of his access to Ira's archive,
agreed with Freed and Levant: Ira should be friendly to Ewen but not
overly cooperative.

The unstated goal was to deflect Ewen from his work. Ira insisted that
he needed to meet the man but agreed to tell Ewen that the scrapbooks
and other items would be unavailable "as we were going to work on them
for another year before the material is ready for our own use."[22] Eager to
retain Ira's good will, Ewen had no choice but to agree to the terms before
making his first visit to Beverly Hills in December 1954.[23] Ira found the
author an "eager beaver but certainly not unsmart" and agreed to read a
sample of his work prior to any in-depth examination of the manuscript.[24]
Although he believed that Ewen would "turn out a fairly presentable job,"
there was to be no "blessing" on the book.[25] Ewen believed otherwise—his
visit with Ira was a seal of approval.[26]

AT AN AFTER-PARTY for *Porgy and Bess* in New York City in 1953, several
women approached Ira and insisted that he should permanently return
there; it was an idea, he admitted, that "Lee would like."[27] Ira's wife had
become increasingly frustrated and enervated by life in Southern California; she desperately wanted to return East. Beverly Hills was dull, she said;

all their friends had moved back to Manhattan, so why were they staying? But Ira was convinced that Lee would soon become bored in Manhattan too; of more concern to him was the thought of leaving sunny California for the cold of the East Coast and the less-than-welcome embraces and out- stretched, begging hands of his relatives. Lee just needed a diversion; the feelings would pass, as they had before.[28] Although Ira was unmoved when Robert Breen asked him to accompany the *Porgy and Bess* troupe through Europe, his wife's excitement at the idea of travel prompted Ira to open his checkbook, hoping that it would ease her distress.[29]

During Lee's six months on the road with the cast and crew of the opera, she often implored Ira to join her, as such an opportunity came just "once in a lifetime and we're still young."[30] But the answer was always no; she got a "much bigger kick" from "parties and opening nights" than he ever did.[31] Back at home, Ira hermetically sealed himself off from the world, emerg- ing to attend a few parties or to watch the broadcast of a new production of *Lady in the Dark* on a neighbor's color television set. The show, starring Ann Sothern as Liza Elliott, was subjected to the network's strict censorship

With Lee and producer Billy Rose at the opening night party for
Porgy and Bess, New York City, March 1953.

standards that prevented the word "mistress" or "any one of the fifty-or-so synonyms in Roget and in the Berry and Van den Bark slang compilation" to be heard on the air, which forced Ira to create a "perfumed version" of the Ringmaster's quatrains to protect the sensibilities of American television audiences in 1954.[32]

THE MOST NOTABLE OUTING of Ira's months as a bachelor was the star-studded opening of *A Star Is Born* at the RKO Pantages Theatre on September 29, 1954, and the after-party at the Cocoanut Grove nightclub. Some of the revelers, including Ira, continued the merry night at Judy Garland's house, finally departing well after sunrise.[33] By the time of the premiere, he had become less sanguine about the movie's success at the box office; Sid Luft's prediction that *A Star Is Born* would become the second-highest-grossing picture in Hollywood history seemed "rather optimistic," an opinion Ira formed at a party not long before the opening when Humphrey Bogart drunkenly asked Jack Warner and Luft "who's going to screw whom" on the movie, to which the veteran producer Walter Wanger replied, "the one with the most experience."[34] Wanger knew his Hollywood: executives at Warner Bros, upset at the length of the movie and its impact on the studio's bottom line, had *A Star Is Born* mercilessly hacked to pieces, eliminating vital scenes and the songs "Lose That Long Face" and "Here's What I'm Here For."[35]

Ira considered his work on *A Star Is Born* little more than "adequate," confessing that "if there's little brilliant it was a job of showmanship [for] a singer who's a good but not great dancer."[36] The song that meant the most to Garland was the ballad "It's a New World." Her performance confirmed the songwriters' idea to create not only a song appropriate to Garland's character and the situation in the plot, but one that gave Garland herself something to hope for. Ira's lyrics dipped into the corners of his catalog, with the song's title coming from a similar line in "Love Walked In" and Esther Blodgett's visions of "joy and blossom and bloom" and "the pleasures we will prove" borrowed from two numbers in *The Firebrand of Florence*. A decade later, in October 1963, he revisited the lyric for two benefit concerts at Carnegie Hall for the civil rights organization SNCC (Student Nonviolent Coordinating Committee). Originally to have been sung by Garland, who had to drop out due to filming commitments on her television show, Ira dedicated the new set of words to August's epoch-making March on Washington for Jobs and Freedom.[37] With Harold Arlen at the piano, Lena Horne sang words that she told Ira were "beautiful and . . . inspiring."[38] The personal references of the original were transformed into terms more relevant to the situation, although the sentiments could be applied to everyone, not just to the Black citizens of the United States struggling for their rights as citizens:

How wonderful that I'm beholding
A vision of a world unfolding—
Where we reach up to the stars
As mountains we move
In a life where all the pleasures
We will prove.

It's a new world I see—
A new world for me!

The tears have rolled off my cheek,
And fears fade away, seeing all I seek.

A new world—though it once was just a dream—
Full of love, full of faith and self-esteem.

LESS THAN THREE MONTHS after the extravagant opening of *A Star Is Born*, Ira attended the more subdued premiere of *The Country Girl*. "It's still a fine job," he wrote, "even tho' the songs are now cut to the bone."[39] Two numbers—"Dissertation on the State of Bliss (Love and Learn)," which appears to be a world-weary response to Irving Berlin's contemporaneous "Count Your Blessings Instead of Sheep," and "The Search Is Through"— were issued by Arlen's publisher but gained little notice. After hearing Bing Crosby's duet with Patti Andrews on the first number, Ira wondered if "maybe the song isn't as good as I thought."[40]

Love and learn, love and learn.
It's a breeze, then a burn.
You retreat, then return.
You may have climbed the Tree of Knowledge,
But when you love you *really* learn.

Love and learn. Learn a lot.
It's the be-and-end-all, then it's not.
It's a dream, it's a plot.
It's something out of Seventh Heaven—
Then Something Misbegot.

Each morning when I count my blessings,
They tally up to none.
I've arrived at this:
What some call bliss
Is somewhat overdone.

As IRA GERSHWIN neared sixty, his memory was becoming what John Steinbeck described as "at best a faulty, waspy reservoir."[41] He was at a creative crossroads: three years of writing songs for the movies had proved professionally unsatisfying; as to Broadway, "he could not convince himself that such an assignment would reward him with anything other than pain and exhaustion."[42]

Long conversations with Lawrence Stewart led Ira to return to an idea that he had considered for two decades. After the successful opening of the revised version of *Strike Up the Band* in 1930, the caricaturist Ralph Barton had written that he would eagerly buy a book of Ira's lyrics, "and find something more than the accident of alphabetical arrangement in the fact that it would be placed on my shelves next to the words of W. S. Gilbert."[43] Ira asked Vincente Minnelli to illustrate such a volume, perhaps in a nod to the work of Constantin Alajálov in *George Gershwin's Song-Book*, but the idea languished.[44]

Publicist Irving Drutman asked Ira in 1952 whether he was now ready for the task, but with Alfred and Blanche Knopf pressing Ira to write a book on George, he asked Drutman to keep silent about it; then, in the summer of 1954, Ira happened to glance through a copy of the Random House collection *103 Lyrics by Cole Porter*. The editor, whom Ira dubbed a lyricologist—"a needed term I've just invented"—was "too narrow" in his thinking. There was "no mention of any name but Cole's and too much explaining of what any reader who'd buy such a book can readily understand himself."[45] Although eager to see a different book, Blanche Knopf thought this a suitable stopgap until Ira was ready to write about his brother.[46]

Persuading Max Dreyfus to approve the publication of so many lyrics for one project was a difficult task, but Ira gained his wily publisher's blessing by carefully constructing a case for the value of such a volume, citing an essay that discussed Lorenz Hart, Porter, Howard Dietz, and Harold Rome and that praised Ira's lyrics as "outstanding for their versatility and verve. They display the same rhythmic and melodic rightness, vitality and range of mood that characterized his brother's music."[47] Ira then explained his reasons for choosing some lyrics from his oeuvre over others: "Embraceable You" not for its popularity but because it contained "four-syllable rhymes"; "I Can't Get Started" because it would be accompanied by "the few lines of dialogue I wrote before and after the song." Half the text would consist of unpublished material, such as the fourth dream sequence from *Lady in the Dark*. Every song would be accompanied by notes that would be of interest to Ira and what he drily referred to as his "six disciples."[48]

But he demurred when Blanche Knopf wanted him to start work immediately: "It would be the better part of valor to lay off for a year or two" to give the matter some thought.[49] It was not like writing lyrics, and "naturally I want my name on a careful and literate job."[50] The undertaking required organization, but he lacked the energy and the will to straighten up his scattered papers and his "collection of dictionaries, encyclopedias, atlases, and other books of reference."[51] It would be a long process, "wad[ing] through a morass of published and unpublished material," and the result? "Could be that it could be something. Could also be that I'll work on such a project most of next year, then weigh the whole thing and say 'Nah!' "[52]

BY CHRISTMAS 1954, Ira and Lee had been apart for more than three months. He rarely indulged in sentimentality, but loneliness caused the composition of a long letter in response to her regular missives from foreign lands. "Who am I to stand in the way of a fabulous trip that has every one of your female friends green with envy but who at the same time join me in being happy that you're able to make it." As the *Porgy* troupe headed for its next engagement in Egypt, "there you are on a slow boat to Alexandria and you must tell me all about the party on the boat and tomorrow when I get back to this letter I'll tell you about tonight's party [at the Bogarts' house] in Holmby Hills."[53] The debut of *Porgy and Bess* in Tel Aviv, Israel, was a momentous occasion: an opera cowritten by two American Jews was being performed in a country whose controversial founding had taken place less than four years earlier. But Ira seemed not to have been prompted to comment about that fact, other than to turn down an offer to update Isaac Goldberg's biography for a Hebrew-language publisher.

WITH *PORGY AND BESS* once again a stage success, the push for a motion picture version gained speed, and Blevins Davis offered $500,000 for a fifteen-year lease on the rights.[54] The biggest hitch in the ensuing debacle turned out to be an agreement signed by Dorothy Heyward at the end of 1953 that granted Davis and Robert Breen a five-year option to purchase her interest in the novel, the play, and the opera's movie and television rights.[55]

Ira had begun "to respect more and more" Breen's "notions about the making of the film when, as and if,"[56] and he told his agent that an option should be sent to Breen "as promised."[57] But negotiations slowed when Ira's fellow trustees became suspicious of what Ira thought was a reasonable request from Irving Lazar: a 10 percent commission if Lazar successfully concluded the Breen option negotiations. Ira could not understand their objections: "Has any agent spent more money and time" on the subject?[58]

Impressed by the reaction to Breen's staging of the opera, Ira considered him to be the best hope for a movie, particularly if Breen were to work with Ira's experienced friends William Perlberg and George Seaton at Paramount.[59] Dorothy Heyward was a firm proponent of Breen, but Lee Gershwin advised her husband to listen to his agent—"he really is the smartest and is the only one that has a clear picture."[60] Heyward would soon fall out of love with Breen and agree with Ira that the movie rights should remain unsold—at least to Breen.[61] Ira and DuBose's widow rarely met, and any feelings of friendliness she felt toward him were inherited from those of her late husband.[62] Her discontent at the delay in selling the movie rights was magnified by Ira's sometimes flippant replies to her complaints that DuBose was being forgotten. In these replies, Ira failed to recall the moments when his own ego had been similarly bruised, such as his response to seeing the sleeve of the 1954 RCA Victor cast recording of *Lady in the Dark*. Ira complained—to his diary—that "outside of about six short spoken lines [on the LP], every word is mine and of course all the music is Kurt's, yet the name of Moss Hart is twice the size of Kurt's and mine."[63]

So IRA SAT BACK, puffed on his cigar, and watched as the competing offers rolled in from producers proven and unproven. Although he held the smallest financial share of the opera, gaining his approval was vital. As George's brother, he was viewed as the *owner* of the opera; while Dorothy Heyward held much of the property and relied on *Porgy* to keep herself financially afloat, she was—in the eyes of the producers—only a woman. Ira was content to wait: an acclaimed, popular stage production with long-term prospects was worth more than a movie. But he eventually grew tired of the arguments: "What with four or five newspapers daily, magazines, books, letters to answer, telephone calls, visitors, market (stock, not song) who has time for so-called creative work? Not me."[64] He asked for no more details: "After listening to over eighty propositions over the years, let the trustees of the two estates finally get together and decide and I'll go along."[65]

But his hopes for a peaceful resolution to the issue were dashed. Ira's friendship with movie producers such as Perlberg and Seaton and his representation by Lazar were resented by the other parties who had a stake in the film rights; Ira thought they were "sore" at Lazar "for not having let them in some of the tentative negotiations" and that they believed Ira was eager to sell the rights for whatever he could get.[66] But his stance that "no movie could promote the good will the present talented troupe and production engender" never wavered.[67] Another twist came when Blevins Davis announced that he was going to produce the movie in Spain, a proposal that cut Robert Breen out of the picture.[68] Ira wired Dorothy Heyward:

It has come to my attention that Blevins Davis is causing considerable agitation in an effort to secure the movie rights to PORGY. *Two years ago, under immediate threat of closing the show by Davis we were willing to give an option to Davis and Breen. However, in view of their personal estrangements plus a cable received yesterday from Breen denying he had withdrawn as claimed by Davis, I am sure you feel as I do that this is an unpropitious time to consider any movie offer.*[69]

Ira recapped their subsequent conversation: "She's unhappily all mixed up. Feels she owes a lot to Blevins and Breen but realizes they aren't on speaking terms and she'd be worried anyway even if they were about their capabilities making a picture; but [John] Rumsey and her other agent [Audrey Wood] are after her, high-pressuring for Davis. Told her to sign if she wanted to; I wouldn't."[70] Dorothy said that Ira was the only one holding out against Davis.[71] Breen revealed that his erstwhile producer was broke and was trying to gain the movie rights to "cash in on them."[72] Ira thought it was too bad that Dorothy's agents continued to high-pressure her into making a sale now. Davis's pleas of urgency—"the services of such-and-such a camera man will be lost, no major studio will accept the terms he offers"— were "all meaningless," and he found John Rumsey ridiculous when he claimed "that if World War III came along, the movie rights might become worthless. I told Dorothy that if WW3 did rear up we'd all be worthless."[73]

Lawrence Langner of the Theatre Guild was convinced that Ira could be forced to sell the rights to Davis, claiming that the Guild had had the original idea to musicalize *Porgy*,[74] but after Ira told Langner of the letter his brother had written to DuBose Heyward in 1926, Langner reluctantly agreed that the concept of an operatic *Porgy* had been conceived "independently."[75] A frustrated Ira told Dorothy Heyward that they were not as opposed as she thought they were: "Neither of us has been responsible for the hanky-panky that's been going on for the past two years."[76]

AFTER *A STAR IS BORN* and *The Country Girl*, Ira joked that he and Arlen would probably "be asked to do the next film that deals with a drunk,"[77] but any negative feelings faded when the two movies picked up thirteen Academy Award nominations (seven for *The Country Girl* and six for *A*

Star Is Born), including one for "The Man That Got Away," Ira's third nomination for Best Original Song. Although happy to be recognized, he confessed that he would "be quite surprised" to win over such popular choices as Jule Styne and Sammy Cahn's "Three Coins in the Fountain" and Irving Berlin's "Count Your Blessings Instead of Sheep."[78] His and Arlen's complicated number, he thought, had to "be heard several times before one gets the construction."[79] It would become a "challenge to the gal night club singers."[80]

> The night is bitter,
> The stars have lost their glitter;
> The winds grow colder
> And suddenly you're older—
> And all because of the man that got away.

> No more his eager call,
> The writing's on the wall;
> The dreams you've dreamed have all
>   Gone astray.

> The man that won you
> Has gone off and undone you.
> That great beginning
> Has seen the final inning.
> Don't know what happened. It's all a crazy game.

> No more that all-time thrill,
> For you've been through the mill—
> And never a new love will
>   Be the same.

Ira joined William Perlberg at the RKO Pantages Theatre for the ceremony, where they and other Academy "old-timers" were disappointed that, when the award for Best Actress was announced, Grace Kelly's name was called instead of Judy Garland's. And when "The Man That Got Away" joined "They Can't Take That Away from Me" and "Long Ago (and Far Away)" as Oscar losers, Ira wondered . . . was it time to say "away with 'away' "?[81]

WHEN DAVID EWEN ARRIVED for a week's stay in Southern California in May 1955, he brought with him the first draft of his biography of George. It was "easy reading," but Ira saw that he would "have to spend lots of time correcting dates and chronologies."[82] He was adamant that Ewen's book was not to be referred to as "official"—Ira was to be no "more than one of the many interviewees." It was imperative that "neither the Estate nor the Gershwin family is involved in any way, officially or financially."[83] Ewen agreed but warned that he could not be blamed for people's later ideas.[84] Ira read through the galleys for two days, admitting that it was too short a time to "read the manuscript with the close attention it deserves." He told the worried author that he had "been too near your words and to the subject to see the story, but my general impression is that the book is exceedingly readable and serves its purpose passing well."[85]

IF IRA'S OWN BOOK was to be as thorough as he wished it to be, his workroom and papers had to be organized. He bristled at the idea of anyone disturbing the sanctuary of the former, but the latter could be done without his active participation, so in the late spring of 1955, he offered Lawrence Stewart a summer position as his literary secretary. Stewart, in search of an alternative to his teaching position at UCLA, readily accepted, happy to be in proximity to the primary sources for the Gershwin book he still hoped to write.[86] As he gathered and collated Ira's papers, Stewart's enthusiasm and intelligence, along with his uncanny ability to soak up facts, turned him into the lyricist's amanuensis.[87]

Ira hoped to begin work on the book during the absence of his "itinerant spouse," who had joined the South American leg of the *Porgy and Bess* tour in the early summer of 1955. Referring to himself as an "old bard," Ira told a friend that Lee, in lines borrowed from his own "The Saga of Jenny," was "only on vacation, but the Latins agree, Mrs. Gershwin is upholding the Good-Neighbor Policy."[88] But lacking the ability to concentrate, it took until August 2, 1955, for his first thoughts, about the origins of "The Bab-

August 2, 1955: the first scribble for what would become Ira's 1959 book, *Lyrics on Several Occasions*.

bitt and the Bromide" (from *Funny Face*), to be scribbled onto "a bedside scratch pad."[89]

As the work continued, Ira became "enmeshed in the footnotes of memories."[90] He pored over his drafts and the published versions of his lyrics, dictated notes about a song's creation and its history, then spent more hours meticulously correcting what he had written to make it less "text-booky."[91] By October, he had narrowed 250 possible lyrics down to between 75 and 125 and hoped to arrange them into categories ("Lyrics Not for Musicologists," "Lyrics of the Polly-Analytical," and "Lyrics about That Certain Feeling"), estimating that it would take six to nine months to complete the job.[92]

But the "comedy of errors and machinations" of the movie rights to *Porgy and Bess* forced him away from the pleasures of reminiscence. Solid offers had been received from experienced producers, but Ira remained adamant, in the face of opposition, that the rights should not be sold until the touring company had completed its performances.[93] The "quixotic" Robert Breen continued to hope that he would get the chance to see his vision on the screen, but Ira began to find Breen's suggestions "increasingly bizarre."[94] Blevins Davis was certain that *he* held the upper hand and could "force" Ira to sell the rights to him.[95]

A further distraction came with Breen's announcement that he had negotiated performances of the opera in the Soviet Union and that he wanted Ira to be on hand. Ira was reluctant to "go abroad to THAT CERTAIN COUNTRY,"[96] but Lee—at Breen's request—convinced him that it would be a feather in the hat of all concerned. When the US State Department expressed uncertainty about the merits of the tour, Ira and Dorothy Heyward waived their royalties to "gain the goodwill" of the federal government.[97] He agreed that he was "more or less committed to go along for a few weeks,"[98] but just sorting through the opera's royalty statements led him to complain, "What a nuisance! and brother how much red tape and bother since I became an executor."[99]

He felt more comfortable when he discovered that Breen had taken the initiative and booked seats for Ira and Irving Lazar on an SAS flight. But Breen quickly soured on Lazar; the agent's public announcements of his impending trip left Breen concerned about bad publicity. How would it look if people knew that Ira's agent was getting a free ride?[100] Two songwriters seemed like a better choice, and Breen persuaded Harold Arlen to take Lazar's place.[101] Ira joked about traveling on the "borscht, caviar (I hope) and black bread circuit," although he admitted that "the odds around town are 8 to 5 that I won't make it." In preparation, he purchased "a fur-lined cap, fleece-lined shoes, and other trappings that are supposed to keep one warm, and hope to stay on through Moscow and Warsaw and, possibly, Prague. Have no idea for how long I'll be able to take it, as the other day Moscow reported thirty below zero."[102]

CHAPTER 19

L ITTLE RAN SMOOTHLY as the hours ticked by toward Ira's departure for the Soviet Union. If the trip itself was not enough to make him nervous, the numerous problems with passports and visas left him unable to act; so he retreated to his workroom and handed off the problems to the indispensable Lawrence Stewart. When Harold Arlen arrived in Beverly Hills with his "last minute purchases" for the journey in hand, Ira marveled that "the most striking" item was "his bronze ski shoes with tartan laces. Less obviously discernable but also startling was his fire engine red woolen underwear." The duo arrived at Los Angeles airport in the late evening of January 6 to be told that Ira's luggage, burdened with the "pills and dictionaries" Robert Breen had requested, required an extra fee. He reluctantly pulled out his checkbook, and after being "marched to the steps of the plane" for photographs, they boarded and took their seats before the half-filled airliner took off for Stockholm just minutes after midnight.[1]

He noted with approval that their in-flight meal was partially catered by the Brown Derby restaurant, then nodded off in a special berth in the aft of the airplane. Winnipeg, the first refueling stop, "looked very Grandma Moses-like—pink dawn and white snow." When they arrived in Greenland for a second refueling, he and Arlen donned heavy coats and boarded a waiting bus that took them to a coffee shop on a nearby army airbase.[2] After twenty-five hours, the airplane landed in Copenhagen to pick up additional passengers; two more hours and they touched down at Stockholm's Bromma Airport, where in his haste to get to the hotel, Ira thought he had left his glasses on the airplane: "Rushed back. Helped by steward and stewardess looked everywhere. No glasses. Said 'The hell with it!' and got back to entrance window and while talking to the official happened to touch my right temple and there were the glasses all the time, right on my face! Who's nervous?" The two men taxied to the venerable Grand Hotel, where, during dinner, Ira indulged in a martini and three beers while listening to the hotel orchestra play selections from *Can-Can*, an incident that inspired Arlen to suggest sending a cable to Cole Porter. "After three bottles of beer I would agree to anything," Ira wrote in his diary. In the lobby, they ran into DuBose and Dorothy Heyward's twenty-five-year-old daughter Jenifer and the opera's stage manager, Ella Gerber, who accompanied Ira and Arlen on the final legs of the journey.[3]

A ninety-minute flight the following morning brought them to Helsinki, where no one at the airport was aware of Arlen's visa; after a series of frantic calls proved fruitless, Ira, whose documents said he had to arrive in the Soviet Union on the ninth, was forced to temporarily leave his friend behind: "By the time I said goodbye to Harold the plane was preparing to leave, so I rushed across to reach it. (Ella had taken my handbags.) But when I got near the plane I felt myself being pushed backwards [by the propellors] on the icy ground. Happily a couple of men materialized, grabbed hold of me and elbowed me to the plane where the ladder was pushed back for me and I got on somewhat out of breath." Ira found himself without a seat belt in an old, twenty-seat, two-motor Aeroflot airplane that never reached an altitude of three thousand feet and rattled throughout the ninety minutes it took to get to Leningrad. The stressful customs examinations that he expected were a mere formality: Ira and his companions "were evidently special as we were given a small room of our own, furnished with a full-length mirror, carpets, and a large painting of Comrade S[talin]."[4]

Ira was greeted by his wife at the Moscow airport three hours later, and they "raced on broad highways and through wide boulevards" to an "elaborate suite of three large rooms" in the prerevolutionary-era Metropole Hotel, "furnished rather bizarrely with an enormous desk in the sitting room and a large wardrobe in the bedroom. The largest room was the dining-room, with red plush curtains on the window, behind which was a small platform with two large throne-like chairs." Ira was told that there had been "much betting" on whether he "would actually make the trip."[5]

The following evening, Ira found Harold Arlen in the lobby, just arrived from Helsinki, "much the worse for wear, unshaved, tired, suit wrinkled—but no time to change," as Arlen insisted he had to be at the Stanislavsky Theatre for the first performance of *Porgy and Bess*. After filing onto the stage to be introduced to the audience, Robert Breen gave "a longish speech . . . about cultural relations and peace among nations," while St. Petersburg native Alexander Smallens received a large round of applause. Ira was amused to hear that "it was announced that I too had been born there." The house was packed, and near the end of the performance, Breen asked Ira to go backstage to observe a "special effect." To his amazement, Ira was grabbed by LeVern Hutcherson, the opera's Crown, who dragged him onto the stage. "I honestly couldn't release my wrist from Hutch's grasp. 'Gawd, what a grip for a piece of a man!'" To his chagrin, Ira made a "quick bow" to the audience before "running quickly upstage and off. (I *really* ran.)"[6]

Ira suspected that the Russians enjoyed the opera due to their preference for Breen's ballet-like staging,[7] but "a couple of bits of business shocked the audience, as obviously they go in for very little sex on stage. (A gasp went through the house when Bess lifted her skirt to get some money for Crown.)"[8] After the performance ended, it was off to a party at the residence of American Ambassador Charles E. Bohlen, with five hundred guests, including the opera's cast and crew, ambassadors, journalists, and officials from the Soviet Ministry of Culture. Ira and Lee departed for their hotel at 2 a.m., "when some of the cast started soloing with Lorenzo Fuller [Sportin' Life] at the piano." He was told that most of the guests stayed for another three hours, "with Arlen in his long ski boots and [Truman] Capote," who was covering the tour for the *New Yorker*, "in his velvet suit making quite a contrast."[9]

Capote turned his experience into a lengthy essay, "Porgy and Bess in Russia," that was published over two consecutive issues of the magazine later that year. (Random House issued it in book form as *The Muses Are Heard* shortly thereafter.) Capote, who thought his piece amusing, portrayed Lee Gershwin as the prototypical ugly American, more interested in her jewelry and furs than the cultural and artistic aspects of the Soviet tour.[10] He acidly quoted Lee as she forlornly fingered her diamonds while gazing at the czar's jewels during a group tour of the Hermitage: "I wish I'd *never* come here. I feel so dissatisfied, I'd like to go home and crack my husband on the head."[11] Lee complained that in Capote's telling, she was little more than "a road company Billie Burke." What Capote failed to understand was that Lee's use of language was shaped in the way an architect designed a building—to "give singular interest to what she said" and nothing more.[12]

Ira was unimpressed by the Dutch ambassador to the Soviet Union, who insisted that, other than *Porgy and Bess*, "we of the West weren't doing enough in the way of cultural propaganda. He didn't seem to get that the West could only do as much as the Soviets would permit, and permission was usually nil." To Ira, anyone who kept up with the press (that is, himself) "knew as much about general political and economic conditions as most ambassadors."[13]

On January 11 he joined a group that walked from the Metropole, accompanied by a group of Soviet photographers and newsreel cameramen who were documenting the Americans' visit. They "passed St. Basil's, then the tomb of Lenin and Stalin," before spending an hour touring the Kremlin museum.[14] A viewing of the embalmed bodies of the two Communist leaders was carefully overseen by a group of soldiers; Ira observed that Stalin's hair must have been dyed, that Lenin looked to be in his late thirties, and that "the nails of both gentlemen had been manicured and were highly polished and cut very short." He was told that the long queue at the tomb may have been made up of Russian factory employees who were brought in to "impress" the Americans. The group returned to the hotel on the Moscow metro, "which went on a greater speed than any I'd known and it was probably the longest one I'd ever been on." A tour through the Pushkin State Museum was unimpressive; Hollywood could put together a more complete show "if Eddie Robinson and [Bill] Goetz and all the others who own French paintings in Southern California pooled their collections."[15]

Anna Karenina at the Moscow Art Theatre was "very good looking, even if we didn't understand quite what was going on."[16] But Prokofiev's

Romeo and Juliet ballet at the Bolshoi, where they sat in boxes as guests of honor, was more enjoyable.[17] Although Ira's visa allowed for a thirty-day visit, he admitted to being tired after only five days, and he determined not to continue with the company to Poland and Czechoslovakia, jokingly blaming the decision on having yet to see a pool table.[18] But obligations still needed to be met, including a meeting of the USSR Society for Cultural Relations with Foreign Countries, during which Russians from the worlds of music, film, theater, radio, and television joined the American contingent in mutually admiring remarks. "A few questions were asked, but nothing that could start any argument."[19] During the event, Ira was introduced to the Russian composer Reinhold Glière, an "affable and charming octogenarian." Lee had told Glière that her husband had mentioned him in one of his lyrics, but Ira was "somewhat embarrassed" by the older man's "profuse thanks," as the Russian was unaware that forty-eight *other* composers were mentioned in "Tschaikowsky."[20]

Ira put on his dinner jacket ("first time I ever had one on so early") to catch a bus to the only Baptist church in Moscow for the afternoon wedding of Helen Thigpen (who played Serena) and Earl Jackson (the opera's other Sportin' Life). The church was crammed, with more than twelve hundred people inside and an equal number outside watching the couple enter the building. Ira found it "quite a spectacle," with "a rich Oriental Arabian Nights splendor." The midnight wedding reception was held at a local restaurant, but "although all the cast were invited, only about one-half showed up as many do not approve of Jackson's minstrel-man behavior." (Ira had demurred when Jackson asked him to be his best man.) The final toast was made by Ambassador Bohlen. As Ira reflected, "everyone was good natured about the reception, but I felt it was the first fizzle of my stay."[21] The next day, there was a large get-together in the Metropole's main dining room. After the Minister of Culture raised his glass to praise the company, "a microphone from Moscow Radio was put in front of me," and Ira delivered an "unstartling toast" that he felt lacked polish—"but then I'm no speaker."[22]

After a whirlwind ten days, Ira and Arlen departed for their flight home while "intrepid Lee, Miss Marco Polo of '54-'55-'56," continued with the tour.[23] Journalist Horace Sutton—who had been traveling through the

Ira and Harold Arlen (*right*) with unidentified companion aboard
their airplane returning from the Soviet Union, January 1956.
Photo by Horace Sutton.

Soviet Union on assignment for the *Saturday Review*—quickly got them
through the required paperwork and onto the plane. The journey to Leningrad was, thankfully, aboard "a Russian two-motor which was in better
condition than the Helsinki-Moscow flight one." An SAS Douglas DC-6B
took them to Stockholm via Copenhagen.[24] Ira didn't get a chance to sleep
on the plane, as he had given the only available berth to Arlen, "who needed
more rest." They landed in Greenland for refueling, then continued to
Winnipeg. As Ira noted in his diary, "On board it was a most satisfactory
sensation to be able to read thick newspapers in English again." Customs,
which had been so easy in the Soviet Union, became problematic at home
when an official "leafed skeptically through a package of Russian books"
Arlen had asked Ira to carry for the wife of an Associated Press reporter.
They turned out to be prerevolution language textbooks. "It was odd that
my only feeling of guilt had to come when I arrived at L.A."[25]

BACK HOME in Beverly Hills, Ira barely looked at his copy of David Ewen's
biography *George Gershwin: A Journey to Greatness*, annoyed that the text of

his early poem, "The Shrine," was rife with typographical errors.[26] What really disturbed him was that Ewen's flawed work might be judged as the definitive take on his brother—as well as on Ira himself—and it prodded Ira into thinking more about his own volume.[27] But the days flew by with little accomplished beyond a possible dedication—"To L.S.G. and A.S.C.A.P."—a line that amused Ira in its acknowledgment that the source of much of his income was as important to him as his wife.[28]

The overarching reason for the delays was Ira's conviction that a lyric was never truly finished. Since some of the songs he wanted to include had never been published and had not often been heard—and if so, typically in less-than-ideal circumstances—he felt that he had the right to improve on what he had originally written, sometimes in the haste of completing a lyric to meet an urgent deadline. Was this cheating his audience? Lawrence Stewart noted that there were times when Ira "wanted to gloss over the issue and pretend that the variant lines were retrieved from old manuscripts" or were "lines taken from discarded attempts.[29] But the lyricist concluded that no one would remember all the lines of such obscure numbers, and this gave him the freedom to pore over his texts for many days and nights, polishing his verse to its ultimate sheen.[30]

IN SPITE OF his efforts, *Porgy and Bess* continued to break into his concentration. Columbia Pictures had made an offer of $700,000 and 10 percent of the gross for the rights to make the motion picture, but Blevins Davis argued that *he* was solely responsible for the Gershwins' worldwide reputation and laid down his claim on the property.[31] Dorothy Heyward pleaded with Ira: she needed the money, and since Robert Breen reportedly owed a substantial amount of back taxes, would it not be in everyone's interests for Ira to join with all concerned and favor Davis?[32] "Ye Gods! What a career *Porgy and Bess* turned out to be!" Ira complained.[33]

When Irving Lazar nudged Columbia to increase their offer to $1 million, Davis was given the chance to meet that figure.[34] Dorothy Heyward considered selling her rights in the movie to Davis,[35] but Robert Breen had an ace up his sleeve when it came to his erstwhile partner: he had photocopies of letters that Davis had written to the New York financier Herman Sartorius, "wherein Mr. D. sold Mr. S. $100,000 worth of *Porgy and Bess* as

an *investment*, promising him big profits. After Mr. S. found out that P&B
was a *non-profit* project, he threatened to have Mr. D. jailed if the money
wasn't returned."[36] By the time the world tour of *Porgy and Bess* ended in
June 1956, it had been revealed that Davis had not "contributed a dime to
the show for over two years."[37]

Ira wanted to "do everything possible" to keep the opera on the road,
"not only for prestige and cultural reasons but for the more than satisfactory" royalties it had provided for the last four years.[38] His siblings supported this stance, but his nemesis, Emanuel Alexandre, continued to be
an "inefficient nuisance."[39] Ira lamented that "as a trustee, I try to be as
conscientious as possible but I can't help thinking how much of my time the
past seven years has been spent on matters that should have been in Alexandre's department."[40] Frustrated, Ira told his attorney that he appreciated
"anything that keeps me from having to get in touch with A. Should it be
decided that Frankie is to move for the removal of A. as a menace to the
Estate, I for one will not impede the path of progress."[41]

In December 1956, Blevins Davis waved the white flag and agreed to
assign his rights in the Dorothy Heyward option to Robert Breen.[42] Ira
was happy to see the back of Davis, and when, a few years later, he heard
about the erstwhile producer's financial problems, he indulged in a rare
moment of cattiness: "Maybe he'll find another rich old lady who'll marry
him and take care of his debts."[43] Although Davis was out of the way, Ira
foresaw dark clouds for the movie business, which "really seems to be at its
lowest ebb these days, thanks not only to TV but, even more important, to
the European market which is being shot to hell by the Suez-Hungarian
imbroglios and economic aftermaths."[44]

Dorothy Heyward continued her efforts to pin Ira down, again playing
on their significantly different financial positions; Ira, she claimed, was a
billionaire whose small share of the rights constantly stymied the majority.[45]
His response was both humorous—"I am only a fraction of a millionaire"—
and a vehement defense of his opinions and actions:

> *When you say that my six and two-thirds percent has always negated
> a possible movie sale, I'm afraid that isn't so. I said O.K. to Columbia
> Films' offer of a million dollars; it seems it was your signed agreement
> with Davis and Breen that stymied that deal—Columbia wanted the*

property for George Sidney to direct, but with no cloud on the title to the property. . . . Columbia told me at that time they would even pay a bonus to Breen if your agreement were torn up. But Breen, when I told him this, turned that offer down. Saxe feels that P&B isn't open to free negotiations until your option expires.[46]

Privately, he called Dorothy Heyward "sweet but full of misinformation"[47] and hoped that she could be convinced that he was "not the heavy they believe me to be."[48] Ira's goal was "the best possible deal from any quarter" when it came to the movie. He liked Robert Breen and admired his "dedication," yet stuck to his conviction that touring the opera would be more lucrative in the long run.[49] As the years passed, he was less sanguine about Breen's direction of the opera, preferring a "legitimate interpretation" to "the jazzed-up version" he had seen in Moscow.[50]

By April 1957, Irving Lazar had persuaded Samuel Goldwyn to make an offer for a fifteen-year lease of the film rights; Ira, exhausted by the endless process, agreed to give his okay, although he remained unconvinced that the aging movie mogul was the ideal choice to bring his brother's career-defining masterwork to the screen. But yet again, the "troublesome—if not unbreakable" Breen-Davis option with Dorothy Heyward blocked progress,[51] and it was not until Breen signed an agreement that transferred his option to Goldwyn, provided that Goldwyn completed his negotiations for the picture, that the announcement of the sale was made: $650,000 as a "down payment" against 10 percent of the gross box office.[52]

Fifteen years of legitimate—and a few fanciful—bids to adapt the opera for the big screen had finally—mercifully—come to an end; the interminable battles, accusations, and recriminations between the rights holders and their attorneys and advisers had taken their toll on Ira, physically and mentally. But even as the contract with Goldwyn was being written, Dorothy Heyward continued to diminish his role by insisting on a clause that her husband's name *always* come before Ira's as the opera's lyricist. She claimed that Ira was not originally intended to be a participant, but that George felt that his brother needed work and added him to write "additional lyrics"; therefore, Ira's involvement was slight. She was concerned—and history *has* proven her correct—that the opera not become known as *The Gershwins' Porgy and Bess*. Leonard Saxe objected, and Heyward relented.[53] Ira was not easily provoked, but he had had his fill; Dorothy Heyward, he vowed, would not deny the importance of his contribution to the opera.[54]

AFTER FIFTEEN YEARS of "tough usage and abusage," Ira's house needed a makeover.[55] But the impetus for what would ultimately become the demolition of the original Spanish-style structure and its re-creation as a neo-Regency mansion was not mere cosmetics; it was another method of soothing Lee Gershwin's negative feelings about Southern California. Her extensive—and expensive—travels were not enough to keep her happy, and if she was to ignore the "crazy genes" that told her to return to New York, Ira was obliged to do more.[56] By the spring of 1956, he had hired John Woolf, a young architect recommended by Fanny Brice.[57] The cost of the work "will doubtless be three times what we bought this house for originally, but what the hell—Comfort and Hospitality must go on."[58]

That summer, the couple moved from their "cluttered-up repository"[59] to a "tumble-down palazzo"[60] once owned by the actor William Powell, at 1113 Tower Road, in Benedict Canyon.[61] Although Ira's library was reassembled to allow for work to continue on his book, the move became yet another impediment to its completion.[62] By October, he had selected more than thirty lyrics and had written notes for more than two-thirds of those, but the struggle of spending "three afternoons on one note" only to find that the result was a mere half page left him reconsidering the entire project.[63]

After almost eight months away from home and having spent more than $120,000 ($1.2 million today), Ira was restless.[64] Although only two rooms had been finished in the new "Taj Mahal" designed to "house Leonore's jigsaw puzzles" and his "cigars and doodlings," he ached for semi-familiar surroundings, even if it meant six more weeks of "living in the midst of carpenters, electricians, painters, and decorators," so in late March 1957, they returned to face "a form of camping out—or should I say camping in?"[65]

The couple's thirtieth wedding anniversary was acknowledged with an exchange of gifts: hers to him was a copy of the *Dictionary of National Biography*, and although the subjects of the entries were all Englishmen, the fact that many of them were notable eccentrics was cause for elation.[66] His to her was a weekend with friends in Las Vegas, and "there wasn't a dull, inexpensive moment."[67] Ira had been among the first gamblers to try his luck at the then-new Sands Hotel on the Strip four years earlier, and he had found the town to be "undoubtedly the most exciting place of its kind in the world." Although he was "not much of a night club habitue," the desert resort was the scene of one of his more unusual evenings when, in 1953, he was persuaded to take in a show at the El Rancho Vegas and was surprised to watch stripper Lili St. Cyr disrobe to the strains of *Rhapsody in Blue.*[68]

HE PROMISED to return to work on his book once he was "completely ensconced in the new plantation,"[69] but another event—one that included much public airing of family matters—took him further away from the act of creation. The consequences of his actions would last for decades and left Ira awkwardly poised between anger, embarrassment, and frustration. It began in the summer of 1955, when he answered an innocuous request to sign an ASCAP membership application. Without giving it much thought, he sent off the inscribed document as requested.[70] Nearly two years later, and just a month before the twentieth anniversary of George Gershwin's death, Walter Winchell informed his millions of readers of an impending lawsuit by a man alleging to be George's son who was now seeking control of his father's estate.[71]

Was it a coincidence that this allegation appeared shortly after the announcement of the sale of the movie rights to *Porgy and Bess?* Three days after Winchell's column appeared, a man who identified himself as Alan Gershwin wrote to Ira from an address in Jackson Heights, New York, insisting that they must meet soon in person.[72] Ira forwarded the missive to his attorney, Leonard Saxe, telling Saxe that he had received other letters—as well as the 1955 ASCAP application—from this man, who had then called himself Alan Schneider, but since the letters also included the familiar suggestion that he could be Ira's next songwriting partner, Ira had deposited the lot into the waste basket. "Ordinarily I would pay no mind to such crazy items and claims," but the fact that the story had been published at the same time as a junior high school in New York City was to be named after his brother left Ira with a "bad taste" in his mouth.[73]

He wanted action to be taken—"without publicity, if possible"—to "[squelch] this hoaxster or mental case" whose story was being believed by people Ira felt should know better.[74] Leonard Saxe advised Ira against making a public response.[75] Ira reluctantly retreated, but wanted "enough on" Schneider "to make him stop embarrassing the Estate and family with his preposterous claim."[76] He convinced Herman Starr of New World Music to pay for a private detective,[77] and Saxe hired Belle Levy, of the Colonial Detective Service, to look into Schneider's background.[78]

For all his claims—including that his grandfather and Ira's had come from the same Russian village, a statement that was rebuffed by Morris Gershwin's half brother Aaron[79]—there has never been a shred of documentary evidence to support the assertion that "Alan Gershwin" was George's son. While it is well known that George had many intimate relationships with women, the story of the "imposter" (as he was known in Gershwin circles)—who magically appeared when the Gershwin name and large sums of money were mentioned in the press—is easily told. Albert Alan Schneider was born in Brooklyn on May 18, 1926.[80] His mother, he said, was the actress Margaret Manners (nee Charleston), who died a few years after his birth; he was raised by his aunt and uncle, Fannie and Ben Schneider.[81] A chorus girl named Margaret Manners appeared in three editions of *George White's Scandals*, including the one that opened on Broadway on June 14, 1926. If Manners truly was Schneider's mother, it seems unlikely that she was simultaneously heavily pregnant and participating in strenuous rehearsals.

The private detective learned that Schneider had served in the US Navy and had received a "disability discharge on account of a mental illness."[82] This was confirmed by Veterans Administration documents. Diagnosed with schizophrenia,[83] Schneider had been a patient in a rest camp for veterans in New York State on five occasions between 1947 and 1955.[84]

The 1959 publication of "I Am George Gershwin's Illegitimate Son" in the tabloid magazine *Confidential* was the last significant appearance of the "imposter," who certainly *looked* like George Gershwin and certainly *believed* that he was his son, but was, in Ira's mind, "either demented or a not too clever opportunist."[85]

HOURS WERE SPENT changing a single line until he discovered the right phrase or rhyme. The result? No new lyrics for the book were delivered for retyping until the middle of the summer of 1957.[86] A few songs required less than extensive commentary and forced Ira to scour his reference books for appropriate tidbits.[87] It was "highly interesting" work, but "tough as hell."[88]

If finding his way into the past was not easy, finding a title was vital. He considered the forthright *Words By* and *Lyrics By*, as well as the self-deprecating *A Bargain Basement of Lyrics*, but the solution only came when he discovered a title that matched the idea of lyrics being written to situations rather than as pure poetry. The book would not be made up of the words of a poet but of a "word mosaicist" who built his structure upon bits and pieces of text that may have been stored away for decades.[89]

I was placing Matthew Prior's *Poems on Several Occasions* to the left of *Puniana* (London, 1867) when I suddenly thought what an appropriate title *Lyrics on Several Occasions* could be, *my* occasions of course being stage and screen. Quite excited at first, my enthusiasm began to wane after a bit: too literary perhaps; also I had visions of Prior turning over in his Westminster Abbey grave. No, it wouldn't be right; I'd better get something else. Then two nights later I was reading an article in

At his desk in Beverly Hills, surrounded by books and stacks of papers, August 1958. Photograph by Sidney Zelinka.

a *Colophon* and saw a reference to *Poems upon Several Occasions* by Mrs. Aphra Behn. Interesting. About a week later I was looking up poet and songwriter Henry Carey—I forget why—and he too had published a *Poems on Several Occasions*. Really interesting now. So I got hold of a *Cambridge Bibliography* and discovered that there was a period a couple of centuries back when at least a dozen others had published *Poems on, &c*. Which freed me for *Lyrics on, &c.*, with no further apprehension about a possible revolving Prior.[90]

By Thanksgiving 1957, a tentative list of more than 110 lyrics had been compiled,[91] but work came to a halt two days after Christmas, when an ambulance arrived to take Ira to Cedars of Lebanon Hospital. Having suffered for days from abdominal discomfort, his doctors quickly suspected that, contrary to the medical records that showed a "complete removal" of his "gangrenous appendix" in 1926, Ira required a second appendectomy:

> *They opened me up and found that there was a hidden part of the appendix that Berg* [Albert A. Berg, the surgeon in 1926] *couldn't have seen, even though he worked 2½ hrs over it; this had now developed, attracting other nauseous material, to form a disgusting and expensive hospitalization. My arms are black and blue with some 30 blood-lettings, also my tiny veins have been slashed to make room for intravenous feedings; I am absolutely fed up on dextrose 5% and saline, plus achromycin 500 mg, &c. These are some of the comforts. I won't go into the discomforts, even though actually all the attending specialists are doing a fine job and it's possible I may be home a week from today.*[92]

When old scar tissue was discovered to be blocking his bowels, Ira's hopes were dashed; peritonitis sent him onto the critical list.[93] Further tests revealed coronary artery disease and that he had suffered a mild stroke.[94] A member of the family feared a repeat of 1937 and asked Leonard Saxe to take Ira's care away from Lee; Saxe refused, saying that Dr. Corday was perfectly capable.[95]

Ira returned home after more than ten days in the hospital, weak but able to say that he was "well on that W.K. [well-known] Road to Recovery,

Calif."[96] Another month passed before he was able to put away his bathrobes and don a pair of trousers.[97] When he began work again, it was to face the struggle of how to write about the creation of "Strike Up the Band." Ira wanted to see more than the chorus of the song in print, yet was reluctant to admit that the idea for the most biting line of the original verse—"We don't know what we're fighting for / But we didn't know the last time"— came from Morrie Ryskind, whose political beliefs had veered to the right. He was also reticent about revealing that he and his brother had shared a hotel room in Atlantic City when the song was written. But since he and George were the only people there, he felt safe in writing that rather than George jumping out of his adjoining bed to exclaim that he had the perfect tune for the refrain, Ira looked "for a slit of light under the door" of the adjoining room before George burst in with the idea.[98]

THE NEW 1021 North Roxbury Drive was a "clearing house for talents and neurotics—more often than not they're indistinguishable; this makes for many exciting evenings but keeps us up all hours."[99] Talent and neuroticism found no greater combination than in the pianist Oscar Levant, who lived on the next block of North Roxbury Drive for many years. Levant left Ira feeling conflicted; his talent, particularly as an interpreter of George's music, was unparalleled, yet his temperament and ubiquitous presence made him a social chore.[100] The long, late nights spent with the depressed pianist were "all very sad because essentially he wants to be liked and would hurt nobody."[101] For his part, Levant accused Ira of "putting up" with him for decades, a statement Ira admitted to making but excused by saying that he "told Oscar that we all say critical things at times of our friends—and if he analyzed this particular statement it might be considered funny."[102]

Being the owner of a "new" house meant constant visits from friends and colleagues, which left Ira with little energy for *Lyrics on Several Occasions*, but he pushed through, until by late May of 1958, three-quarters of the manuscript was complete.[103] There was joy in recalling his brother and the songs they had written, but the fear that Alfred Knopf would insist that Ira write his autobiography continued to nag at him.[104]

A BRIEF RESPITE from his book came with a request from Horace Sutton, the editor of the *Saturday Review,* for a brief essay on why Ira chose to live in California rather than New York. When the essay "California, Here I Came" was published on October 18, 1958, he sent a facetious letter of complaint to Sutton:

> *This is not that I'm not pleased to appear in* SR, *but it's been a pretty expensive proposition—that article. I figured that the $150 receivable would leave me a net of $15.50 (6% off for State Franchise Tax, leaving a balance of $141, taxable at 89% Federal—net, $15.50.) Still not too bad—it would pay for one office visit to the doctor to tell me I'm in good shape, considering; and 50¢ for parking. But I decided I was feeling fine, canceled the doctor, and felt $15.50 richer.*
>
> *It happened that we had guests that weekend. After dinner the wives went upstairs to Lee's sitting-room to gossip, and, unfortunately, one of the husbands suggested a game of blackjack. Feeling I could spare $15.50, I agreed. The dealers' limits kept getting larger and larger and at 1:30 a.m. I quit and signed checks for $600. (Actually one on Bank of America for $300, plus three $100 left-over American Express checks I couldn't find anything to buy with in Moscow.) So now I'll have to earn about $5,400 to make up for the night's loss.*
>
> *All this is certainly not your fault, but the lesson I've learned is: Turn down Horace Sutton, should he ever insist on another piece for* SR, *unless* SR *pays $5,400.*[105]

THE FINAL NOTE for *Lyrics on Several Occasions* was completed on January 28, 1959; its paucity matched its subject: "I Can't Be Bothered Now." Exhausted, Ira sent Lawrence Stewart with Lee to New York to deliver the manuscript to Blanche Knopf.[106] The book was good, she told him, but it lacked his personality.[107] Although unhappy at the extra work, he remained in a mood for reminiscing, telling a reporter that "people still feel personally close" to George, even after twenty-two years. "They come up to me and say, 'Isn't it too bad about your brother?'—as if it happened yesterday." He was more circumspect about his own accomplishments; he would be "very happy" if his book sold three thousand copies: "It's quite informative, if anybody can live through it."[108]

After making the necessary changes, and with what he hoped were the final words to the book off his desk, Ira again checked himself into Cedars of Lebanon, where on April 28 he went under the knife for a two-hour operation on his prostate.[109] The biopsy proved negative,[110] but the surgery and postoperative recovery were painful,[111] and he did not return home for ten days.[112] "The worst is over," he said, "but the doctors tell me it will be four or five weeks before I will be in control of the situation."[113] A few years later, his ailment was the cause of some lighthearted remarks made after waiting in a long line to visit a small first-floor bathroom at the Guggenheim: "Frank Lloyd Wright probably never had prostate trouble."[114]

IRA HAD LITTLE to do with the production of Samuel Goldwyn's movie of *Porgy and Bess*: other than the occasional meeting with the producer and André Previn, the movie's musical director, his most significant contribution was to make some necessary adjustments to the lyrics. "The world changes," he said, "and peoples' ideas change. When we worked on *Porgy* in 1935, it didn't matter whether the audience we were writing for was yellow, white *or* black. We thought, and wrote, in the acceptable fashion of the day. And the idea that what we were doing would in any way offend or hurt anybody was farthest from our minds. . . . Today . . . all words that might be construed offensively would go out altogether."[115]

The mysterious fire that destroyed the Catfish Row set in July 1958 and delayed production of the movie was, in Ira's estimation, the result of "spontaneous combustion," not "human malice," as some had rumored.[116] He had little to say about the firing of Rouben Mamoulian as the film's director, other than to defend Mamoulian from the rumors that he had instigated some of the negative publicity the production received in the Black press.[117] But Ira was encouraged by the excerpts he saw of the film as it was being made; if they were an "indication of future footage, we're going to have a great picture."[118] His positive outlook grew after viewing some of the scenes in the deluxe, widescreen Todd-AO process,[119] and after a showing in May of 1959, he concluded that the film went beyond his original expectations.[120]

Ira's pride in his brother and his place in the world was palpable, never more so than when he said that he planned to get an extra seat for the gala Hollywood premiere in July 1959; he wanted "to think that George will be sitting beside me. It will be the greatest of all his great first nights."[121] Those high hopes were dashed; Goldwyn's film was panned by the critics and performed poorly at the box office, both domestically and in foreign markets. Less than two years later, the producer withdrew the movie from release.[122] Ira's prediction that "no returns from the film" would be seen "for many and many a year—if ever in this lifetime" proved correct;[123] the only profit the estates made after the movie opened was derived from the success of the soundtrack recording.[124] And the clause in the contract that allowed Goldwyn to block any stage versions from cities where the film hadn't played left valuable theatrical markets off the books. A year after the film opened, Dorothy Heyward finally admitted that Ira had been correct all along—the royalties from touring the opera *were* far more valuable than the movie rights ever would be.[125]

FOUR YEARS OF WORK ended when the corrected proofs of *Lyrics on Several Occasions* were returned to the publishers in August 1959. Ira joked that if he had been aware of what the job would entail, he might never have started it.[126] He rejected the suggestion to use his sketch of himself taking a bow—something he occasionally added at the end of a letter to a friend—as the heading of each category of lyrics,[127] and he deflected most of the suggestions put forth by his press agent Irving Drutman, who had taken on the ultimately thankless job of promoting the book: "With so much publicity I feel I'm being undressed in public, so please take it easy."[128] Although he consented to interviews, he turned down the idea of making a spoken word recording of excerpts for Caedmon Records, claiming that his voice was not beautiful enough to join those of Dylan Thomas, Thomas Mann, Ogden Nash, and Tennessee Williams.[129] He also avoided Lawrence Stewart's efforts to add him to the list of spoken word recordings—Evelyn Waugh and Alice B. Toklas among them—that Stewart was making for Verve Records.[130]

The postman delivered Ira's first copy of the book on September 16; the author glanced at it, initially expressing little interest, but soon sat down to

A late 1950s version of Ira's "bowing man" illustration, drawn
during the writing of *Lyrics on Several Occasions*.

peruse the volume with an occasional surprised exclamation at how good it
was.[131] Nine days later, he and Lee arrived in New York City for three and
a half weeks of "highlights, lowlights and at times shades of nightmare,"
filled with reluctantly performed obligations: meetings, book signings, and
newspaper and magazine interviews.[132] (The first publicity for the volume
came via excerpts published under the title "Which Came First?" in the
Saturday Review.) He was a "bit of a wreck" by the time the last conversation had been concluded: "It's all too much."[133]

Alfred and Blanche Knopf celebrated the official publication with a
cocktail party in honor of the author, during which he was toasted by family
(a rare visit with his brother Arthur), writers (Dashiell Hammett, Lillian
Hellman, Arthur Kober), songwriters (Arthur Schwartz, Betty Comden,
Adolph Green), performers (Lotte Lenya), critics (Kenneth Tynan), con-
ductors (Andre Kostelanetz), artists (Al Hirschfeld), record company executives (Goddard Lieberson), and more pesky journalists. More "hectivity"
(*sic*) took place the next day: the door of his suite was in constant motion as
he fielded congratulatory telephone calls and signed a mountain of books,
a chore that soon reduced his inscription to an impersonal "To Whom It
May Concern."[134]

Lyrics on Several Occasions was issued as part of Knopf's October 1959
list alongside John Hersey's novel *The War Lover* and another in a popular

series of cookbooks by Alfred Knopf's sister-in-law and shared bookstore shelf space with recent volumes by several of Ira's friends: Moss Hart (*Act One*), Herman Wouk (*This Is My God*), and Groucho Marx (*Groucho and Me*).[135] The reviews were not as numerous as he had hoped, and although largely positive, they did little to help sales, which reached only 3,700 copies by the end of the year.[136] One of the few notable assessments came from Ira's old friend Newman Levy, who placed Ira's lyrics above those of Larry Hart, Oscar Hammerstein, and Yip Harburg, while the "commentary, written with charm, wit and modesty, presents a revealing portrait of an urbane and erudite philosopher."[137]

PART SIX

Bidin' My Time

CHAPTER 20

B Y THE EARLY 1960s, Ira Gershwin's semifacetious remark that he was "really a bookkeeper" had more than a grain of truth in it.[1] His career as a lyricist, dormant for more than half a decade, showed little signs of revival, and the publication of *Lyrics on Several Occasions* was but a reminder of past glories. The book sold at a steady, if unspectacular pace, for nearly a year after publication, but returns eventually outweighed sales, and by the spring of 1961, its author was responsible for most of the purchases.[2] When a year later Ira's "first and only book" was remaindered, his disappointment was palpable.[3]

He was now content to spend his days behind his desk, following the stock market, answering correspondence, approving or rejecting the use of his songs or his brother's concert works, and working to bring some of George's unpublished music into the public eye. His activities in this area had begun in the early 1940s with *Porgy and Bess: A Symphonic Picture*, Robert Russell Bennett's popular suite arranged from the opera score. Bennett's work left George's own suite from the opera, composed after its closure, in the dark until the mid-1950s, when the orchestral parts were discovered in a closet in Ira's house. He brought the piece to the attention of conductor Maurice Abravanel and suggested it be called *Catfish Row*.[4] It was, he thought, "more musicianly than Bennett's synthesis."[5]

Due to Ira's persuasion, or with his cooperation, the Gershwin songs "Just Another Rhumba," "The Real American Folk Song (Is a Rag)," and "Hi-Ho!"; George's piano pieces "Walking the Dog" (as "Promenade"), "Merry Andrew" (renamed by Ira from *Rosalie*'s "Setting-Up Exercises"), and "Three-Quarter Blues" (from the 1920s "Irish Waltz"); and his broth-

Presenting Tony Bennett with the limited edition of "Hi-Ho!,"
New York City, May 1968.

er's *Lullaby* for string quartet all found their way to a still-clamoring-for-Gershwin audience. These years also saw the publication of a new edition of the *Porgy and Bess* vocal score that included the replacement words and phrases that he had labored to find for Goddard Lieberson's popular Columbia cast recording in 1951.[6]

A revised version of *Oh, Kay!* that opened off-Broadway in the spring of 1960 received Ira's approval, but he suspected that "some who know the score (especially after that well-made Columbia recording two years ago) will be a bit puzzled" by the interpolation of songs from *A Damsel in Distress* and *Lady, Be Good!* as well as two tunes from *Primrose* that he allowed P. G. Wodehouse to relyricize.[7] The low-budget production also added Wodehouse's famous character, the Earl of Blandings, to the plot, but the production failed to transfer to Broadway, leaving Ira cautious about librettist Guy Bolton's ideas for revivals of other Gershwin shows: "I still can't visualize whether the new setup would amount to anything."[8]

In his increasingly numerous hours of leisure, Ira hosted weekly poker games and pocket billiards tournaments, got "lots of exercise traipsing to the sellers' windows" at Santa Anita and Hollywood Park racetracks, but—due to his "sunny disposish"—avoided getting "too exercised not getting to the cashiers' windows."[9] He also frequently escaped to Las Vegas to play blackjack and roulette between watching the Rat Pack perform at the Sands Hotel: "I've never won there but have really had a good time not losing too much."[10] That streak of failure ended after New Year's Day 1961, when he returned to Beverly Hills in the black. Was this a good sign, he joked, or the end of the world as he knew it?[11] Ira's sixty-fifth birthday was celebrated with another trip to the desert: "I was out more thousands than I care to mention, but New Year's Eve I won back all my losses plus enough to pay all expenses. The game was baccarat and I had to play from midnight to 8 a.m., but despite aching back I managed to survive, tottered back to the hotel, slept three hours and got up to watch the Rose Bowl game on T.V. Pretty good going for an old man say I."[12] But age and a sedentary lifestyle *were* catching up with him; pinched nerves in his back and left leg and the aftereffects of three falls left him bedridden for several weeks.[13]

LEE GERSHWIN HAD no wish to descend into the depths of memory as her husband had done over the past few years, and the many charms of the rebuilt house in Beverly Hills eventually wore off, leaving her with a renewed itch to travel. Throughout the 1960s, Lee made lengthy journeys through Asia, Europe, and North Africa, all expensive propositions—no second-class traveler was she—and she told her husband, in letters and cards postmarked from far-off places, that she missed him, thanking him "again and again" for paying the bills that made all of it possible.[14] But for every "I'm a fool to be wandering around like this without you," there was a "maybe if you'd take me out to dinner once a week—or once every two weeks I wouldn't need the world."[15] Ira knew that his restless wife would eventually return "to unexotic Beverly Hills and unexciting (however charming) me,"[16] but he was also aware that she would never be content with the things that kept him—unproductively in her opinion—occupied.

Ira and Lee in the backyard of Lawrence D. Stewart's
Beverly Hills house, October 20, 1960. Photograph by
Lawrence D. Stewart.

Two YEARS AFTER the failure of the movie adaptation of *Porgy and Bess*,
Dorothy Heyward was still making insinuations. A new production of
the opera had opened at New York's City Center in the spring of 1961, yet
she was saying that Ira's intransigence in approving bookings had cost her
$100,000 annually.[17] Fed up, he replied that he was "a bit tired of having
you write irresponsible nonsense about me to the trustees of the Gershwin
Estate and to others." He reminded her that *she* had "stymied" many of
the movie deals by the "silly piece of paper" she had given Robert Breen:

> *And as for your insisting that . . . Breen made P&B, I must remind you
> that the . . . Crawford-Wildberg production, which was an inexpensive
> and even thinned-down presentation, played on & off for some 3 years,*

again to great notices. Meanwhile, continuously my brother's P&B music was heard on the airwaves and in concert halls and was climaxed in 1951 by Goddard Lieberson's wonderful 6 side LP album of the opera. Bob studied this album carefully and thus was able to present his *and Davis's excellent production of the opera. . . . I'm not taking anything away from Bob, I'm just insisting that P&B is more important than Bob Breen or any other director or producer of it.*[18]

Dorothy Heyward died in New York City in November 1961. Ira's attorney visited her grave, next to DuBose's, at St. Philip's Episcopal Church in Charleston, South Carolina, and told Ira that he "prayed that she get her story correct on the Gershwins, wherever she might be."[19]

IRA GERSHWIN WAS always a reluctant celebrity. Taking a bow was a joke; he would "be an addled rather than an added attraction."[20] But in the spring of 1963, he agreed to return to Manhattan for the first time in four years to help celebrate the forthcoming sixty-fifth anniversary of George Gershwin's birth. When a large party was held at his sister-in-law's apartment in Greenwich Village, Ira's friends were dumbstruck—he had actually left home! The highlight of the evening was when he was "pushed over to the piano," a copy of *Lyrics of Several Occasions* was found, and to the accompaniment of Burton Lane, Ira sang twenty of his songs, with friends and family joining in on the choruses. The following evening, he visited his sister Frankie and her family at their home in Westport, Connecticut, for another extended party in his honor. And once again, Ira held everyone's attention with his unique vocalizing. Frankie added her own take on some early Gershwin numbers, but Ira was more impressed by the "combination of figure and abstraction" that he saw in the paintings she had created.[21]

He was "busy every moment, recalling faces, being introduced, being kissed and being charming" at a Lincoln Center exhibition of paintings by his brother, but he was unimpressed when the poet Carl Sandburg cut in half one of Ira's prized Punch Royal Coronation cigars: "I doubt if I'll waste another pre-Castro on him." Three days later, he returned to the venue for a concert conducted by Andre Kostelanetz, where after the New York debuts of *Catfish Row* and *Promenade*, the maestro motioned for the lyricist to take a bow. Ira "got up halfway from my chair but hardly anyone could see me other than those in the immediate vicinity." After the encore, Kostelanetz again announced Ira's presence, so he "got up again, this time only ¼ up."[22]

BY 1963, A DECADE had elapsed since Ira's last work for the screen; *Park Avenue*, his last stage musical, was seventeen years in the past. Much had changed on Broadway. The lighthearted musicals he knew were disappearing, and when he visited New York City that year, he was introduced to one of the men who was responsible for the genre's transformation. Ira's friend Zero Mostel invited him to a performance of Stephen Sondheim's *A Funny Thing Happened on the Way to the Forum*, in which Mostel was starring. Ira thought that the "score even though not generally acclaimed worked well." After the show, Mostel introduced him to the composer/lyricist, who joined them at Sardi's. Sondheim knew "a lot of pretty special songs," and Ira was surprised, and no doubt pleased, to hear that one of his favorites was the obscure "There's No Holding Me" from *Park Avenue*.[23]

Ira's reluctance to again pick up his pen did not mean that he was being ignored. The late 1950s and early 1960s saw numerous offers. 1956: George S. Kaufman wanted to work with him and Alan Campbell on *The Lipstick War*; composer Sammy Fain thought about him for a musical version of *The Shop around the Corner* at MGM; and Broadway producers Cy Feuer and Ernest H. Martin inquired about his interest in *Whoop-Up*.[24] 1957: Ben Hecht asked Ira to be the lyricist on a Broadway version of *Twentieth Century*. 1959: Harold Arlen discussed an animated version of *A Christmas Carol* adapted by the playwright Christopher Fry.[25] 1961: producer Herman Levin suggested that Ira team up with Arlen and Harry Kurnitz on a musical version of Terence Rattigan's 1953 play, *The Sleeping Prince*.[26]

All were turned down with the well-known-to-his-friends excuse that he was working on another score. The closest he ever came to saying yes was in 1957, when he was offered *Merry Andrew*, a Danny Kaye movie musical about an eccentric college professor. Ira liked the idea and the script, but when producer Sol Siegel left the choice of composer to Ira and wanted a decision quickly, the lyricist became nervous and sickly; wondering if he had created a situation he could not get out of, he said no, and immediately felt better. This rejection of a solid project caused his agent to angrily predict that his client's days as a lyricist had come to an end.[27]

The type of songwriting that became increasingly important during this period was the writing of movie title songs, a field that lyricists Sammy Cahn and Johnny Mercer were successfully mining to their great financial benefit. But Ira needed a larger canvas; he felt uncomfortable finding ideas for songs that had little or no connection to a story. It was too much work for too little reward, and his natural lethargy prevented him from turning out lyrics to order.

THE GENESIS OF Ira Gershwin's final published work as a lyricist began at a wedding anniversary party for director William Wyler and his wife Talli in the fall of 1963, when director Billy Wilder asked Lee Gershwin how her husband could be persuaded to get back in the harness again: "To be asked by someone he admires," she responded.[28] Wilder, with an impeccable Hollywood track record (*Double Indemnity*, *The Lost Weekend*, *Sunset Boulevard*, *The Seven-Year Itch*, *Some Like It Hot*, and *The Apartment*) asked and Ira—surprisingly—agreed, even if Wilder had little idea what type of songs he wanted.

It was assumed that Ira would choose a composer with whom he had previously worked (Harry Warren) or a younger one who was familiar or currently popular (André Previn or Henry Mancini); instead, he opted to develop another set of songs from his brother's sketches. Once again, he needed the assistance of a seasoned composer to fashion the material; in this instance, Roger Edens. Unfortunately, it quickly became clear that no script had been "prepared in advance nor was the story line itself precisely laid out." Instead, Ira would have to devise a few novelty numbers to give Wilder and his screenwriting partner, I. A. L. Diamond, "ideas for building the story," which they eventually based on *L'ora della fantasia*, a 1944 play by Anna Bonacci, and which they gave the title *Kiss Me, Stupid*.[29]

SONGWRITING TOOK a back seat to the assassination of President John F. Kennedy in November 1963. Friends gathered at Ira's house to mourn and commiserate. He told his attorney that "we here like all good Americans have been devastated . . . and it'll take a long time—if ever—to get over it," an echo of comments Ira had made in the wake of his brother's passing.[30]

But life in Hollywood continued amid sorrow. Wilder told Ira that he thought an Italian-style waltz would ideally suit the film's star, Dean Martin, playing a Las Vegas lounge singer who gets stuck in a backwater Nevada town and meets two amateur songwriters who attempt to sell their songs to him. The waltz idea seemed okay, if a deliberate attempt to milk Martin's success with pastiches of Italian songs ("That's Amore" and "Volare" being the most successful). Ira was unhappy that "the ballad which I thought was required suddenly didn't seem needed." Depressed, he told his agent that Wilder could have the waltz, but that he wanted out of the project. Irving Lazar suggested that Ira should not be bothered by the director's mood changes, advice that gave Ira time to develop other treatments of the ballad that Wilder could play with.[31]

Perhaps he should have been more wary of the project, but his initial enthusiasm had yet to wear off, and when Wilder asked for one number "to be a rather 'nutty' one," Ira recalled an idea that he and George had worked up in the 1930s "for no particular show or reason." The phrase "I'm a poached egg without a piece of toast" had made its way into two songs that never reached Broadway—"You Know How It Is" (for *Rosalie*, 1928) and "It's Never Too Late to Mendelssohn" (*Lady in the Dark*, 1941); perhaps the right music could finally get it to work. Roger Edens played through almost two dozen of George's unpublished tunes before Edens and Ira settled on those intended for "I Can't Be Bothered Now" (1937) for the verse and "Are You Dancing?" (1930) for the chorus.[32]

Two songs—"Sophia" (the Italian number) and the ballad "All the Livelong Day (and the Long, Long Night)"—were largely complete by the end of 1963. The waltz tune for "Sophia" came from Ira's impression that the original opening bars of "Wake Up Brother, and Dance," which George had written in 4/4 time, had a Neapolitan flavor.[33] He took the music for the verse of "All the Livelong Day" from "Phoebe," a number he, George, and Lou Paley wrote during a visit to a summer camp in the Adirondacks in 1921.[34] A few days before *Kiss Me, Stupid* began filming at Goldwyn Studios, Ira sang the numbers to Wilder, Dean Martin, and the English actor and comedian Peter Sellers, coming off his success as Inspector Clouseau in *The Pink Panther* and slated to play one of the amateur songwriters.[35]

But Ira was already fed up: after three months of work, and no contract, Wilder still wanted him to "more-or-less jump" whenever he was needed.[36] And there was another problem—the movie's title, *Kiss Me, Stupid*, which Ira hoped Wilder would "think about twice—and change."[37] After seeing a preview of the bawdy film, Ira came up with more apposite titles: what about *Lust for Lust, Lust Horizon, Get Lust*, or *Dino's Didoes?*[38] Wilder stuck with the original, but the loss of Peter Sellers to a massive heart attack a few weeks into production altered everything; it was another bad omen, and Ira found it increasingly difficult to explain his participation.

Although he prepared the manuscripts of the three songs for publication and recordings in his usual meticulous way, he was unhappy with the lyrics that were to be sung in the movie and wanted Dean Martin's proposed Reprise disc to include the lines from the sheet music that Ira thought were better.[39] He began to reduce his expectations: "If the songs turn out to be n.s.g. [not so good] I want credit for good showmanship" but "don't blame the Gershwins—blame the high school music teacher and the garage man [the amateur songwriters] in the film."[40]

Released at the end of 1964, *Kiss Me, Stupid* left a bitter aftertaste, but Ira's thoughts of the movie's failure were deflected by the critics who, happily for him, focused on the risqué plot and wasted little ink on the songs. But it was an indication that Ira might have written his last lyric, whether his musical partner was alive or dead: "I don't want to tackle any further Broadway or Hollywood commitments. It is too tough struggling with most of the unpublished music without having the composer at my side."[41]

"ONE THING the IRS has never had to worry about is my statement of income: even the dollar or two I usually get from Harry Warren's company is always declared."[42] Money—even if it came in regularly and in amounts that continually surprised him, given the new world of music of which he had little understanding—was rarely far from Ira's thoughts. Although he was fond of his longtime publisher Max Dreyfus—a "most accommodating and sociable soul" when in a friendly mood—the annual publishing contract renewal that he had been signing since 1919 had become a deterrent if a songwriting partnership required him to publish with a firm other than Chappell.[43] "As you know," he told his attorney, "this does not make me a good business man, but I have always signed for sentimental reasons."[44]

The subject that worried Ira more than any other was how—if he was no longer going to make money from new writing—to secure a solid financial future for himself and, after his death, for Lee. For most of their careers, he and George had relied on agents, some of whom may not have completely understood the complex agreements prepared for the Gershwins' signatures.[45] Ira became convinced that, for many decades, he and his brother's estate had been "taken terrible advantage of" by their publishers.[46] In an attempt to prove this theory, he asked Leonard Saxe to analyze hundreds of George and Ira's royalty statements; after much effort, Saxe concluded that, since 1937, the allocation of George's copyrights to the New World Music and Gershwin Publishing Corporation imprints had resulted in the family's being underpaid by at least $500,000.[47]

Saxe and Ira suggested to Ira's siblings (whom Saxe was also representing in the matter) that a new corporation be created to hold all the renewed domestic copyrights of the Gershwin Publishing Corporation as well as all of George and Ira's unpublished compositions; by this method, the monetary losses would be returned over time in the form of dividends, rather than in a lump sum that would be depleted by income taxes. Sixty percent of the new company would be owned by the Gershwin siblings and 40 percent by Chappell.[48]

The initial discussions between Saxe and some of Chappell's executives were encouraging, but Ira insisted that he did not want a repeat of what had occurred in the early 1930s, when Max Dreyfus sold his publishing interests to Warner Bros. without giving the Gershwins a chance to profit from the deal; he asked that the new agreement include a clause that gave him and his siblings the chance to pull their publishing out of any sale of Chappell to another company or that would, at the very least, provide them with a benefit from such a transaction.[49] Ira was certain that his publisher would "bend backwards" to retain his rights in the Gershwin catalog.[50] But the death of Max Dreyfus in the spring of 1964 and the ramifications of the sale of his holdings to his brother Louis brought negotiations to a crashing halt. Louis Dreyfus, Ira said, may have been worth $100 million, but "still hasn't changed when it comes to dimes and quarters."[51]

It took another year to conclude the deal and to create the new publishing concern, New Dawn Music. Ira reluctantly returned to Manhattan to sign the documents, complaining that it was "all terribly complicated."[52] The internal family agreement for the creation of New Dawn was signed by all the parties in June 1965, but when Leonard Saxe laid out his expectations of what the family would recoup in lost revenue and what he expected as payment for his five years of work on the deal, it was clear that Ira, Arthur, and Frankie had no true concept of what they had agreed to.[53]

The attorney explained that all three would share in the funds that could be obtained from the point in July 1962 when the money that had been siphoned off was returned to GPC; Saxe thought a reasonable fee for his services was 10 percent of the total from each sibling, and another 5 percent if the returned funds were paid out in capital gains rather than as a lump sum.[54] Ira, thinking in the short term, wondered how he could be expected to pay up front for returns he would see over time. His siblings asked to have the payments extended over two or three years. Saxe stood his ground; any other lawyer would have charged them much more than he was asking.[55]

Ira's reluctance to part with his money began to rot the almost fraternal relationship that he had developed with his attorney. Saxe agreed to accept $25,000 but reminded Ira that he could deduct half of the amount from his taxes; he was surprised that Ira failed to comprehend what had been done on his behalf. Ira claimed that he had never been told how much the work would cost and begged off paying so much; it had been an expensive year, and this amount, on top of the raise in salary that Lawrence Stewart wanted, was just too much.[56] Saxe suspected that Sam Berke, Ira's financial adviser, was behind the negativity; it seemed that Ira had conveniently forgotten how much money Saxe had made for him over the years, not just as his attorney, but through his frequent investment tips.[57] Lee Gershwin joined the battle, berating Saxe for insisting on a fee and thus causing Ira to become depressed and take to his bed.[58] Although he tried to mend the fences, Ira's relationship with Leonard Saxe dissolved into a strictly attorney/client one as the decade continued.

EVEN WITH MONEY at the forefront of his thoughts during his 1965 visit to
New York City, he still made his rare presence felt in the city of his birth,
even if it had changed in his eyes. Emily Paley gave another party for him
in Greenwich Village, but he found the neighborhood now "full of weird-
ies, mostly fairies."[59] He also visited his sister again, and Frankie expressed
amazement, after reading *Lyrics on Several Occasions*, at her older brother's
intellect.[60] For his part, Ira adored Frankie, but an aversion to disharmony
meant that the lack of affection between his wife and his sister kept him
from expressing it as much as he may have wished.[61]

He once again attended the *Promenade* concert, and once again, while
conductor Andre Kostelanetz held up a copy of Ira's book during his introduction of its author, he was persuaded to step into "a pink light . . . from
the gallery or somewhere" and take a few bows.[62] A visit to the World's Fair
saw a food indulgence that matched that of Europe in 1928:

Ira with his sister-in-law, Emily Paley, Beverly Hills, August 1964.

*I ordered the smorgasbord . . . and I got a heaping plate of shrimp, pate,
salami, etc. & draught beer, all of which I downed. Then came a plate
of smoked salmon with dill sauce. "For me?" So I ate that. Then came
a plate of veal and pork sausage. "Not for me again?" "Yes, sir." So I ate
that too and ordered coffee and with coffee came a big triangle of rich
chocolate, apple and what-not else in it and several kinds of cheese. So
I ate that too, leaving just a small piece of the cake. I figured, what the
hell, I'll gain 3 or 4 lbs., so what? And woefully I undressed and weighed
myself and the register showed 181 lbs. which was exactly 5 pounds more
than I carried after this morning's coffee.*[63]

He also reacquainted himself with the joys of peregrination: a forty-minute walk from his hotel to the Chappell offices on Fifth Avenue and back again merited this comment from the typically sedentary lyricist: "Should you think this isn't much of a feat (good spot for a lousy pun), let me add that the temp. was about 87° while the humidity had everyone who walked more than 3 or 4 blocks, dripping. Even my community-property spouse was impressed."[64]

THE 1960S WERE also occupied by Ira's discussions with cultural institutions about George Gershwin's original manuscripts and memorabilia. The Gershwin Collection that took shape at the Library of Congress in 1939 had expanded via manuscript donations from numerous sources, including Ira, but it was a surprise—and a cause for quiet, personal celebration—when, in 1962, the head of the Music Division asked for items related to *Ira's* career.[65] Three years later, during a brief trip to Washington, DC, he was thrilled to see his brother's desk, looking "smart" between those of Rachmaninoff and Victor Herbert, while George's portrait of Arnold Schoenberg hung on the wall above it.[66]

Ira was proud; George richly deserved the acclaim, and he remained on guard against anyone who claimed to have had a significant influence on George's compositions. In 1949, he had refuted an assertion that George had borrowed rhythms and themes from Darius Milhaud's 1923 ballet *Creation of the World* in writing *Rhapsody in Blue*; George, he said, "was about as influenced by 'Creation of the World' as by Frescobaldi's 'Chaconne and Passacaglia' or Patagonian Bebop."[67] Another such claimant was the composer and music theorist Joseph Schillinger, with whom George studied in the 1930s; Schillinger's lessons, Ira wrote, "unquestionably broaden musical horizons, but they don't inspire an opera like *Porgy and Bess* or a symphonic piece like *Concerto in F.*"[68]

THE FINANCIAL STATEMENTS for the Rose Gershwin Testamentary Trust in 1965 were a pleasant surprise: a gross income of $430,000, the largest annual amount it had ever earned.[69] The figure was a tribute to the continuing popularity of his brother's music. As the work of the composers and lyricists of the 1920s through the 1940s morphed into what is now known as the Great American Songbook, the Gershwins were among those who found the most appreciation, from singers as well as from jazz musicians, who took George's rhythms and melodies and turned them inside out.

Ira preferred to hear his songs in their original context; he appreciated their afterlife, but was not always pleased by what was done to his carefully crafted words. He generally obliged requests for changes to create duets or to make a song fit the gender of the singer, but took umbrage at the abuse to which his lyrics were subjected by those who changed "tense and sense, and suddenly rhyme doesn't chime."[70] Not even Frank Sinatra was immune from criticism; Ira blanched when he heard Sinatra's recording of "A Foggy Day," in which the singer added a beat to the tune and changed Ira's original line "I viewed the morning with alarm" to "I viewed the morning with *much* alarm."[71]

In a 1959 interview published in the jazz magazine *Down Beat* as part of a special *Porgy and Bess* issue that coincided with the opening of Samuel Goldwyn's movie, Ira was described as "the comfortable custodian of the Gershwin estate and saga" who had begun a new hobby: collecting all the new recordings of songs from his brother's opera. "But there are so many of them," Ira lamented, "where does it end?" Although he was never a jazz fan, Ira acknowledged that repeated listening to Miles Davis's Columbia disc had given him a greater appreciation of what the trumpeter and arranger Gil Evans had accomplished, and while he had at first been surprised by Ella Fitzgerald taking on some of the male parts in her Verve set with Louis

Armstrong, he eventually found it "effective," and their duet on "There's a Boat Dat's Leavin' Soon for New York" was "really quite unexpected, to put it mildly."[72]

That same year, Ira was approached by the jazz impresario and modern art collector Norman Granz with the idea of having Fitzgerald continue her successful multidisc *Songbook* recordings with an all-Gershwin set. While it was not the first such project—the vocalist Lee Wiley had released an octet of Gershwin songs for the Liberty Music Shop label in 1939, and Fitzgerald herself had made a single disc of Gershwin numbers for Decca in 1950—Ira was encouraged by the notion that what Granz had in mind was a "comprehensive" survey of his and George's catalog.[73] He eagerly made suggestions on repertoire and interpretation: although his lyrics for "Just Another Rhumba" were "somewhat dated," George's music was not,[74] and he asked Fitzgerald to do the verse of "The Real American Folk Song (Is a Rag)," as the point of the song "was to contrast the sweet and barcarolle verse with the ragtime chorus."[75]

The income surge of the 1960s was also the result of publishing deals that exploited the Gershwin catalog in new ways. Ira had approved the use of "They Can't Take That Away from Me" for a Kodak commercial in 1963 in what appears to be the first use of a Gershwin song in that medium.[76] The following year, he gave his blessing to the recording of "Your Mother's Here to Stay" by the satirist Allan Sherman. Ira found him a "most charming gent" when he came to visit,[77] but after hearing complaints that the parody of "Love Is Here to Stay" had "cheapened a standard," he agreed to say no to any further parodic attempts.[78] And in 1965, the mechanicals and small performance rights to the Gershwin songs used in *When the Boys Meet the Girls*, an updated MGM movie adaptation of *Girl Crazy*, were accompanied by the rights to non-Gershwin songs by other performers in the film. When the recording of "Listen People" by Herman's Hermits became a top-ten hit, New World Music—and the Gershwin family—reaped the financial benefit. Ira remained ambivalent: "As for Herman and his ubiquitous Hermits," he wrote, "We'll overlook their tresses / If their sales are big successes."[79]

CHAPTER 21

I N EARLY JUNE 1966, Ira traveled to the University of Maryland in College Park to be awarded an honorary degree of Doctor of Fine Arts, in a ceremony that took place at 10 a.m.—an early hour for the inveterate late riser. The gathered spectators heard the reading of a citation that stated that Ira "has charmed us with a unique mixture of wisdom and whimsicality, of satire and sentiment. He has laughed at man's foibles, been amused by his peccadilloes, but has never failed in fun and good humor." Columnist Leonard Lyons joked that the walk that Ira took from his seat to the stage to pick up the degree was the lengthiest of his life.[1]

If Ira wondered how he "deserved such an accolade," Lee Gershwin had no such doubts; she watched with pleasure as her husband received his hood from the university's dean and president.[2] Although he often made a joke of the award—saying that his "old friends . . . can slap me on the back and call me 'Doc,'"[3] that DFA stood for "Division Freight Agent,"[4] and that the chart success of a pop group's recording of "I Got Rhythm" might have given the university doubts about giving him the degree[5]—the honors were "pretty good for a man" whose "greatest claim to fame was that he had two emergency appendectomies, the second, thirty years after the first."[6]

EVEN AFTER RECEIVING the additional honor of being feted at the Library of Congress prior to the degree ceremony, Ira considered placing at least some of his "Gershwiniana" in another institution. Lee and publicist Irving Drutman were sent East to evaluate the merits of the Brooklyn Museum, the George Gershwin Theatre at the University of Brooklyn, the Museum

Posing with Testudo, the University of Maryland's terrapin mascot, during the celebrations surrounding Ira's receiving an honorary doctorate of fine arts, June 1966.

of the Performing Arts at Lincoln Center, Columbia University's archives, and the Museum of the City of New York (MCNY). The last was judged the most impressive, and Lawrence Stewart was directed to inform the head of the Music Division at the Library of Congress about the decision, thus beginning a two-year tug-of-war between the city of the Gershwins' birth and the nation's capital.[7]

The following year, Ira loaned the etched sterling silver tray that his brother had received after the opening night of *Porgy and Bess* for an MCNY exhibition on the musicals of the 1930s. He was told that space would be set aside in the museum's existing building for the tray until a new wing and a new "Gershwin Room" to house George and Ira's memorabilia was built. The cost was expected to be approximately $50,000; Ira was encouraged to contribute money for the construction,[8] and he agreed to donate the tray and to give the museum $5,000.[9]

Ira and Lee could never manage such a project themselves, and when a reporter from the *New York Times* asked Ira to speak about the museum, Lawrence Stewart was deputed to answer on the lyricist's behalf.[10] The *Times* article indicated that Ira would give the New York museum nearly all his Gershwin memorabilia as well as George's "favorite piano." The Library of Congress was "not 100 per cent enthusiastic about dividing the collection" but "deferred to Ira's wishes."[11] Shortly thereafter, Stewart was forced to say that the reporter had misunderstood or mischaracterized some of what he had been told.[12]

The wisdom of Ira's decision was quickly called into question: the *Times* published a second article in which the haphazard state of the MCNY theater collection was emphasized, revealing that "valuable memorabilia amid clutter" was "commonplace" and that only one full-time employee worked on the collection. "If I dropped dead tomorrow," curator Sam Pearce admitted, "I haven't any idea how anybody would find anything." But the hiring of an assistant allowed Pearce to hint that "the chaos that we are in now is leading somewhere."[13]

The success of the *Musicals of the 1930s* exhibition convinced Pearce that "somewhere" was a separate building to house the theater collection, but where was the money to come from to make that dream a reality? One solution was to again ask Ira, this time by promising him that an exhibition dedicated to the Gershwins would become the foundation for a future Gershwin Room. With no existing display of Gershwin material at the Library of Congress, Ira agreed to pledge $10,000 for the project beginning in 1968.[14]

THE THEATER COLLECTION would never move to another building, but when Ira was assured that space would be found for the Gershwin material in the existing structure, he agreed to lend hundreds of items from his archive for the lavish exhibition, to persuade others to do so, and to appear at the opening. Again, Lawrence Stewart handled most of the details.[15] Although regretting that the walls of his house would "be as bare as *Playboy*'s centerpieces," Ira was content, knowing that he could put off any decisions about future donations to the museum.[16] The publicity about the decision to give his memorabilia to the Museum of the City of New York still rankled at the Library of Congress, and it took Ira's personal intervention to convince Harold Spivacke, the head of the Music Division, to loan anything from its collection.[17] In the end, Spivacke agreed to provide only those Gershwin manuscripts that Ira had personally donated.[18]

The lyricist rebuffed attempts by the museum staff to burnish his ego by putting his name first in the exhibition title; Ira said that he would never deserve top billing over his brother. He joked about calling the exhibition *Principally George (and Incidentally Ira)*[19] but insisted that he would not attend the opening unless they agreed to *GERSHWIN / George the Music / Ira the Words*, a reversal of the inscription George had had etched on a lighter he gave to his older brother to celebrate the opening night of *Girl Crazy*.[20]

Ira assured the museum that he would supply the necessary funds to make the exhibition a reality,[21] but when he arrived in New York City for the opening in early May, he found Lee in a rage over the prominence of Edward Jablonski's name on the wall labels. A stunned Ira looked away, puffed on his cigar, and said nothing.[22] Her harsh judgments were not uncommon; Lee often left others with a "dread of being in her presence,"

With bandleader Skitch Henderson and Harold Arlen
at the opening of the Gershwin exhibition at the Museum of the
City of New York, May 5, 1968.

so it was with a sense of relief that when Ira visited the apartment of his nephew, Leopold Godowsky III, and his recent bride, Elaine, he came alone and enjoyed an evening with friends and family in which everyone became "a little loopy because Lee wasn't around."[23]

Ira found the attention aimed at him during a private reception and preview of the exhibition "all very embarrassing," admitting that "I'm not as shy as I used to be but I'm still pretty shy." But he agreed to pose for pictures and happily chatted with Sam Behrman, Anita Loos, Adele Astaire, Arthur Schwartz, Roddy McDowell, Betty Comden, Adolph Green, Dorothy Fields, Robert Breen, and Eva Jessye, while Harold Spivacke "prowled around casing the opposition."[24] Although Ira and Lee were heard in public praising the exhibition, privately she demanded that Jablonski's name be removed from the wall labels and had her sister return to the museum to verify that this had been done. She complained that alphabetizing the names of those who had loaned items for the exhibition meant that Ira's contribution—much larger in numbers than any other lender—went unrecognized; she also kowtowed the museum staff into dimming the lights of George's portrait of Emily Paley, while raising them over her own.[25] These outbursts reached a boiling point when three staffers from the museum came to see the couple at their hotel; they were shocked by Lee's intensity and had little to offer to relieve the difficult situation.[26]

IRA RETURNED to Beverly Hills "pretty much exhausted" physically and mentally.[27] Emotions were raw, and he wished that these problems would disappear, leaving him to contentedly resume sorting through his papers and watching television. But reality continued to break through the walls that he had so meticulously raised around his life. The assassination of Robert F. Kennedy stunned them all, yet failed to prevent Lee from fuming over what had occurred in New York City; she took verbal jabs at everyone, while Lawrence Stewart—after thirteen years of working at an unrealistically low salary—considered his future. Emily Paley and Leo Godowsky suggested that he ask Ira for a pension, but Stewart knew that Ira lived in a fantasy world when it came to money: a higher wage—maybe; long-term financial assistance—unlikely.[28] When a contract was suggested, Stewart was told that it might be better to wait and see if he was left something in

Ira's will; this worried Stewart too; did he want his future placed in the
hands of Ira's increasingly hostile wife?[29]

IRA'S ATTORNEY Leonard Saxe was taken ill with multiple attacks of angina
in the months following the tumultuous birth of New Dawn Music in
1966.[30] When Saxe unexpectedly passed away at the age of sixty-nine on
June 29, 1968, Ira was left to wonder whether the bitter words of two years
earlier had somehow contributed to his death. Stunned by the loss of the
man he considered his "guardian angel when it comes to my job as an Estate
Trustee," Ira became paralyzed.[31] Lee's coldness and the uncertainty about
Lawrence Stewart's future only added further weight onto his shoulders.[32]

Saxe had no legal partner to take over his affairs, which left an increasingly puzzled Ira to deal with "more legal and other matters . . . than ever
before."[33] He sought advice from his brother-in-law, but Lee objected to
Leo Godowsky playing any part in her husband's business affairs.[34] At the
recommendation of Ira's business manager, a young Los Angeles tax lawyer
named Ron Blanc, a specialist in the fields of entertainment, television, and
movies, was hired a few weeks after Saxe's death to handle a dispute over
the ownership of a set of manuscripts from George and Ira's final work
together.[35] Four years later, Blanc's work led to the federal government
gaining custody of the manuscripts from the public administrator in New
York County, and Ira was able to get a tax break on the donation to the
Library of Congress.[36]

At the same time, Ira was considering which items to donate to the
Museum of the City of New York; to that end, Lawrence Stewart was again
sent to New York City, to introduce Ron Blanc to the East Coast members
of the Gershwin family and their representatives and to coordinate the
disposition of the items from the exhibition.[37] Stewart was reluctant to go,
but acceded to Ira's wishes—if nothing else, it would take him away from
the madness that was enveloping 1021 North Roxbury Drive.[38]

A week after his arrival, Ira and Stewart spoke on the telephone, a conversation so full of shocks and surprises that Stewart felt the need to follow
it up with a full-length report. He had met with Ralph Miller, the museum's director, expecting to hear that a temporary location for a Gershwin
Room had been selected; instead, he was told that the museum trustees and

its chairman, Louis Auchincloss, were dismayed to see most of the items loaned for the exhibition being returned to their owners. Although Miller tried to alleviate their concerns—some of the loaned material would be donated later, he said—he was told to inform Stewart that even a *temporary* Gershwin Room would not happen unless most of the money came from Ira. Stewart advised Miller that Ira would not give the museum a large sum of money, but he asked Ira if it were possible to add a bequest to the museum in his will. Stewart concluded his report by suggesting an alternative solution: make it known that the creation of a Gershwin Room was no longer something Ira was interested in but that he would donate some of his memorabilia to the museum's general collection.[39]

It was the final straw. When Lee heard what had been suggested, her anger intensified. But the target of her outbursts was not Ira, on whom she was financially dependent and who once again was physically ailing and unwilling to argue—having taken a fall that kept him largely confined to his bedroom—but Lawrence Stewart.[40] After hearing Lee accuse him of partial responsibility for the mismanagement of the exhibition, Stewart walked out.[41] On January 10, 1969, he returned to pick up his severance check and found his former employer flat on his bed, curtains closed and lights low—a mirror image of the final days of George Gershwin. The two men exchanged a few words. As Stewart departed, Lee's laughter was symbolic of their triangular relationship: Stewart had fashioned a way to deal with Ira's passivity and his willful ignorance of reality, as well as with Lee's resentments and unforgiving nature.[42] But the relationship had finally—permanently—fractured, and it took Emily Paley's influence—at the risk of her own financial dependence on her brother-in-law—to convince a reluctant Ira to even write Stewart's final check.[43]

THE FULL DAYS that had once been spent at his desk were drastically reduced in 1969. Although Ira felt better by summer, he still required a cane to get around.[44] Then in October, after completing a rare radio interview, he was diagnosed with Bell's palsy, a paralysis of the facial muscles that led to a constant tearing up of one eye and a noticeable droop on one side of his face. To cover this deformity, he grew a moustache, something he had not done since he was twenty years old, and worked with a physical therapist to strengthen his facial muscles.[45] Always a reluctant subject for photographs, he could now use the Bell's palsy as an excuse: "If I was not photogenic at that time [1954] I am far less so today."[46]

The turbulent decade that saw the last new lyrics from Ira Gershwin's pen ended on a rare personal note when Ira reminded his wife that "43 years ago—and 5 months before we were married—you wrote the 14 words contained in the attached envelope [that held the visiting card she had left him in 1926]. And of course I felt about you as you felt about me; and 43 years from now I'll feel the same way about you and hope you'll feel the same way about me."[47] It was an acknowledgment of the debt he owed her; after all, Lee Gershwin had created the unique atmosphere that provided Ira with the opportunity to exist in his private world of words.

CHAPTER 22

IRA GERSHWIN ENTERED the 1970s a man adrift. A price had finally been paid for his penury; for the want of a few thousand dollars, he had lost the two men who had been the most significant barriers between him and the outside world. Leonard Saxe, his contemporary and friend, the man who had helped him navigate the treacherous shoals of finance and contracts for twenty years, was dead; Lawrence Stewart, the younger man who, for seventeen years, was simultaneously Ira's greatest fan and a scholarly presence in whom the lyricist could confide, had been condemned to a purgatory that rendered him nameless in the lives of those he had come to know and love. Edgar Carter, a former literary agent—most notably for the celebrated mystery writer Raymond Chandler—took over as Ira's secretary. Carter was "a gentleman and a good guy to be around," but could not replace them.[1]

His sense of isolation was enhanced by other instances of mortality among his friends and colleagues at the end of the 1960s. The January 1967 death of Albert Sirmay, George and Ira's devoted music editor at Chappell, was followed, thirteen months later, by that of Ira's friend, the writer and raconteur Harry Kurnitz. The September 1968 suicide of the author Charles Jackson (*The Lost Weekend*)—a frequent visitor to Beverly Hills during the 1940s—was followed shortly thereafter by the death of producer William Perlberg. Ira acknowledged the passing of these friends but remained outwardly unaffected, except in the case of Kurnitz; in a rare public display, he functioned as one of the honorary pallbearers at the memorial service. It was "a sad but dignified occasion." Kurnitz "was so beloved that not only all of his friends here were there but many flew out

In the back garden of his Beverly Hills home, 1970s. Note the mustache
and the initials sewn on his shirt pocket.

from New York, and one even from Spain. I know no one who didn't feel
it was a privilege to know Harry."[2]

In addition, there were his ever-encroaching health issues: the Bell's
palsy, bursitis-induced spasms in his right arm and leg, accidents that led
to hospitalizations, and an increased reliance on prescription medications
all combined to make Ira unwilling to leave his house for more than a brief
time.[3] The world now increasingly came to him—his barber, his tailor,
his doctor—and the premiere of George Balanchine's ballet *Who Cares?*
at Lincoln Center in 1970 passed largely without his input or notice. The
idea of using a selection of his brother's unpublished tunes for a ballet had
once been the lyricist's "Project #1" when he suggested that Balanchine
might create a "group of short choreographic vignettes" of New York City,
but the 1964 recording of "A Frenchman in New York," Darius Milhaud's

homage to George that used titles for its six movements that were similar to those Ira had suggested, left the idea in limbo. Balanchine returned to the concept in the late 1960s, and Ira gave his blessing to a work that was largely based on songs from the 1932 *Song-Book*.[4]

By March 1970, Ira had been having daily sessions with a physical therapist and hoped to soon be "getting the better" of his ailment.[5] But the following month he was back at Cedars of Lebanon to be treated for more spasms by Dr. Corday, a stay that was extended when he took a fall; upon his release, he began taking the prescription blood thinner Coumadin and resumed physical therapy.[6] "I haven't been functioning 100%, or even 75%, the past few months," he told a correspondent.[7] What may have disturbed him even more than his ailments was the time he committed to correcting the galleys of David Ewen's revised biography of George Gershwin: three hours for one paragraph about the 1924 chronology of *Rhapsody in Blue* left him asking, "How did I ever get into this thing?"[8] He remained unhappy when *George Gershwin: His Journey to Greatness* was published in the fall of 1970: the book was as sloppy about facts as the original had been; the appendix listed songs that incorrectly credited Ira or failed to include his collaborators, an oversight he considered "terribly important and very embarrassing to me."[9] The situation was made worse by Ewen's statements that his book was "authorized [and] definitive" and that he had been "chosen to write it," implying that Ira had blessed both it and its author.[10]

"The past three years have been most unkind, to put it mildly, to corporeal me," he told a correspondent. Unable to travel, Ira was reduced to walking "around the block once a day."[11] But his sedentary life was brightened by regular visits from nephews and nieces; from friends like Angie Dickinson, Norman Granz, Arthur Freed, Yip Harburg, Richard Conte, Marianne Stewart, Irving Lazar, Paul Stewart, and Sam Marx, who joined him for poker and reminiscences; and from business associates Ron Blanc and Sam Berke, who sought Ira's advice on contracts and kept him informed of the still steady popularity of his songs and his brother's concert works.

Although he continued to be bothered by what his doctor was "pleased to call a slight spasm," Ira was able to spend a brief period at his desk every day to check his stocks and to try and keep up with the steady flow of business correspondence and letters from Gershwin fans. By the spring of

1971, he was nearing a full recovery.[12] But on May 21, just eleven days after finishing a lengthy series of physical therapy appointments, he fractured the upper humerus in his right arm in a bathroom fall. By the end of the month, a male nurse was hired for twelve-hour overnight duty.[13] Although prevented from using a typewriter due to his fractured arm and recurrent spasms, he continued his correspondence by pen, the humor still present even though the body was failing, as evidenced by a reference to his attorney having been on the Grand Tour "as we used to call it in the 18th century."[14] But by 1973, most of Ira's written communications with the outside world were handled by his secretary.

HIS FAVORITE VISITOR was always his sister-in-law Emily Paley, who frequently spent her summers with Ira and Lee in Beverly Hills after the death of her husband in 1952. Of all the women in the world, Ira had more love for Emily than any other; she brought a welcome sunniness to an otherwise often chilly household. When Ira turned seventy-five, she playfully reminded him of their first meeting, writing that he would "always be the darling young man of May 27, 1917. You were adorable then; you were witty and erudite and gifted, and you liked lox. To me you have changed hardly at all."[15] Although he received many congratulatory messages and telephone calls, and songwriter Arthur Hamilton ("Cry Me a River") presented him with a proclamation declaring "Ira Gershwin Week" in Los Angeles, Emily's heartfelt words were the most precious.[16]

Less than three months after that birthday, Dr. Corday and a nurse were summoned to the house after Ira complained of chest pain. An EKG was taken, and an ambulance arrived to whisk the patient to the hospital, where, for nearly a week, Ira underwent cardiac care, at times in the intensive care unit.[17] A few weeks after returning home, his longtime business manager, Sam Berke, died of a heart attack, and more responsibility was placed on the shoulders of Ron Blanc. Since Ira "never left the house," the pair's meetings were held in the late afternoons around the table in the family room or in Ira's bedroom. It was easy to talk with him, Blanc recalled. While the lyricist was clearly slowed down by his ailments, his physical deterioration did not affect the quality of his thinking. If an issue became overly technical or family-oriented, Lee would sit in, and Ira frequently consulted her about the suitability of a particular piece of music for an intended project.[18]

Although more reluctant than ever to be interviewed, fearing that he would "say something that will offend someone,"[19] and still recovering from his numerous maladies ("for the past three years this AK has been N.S.G."),[20] Ira agreed to a request from his friend Alfred Simon and the young musical theater historian Robert Kimball to allow them to pay extended visits to Beverly Hills in the summer of 1972 to do research for *The Gershwins*, an elaborate coffee-table book published by Atheneum the following year. Kimball found Ira to be modest and self-deprecating: "He said, 'Look, the book should be about my brother, not me,'" but "reluctantly accepted" that his own career should be explored. "Ira was supportive, without ever really asking us to tell him what we were doing." The pair worked in the billiard room in the basement that had been partially converted into an area for Ira's assistants. Ira made an appearance in the early afternoons to say "Boys, I hope I'm not disturbing you." Kimball recalled the day when Ira had a modicum of energy and asked Al Simon if he remembered the score to *Of Thee I Sing*. "Al at the piano, without a score, and Ira, just sitting there, remembering everything. Ira set the tempi, and I remember different parts of it where he sounded like a Jewish cantor doing 'The Senatorial Roll Call.' It was mind-blowing."[21] A recent CBS television production of the musical may have triggered the performance. It had been difficult to produce any of the three political shows due to the divide between Ira and the archconservative Morrie Ryskind (George S. Kaufman had passed away in 1961), but this production—broadcast in a presidential election year and with the lead roles played by the popular actors Carroll O'Connor (*All in the Family*) and Cloris Leachman (*The Mary Tyler Moore Show*)—met with approval, and Ira was in front of his television set when it aired.

DUE TO copyright issues in the late 1950s, *Lyrics on Several Occasions* was originally published only in the United States and Canada. A glimmer of hope for a British edition was W. H. Auden's attempt to have the volume issued by his book club, the Readers' Subscription; the poet also offered his assistance in trying to interest Faber & Faber, even suggesting that he might write an introduction.[22] But the 1960 sale of Knopf to Random House halted any progress at the time.

Every so often, Ira wondered if his book could find a new audience, but his suggestion of a paperback edition was quickly shot down, and he reluctantly agreed; it "would possibly be too limited to make it worth any while."[23] Five years after publication, he was disappointed to learn that Knopf's stock of the book would last thirty years and that the remaining sets of unbound sheets were to be pulped.[24] By the early 1970s, the meager sales of Ira's "one and only hard-cover classic"[25] caused him to purchase the remaining stock before the title was taken off the market.[26] It was only in 1977 that a small British publisher, Elm Tree Books, issued *Lyrics on Several Occasions* in the United Kingdom, but the volume sold so poorly that, shortly before his death, Ira once again purchased the remaining copies.[27]

In 1973, the seventy-fifth anniversary of George's birth was celebrated by the publication of *The Gershwins*, an updated edition of *The Gershwin Years*, and—surprise—a Viking Press paperback edition of *Lyrics on Several Occasions*, with a new introduction by Betty Comden and Adolph Green. It sold only a few thousand copies.[28]

Ira wanted to try to continue working on George's unpublished tunes, but by the early 1970s, his intake of medications for high blood pressure and a heart condition, combined with his use of sedatives and Valium, left him incapable of making any concerted effort on the project.[29] April 1975 saw another fall; he was again a "rhapsody in bruise."[30] He broke several ribs, punctured a lung, and spent ten days at the UCLA Medical Center to be treated for internal bleeding.[31] This slow recovery gave him the excuse he needed to avoid charity tribute concerts held in his honor in Los Angeles and New York later that year.

PRODUCTIONS OF *Porgy and Bess* attracted audiences throughout the world—barring the United States—through the 1960s; by the following decade, American producers were avoiding the opera for fear of offending Black audiences who saw it as racially insensitive. But during 1975, producer Sherwin Goldman came to Ira with the idea of restoring *Porgy and Bess* to the way audiences in Boston had heard it before it was cut for Broadway. Ira was skeptical: why "tamper" with the version that everyone knew and loved? Lee suggested an experimental production in an out-of-the-way location.[32] This small idea grew into a full-scale, magnificently received production at the Houston Grand Opera in July 1976, followed by an equally enthusiastic response in New York City. Almost thirty years after George Gershwin's death, Ira was justifiably proud that his brother's magnum opus was now regarded as what its creators believed it to be all along—a true American operatic masterpiece.

IN EARLY 1977, Edgar Carter resigned from his secretarial job after a cancer diagnosis; the hiring of his replacement, Walter Reilly, who had once worked for the Theatre Guild, was not as vital to Ira's future comfort as the appearance that summer of a young man from Ohio. Michael Feinstein had moved to California at the age of twenty to pursue a singing career, and on July 18, 1977, he knocked on the front door of 1021 North Roxbury Drive, having been introduced to Lee Gershwin via Oscar Levant's widow, June.[33] At a young age, Feinstein had become obsessed with the Great American Songbook and was familiar with obscure corners of George and Ira's song catalog that the ailing eighty-year-old lyricist had forgotten. Ira took an instant liking to him; Lee, seeing the positive effect Feinstein's enthusiasm had on her husband, asked if he would like to come work for them. Although he spent a significant amount of his time working with Ira's archives, becoming his "demon discographer," Feinstein's most important mission was to "keep Ira happy" by engaging him with the recordings, manuscripts, and sheet music in Ira's vast collection.[34] Hearing his brother's melodies played and his own lyrics sung with such feeling brightened Ira's mood. Over the next few years, Feinstein became the last recipient of Ira's storehouse of memories.

THE FINAL YEARS of Ira Gershwin's life echoed some aspects of the final days of George Gershwin, who was never far from Ira's thoughts. No matter how hard he may have tried to steer his mind away from the events of 1937, they never failed to come back to haunt him. At times, Ira could be heard talking in his sleep, "filled with anger" as he told George that he no longer wished to live, while George "insiste[d] that he stay."[35] Although he was not suddenly struck down in his prime as his brother was, by the late 1970s, Ira was under around-the-clock nursing care, the curtains in his bedroom almost always drawn shut and his handwriting now a scrawl, much as George's had been at the end.

Lee kept most visitors away; she was uncomfortable with any sort of illness, and Ira was easily tired. One of the last people to visit who was not part of Ira's Beverly Hills social circle was Kay Swift. They happily talked about old times, but Ira was not "as well as he could be, *if* he believed it possible. His doctor says many people with his ailments are *much* better— but it varies according to temperament and amount of faith in one's basic core of health."[36] His sister Frankie appeared at the house in the spring of 1983, in the company of her son, Leopold Godowsky III, whose wife Elaine found Ira, at the age of eighty-four, "accepting of his life, quiet about things."[37]

On May 1, 1983, *My One and Only*, the last project in which Ira was involved, opened on Broadway, but without the maverick director Peter Sellars, who had been fired after the opening night of the out-of-town run in Boston. Ira was pleased by the reception that this "new" Gershwin musical, based loosely on the plot of *Funny Face*, received, but was uncertain about the random use of his songs in new musicals; they "might hurt the chances of reviving those other musicals in their original form." But Lee insisted that the show—and keeping its star, Tommy Tune—was more important than Ira's feelings. They could not "interfere with" the artists; they had to "give them what they want." But when Ira saw the tossed-off, improper rhymes that had been written to replace his carefully considered ones, he took pen in hand for a final time, making corrections in the hopes that his words would be, as they should have been, final. When his corrections were ignored, Ira shrugged, "threw up his hands and said, 'Let them do their worst.'"[38] Nevertheless, *My One and Only* enjoyed lengthy runs on Broadway and in London, and in June 1983, it received three Tony Awards. That same evening, the Uris Theatre on West 51st Street, where the ceremony was held, was renamed the Gershwin Theatre.

THE FORTY-SIXTH ANNIVERSARY of George Gershwin's death would be the last time Ira Gershwin would have to relive the trauma of the summer of 1937. At 7:57 a.m. on August 17, 1983, he suffered a heart attack in his sleep at his Beverly Hills home and died at the age of eighty-six.[39] It was a hot afternoon by the time Michael Feinstein—who, by this time, was somewhat estranged from Lee—arrived at the house, where he saw the ambulance waiting to remove Ira's body. Lee, as usual the face of "nothing is wrong," told Feinstein to go upstairs and give her husband a farewell kiss; when he returned, she ordered him to play the slow movement of the Concerto in F as the undertakers did their work. "As they were going through the living room," Feinstein recalled, "I turned my head, and Lee said, 'Don't look!' So I turned my head back to the piano and finished playing. And that was the end of the golden days at what Ira always called the Gershwin plantation."[40]

THE FUNERAL WAS, deliberately, no match for the lavish ceremony that was held for his brother forty-six years earlier. There was no service, and although Ira had lived half his life in California, the internment of his ashes in the Gershwin crypt at the Westchester Hills Cemetery had already been decided upon. Six limousines followed the hearse from the Frank E. Campbell Mortuary to the cemetery; the limousines carried Ira's widow and the twenty family members and friends who chose to make the fifty-minute trip from Manhattan. Ira was unknown to the rabbi assigned by the funeral home; only the briefest of words were spoken during the private ceremony.[41] Ira's peregrinations—his search for a temporal paradise—had ended.

AS IRA GERSHWIN NEARED his seventieth birthday, a reference to Dorothy Parker's self-composed epitaph "Excuse My Dust!" encouraged him to find an equally pithy phrase that would sum up *his* life. The result was "Words Failed Me."[42] He knew it was a joke: words—those lyrics developed in his ever-fertile mind and honed to perfection with the skill of a diamond cutter—*never* failed him. Those timeless words remain his legacy. They will live, as his friends Betty Comden and Adolph Green said, "as long as anyone remembers anything about the twentieth century."[43]

The more I read the papers,
The less I comprehend
The world and all its capers
And how it all will end.
Nothing seems to be lasting,
But that isn't our affair;
We've got something permanent—
I mean, in the way we care.

It's very clear
Our love is here to stay;
Not for a year,
But ever and a day.

The radio and the telephone
And the movies that we know
May just be passing fancies—
And in time may go.

But oh, my dear,
Our love is here to stay.
Together we're
Going a long, long way.

In time the Rockies may crumble,
Gibraltar may tumble
(They're only made of clay),
But—our love is here to stay.

EPILOGUE

I RA GERSHWIN OFTEN FOUND it difficult to believe that decades after their creation, his lyrics were still being sung; he would be amazed to discover that forty years after his death, those same words still delight and continue to reach the hearts of new, multigenerational audiences.

Much of the credit for keeping Ira's legacy alive belongs to his widow, Leonore Strunsky Gershwin. In 1987, she created a series of trusts that, along with providing much-needed funds to charitable organizations and to the Music Division of the Library of Congress, gave birth to a series of meticulous restorations of many of George and Ira Gershwin's musical theater works. Much of the material used to create these restorations came from a wealth of original Gershwin scores and manuscripts that were located in a Warner Bros. warehouse in Secaucus, New Jersey, a year before Ira's death; this treasure trove, combined with items from the Gershwin Collection at the Library of Congress, other scattered collections, and Ira's own archive, housed in his Beverly Hills home and later in San Francisco, were key elements in bringing back to life Gershwin shows and songs that had seemingly been lost to time.

The cast recordings that followed the restorations, inspired by the 1987 CBS Records release of *Of Thee I Sing* and *Let 'Em Eat Cake* (conducted by Michael Tilson Thomas), began in the 1990s on the Roxbury Recordings label (*Girl Crazy, Strike Up the Band, Lady, Be Good!, Pardon My English*, and *Oh, Kay!*) and have continued into the twenty-first century with *Ziegfeld Follies of 1936* (Decca Broadway), *Tip-Toes* and *Tell Me More* (New World Records), and most recently, *Life Begins at 8:40* and the 1930 revised version of *Strike Up the Band* (PS Classics).

Rarely has a recording of material from the Great American Songbook been released without at least one Ira Gershwin song. In addition, all-Gershwin recordings have been released in the past decade by Michael Feinstein, Willie Nelson, Brian Wilson, and the team of Tony Bennett and Diana Krall. Ira's songs have found their way into commercials, as well as countless movies and television series—from period pieces (*The Marvelous Mrs. Maisel*) to unlikely contemporary comic book adaptations (*The Boys*).

Theatrical audiences have laughed or been thrilled by the musical *Crazy for You* (1992, based on *Girl Crazy*), a London production of *Porgy and Bess: The Musical* (2006), *Nice Work If You Can Get It* and a Broadway-style adaptation of *Porgy and Bess* (both 2012), and a reimagining of *An American in Paris* (2015). Collectively, these shows, as well as *My One and Only*, garnered fourteen Tony Awards and a host of domestic and foreign prizes. *Crazy for You* remains one of the most popular musical theater shows around the world, and a revival of the original production opened to acclaim in London in 2023. Might a return to Broadway be in the offing? Even *Lady in the Dark* has found new life, with recent European productions in Vienna, Basel, and Maastricht.

The Jefferson Building of the Library of Congress is the home of the Gershwin Gallery, which opened in 1998 for the centennial of George Gershwin's birth; there visitors can find Ira's writing table and typewriter in the center of the space, opposite his brother's piano. The library houses the largest collection of Gershwin material in the world, consisting of more than 165,000 items, much of it coming directly from Ira or his estate. In 2007, the library, in conjunction with the Gershwin families, created the Library of Congress Gershwin Prize for Popular Song. Recipients of the award to date have been Paul Simon, Stevie Wonder, Paul McCartney, Burt Bacharach and Hal David, Carole King, Billy Joel, Willie Nelson, Smokey Robinson, Tony Bennett, Emilio and Gloria Estefan, Garth Brooks, Lionel Richie, Joni Mitchell, and Elton John and Bernie Taupin.

Books about George Gershwin have been published at a constant rate since 1983. Among the most recent and comprehensive are biographies by Howard Pollack (*George Gershwin: His Life and Work*; University of California Press) and Richard Crawford (*Summertime: George Gershwin's Life in Music*; W. W. Norton), *The Cambridge Companion to Gershwin*, a volume of essays edited by Anna Harwell Celenza (Cambridge University Press), as well as Michael Feinstein's more personal *The Gershwins and Me* (Simon & Schuster); all include significant sections about Ira's contribution to his brother's career. Ira himself has been the subject of a scholarly analysis of his lyrics by Philip Furia (*Ira Gershwin: The Art of the Lyricist*; Oxford University Press), while musical theater historian Robert Kimball has collected the lyrics in the compendiums *The Complete Lyrics of Ira Gershwin* (Da Capo) and *Ira Gershwin: Selected Lyrics* (Library of America). In addition, The Kurt Weill Foundation for Music has issued critical edition volumes of *Lady in the Dark* and *The Firebrand of Florence*.

In 2015, the University of Michigan's School of Music, Theatre & Dance, in conjunction with the Gershwin families, created the Gershwin Initiative, a multidisciplinary program that includes the publication of scholarly editions of the Gershwins' music and lyrics. The first volumes of the George and Ira Gershwin Critical Edition—the full score and two-piano score of *Rhapsody in Blue* (edited by Ryan Raul Bañagale)—were published in 2023, with Ira's *The Gershwins Abroad, or Four Americans in Paris (and Several Other Cities): A 1928 Notebook*, edited and annotated by the author of this biography, to follow in 2024.

More than forty years after Ira Gershwin's death, his words, with all their wit and romance, remain a touchstone of American culture.

ACKNOWLEDGMENTS

I N THE SUMMER OF 2000, I was hired for a temporary position at the newly opened San Francisco office of the Ira and Leonore Gershwin Trusts. The job entailed photocopying the entire contents of fourteen bankers' boxes containing the papers of Leonard Saxe, one of Ira Gershwin's attorneys. Little did I know that this short-term project would turn into four years of work and that, in 2005, I would be asked to manage Ira's archive. Even less likely was that eleven years later I would be asked to write a biography of Ira and that my archival work would pay off for *me*, rather than helping others, as it had for so many years.

There are many people to thank, but my primary gratitude goes to Mark Trent Goldberg, who took a chance on me for the "copy job from hell." He gave me books on the Gershwins and never failed to encourage my interest in their work and lives. I miss him dearly.

I met Ira Gershwin's longtime archivist and assistant Lawrence D. Stewart only once, but his collection of Gershwiniana, which I processed when it was given to the Gershwin Trusts after his death, was invaluable. (It is now at the Library of Congress.) To him, I say "thank you" for being the first person to organize Ira's archive.

Following Ira's example, I extend a deep bow to Jean Z. Strunsky, the trustee of the Ira and Leonore Gershwin Trusts, and to LJ Strunsky, the Trusts' Managing Director, for their enthusiasm for this project, as well as for their permission to quote extensively from Ira's writings and to use photographs from the Trusts' archive. A special thank you to Vinny Fajardo, Martha Buck, and Olivia Smith for their friendship and assistance over the years.

This book would never have been researched without the assistance of all the librarians, archivists, and curators whose paths intersected with mine during this journey; their knowledge and courtesy are models of professionalism.

My greatest appreciation goes to archivist Janet McKinney, of the Music Division of the Library of Congress; gracious with her time during my on-site visits to the library, when the pandemic closed physical access to the collections in 2020, Janet provided an endless stream of important documents via email.

Thank you as well to Allison DeArcangelis, Special Collections library assistant, Newberry Library; Barbara Bair, Manuscript Division, Library of Congress; Fran Barulich, the Morgan Library & Museum; Sam Bessen, curator, Lester Levy Sheet Music Collection, Special Collections, Sheridan Libraries, Johns Hopkins University; Richard Boursy, archivist, Irving S. Gilmore Music Library of Yale University; Joshua Caster, archives manager, Archives & Special Collections, University of Nebraska–Lincoln Libraries; Ned Comstock, Cinema-Television Library, University of Southern California; Graham Duncan, curator of Manuscripts/head of Collections, South Caroliniana Library at the University of South Carolina; Jessica Getman, California State University, San Bernardino (former managing editor of the Gershwin Critical Edition at the University of Michigan); Harlan Greene, College of Charleston, Charleston, South Carolina; Mark Eden Horowitz, senior music specialist, Music Division, Library of Congress; Warren Klein, curator of the Bernard Museum of Judaica at Congregation Emanu-El of the City of New York; James Maynard, PhD, curator, The Poetry Collection, University of Buffalo; the staff of the Billy Rose Theatre Division of the New York Public Library; Anne Rhodes, research archivist, Oral History of American Music, Yale University Library; Matthew Rowe, Beinecke Rare Book & Manuscript Library, Yale University; Jay Satterfield, Rauner Special Collections Library, Dartmouth; Loras Schissel, senior musicologist, Music Division, Library of Congress; Jennifer Tran, John F. Kennedy Presidential Library; Anita Weber, music archivist, Library of Congress; and Ray White, senior music specialist, Music Division, Library of Congress.

Additional thanks to those who agreed to speak with me about Ira and other Gershwin-related matters, who provided helpful material from their own collections, gave me feedback on the manuscript, or just listened: the family of Nan Apotheker (particularly Cara Flanagan), Ron Blanc, Anna Celenza Harwell, Eric and Steve Dibner, Michael Feinstein, George

Ferencz, the late Alexis Gershwin, Elaine Godowsky, Joseph Goodrich, Harvey Granat, Eric Harrington, Roger Howlett, Robert and Abigail Kimball, Nadia Natali, Frankie Wolpin Ross, the late Stephen Saxe, Alan Wald, Katharine Weber, and Marianne Wurlitzer. My thanks as well to Joyce Dollinger, of Alter, Kendrick and Baron, LLP, for her assistance in getting me through the final stages of lyric licensing.

My wife, Libbie Hodas, is a never-ending source of love and support. She always helped me to find the right path when I was lost—something that happened more often during the writing of this book than I care to remember! Thanks, sugar.

At W. W. Norton/Liveright, the lengthy process of turning my unwieldy manuscript into a solid book was guided by my patient editor, Chris Freitag. (And thanks to Mark Clague for the introduction.) Chris's advice—to find the story inside the potentially interesting (to me) details—was just what I needed. Thanks for getting me to the finish line. And grateful nods to Janet Greenblatt for her expert copy editing and to Robert Byrne for seeing the book through to publication. Additional thanks to Jessica R. Friedman for her help sorting out a tricky situation.

One final note: when Chris Freitag told me that there was interest in my manuscript at Liveright Publishing, I remembered that Ira, in one of his letters, had referred to Horace Liveright as a "dope." (See the story in chapter 7.) I wondered what the publisher had done to provoke this rare disparaging remark from the easygoing lyricist. After I signed the deal for this book—exactly thirty-eight years after Ira Gershwin's death—I acquired a copy of Tom Dardis's excellent biography, *Firebrand: The Life of Horace Liveright*, and there it was—the background that explained the comment. Life comes full circle.

SONGS BY IRA GERSHWIN

(Only those with extant music)

1918

LADIES FIRST (SHOW)
The Real American Folk Song (Is a Rag) (MUSIC BY
GEORGE GERSHWIN)

HALF PAST EIGHT (SHOW)
There's Magic in the Air (MUSIC BY GEORGE GERSHWIN)

1920

THE SWEETHEART SHOP (SHOW)
Waiting for the Sun to Come Out (MUSIC BY GEORGE GERSHWIN;
LYRICS BY "ARTHUR FRANCIS")

PICCADILLY TO BROADWAY (REVUE)
Mr. and Mrs. (MUSIC BY VINCENT YOUMANS; LYRICS BY
"ARTHUR FRANCIS")
Who's Who with You? (MUSIC BY VINCENT YOUMANS; LYRICS
BY "ARTHUR FRANCIS")

1921

A DANGEROUS MAID (SHOW), music by George Gershwin; lyrics
by "Arthur Francis"
Boy Wanted
Dancing Shoes
Just to Know You Are Mine
The Simple Life
Some Rain Must Fall

UNUSED: *Anything for You; The Sirens*

TWO LITTLE GIRLS IN BLUE (SHOW), music by Vincent Youmans and Paul Lannin; lyrics by "Arthur Francis"
> *Dolly* (MUSIC BY VINCENT YOUMANS; LYRICS WRITTEN WITH SCHUYLER GREENE)
> *Honeymoon* (MUSIC BY PAUL LANNIN)
> *Just Like You* (MUSIC BY PAUL LANNIN)
> *Oh Me! Oh My!* (MUSIC BY VINCENT YOUMANS)
> *Rice and Shoes* (MUSIC BY VINCENT YOUMANS; LYRICS WRITTEN WITH SCHUYLER GREENE)
> *Two Little Girls in Blue* (MUSIC BY VINCENT YOUMANS)
> *We're Off on a Wonderful Trip* (MUSIC BY VINCENT YOUMANS)
> *We're Off to India* (MUSIC BY VINCENT YOUMANS)
> *When I'm with the Girls* (MUSIC BY VINCENT YOUMANS)
> *Who's Who with You?* (MUSIC BY VINCENT YOUMANS)
> *You Started Something* (MUSIC BY VINCENT YOUMANS)
>
> UNUSED: *Make the Best of It* (MUSIC BY VINCENT YOUMANS); *Mr. and Mrs.* (MUSIC BY VINCENT YOUMANS)

PEACOCK ALLEY (MOVIE)
> *Peacock Alley* (MUSIC BY LOUIS SILVERS; LYRICS BY "ARTHUR FRANCIS")

1922

PINS AND NEEDLES (REVUE)
> *The Piccadilly Walk* (MUSIC BY EDWARD A. HORAN; LYRICS BY "ARTHUR FRANCIS" AND ARTHUR RISCOE)

FOR GOODNESS SAKE (SHOW), music by George Gershwin; lyrics by "Arthur Francis"
> *French Pastry Walk* (MUSIC BY WILLIAM DALY AND PAUL LANNIN; LYRICS BY ARTHUR JACKSON AND "ARTHUR FRANCIS")
> *Someone*
> *Tra-La-La*

MOLLY DARLING (SHOW)
> *When All Your Castles Come Tumbling Down* (MUSIC BY MILTON SCHWARZWALD; LYRICS BY "ARTHUR FRANCIS")

FASCINATION (MOVIE)
> *Fascination* (MUSIC BY LOUIS SILVERS; LYRICS BY "ARTHUR FRANCIS" AND SCHUYLER GREENE)

GEORGE WHITE'S SCANDALS OF 1922 (REVUE)
(I'll Build a) Stairway to Paradise (MUSIC BY GEORGE
GERSHWIN; LYRICS BY B. G. DESYLVA AND
"ARTHUR FRANCIS")

Mischa, Jascha, Toscha, Sascha (STAND-ALONE SONG), music by
George Gershwin

1923

GREENWICH VILLAGE FOLLIES (REVUE)
Hot Hindoo (MUSIC BY LEWIS GENSLER; LYRICS BY
"ARTHUR FRANCIS")

LITTLE MISS BLUEBEARD (SHOW)
I Won't Say I Will, but I Won't Say I Won't (MUSIC BY
GEORGE GERSHWIN; LYRICS BY B. G. DESYLVA AND
"ARTHUR FRANCIS")

NIFTIES OF 1923 (REVUE)
Fabric of Dreams (MUSIC BY RAYMOND HUBBELL; LYRICS BY B. G.
DESYLVA AND "ARTHUR FRANCIS")

THE SUNSHINE TRAIL (MOVIE)
The Sunshine Trail (MUSIC BY GEORGE GERSHWIN; LYRICS BY
"ARTHUR FRANCIS")

1924

TOP HOLE (SHOW)
UNUSED: *Imagine Me without My You* (MUSIC BY LEWIS GENSLER)

THE FIREBRAND (SHOW)
The Voice of Love (MUSIC BY ROBERT RUSSELL BENNETT AND
MAURICE NITKE)

PRIMROSE (SHOW), music by George Gershwin
Boy Wanted (LYRICS WRITTEN WITH DESMOND CARTER)
Four Little Sirens
Isn't It Wonderful (LYRICS WRITTEN WITH DESMOND CARTER)
Naughty Baby (LYRICS WRITTEN WITH DESMOND CARTER)
Some Far-Away Someone (LYRICS WRITTEN WITH B. G. DESYLVA)
Wait a Bit, Susie (LYRICS WRITTEN WITH DESMOND CARTER)

BE YOURSELF (SHOW)
  I Came Here (MUSIC BY LEWIS GENSLER; LYRICS WRITTEN
    WITH MARC CONNELLY AND GEORGE S. KAUFMAN)
  Uh-Uh (MUSIC BY MILTON SCHWARZWALD; LYRICS WRITTEN
    WITH MARC CONNELLY AND GEORGE S. KAUFMAN)
  The Wrong Thing at the Right Time (MUSIC BY MILTON
    SCHWARZWALD; LYRICS WRITTEN WITH MARC CONNELLY
    AND GEORGE S. KAUFMAN)

LADY, BE GOOD! (SHOW), music by George Gershwin
  End of a String
  Fascinating Rhythm
  The Half of It, Dearie, Blues
  Hang On to Me
  Juanita
  Linger in the Lobby
  Little Jazz Bird
  Oh, Lady, Be Good!
  Seeing Dickie Home
  So Am I
  Swiss Miss (LYRICS WRITTEN WITH ARTHUR JACKSON)
  We're Here Because
  A Wonderful Party

  UNUSED: *The Bad, Bad Men; Evening Star; The Man I Love;
    Rainy Afternoon Girls; Singin' Pete; Weatherman; Will You
    Remember Me?*

1925

CAPTAIN JINKS (SHOW)
  You Must Come Over Blues (MUSIC BY LEWIS GENSLER)

A NIGHT OUT (SHOW)
  I Want a Yes Man (MUSIC BY VINCENT YOUMANS; LYRICS
    WRITTEN WITH CLIFFORD GREY AND IRVING CAESAR)

TELL ME MORE (SHOW), music by George Gershwin; lyrics
written with B. G. DeSylva
  Baby!
  How Can I Win You Now?
  In Sardinia
  Kickin' the Clouds Away

Love Is in the Air
My Fair Lady
Mr. and Mrs. Sipkin
Once
The Poetry of Motion
Shopgirls and Mannequins
Tell Me More
Three Times a Day
Ukulele Lorelei
When the Debbies Go By
Why Do I Love You?

UNUSED: *Gushing*; *The He-Man*; *I'm Somethin' on Avenue A*

TIP-TOES (SHOW), music by George Gershwin
It's a Great Little World
Lady Luck
Looking for a Boy
Nice Baby
Nightie-Night!
Our Little Captain
Sweet and Low-Down
That Certain Feeling
These Charming People
Tip-Toes
Waiting for the Train
When Do We Dance?

UNUSED: *Gather Ye Rosebuds*; *Harlem River Chanty*

1926

AMERICANA (REVUE)
Blowin' the Blues Away (MUSIC BY PHILIP CHARIG)
That Lost Barber Shop Chord (MUSIC BY GEORGE GERSHWIN)
Sunny Disposish (MUSIC BY PHILIP CHARIG)

OH, KAY! (SHOW), music by George Gershwin; some lyrics written
with Howard Dietz (HD)
Bride and Groom
Clap Yo' Hands
Dear Little Girl
Do, Do, Do

Don't Ask!

Fidgety Feet

Heaven on Earth (HD)

Maybe

Oh, Kay! (HD)

Someone to Watch Over Me

The Woman's Touch

UNUSED: *Ain't It Romantic?*; *Bring on the Ding Dong Dell*; *The Moon Is on the Sea*; *Show Me the Town*; *When Our Ship Comes Sailing In*

1927

STRIKE UP THE BAND (SHOW), music by George Gershwin

17 and 21

Fletcher's American Cheese Choral Society

Homeward Bound

Hoping That Someday You'd Care

How About a Man?

Jim, Consider What You Are Doing!

The Man I Love

Meadow Serenade

Military Dancing Drill

Oh, This Is Such a Lovely War

Patriotic Rally

Strike Up the Band

Typical Self-Made American

The Unofficial Spokesman

The War That Ended War

Yankee Doodle Rhythm

UNUSED: *Come-Look-at-the-War Choral Society*; *Nursie, Nursie*

FUNNY FACE (SHOW), music by George Gershwin

The Babbitt and the Bromide

Birthday Party

Funny Face

He Loves and She Loves

High Hat

In the Swim

Let's Kiss and Make Up

My One and Only

Once
'S Wonderful
Tell the Doc

UNUSED: *Acrobats*; *Aviator*; *Dance Alone with You*; *Finest of the Finest*; *How Long Has This Been Going On?*; *When You're Single*; *The World Is Mine*; *Your Eyes! Your Smile!*

1928

ROSALIE (show), music by George Gershwin; lyrics by Ira Gershwin and P. G. Wodehouse
At the Ex-Kings' Club
Ev'rybody Knows I Love Somebody (LYRICS BY IRA GERSHWIN)
Follow the Drum
How Long Has This Been Going On? (LYRICS BY IRA GERSHWIN)
Hussar March
New York Serenade (LYRICS BY IRA GERSHWIN)
Oh Gee! Oh Joy!
Say So!
Show Me the Town

UNUSED: (ALL LYRICS BY IRA GERSHWIN): *Beautiful Gypsy*; *I Forgot What I Started to Say*; *The Man I Love*; *Rosalie*; *When Cadets Parade*; *Yankee Doodle Rhythm*; *You Know How It Is*

THAT'S A GOOD GIRL (show), music by Joseph Meyer and Philip Charig; lyrics written with Douglas Furber
Chirp-Chirp (LYRICS BY IRA GERSHWIN)
Let Yourself Go!
The One I'm Looking For
Sweet So-and-So
Whoopee (LYRICS BY IRA GERSHWIN)

TREASURE GIRL (show), music by George Gershwin
According to Mr. Grimes
Feeling I'm Falling
Got a Rainbow
I Don't Think I'll Fall in Love Today
I've Got a Crush on You
Kr-a-zy for You
Oh, So Nice!
Place in the Country

Skull and Bones
What Are We Here For?
Where's the Boy? Here's the Girl!

UNUSED: *Dead Men Tell No Tales*; *Good-bye to the Old Love*;
I Want to Marry a Marionette; *What Causes That?*

1929

SHOW GIRL (SHOW), music by George Gershwin; lyrics written
with Gus Kahn

Do What You Do!
Happy Birthday
Harlem Serenade
Home Blues
How Could I Forget?
I Must Be Home by Twelve O'Clock
Liza
Lolita, My Love
One Man
My Sunday Fella
So Are You!

UNUSED: *Adored One*; *At Mrs. Simpkin's Finishing School*; *Feeling
Sentimental*; *Follow the Minstrel Band*; *I Just Looked at You*;
Magnolia Finale; *Minstrel Show*; *Somebody Stole My Heart
Away*; *Stage Door Scene*; *Tonight's the Night!*

In the Mandarin's Orchid Garden (STAND-ALONE SONG), music by
George Gershwin

Late 1920s or early 1930s

Ask Me Again (STAND-ALONE SONG), music by George Gershwin

1930

THE GARRICK GAIETIES (REVUE)

I Am Only Human after All (MUSIC BY VERNON DUKE; LYRICS
WRITTEN WITH E. Y. HARBURG)

SWEET AND LOW (REVUE)

Cheerful Little Earful (MUSIC BY HARRY WARREN; LYRICS
WRITTEN WITH BILLY ROSE)

STRIKE UP THE BAND [revised version] (SHOW), music by
George Gershwin

Fletcher's American Chocolate Choral Society
Hangin' around with You
He Knows Milk
How about a Boy?
I Mean to Say
I've Got a Crush on You
If I Became the President
In the Rattle of the Battle
Mademoiselle in New Rochelle
A Man of High Degree
Military Dancing Drill
Official Résumé
Ring-a-Ding-a-Ding-Dong Bell
Soon
Strike Up the Band
This Could Go on for Years
Three Cheers for the Union!
Typical Self-Made American
The Unofficial Spokesman

UNUSED: *I Want to Be a War Bride*; *Thanks to You*; *There Never
Was Such a Charming War*

GIRL CRAZY (SHOW), music by George Gershwin

Barbary Coast
Bidin' My Time
Boy! What Love Has Done to Me!
Bronco Busters
But Not for Me
Cactus Time in Arizona
Could You Use Me?
Embraceable You
Goldfarb, That's I'm!
I Got Rhythm
Land of the Gay Caballero
The Lonesome Cowboy
Sam and Delilah
Treat Me Rough

UNUSED: *Are You Dancing?*; *The Gambler of the West*; *You Can't Unscramble Scrambled Eggs*

1931

CRAZY QUILT (REVUE)
In the Merry Month of Maybe (MUSIC BY HARRY WARREN; LYRICS WRITTEN WITH BILLY ROSE)

GIRL CRAZY (MOVIE), music by George Gershwin
You've Got What Gets Me

THE SOCIAL REGISTER (SHOW)
The Key to My Heart (MUSIC BY LOUIS ALTER)

DELICIOUS (MOVIE), music by George Gershwin
Blah, Blah, Blah
Delishious
Dream Sequence
Katinkitschka
Somebody from Somewhere
You Started It

OF THEE I SING (SHOW), music by George Gershwin
As the Chairman of the Committee
Because, Because
The Dimple on My Knee
Entrance of the French Ambassador
Entrance of the Supreme Court Judges
Exit, Atlantic City Scene
Garçon, S'il Vous Plaît
Hello, Good Morning
How Beautiful
I Was the Most Beautiful Blossom
I'm About to Be a Mother
The Illegitimate Daughter
Impeachment Proceeding
Jilted
A Kiss for Cinderella
Love Is Sweeping the Country
Never Was There a Girl So Fair
Of Thee I Sing
On That Matter No One Budges

Posterity Is Just around the Corner
The Senatorial Roll Call
Some Girls Can Bake a Pie
Trumpeter, Blow Your Golden Horn
We'll Impeach Him
Who Cares? (So Long as You Care for Me)
Who Is the Lucky Girl to Be?
Wintergreen for President
Zwei Hertzen

UNUSED: *Entrance of Wintergreen and Mary*

1933

PARDON MY ENGLISH (SHOW), music by George Gershwin
Dancing in the Streets
The Dresden Northwest Mounted
Hail the Happy Couple
He's Not Himself
I've Got to Be There
In Three-Quarter Time
Isn't It a Pity?
The Lorelei
Luckiest Man in the World
My Cousin in Milwaukee
Pardon My English
So What?
Tonight
What Sort of Wedding Is This?
Where You Go, I Go

UNUSED: *Fatherland, Mother of the Band*; *Freud and Jung and Adler*; *He's Oversexed!*; *No Tickee, No Washee*; *Together at Last*; *Watch Your Head*

LET 'EM EAT CAKE (SHOW), music by George Gershwin
All of the Mothers of the Nation
Blue, Blue, Blue
Climb Up the Social Ladder
Comes the Revolution
The Double Dummy Drill
Down with Everyone Who's Up
Fashion Show / Finale Ultimo

The General's Gone to a Party
Hanging Throttlebottom in the Morning
A Hell of a Hole
I Know a Foul Ball
I've Brushed My Teeth
It Isn't What You Did
Let 'Em Eat Cake
Mine
Nine Supreme Ball Players
No Better Way to Start a Case
No Comprenez, *No* Capish, *No* Versteh!
On and On and On
Oyez, Oyez, Oyez!
Play Ball!
Shirts by Millions
That's What He Did!
There's Something We're Worried About
Throttle Throttlebottom
Tweedledee for President
The Union League
Union Square
Up and at 'Em, on to Victory
What's the Proletariat?
Who's the Greatest?
The Whole Truth
Why Speak of Money?
Yes, He's a Bachelor

UNUSED: *First Lady and First Gent*

Till Then (STAND-ALONE SONG), music by George Gershwin

1934

LIFE BEGINS AT 8:40 (REVUE), music by Harold Arlen; lyrics written with E. Y. Harburg
All the Elks and Masons
C'est la Vie
Fun to Be Fooled
I Couldn't Hold My Man
I'm Not Myself
It Was Long Ago
Let's Take a Walk around the Block

Life Begins (At Exactly 8:40 or Thereabouts)
Life Begins at City Hall
My Paramount-Publix-Roxy Rose
Quartet Erotica (We're Not What We Used to Be)
Shoein' the Mare
Spring Fever
Things!
What Can You Say in a Love Song? (That Hasn't Been
  Said Before?)
You're a Builder Upper

UNUSED: *I Knew Him When; A Weekend Cruise*

1935

PORGY AND BESS (OPERA), music by George Gershwin; some
lyrics written with DuBose Heyward
  Bess, You Is My Woman Now (WITH DUBOSE HEYWARD)
  I Got Plenty o' Nuttin' (WITH DUBOSE HEYWARD)
  I Loves You, Porgy (WITH DUBOSE HEYWARD)
  It Ain't Necessarily So
  Oh, Bess, Oh Where's My Bess?
  Oh, Heav'nly Father (WITH DUBOSE HEYWARD)
  Oh, I Can't Sit Down
  A Red Headed Woman
  There's a Boat Dat's Leavin' Soon for New York

1936

ZIEGFELD FOLLIES OF 1936 (REVUE), music by Vernon Duke
  Dancing to the Score
  The Economic Situation
  Fancy! Fancy!
  Five A.M.
  The Gazooka
  He Hasn't a Thing Except Me
  I Can't Get Started
  Island in the West Indies
  It's a Different World
  Maharanee
  Modernistic Moe (LYRICS WRITTEN WITH BILLY ROSE)
  My Red-Letter Day
  Sentimental Weather
  That Moment of Moments

Time Marches On!
Trailer for the 1936 Broadway Gold Melody Diggers
Words without Music

UNUSED: *The Ballad of Baby Face McGinty (Who Bit Off More*
Than He Could Chew); Does a Duck Love Water?; Hot
Number; The Knife-Thrower's Wife; The Last of the Cabbies;
Please Send My Daddy Back to Mother; Sunday Tan; Why Save
for That Rainy Day?; Wishing Tree of Harlem

I Used to Be Above Love (STAND-ALONE SONG), music by Vernon Duke

Strike Up the Band for UCLA (STAND-ALONE SONG), music by
George Gershwin

THE SHOW IS ON (REVUE)
By Strauss (MUSIC BY GEORGE GERSHWIN)

1937

SHALL WE DANCE (MOVIE), music by George Gershwin
(I've Got) Beginner's Luck
Let's Call the Whole Thing Off
Shall We Dance
Slap That Bass
They All Laughed
They Can't Take That Away from Me

UNUSED: *Hi-Ho!; Wake Up, Brother, and Dance*

A DAMSEL IN DISTRESS (MOVIE), music by George Gershwin
A Foggy Day (in London Town)
I Can't Be Bothered Now
The Jolly Tar and the Milkmaid
Nice Work If You Can Get It
Put Me to the Test
Sing of Spring
Stiff Upper Lip
Things Are Looking Up

UNUSED: *Pay Some Attention to Me*

1938

THE GOLDWYN FOLLIES (MOVIE), music by George Gershwin
and Vernon Duke
    I Love to Rhyme
    I Was Doing All Right
    Love Is Here to Stay
    Love Walked In
    Spring Again (VERNON DUKE)

    UNUSED: *I'm Not Complaining* (VERNON DUKE); *Just Another
       Rhumba*; *Night of Nights* (VERNON DUKE)

Dawn of a New Day (STAND-ALONE SONG), music by
George Gershwin

*Hard to Replace; I Was Naïve; I've Turned the Corner; No Question in
My Heart; Now That We Are One; Once There Were Two of Us; People
from Missouri; Something's Wrong* (STAND-ALONE SONGS), music by
Jerome Kern

1939

STICKS & STONES (REVUE)
    Baby, You're News (MUSIC BY JOHNNY GREEN; LYRICS
      WRITTEN WITH E. Y. HARBURG)

I'll Supply the Title (You'll Supply the Tune); Let It Rain! Let It Pour!
(STAND-ALONE SONGS), music by Harold Arlen

1940

LADY IN THE DARK (SHOW), music by Kurt Weill
    The Best Years of His Life
    Girl of the Moment
    The Greatest Show on Earth
    Huxley
    It Looks Like Liza
    Mapleton High Chorale
    My Ship
    Oh, Fabulous One
    One Life to Live
    The Princess of Pure Delight
    The Saga of Jenny
    This Is New

Tschaikowsky (and Other Russians)
The Woman at the Altar

UNUSED: *Bats about You; The Boss Is Bringing Home a Bride;*
Home in San Fernando Valley; It's Never Too Late to
Mendelssohn; Minstrel Dream; No Matter under What Star
You're Born; Party Parlando; Song of the Zodiac; A Trial
Combined with Circus; Unforgettable; The Unspoken Law

Honorable Moon (STAND-ALONE SONG), music by Arthur Schwartz;
lyrics written with E. Y. Harburg

If That's Propaganda (STAND-ALONE SONG), music by Harold Arlen

1942

Women of America (STAND-ALONE SONG), music by Ted Grouya

1943

THE NORTH STAR (MOVIE), music by Aaron Copland
No Village Like Mine
Song of the Fatherland
Song of the Guerillas
Village Scene Jingles
Younger Generation

UNUSED: *Collective Loading-Time Song; Wagon Song*

1944

COVER GIRL (MOVIE), music by Jerome Kern
Cover Girl
Long Ago (and Far Away)
Make Way for Tomorrow (LYRICS WRITTEN WITH E. Y. HARBURG)
Put Me to the Test
The Show Must Go On
Sure Thing
Who's Complaining?

UNUSED: *Any Moment Now; Midnight Madness; Midnight Music;*
That's the Best of All; Time: The Present; Tropical Night

1945

WHERE DO WE GO FROM HERE? (MOVIE), music by
Kurt Weill
All at Once
If Love Remains

Morale / Dancing with Lucilla
The Nina, the Pinta, the Santa Maria
Song of the Rhineland

UNUSED: *It Could Have Happened to Anyone; That's How It Is /*
   Telephone Passage; Woo, Woo, Woo, Woo, Manhattan

THE FIREBRAND OF FLORENCE (SHOW), music by Kurt Weill

Alessandro the Wise
Come to Florence
Come to Paris
Dizzily, Busily
Duchess's Entrance
Hear Ye! Hear Ye!
How Wonderfully Fortunate
I Am Happy Here
I Know Where There's a Cozy Nook
Just in Case
The Little Naked Boy
Love Is My Enemy
My Dear Benvenuto
My Lords and Ladies
The Nighttime Is No Time for Thinking
Our Master Is Free Again
A Rhyme for Angela
Sing Me Not a Ballad
Song of the Hangman
Souvenirs
There Was Life, There Was Love, There Was Laughter
There'll Be Life, Love, and Laughter
This Night in Florence
When the Duchess Is Away
The World Is Full of Villains
You Have to Do What You Do Do
You're Far Too Near Me

UNUSED: *I Had Just Been Pardoned*

1946

PARK AVENUE (SHOW), music by Arthur Schwartz

The Dew Was on the Rose
Don't Be a Woman If You Can

For the Life of Me
Good-bye to All That
Hope for the Best
The Land of Opportunitee
My Son-in-Law
Sweet Nevada
There's No Holding Me
There's Nothing Like Marriage for People
Tomorrow Is the Time

UNUSED: *The Future Mrs. Coleman; Heavenly Day; Remind Me Not to Leave the Town; Stay as We Are*

1947

THE SHOCKING MISS PILGRIM (MOVIE), music by George Gershwin

Aren't You Kind of Glad We Did?
The Back Bay Polka
Changing My Tune
Demon Rum
For You, For Me, For Evermore
One, Two, Three
Stand Up and Fight
Sweet Packard
Waltzing Is Better Sitting Down

UNUSED: *Tour of the Town; Welcome Song*

1949

THE BARKLEYS OF BROADWAY (MOVIE), music by Harry Warren

Manhattan Downbeat
My One and Only Highland Fling
Shoes with Wings On
Swing Trot
Weekend in the Country
You'd Be Hard to Replace

UNUSED: *Call On Us Again; The Courtin' of Elmer and Ella; Minstrels on Parade; Natchez on the Mississip'; The Poetry of Motion; Second Fiddle to a Harp; Taking No Chances on You; There Is No Music; These Days; The Well-Known Skies of Blue*

1953

GIVE A GIRL A BREAK (MOVIE), music by Burton Lane
Applause! Applause!
Give a Girl a Break
In Our United State
It Happens Ev'ry Time
Nothing Is Impossible

UNUSED: *Ach, Du Lieber Oom-Pah-Pah; Dreamworld; Woman,*
There Is No Living with You

1954

A STAR IS BORN (MOVIE), music by Harold Arlen
Gotta Have Me Go with You
Here's What I'm Here For
It's a New World
Lose That Long Face
The Man That Got Away
Someone at Last
The TV Commercial

UNUSED: *Dancing Partner; Green Light Ahead; I'm Off*
the Downbeat

THE COUNTRY GIRL (MOVIE), music by Harold Arlen
Commercials
Dissertation on the State of Bliss (Love and Learn)
It's Mine, It's Yours
The Land around Us
The Pitchman
The Search Is Through

1964

KISS ME, STUPID (MOVIE), music by George Gershwin
All the Livelong Day (and the Long, Long Night)
I'm a Poached Egg
Sophia

Lyrics for which music is not extant can be found in Robert Kimball, ed., *The Complete Lyrics of Ira Gershwin* (New York: Da Capo, 1998).

NOTES

Abbreviations Used in Notes

AMW—A. M. Wattenberg
BB—Benjamin Botkin
CLIG—*The Complete Lyrics of Ira Gershwin*
CW—Carl Williams
DBH—DuBose Heyward
DE—David Ewen
DH—Dorothy Heyward
EA—Emanuel Alexandre
EJ—Edward Jablonski
EP—Emily Paley
FG—Frances Godowsky
GCLC—George and Ira Gershwin Collection, Library of Congress, Washington, DC
GG—George Gershwin
GP—George Pallay
GPC—Gershwin Publishing Corporation
GTLC—Ira and Leonore Gershwin Trust Archive, Music Division, Library of Congress, Washington, DC
GTSF—Ira and Leonore Gershwin Trusts, San Francisco
HB—Henry Botkin
IG—Ira Gershwin
ISGO—Isaac Goldberg
KS—Kay Swift
KW—Kurt Weill
LDS—Lawrence D. Stewart
LDSGTLC—Lawrence D. Stewart papers, Ira and Leonore Gershwin Trust Archive, Music Division, Library of Congress, Washington, DC
LL—Lotte Lenya
LOSO—*Lyrics on Several Occasions*
LP—Lou Paley
LSG—Leonore S. Gershwin
LSS—Leonard S. Saxe
LSSLC—Ira Gershwin files from the law office of Leonard Saxe, Library of Congress, Washington, DC

343

MD—Max Dreyfus
MS—Mabel Schirmer
RG—Rose Gershwin
SNB—S. N. Behrman
VD—Vernon Duke
YH—Yip Harburg

Chapter 1

1. Aaron Gershwin to IG, January 25, 1954 (GTLC).
2. Mary emigrated to the United States in 1895 and married into the Wolpin family, as did Rose Gershwin's sister Kate (1910 US census for New York).
3. Aaron emigrated to the United States in 1913 (US military draft registration card, 1917). Kolya became an entertainer in Saint Petersburg (Aaron Gershwin to IG, January 25, 1954).
4. Irving Howe, *World of Our Fathers* (New York: Schocken Books, 1989), 24–32.
5. Morris Gershwin naturalization certificate, January 15, 1898 (GCLC); Edward Jablonski and Lawrence D. Stewart, *The Gershwin Years: George and Ira* (New York: Da Capo, 1996), 29–30.
6. Aaron Gershwin to IG, January 25, 1954.
7. SS *Sorrento* ship manifest (arrival); Frankie Wolpin Ross, interviewed by author, October 6, 2018 (steerage).
8. Howe, *World of Our Fathers*, xix.
9. Howe, *World of Our Fathers*, 59.
10. IG's birth certificate, transcript, January 31, 1928 (GTLC). A plaque reading "Not for a year, but ever and a day" was placed on the building in 1987, when LSG established the Ira Gershwin Literacy Center at the nearby University Settlement with a gift of $10,000. ("Widow of Ira Gershwin Endows Literary Center," *New York Times*, March 25, 1987.)
11. For a time, Ira referred to himself as Isaac (IG postcard to RG, August 13, 1912, private collection).
12. Howe, *World of Our Fathers*, 131.
13. IG to J. Gordon Leahy, February 15, 1963 (LDSGTLC).
14. IG, " . . . But I Wouldn't Want to Live There," *Saturday Review*, October 18, 1958.
15. IG to J. Gordon Leahy, November 8, 1962 (LDSGTLC). A plaque was added to George's birthplace in 1963 on what would have been his sixty-fifth birthday. The house was later demolished.
16. 1900 US census for New York.
17. Kate Wolpin interviewed by Vivian Perlis, January 30, 1986 (Yale University Oral History of American Music).
18. Howe, *World of Our Fathers*, 139.
19. IG, "But I Wouldn't."
20. Jablonski and Stewart, *The Gershwin Years*, 28.
21. Ira Gershwin, *Lyrics on Several Occasions: A Selection of Stage & Screen Lyrics Written for Sundry Situations; and Now Arranged in Arbitrary Categories, to Which Have Been Added Many Informative Annotations & Disquisitions on Their Why & Wherefore, Their Whom-For, Their How; and Matters Associative* (New York: Knopf, 1959), 67.
22. Milt Cohen to IG, September 10, 1949 (GTLC).
23. [Isaac Goldberg], "In Which Ira Gershwin Is Considered," *New York Times*, January 19,

1930. Clearly a product of Isaac Goldberg's pen, as much of the content is used in chapter 6 ("Ira Gershwin: Tricks of the Words-and-Music Trade") of his biography of George Gershwin the following year.

24. IG, notes for "California, Here I Came" [early draft of the *Saturday Review* essay], September 15, 1958 (LDSGTLC).

25. Howe, *World of Our Fathers*, 131.

26. IG, "But I Wouldn't."

27. 1905 New York City directory.

28. IG to DE, October 11, 1955 (GTLC).

29. IG, "California."

30. IG quoted in Robert Kimball, ed., *The Complete Lyrics of Ira Gershwin* (New York: Da Capo, 1998), xii.

31. Transcript of IG conference with Robert Rossen, August 13, 1941 (LDSGTLC).

32. IG, "But I Wouldn't."

33. Isaac Goldberg, *George Gershwin: A Study in American Music* (New York: Simon & Schuster, 1931), 169.

34. IG, "Everyman His Own Boswell" [diary], April 22, 1917 (GTLC).

35. IG, "California." Affable as they were, "Gyp the Blood" and "Leftie Louie" (the gangsters Harry Horowitz and "Lefty" Louis Rosenberg) were executed at Sing Sing Prison in 1914.

36. "An Artful Dodger Caught," *New York Times*, October 4, 1905.

37. IG, "But I Wouldn't."

38. IG, "Everyman," September 27, 1916.

39. IG to Roy Jansen, March 24, 1967 (GTLC).

40. Jablonski and Stewart, *The Gershwin Years*, 35.

41. David Ewen, *George Gershwin: His Journey to Greatness* (Englewood Cliffs, NJ: Prentice-Hall, 1970), 10; ISGO, *George Gershwin*, 169–70.

42. Howe, *World of Our Fathers*, 128.

43. IG, "Everyman," April 9, 1917. In this entry, IG put quotation marks around his spelling of seder, as if uncertain of the pronunciation or as if trying to emphasize his parents' accents.

44. IG to EJ, April 16, 1949 (GTLC). Ira's siblings did not have bar or bat mitzvahs.

45. LDS, journal transcript, April 26, 1953 (GTSF).

46. IG to LSS, October 10, 1966 (GTLC).

47. Michael Feinstein, *The Gershwins and Me: A Personal History in Twelve Songs* (New York: Simon & Schuster, 2012), 25.

48. Jablonski and Stewart, *The Gershwin Years*, 31. The original Zeitlin's at 126 Canal Street closed in December 1908 to make way for the construction of the Manhattan Bridge ("Passing of Zeitlin's," *New York Sun*, December 13, 1908).

49. LSS journal, May 31, 1963 (LSSLC). Decades later, Arthur Gershwin surprised Ira by giving him his bar mitzvah book, telling him that their mother had saved it: IG diary, May 28, 1963 (GTLC).

50. Jablonski and Stewart, *The Gershwin Years*, photograph after p. 33.

51. IG diary, June 7, 1965 (GTLC).

52. Robert Kimball and Alfred Simon, *The Gershwins* (New York: Atheneum, 1973), 8.

53. *The Harris Annual*, Vol. 1, June 1914.

54. Sandra Shoiock Roff, Anthony M. Cucchiara, and Barbara J. Dunlap, *From the Free Academy to CUNY: Illustrating Public Higher Education in New York City, 1847–1997* (New York: Fordham University Press, 2000), 9.

55. IG to YH, January 27, 1935 (MSS 83, The E. Y. Harburg Collection in the Irving S. Gilmore Music Library of Yale University).

56. [ISGO], "In Which Ira."

57. [ISGO], "In Which Ira." All copies of *The Leaf* disappeared during one of Ira's household moves as an adult.

58. IG, "Everyman," May 20, 1917.

59. IG to Roy Jansen, March 24, 1967.

60. IG, "Everyman," November 4, 1916.

61. "Personals," *The Survey* 30, no. 17 (July 26, 1913).

62. Harold Meyerson and Ernie Harburg, *Who Put the Rainbow in* The Wizard of Oz?: *Yip Harburg, Lyricist* (Ann Arbor: University of Michigan Press, 1993), 15–17.

63. Harriet Hyman Alonso, *Yip Harburg: Legendary Lyricist and Human Rights Activist* (Middletown, CT: Wesleyan University Press, 2012), 14.

64. Sally Ashley, *F.P.A.: The Life and Times of Franklin Pierce Adams* (New York: Beaufort Books, 1986), 55.

65. F. Scott Fitzgerald, "My Lost City," in *The Jazz Age* (New York: New Directions, 1996), 21.

66. IG, "Everyman," January 10, 1917.

67. Ashley, *F.P.A.*, 119.

68. IG, "Everyman," February 23, 1917. George Ade (1866–1944) was an American writer noted for his use of slang.

69. *The Harris Annual*, Vol. 1, June 1914.

70. IG, *LOSO*, 270–71.

71. IG to YH, December 23, 1940 (Harburg Collection).

72. IG to BB, August 18, 1966 (GCLC).

Chapter 2

1. Howe, *World of Our Fathers*, 127.

2. IG, foreword to *The George and Ira Gershwin Song Book* (New York: Simon & Schuster, 1960), vi–x.

3. Jablonski and Stewart, *The Gershwin Years*, 319.

4. IG, "Everyman," May 5, 1917.

5. Jablonski and Stewart, *The Gershwin Years*, 33.

6. ISGO, *George Gershwin*, 167.

7. Edward Jablonski, *Gershwin* (New York: Da Capo, 1998), 13. The club was formed in 1914 in honor of the college's former president, John Finley.

8. IG to HB, January 2, 1915 (GCLC).

9. IG, " . . . But I Wouldn't Want to Live There."

10. LDS, journal transcript, February 10, 1960.

11. IG, transcript of interview by Max Wilk, August 1971 (LDSGTLC).

12. *The College of the City of New York Sixty-Fifth Annual Register 1913–1914.*

13. Edson took over the column when F.P.A. moved to the *New York Tribune*.

14. *New York Mail*, October 13, 1914 ("Colored Pugilist") and October 14, 1914 ("Feature Story").

15. IG to BB, February 12, 1915 (GCLC).

16. IG to Professor William Bradley Otis, April 30, 1955 (GTLC). Ira attended one of Otis's classes at CCNY, ca. 1915.

17. *CCNY Mercury*, October 26, 1915.

18. IG, *LOSO*, 215.

19. *The Campus* 17, no. 10, November 24, 1915. This was rewritten and published under the Arthur Francis pseudonym in 1923 as "Rondeau to Rosie."

20. Transcript of IG conference with Robert Rossen, August 13, 1941.

21. ISGO, *George Gershwin*, 57.

22. HB to IG, October 26, 1958 (GTLC); Arthur Gershwin quoted in John S. Wilson, introduction to Kimball and Simon, *The Gershwins*, xvi.

23. IG to HB, January 2, 1915.

24. IG, "Everyman," October 4, 1916. Ira was a regular reader of both the *New Republic* and *The Masses*.

25. HB to Aaron and Annie Botkin, December 26, 1916 (Henry Botkin papers, 1917–1979. Archives of American Art, Smithsonian Institution).

26. IG, "Everyman," December 30, 1916.

27. Oscar Wilde, "The Critic as Artist," in *Intentions*, 4th ed. (London: Methuen, 1909), 98.

28. Quoted by IG in "Everyman," March 2, 1918. The origin of this quote is unknown.

29. Ashley, *F.P.A.*, 86.

30. "Coney Island Partners in Bankruptcy Court," *Brooklyn Daily Standard Union*, November 1, 1915.

31. Undated notice in *Variety*, 1915. Kobre's sons, Sam and Ben, were relief cashiers at the bank. Ira had a rocky relationship with Sam over tips (IG, "Everyman," November 7, 1916).

32. "New Turkish Baths in Harlem," *Real Estate Record and Business Guide*, November 27, 1915.

33. IG to Jerome Golding, November 3, 1973 (GTLC).

34. IG to HB, August 30, 1916 (GCLC).

35. IG, "Everyman," September 5, 1916. Yellowbacks were gold certificates.

36. IG, "Everyman," October 2, 1916.

37. IG, "Everyman," November 12, 1916.

38. IG, "Everyman," December 10, 1916.

39. IG, "Everyman," March 27, 1917.

40. "Suicide Brings End of Lafayette Baths," *New York Times*, December 8, 1916.

41. "Court Calendars," *New York Times*, April 3, 1917.

42. IG, "Everyman," April 20, 1917.

43. IG, "Everyman," June 2, 19, and 30, 1917.

44. "Receiver Named for Lafayette Baths," *New York Times*, July 3, 1917.

45. IG to HB, July 17, 1917 (GCLC).

46. IG, "Everyman," January 29, April 15, and July 4, 1917.

47. Arthur Rimbaud, *I Promise to Be Good: The Letters of Arthur Rimbaud*, ed. Wyatt Mason (New York: Random House, 2007), 28 (letter to George Izambard, May 1871).

48. IG, "Words and Music," *New York Times*, November 9, 1930.

49. IG, "Everyman," June 23, 1917.

50. IG, "Everyman," November 14–15, 1917.

51. Hal Boyle, "Glad I Have Inferiority Complex, Says Lyric Genius Ira Gershwin," *New York World-Telegram*, October 21, 1959.

52. IG, "Everyman," November 14, 1917.

53. IG, "Everyman," March 21, 1917.

54. IG, "Everyman," March 20 and 30, 1917. The student was Samuel H. Friedman, who twice ran for vice president of the United States on the Socialist Party ticket.

55. IG, "Everyman," April 11 and 23, 1917.

56. "Isidor Gershvin," State of New York Notice of Enrollment under Military Law, June 12, 1917 (GTLC).

57. IG, "Everyman," June 12, 1917.

58. IG, "Everyman," June 13 and 16, 1917.

59. ISGO, *George Gershwin*, 56.

60. Transcript of IG conference with Robert Rossen, August 13, 1941.

61. IG, "Everyman," December 31, 1917.

62. IG, "Everyman," February 8, 1917.

63. IG to BB, August 18, 1966.

64. IG, "Everyman," September 22, 1916; Joseph C. Lincoln, *Kent Knowles: Quahaug* (New York: A. L. Burt, 1914), 2.

65. IG to BB, August 18, 1966.

66. IG, "Everyman," November 9 and 13, 1916.

67. IG to BB, August 18, 1966. Ira told this story to the writer Arthur Kober, who used a variation on Rose's line in a story published in his 1935 book *Thunder over the Bronx*. In his diary for June 25, 1917, Ira wrote these lines as "If you're not serious (you don't mean it) don't do it, if you do, think of me."

68. IG, "Everyman," March 15, 1918. Eisen spent two years studying the piano in Europe during the early 1920s; what followed was a sporadic career as a concert pianist. Other than a letter to Ira from the early 1920s when she was in Paris and a condolence sent after his brother's death in 1937, it appears that there was no further contact, although he clearly remembered her with fondness.

69. IG, "Everyman," June 14, 1917.

70. ISGO, *George Gershwin*, 171.

71. Vivian Perlis and Libby Van Cleve, *Composers' Voices from Ives to Ellington: An Oral History of American Music* (New Haven: Yale University Press, 2005), 206.

72. [ISGO], "In Which Ira."

73. FG, quoted in Perlis and Van Cleve, *Composers' Voices*, 196.

74. IG, "Everyman," August 8, 1917 ("small dead town"); IG to BB, September 21, 1917 (GCLC).

75. IG, "Everyman," September 1, 14–15, and 28, 1917.

76. IG to BB, September 21, 1917.

77. IG, "Everyman," September 25, 1917.

78. IG, "Everyman," October 19, 1917.

79. IG, "Everyman," November 17, 1917.

80. ISGO, *George Gershwin*, 174.

81. ISGO, *George Gershwin*, 78.

82. IG, "Everyman," May 26, 1918.

83. IG, "Everyman," May 6, 1917.

84. IG, "Everyman," October 23, 1916.

85. IG, "Everyman," September 22, 1916.

86. IG, "Everyman," January 3, 1917.

87. Jablonski and Stewart, *The Gershwin Years*, 59.

88. GG to Irving Caesar, "Tuesday" [September 17 or 24, 1918] (Irving Caesar Papers in the ASCAP Foundation Collection, Library of Congress, Music Division).

89. Military draft registration for Isidore B. Gershwin, June 5, 1918 (www.ancestry.com); classification document, July 15, 1918 (LDSGTLC).

90. 1918 Pandemic Influenza Historic Timeline, available at https://stacks.cdc.gov/view/cdc/119435.

91. IG to EJ, November 10, 1942 (GTLC).

92. 1918 Pandemic Influenza Historic Timeline.

Chapter 3

1. Benjamin Welles, "Lyricist of 'The Saga of Jenny' et al.," *New York Times*, May 25, 1941.

2. IG, "Everyman," February 10, 1918.

3. Transcript of IG conference with Robert Rossen, August 13, 1941.

4. ISGO, *George Gershwin*, 174.

5. [ISGO], "In Which Ira."

6. IG, "Everyman," June 2, 1917.

7. *New York Clipper*, July 2, 1919. A *Billboard* article on August 16 of the same year referred to him as "Irv. Gerschwin."

8. IG to Max Abramson, July 6, 1919 (GTLC). A '49 show gave a purported glimpse at life during the California Gold Rush days of 1849.

9. George Newell, "George Gershwin and Jazz," *Outlook*, February 29, 1928.

10. IG to Max Abramson, July 6, 1919. Frank Tinney was a popular American comedic actor (1878–1940). "When a Feller Needs a Friend" was a popular *New York Tribune* cartoon drawn by Clare Briggs (1875–1930).

11. IG, transcript of interview by Max Wilk, August 1971.

12. IG to B. A. Bergman, October 9, 1967 (GTLC).

13. ISGO, *George Gershwin*, 173–74.

14. IG, *LOSO*, 313–14.

15. IG, "Everyman," January 15, 1917.

16. IG, "Everyman," February 10 and March 15, 1918. Before he retired from the songwriting game in favor of his students, Lou Paley supplied the words to George's patriotic "We're Six Little Nieces of Our Uncle Sam" (1917) and to "Something about Love" and "Come to the Moon" (both 1919). The melody for "Something about Love" was given a new lyric by Ira and became "He Loves and She Loves" in *Funny Face*.

17. IG, *LOSO*, 188–89.

18. Welles, "Saga of Jenny."

19. IG, *LOSO*, 188.

20. Agreement, GG and T. B. Harms and Francis, Day & Hunter, February 21, 1918 (GCLC).

21. IG, *LOSO*, 189.

22. [ISGO], "In Which Ira."

23. Jablonski and Stewart, *The Gershwin Years*, 74.

24. Edward Jablonski, *Happy with the Blues* (New York: Da Capo, 1986), 43.

25. Jablonski and Stewart, *The Gershwin Years*, 75.

26. Gerald Bordman, *Days to Be Happy, Years to Be Sad: The Life and Music of Vincent Youmans* (New York: Oxford University Press, 1982), 27.

27. Jablonski and Stewart, *The Gershwin Years*, 75.

28. IG, *LOSO*, 119.

29. Agreement, February 16, 1921 (GCLC).

30. *New York Clipper*, March 2, 1921.

31. Bordman, *Days to Be Happy*, 33.

32. Jablonski and Stewart, *The Gershwin Years*, 75.

33. IG, *LOSO*, 335.

34. Letter to Alex Aarons signed by Paul Lannin, Vincent Youmans, Fred Jackson, and Isidor Gershwin to show to Abraham L. Erlanger "as an inducement to him to execute a contract with you" for *All at Sea*, February 17, 1921 (GCLC).

35. [ISGO], "In Which Ira."

36. *Billboard*, April 23, 1921.

37. *New York Evening Sun*, May 4, 1921.

38. IG, *LOSO*, 149.

39. Bordman, *Days to Be Happy*, 47.

40. LDS, journal transcript, March 20, 1968.

41. *New York Clipper*, February 23, 1921.

42. ASCAP/Arthur Francis assignment of performing rights, February 28, 1921 (GTLC).

43. MacGregor produced the show on Broadway in 1923 as *Elsie* with a new score by Noble Sissle and Eubie Blake.

44. The slower pace of Ella Fitzgerald's rendition in 1959, for which Ira wrote a new set of lyrics, was not the original one.

45. IG financial documents (GTLC).

46. LDS, journal transcript, October 3, 1956.

47. Fitzgerald, "My Lost City," 20.

48. IG, *LOSO*, 295.

49. Royalty statements, September 30 and December 31, 1922 (GCLC).

50. IG, *LOSO*, 296.

51. IG, description on verso of photograph of William Daly, n.d. (GTLC).

52. My thanks to Michael Rafter, who matched "Man, the Master" to its musical setting.

53. Chopin's story was brought to Broadway in 1928 by the Shubert brothers (producers of *Blossom Time*) in the show *White Lilacs*, but without the assistance of IG or William Daly.

54. Goldbeck's son-in-law was the composer Marc Blitzstein (*The Cradle Will Rock*).

Chapter 4

1. Jablonski and Stewart, *The Gershwin Years*, 89; "Whiteman Judges Named: Committee Will Decide 'What Is American Music,'" *New York Tribune*, January 4, 1924.

2. IG to Virginia Doffort, August 13, 1962 (GTLC).

3. IG to DE, October 11, 1955 (GTLC).

4. It was George Gershwin's second visit to London; he had written the score to *The Rainbow* there in 1923, a revue in which Ira was not involved.

5. IG to GG, June 25, 1924 (GTLC).

6. GG to IG, July 9, 1924 (GTLC).

7. "Butt's 'Goodness Sake,'" *Variety*, March 23, 1923.

8. Alex Aarons to IG, May 19, 1923 (GTLC).

9. IG to GG, August 27, 1924 (GTLC). The real identity of Arthur Francis had been revealed in a small news item in the December 23, 1921, issue of *Variety*.

10. Jablonski and Stewart, *The Gershwin Years*, 97.

11. Ira's early scrapbook, ca. 1908, includes a clipping entitled "Boys' Names and Their Signification" (GCLC).

12. IG to GG, August 27, 1924.

13. Kimball, *CLIG*, 38–39.

14. IG to GG, August 27, 1924.

15. IG to LP and EP, November 26, 1924 (GTLC).

16. Ewen, *George Gershwin*, 95.

17. IG to GG, June 25, 1924.

18. IG to GG, August 24, 1924 (GTLC).

19. "Astaires Will Appear in *Black-Eyed Susan*," *New York Sun*, October 9, 1924.

20. Agreement dated September 30, 1924 (GCLC).

21. IG to Alex Aarons and Vinton Freedley, October 8, 1924 (GCLC).

22. IG, notes, September 1967, accompanying donation of George Gershwin's Red Tune Book (dated) September 26, 1922 (GCLC).

23. Kimball and Simon, 46.

24. "Most Important Things about a Song Are the Idea and Title," *New York Herald Tribune*, April 26, 1925.

25. ISGO, *George Gershwin*, 201–2. A spondee is "a metrical foot consisting of two long or two stressed syllables" (*Oxford English Dictionary*).

26. IG, *LOSO*, 136.

27. "Most Important Things."

28. ISGO, *George Gershwin*, 201–2.

29. Fred Astaire, *Steps in Time* (New York: itbooks, 2008), 187.

30. S[tephen] Rathbun, *New York Sun*, December 2, 1924, quoted in Deena Rosenberg, *Fascinating Rhythm: The Collaboration of George and Ira Gershwin* (New York: Dutton, 1991), 108.

31. IG to LP and EP, November 26, 1924.

32. IG, *LOSO*, 5.

33. IG interview, "Problems with *The Man I Love*," *George and Ira Gershwin (Australia)* CD (GTLC).

34. IG, *LOSO*, 4.

35. Astaire, *Steps in Time*, 128.

36. "News and Gossip of the Rialto," *New York Times*, December 7, 1924.

37. W. R., *New York World*, December 2, 1924.

38. IG, *LOSO*, 119.

39. Astaire, *Steps in Time*, 130.

40. IG to Max Abramson, July 18, 1925 (GTLC).

41. Ashby Deering, "Brothers as Collaborators," *New York Morning Telegraph*, February 1, 1925. Emphasis added.

42. LDS, note, October 4, 1967 (LDSGTLC).

43. Tommy Krasker, liner notes to *Tell Me More* recording (New World Records, 2001).

44. M. L., "Gay Gershwin Music in Musical Comedy at Gaiety Theatre," *New York Daily News*, April 18, 1925.

45. IG, notes, May 14, 1965, regarding a letter from GG to Ring Lardner, March 31, 1925 (GCLC).

46. "*Tell Me More* Is Bright Musical Play," *New York Times*, April 14, 1925.

47. Data from *Variety*, April to July 1925.

48. "Most Important Things."

49. IG to LP and EP, June 8, 1925.

50. IG to LSS, October 11, 1961 (LSSLC).

51. IG, quoted in *CLIG*, xvi.

52. IG, *LOSO*, 120.

53. IG, *LOSO*, 176.

54. ISGO, *George Gershwin*, 181.

55. IG, *LOSO*, 183.

56. Babette Deutsch, *Poetry Handbook: A Dictionary of Terms*, 2nd ed. (New York: Grosset & Dunlap, 1962), 125 (quoted in IG, *LOSO*, 9).

57. IG, *LOSO*, 9. The reference is to Moliere's 1670 play *Le Bourgeois gentilhomme*.

58. Box office data from issues of *Variety*, January–June 1926.

59. *Tip-Toes* contract, September 10, 1925 (GCLC).

60. Leonard Hall, "A Thoroughbred," *Washington Daily News*, November 25, 1925.

61. Alexander Woollcott, "Mr. Gershwin's Latest," *New York World*, December 29, 1925.

62. IG, *LOSO*, 120.

63. "'Tip-Toes' Opens at the Forrest," *Philadelphia Public Ledger*, December 8, 1925.

64. IG, "Words and Music."

65. IG, transcript of interview by Max Wilk, August 1971. Oscar Hammerstein II revised Wodehouse's lyrics when the song was included in the score of *Show Boat* in 1927.

66. IG, *LOSO*, 120.

67. Lorenz Hart to IG, March 31, 1926 (GTLC).

68. IG to GG, April 1, 1926 (GTLC).

Chapter 5

1. IG to GG, February 27, 1926 (GTLC).

2. IG to GG, March 16, 1926 (GTLC). Ira passed on *Mama Loves Papa*.

3. Ira Gershwin, "Ira Pleads Innocent," in Abner Silver, *All Women Are Wolves* (New York: The Readers Press, 1945), 16.

4. LSG passport application, September 18, 1923 (Ancestry.com).

5. Lawrence D. Stewart, "Ira and Leonore Gershwin: The Happy Amalgam of Opposite Natures," essay for the program for the opening of the Ira and Leonore S. Gershwin Theater at the University of San Francisco, March 19, 1997 (LDSGTLC).

6. Lawrence D. Stewart, *Something about Leonore*, booklet for a tribute to Leonore Gershwin at the Library of Congress, 1995.

7. IG to Max Abramson, July 18, 1925; Walter Rimler, *George Gershwin: An Intimate Portrait* (Urbana: University of Illinois Press, 2009), 20.

8. Card addressed to "Ira B. Gershwin," April 6, 1926 (GTLC).

9. IG, *LOSO*, 261 (timing of song); ISGO, *George Gershwin*, 202–3 ("jingly").

10. LDS, journal transcript, August 27, 1958.

11. Ewen, *George Gershwin*, 120–21.

12. LDS, *Something about Leonore*. Ira was upset when he discovered that his mother had purchased the engagement ring; he had not intended to buy his fiancée a diamond (LSG/EP oral history, December 1984, tape #5; GTSF).

13. IG, *LOSO*, 111; IG to LSS, December 27, 1957 (GTSF).

14. Howard Dietz, *Dancing in the Dark* (New York: Quadrangle/New York Times Book Company, 1974), 74.

15. IG, *LOSO*, 111.

16. Irving Drutman, *Good Company: A Memoir, Mostly Theatrical* (Boston: Little, Brown, 1976), 69.

17. IG, *LOSO*, 77.

18. IG, *LOSO*, 185. Charles Pike Sawyer's review appeared in the *New York Evening Post* on July 27, 1926.

19. IG to GG, March 16, 1926.

20. IG, *LOSO*, 252.

21. Kimball, *CLIG*, 76. Paul Whiteman's recording of "(I'll Build a) Stairway to Paradise" was also included by O'Hara.

22. A short-lived 1928 edition featured Frances Gershwin, who also made a brief appearance in Herndon's earlier revue *Merry-Go-Round*.

23. LDS, journal transcript, September 14, 1956.

24. New York marriage license index (Ancestry.com); Ewen, *George Gershwin*, 117–18.

25. "Gertrude Lawrence Scores in Comedy," *Philadelphia Evening Public Ledger*, October 19, 1926.

26. Burns Mantle, "Oh, Brother, Do Not Overlook 'Oh, Kay!,'" *New York Daily News*, November 15, 1926.

27. Bide Dudley, *New York Evening World*, November 9, 1926.

28. Charles Brackett, *New Yorker*, November 20, 1926.

29. Box office data from issues of *Variety*, November 1926–June 1927.

30. Income report from Ralph Kravette, January 18, 1927. Another song from the show, "Dear Little Girl," was published in 1968 when *Star!*, the movie biopic of Gertrude Lawrence, was released.

31. Ewen, *George Gershwin*, 118.

32. Kimball, *CLIG*, xi.

33. Arthur Kober, "'Strike Up the Band' Reaches Broadway after Long Travail," *New York Telegram*, January 14, 1930.

34. *New York Sun*, August 20, 1926.

35. Ira's fear of the interplay of drivers can be traced to an incident in May 1917 when, taking an afternoon bike ride through New York City, he was nearly run over by a speeding taxi on Fourth Avenue near 14th Street. "I was deeply indebted to [the driver] for not cursing" (IG, "Everyman," May 6, 1917).

36. Jablonski and Stewart, 122.

37. GG to Jean O'Brien, August 10, 1927 (GCLC).

38. Austin, "Plays Out of Town: *Strike Up the Band*," *Variety*, September 7, 1927.

39. Kober, "'Strike Up the Band.'"

40. "New Musical Comedy Enjoyed at Shubert," *Philadelphia Record*, September 6 (?), 1927.

41. "Shubert—'Strike Up the Band,'" *Philadelphia Evening Bulletin*, September 6, 1927.

42. Arthur B. Waters, unidentified Philadelphia newspaper, September [day unknown], 1927.

43. Kober, "'Strike Up the Band.'"

44. Jablonski and Stewart, *The Gershwin Years*, 124–26.

45. "'Band' Taken Off," *Variety*, September 21, 1927.

46. "Future Plays," *Variety*, December 7, 1927; "Future Plays," *Variety*, May 28, 1928.

47. Ewen, *George Gershwin*, 122.

48. IG, *LOSO*, 24. As much of this text was used in Isaac Goldberg's biography of George Gershwin, it can probably be assumed that Goldberg was responsible for this article, taking

quotes from interviews with Ira. An earlier, much the same, version, appeared in the *New York Telegram* as "Which Comes First?" on October 25, 1930. See IG, "Notes on Collaborating with G.G." for Isaac Goldberg, June 1931 (?) (GCLC).

49. "The Passing Show," *The Tatler*, November 28, 1928.
50. IG, *LOSO*, 252.
51. George Harwood Phillips, *The Tunesmith & the Lyricist: Vernon Duke, Ira Gershwin and the Making of a Standard* (Camano Island, WA: Coyote Hill Press, 2016), 44–45.
52. IG to EJ, November 8, 1954 (GTLC).
53. IG, "Words and Music."
54. IG, *LOSO*, 24.
55. IG to YH, January 27, 1935 (Harburg Collection). The number was performed by Fred Astaire and Gene Kelly in MGM's 1945 all-star movie musical *Ziegfeld Follies*.

Chapter 6

1. "Zieggy Tangled Up with Two Writers," *Variety*, February 15, 1928.
2. LDS, journal transcript, February 24, 1953.
3. Box office data taken from issues of *Variety*, January–October 1928; Florenz Ziegfeld to GG, March 4, 1928 (GTLC).
4. LDS, note [ca. 1996] to journal transcript, December 11, 1953 (GTSF).
5. Michael Owen, "Before They Sailed," in Ira Gershwin, *The Gershwins Abroad, or Four Americans in Paris (and Several Other Cities): A 1928 Notebook* (Mainz: Schott Music, in press).
6. IG, "Everyman," June 16, 1917.
7. IG diary, March 16, 1928.
8. IG diary, March 20, 1928.
9. Noël Coward, *Present Indicative* (New York: Doubleday Doran, 1937), 112.
10. IG diary, March 20–24, 1928. The London production of *The Girl Friend* bore little resemblance to the Broadway original.
11. IG diary, March 19, 1928. Ira was wrong; Buchanan returned to New York in late 1929 to star in the Cole Porter musical *Wake Up and Dream*.
12. Jablonski and Stewart, 131.
13. A seventh song, "Why Be a Good Girl?," was dropped after the show played in Glasgow.
14. IG to Irving Drutman, June 4, 1951 (Irving Drutman letters from colleagues, 1943–1987, Eda Kuhn Loeb Music Library, Harvard University).
15. Agreement with Harms, January 4, 1928 (GCLC).
16. IG diary, March 17, 1928. This change was in the second refrain of "Sweet So-and So." Ira's original lyric was used when the song was performed in the 1930 revue *Sweet and Low*. "Chirp-Chirp!" was used again in the 1931 revue *Shoot the Works*.
17. IG diary, March 25, 1928.
18. IG diary, March 31, 1928.
19. IG diary, April 6, 1928.
20. IG diary, April 16, 1928.
21. Alan Hutchinson, "A Song-Writer Listens to Some Foreign Melodies," *Paris Comet*, July 1928.
22. IG diary, April 29 and May 1, 1928.
23. IG diary, April 25, 1928.
24. IG, "Notes to Walter Damrosch—George Gershwin Correspondence (1928–1932)," May 10, 1965 (GTLC).

25. IG diary, May 6–8, 1928.
26. IG diary, May 16, 1928.
27. IG diary, May 31, 1928.
28. IG diary, June 6, 1928.
29. IG diary, June 17, 1928.
30. Robert Littell, "The Play: *Treasure Girl*," *New York Post*, November 9, 1928.
31. IG, *LOSO*, 37. Cain's Warehouse was a New York company that specialized in housing scenery from shows that had closed on Broadway.
32. Robert Benchley, "The Theatre," *Life*, November 30, 1928.
33. IG, *LOSO*, 36.
34. IG, *LOSO*, 94.
35. IG to LSS, August 8, 1959 (LSSLC). A "double A" member of ASCAP—the highest ranking—received larger royalty payments from the organization than members who were rated "A" or "B."
36. S. N. Behrman, "Troubadour," *New Yorker*, May 25, 1929.
37. 1930 US census, April 2, 1930.
38. ISGO, *George Gershwin*, 7.
39. GG to Rosamund Walling, March 21, 1930 (GTLC).
40. Ewen, *George Gershwin*, 153.
41. Carl Hovey to IG, May 13, 1932 (GTLC).
42. Unsigned agreement, May 1927 (GCLC).
43. "Too Many Musicals," *Variety*, February 15, 1928; IG diary, March 9, 1928.
44. IG diary, March 21, 1928.
45. "'East Is West' with Music," *New York Times*, May 23, 1928.
46. GG to Rosamond Walling, January 29, 1929 (GCLC).
47. IG, *LOSO*, 30.
48. IG, *LOSO*, 152.
49. Isaac Goldberg, "All about the Gershwins: Principally George, Incidentally Ira," *Boston Evening Transcript*, December 21, 1929.
50. IG, *LOSO*, 152.
51. Kimball, *CLIG*, 143.
52. "'Show Girl' Ziegfeld's Latest," *Boston Globe*, June 26, 1929.
53. *Variety*, September 11, 1929.
54. Kimball, *CLIG*, 143.
55. IG, *LOSO*, 31.
56. IG to YH, January 27, 1935.
57. IG, *LOSO*, 237–38. A melody Ira lyricized as "Yellow Blues" was published as the piano piece *Impromptu in Two Keys* in the early 1970s.
58. IG, *LOSO*, 314.
59. IG diary, March 28, 1928.
60. LDS, journal transcript, November 22, 1953; James R. Gaines, *Wit's End: Days and Nights of the Algonquin Round Table* (New York: Harcourt Brace, 1977), 195.
61. Groucho Marx, "Buy It, Put It Away, and Forget It," *New Yorker*, May 4, 1929; Groucho Marx, *Groucho and Me* (New York: Da Capo, 1995), 197.

Chapter 7

1. IG to Benny Green, August 30, 1962 (GTLC).
2. Harlan Thompson, "The State of Musical Comedy," *Billboard*, December 10, 1927.
3. Quoted in Lawrence Maslon, "George S. Kaufman: The Gloomy Dean of American Comedy" (liner notes for *Strike Up the Band*; Roxbury Recordings/Elektra Records, 1991).
4. Ward Morehouse, "Broadway after Dark," *New York Sun*, January 15, 1930.
5. Box office data from *Variety*, January–June 1930.
6. IG contract with Strike Up the Band, Inc., December 2, 1929 (GCLC).
7. Robert Benchley, "Satire to Music," *New Yorker*, January 25, 1930.
8. Ralph Barton, "Theatre," *Life*, February 7, 1930.
9. Bernard C. Clausen, "Strike Up the Band!," *The Christian Century*, July 8, 1931.
10. IG, *LOSO*, 39.
11. Isaac Goldberg, "Gebrüder Gershwin," *Vanity Fair*, June 1932.
12. Douglas Watt, "Ira Reminisces about George," *New York Daily News*, May 27, 1953.
13. IG diary, August 22, 1955.
14. Frank Lee Donoghue, "Ira Gershwin's Home Still Glorifies George," *Los Angeles Examiner*, July 13, 1959. *My Body* is on display in the Gershwin Gallery of the Library of Congress, opposite a self-portrait of George Gershwin in a checkered sweater.
15. Newman Levy, "Drama: Three Shows with Music," *The Nation*, October 29, 1930.
16. IG, *LOSO*, 235.
17. IG, *LOSO*, 31.
18. IG to Goddard Lieberson, March 14, 1951 (MSS 69, the Goddard Lieberson Papers in the Gilmore Music Library of Yale University).
19. IG, *LOSO*, 342.
20. IG, *LOSO*, 271.
21. Percy Hammond, "The Theatres," *New York Herald Tribune*, November 2, 1930.
22. Alison Smith, "Words and Music," *New York World*, November 9, 1930.
23. IG to Raymond S. Koff, February 26, 1958 (GTLC).
24. J. Brooks Atkinson, "They Say It with Music," *New York Times*, December 28, 1930.
25. Agreement with RKO Radio Pictures, March 9, 1931 (GTLC).
26. Agreement with RKO Radio Pictures, November 27, 1931 (GCLC).
27. Kimball, *CLIG*, 109.
28. Agreement with Fox Film Corporation, April 10, 1930 (GCLC). George received $70,000; Ira, $30,000.
29. Jablonski and Stewart, *The Gershwin Years*, 159.
30. IG to LP and EP, January 16, 1931 (GTLC).
31. IG, "Words and Music."
32. IG to LP and EP, January 16, 1931.
33. Louis Sobol, "Hollywood Cavalcade," *Harrisburg Evening News*, March 31, 1941.
34. A 1943 article about the *Rhapsody in Blue* biopic and Herbert Rudley, the actor playing Ira.
35. Jay Gorney to IG, January 14, 1931 (GTLC).
36. Tom Dardis, *Firebrand: The Life of Horace Liveright* (New York: Random House, 1995), 330–31; IG to LP and EP, January 16, 1931.
37. GG to HB, September 9, 1931 (GTLC). Aarons and Freedley *did* produce a show that season: *Singin' the Blues*, a "melodrama with music" that starred Frank Wilson (the original Porgy in the Theatre Guild play) and an all-Black cast.

38. IG to DE, February 27, 1970 (GTLC).

39. IG to ISGO, July 9, 1931 (GTLC). A nonmusical movie was made of *Turnabout* in 1940 starring Adolphe Menjou and Carole Landis.

40. Heywood Broun, "The Stagehands Do Their Bit," *New York World-Telegram*, June 16, 1931.

41. GG to ISGO, June 15–16, 1931 (GG Letters to ISGO [MS Thr 222], Harvard Theatre Collection, Houghton Library, Harvard University).

42. IG to Leopold Godowsky Jr., Tuesday [August 18, 1931?] (GTLC).

43. GG to Sonya Levien, August 21, 1931 (Sonya Levien Papers, The Huntington Library, San Marino, California). Levien received the final screenplay credit for *Delicious*.

44. LSG to GP, n.d. [October/November 1931] (GTLC).

Chapter 8

1. Percy N. Stone, "Ira Gershwin's Light Is Shining without George's Reflected Glory," *New York Herald Tribune*, December 27, 1931.

2. IG, *LOSO*, 351–52.

3. IG, notes on galleys of *George Gershwin: His Journey to Greatness*. *Of Thee I Sing* cost $88,000 to produce; $50,000 in cash and $38,000 in credit. George took 10 percent of the show.

4. IG to George Frazier, August 4, 1965 (GTLC).

5. Stone, "Ira Gershwin's Light."

6. IG to ISGO, April 27, 1932 (GCLC).

7. Kimball, *CLIG*, 172–73.

8. Howard Teichmann, *George S. Kaufman: An Intimate Portrait* (New York: Atheneum, 1972), 99.

9. LDS, journal transcript, October 11, 1953.

10. Frank D. Fackenthal to Morrie Ryskind, April 28, 1932 (*T-Mss 1996-024, Morrie Ryskind Papers, Billy Rose Theatre Division, The New York Public Library for the Performing Arts).

11. "Musical Play Gets the Pulitzer Award," *New York Times*, May 3, 1932.

12. LDS, journal transcript, October 11, 1953.

13. A posthumous Pulitzer Prize was awarded to George Gershwin in 1998 in honor of the centenary of his birth.

14. LDS, journal transcript, October 11, 1953.

15. Carl Hovey to IG, May 13, 1932.

16. IG to Sonya Levien and Carl Hovey, July 19, 1932 (Levien Papers).

17. IG to SNB, May 4, 1932 (S. N. Behrman Papers, Manuscripts and Archives Division, The New York Public Library, Astor, Lenox and Tilden Foundations).

18. Morris Gershwin death certificate (GTLC).

19. LDS, journal transcript, April 26, 1953.

20. Jablonski and Stewart, *The Gershwin Years*, 332.

21. LDS, journal transcript, October 11, 1953.

22. IG to ISGO, April 27, 1932.

23. "'Of Thee I Sing' Authors Sued as Plagiarists," *New York Herald Tribune*, August 9, 1932. A month later, Ira and George were defendants in a second lawsuit, filed by a woman who claimed that a story she had written had been stolen and turned into *Delicious*. ("Says Picture Theme Stolen," *San Bernardino Sun*, September 21, 1932.)

24. Lowenfels v. George Jean Nathan, George S. Kaufman, et al., December 28, 1932 (GCLC).

Woolsey issued a monumental literary decision the following year when he allowed the publication of James Joyce's controversial novel *Ulysses* in the United States.

25. Oscar Levant, *The Memoirs of an Amnesiac* (New York: G. P. Putnam's Sons, 1965), 124.

26. GG to ISGO, May 6, 1932 (GTLC).

27. GG to GP, August 17, 1932 (GTLC).

28. GG to ISGO, October 8, 1932 (GCLC).

29. *New York Sun*, October 28, 1932.

30. "'English' Unready but Gets Philly Break; $12,000 in Three Times," *Variety*, December 6, 1932.

31. GG to ISGO, December 21, 1932 (GCLC).

32. IG, *LOSO*, 325; "Stardom for Pearl," *Variety*, January 17, 1933.

33. "Billing Row, Buchanan Out for 'English' Role," *Variety*, January 10, 1933.

34. IG, *LOSO*, 325.

35. Gilbert Gabriel, *New York American*, January 21, 1933.

36. IG, *LOSO*, 325.

37. "Leasing Active in Apartments on East Side," *New York Herald Tribune*, May 25, 1933.

38. IG, *LOSO*, 162.

39. IG, *Let 'Em Eat Cake* lyrics notebook (GCLC).

40. Rosenberg, *Fascinating Rhythm*, 251.

41. GG to ISGO, August 16, 1933 (GCLC).

42. GG to ISGO, August 25, 1933 (GCLC).

43. H. T. P. [H. T. Parker], "'Let 'Em Eat Cake' Cheered in Boston," *New York Times*, October 3, 1933.

44. IG to Albert Sirmay, Wednesday [October 1933] (GCLC).

45. Jablonski and Stewart, *The Gershwin Years*, 202.

46. Whitney Bolton, "'Let 'Em Eat Cake': Surpasses as Sequel," *New York Morning Telegraph*, October 24, 1933; in Gregory R. Soriano (ed.), *Gershwin in His Time: A Biographical Scrapbook, 1919–1937* (New York: Gramercy, 1998), 100.

47. Brooks Atkinson, "'Let 'Em Eat Cake': Being a Few Further Considerations of the Sequel to 'Of Thee I Sing' Based on a Second Visit," *New York Times*, November 12, 1933.

48. IG check, September 18, 1933 (GTLC); agreement between GG and Sam H. Harris, July 21, 1933 (GCLC).

49. Ewen, *George Gershwin*, 209.

Chapter 9

1. GG to ISGO, November 2, 1933 (GCLC).

2. Walter Rimler, *The Man That Got Away: The Life and Songs of Harold Arlen* (Urbana: University of Illinois Press, 2015), 41.

3. Agreement, March 1, 1934 (GCLC); LDS, journal transcript, February 12, 1960 (billing dispute).

4. William K. Zinsser, "The Secret Music Maker," *Harper's*, May 1960.

5. Jablonski, *Happy*, 89.

6. LDS note, September 14, 1996, to his journal transcript, March 30, 1961.

7. Jablonski, *Happy*, 95; Edward Jablonski, *Harold Arlen: Rhythm, Rainbows, and Blues* (Boston: Northeastern University Press, 1996), 85.

8. "The Stage: Shubert Theatre 'Life Begins at 8:40,'" *Boston Globe*, August 7, 1934.

9. Gilbert Gabriel, "Life Begins at 8:40 and Very Nicely," *Syracuse American*, September 9, 1934.

10. "'8:40' Too Good, Winter Garden Conversion to Nitery Put off," *Variety*, October 30, 1934.

11. GG to DBH, March 8, 1934 (GTLC).

12. DuBose Heyward, "Porgy and Bess Return on Wings of Song," *Stage*, October 1935.

13. DBH to GG, March 19, 1934 (GTLC).

14. Kimball, *CLIG*, 239.

15. GG to IG, June 27, 1934 (GTLC).

16. Alexander Steinert, quoted in Merle Armitage, ed., *George Gershwin* (New York: Da Capo, 1995), 46.

17. GG to DBH, November 5, 1934 (GTLC).

18. Kimball and Simon, *The Gershwins*, 180–81.

19. Armitage, *George Gershwin*, 49–50.

20. GG to Kay Halle, September 17, 1934 (Kay Halle Personal Papers, The John F. Kennedy Library).

21. Kimball, *CLIG*, 222.

22. YH to IG, January 18, 1935 (GTLC). Universal's black-and-white *Show Boat*, directed by James Whale (*Frankenstein*), has been overshadowed by MGM's 1951 color version.

23. IG to YH, January 27, 1935.

24. Vernon Duke, *Passport to Paris* (Boston: Little, Brown, 1955), 223.

25. IG to GG, February 16, 1935 (GTLC).

26. IG, *LOSO*, 187.

27. IG to GG, February 16, 1935.

28. IG to YH, January 27, 1935. One of the young men was the future novelist Herman Wouk, a fellow alum of Townsend Harris Hall.

29. IG to GG, March 18, 1935 (GTLC).

30. IG to YH, March 29, 1935 (Harburg Collection).

31. Duke, *Passport to Paris*, 315–16.

32. IG to DE, October 11, 1955.

33. IG to YH, July 3, 1935 (Harburg Collection).

34. IG to YH, July 3, 1935.

Chapter 10

1. *New York Daily News*, May 6, 1935; "Anne Brown to Sing in Gershwin Opera," *The Afro-American*, May 25, 1935.

2. DBH, "Porgy and Bess Return on Wings of Song."

3. LDS, journal transcript, February 9, 1956; Michael Feinstein "interview" of Ira for UPI, May 31, 1983 (questions submitted by UPI; became the basis for a syndicated article published just before the broadcast of the Tony Awards) (LDSGTLC).

4. Armitage, *George Gershwin*, 166–67.

5. *Variety*, October 9, 1935.

6. Murray Schumach, "Hollywood Recall: Ira Gershwin Provides 'Notes' for 'Porgy,'" *New York Times*, June 21, 1959.

7. IG to EJ, April 5, 1947 (GTLC); IG diary, January 10, 1956.

8. Box office data from *Variety*, October–December 1935.

9. Warren Munsell to IG, December 18, 1935 (GTLC).

10. Agreements dated April 22, 1935 (GTLC).
11. Contract, June 28, 1935 (LSSLC); Schumach, "Hollywood Recall."
12. LSS journal, March 30, 1952.
13. LDS to LSS, December 5, 1960 (LDSGTLC).
14. KS to IG, June 29, 1959 (GTLC).
15. IG to Frank Durham, June 18, 1951 (GTLC).
16. IG, *LOSO*, 149.
17. IG, *LOSO*, 193–95.
18. IG to Arthur Freed, November 6, 1944 (Arthur Freed papers, Cinematic Arts Library, USC Libraries, University of Southern California).
19. Libbey, "Plays Out of Town: 1936 Ziegfeld Follies," *Variety*, January 8, 1936. Moss Hart's only contribution, the sketch "Pulitzer Prize Announced," was cut before New York.
20. Box office data from *Variety*, February–May 1936; *Variety*, May 13, 1936.
21. IG to YH, June 12, 1936 (Harburg Collection).
22. IG to VD, October 6, 1936 (Vernon Duke Collection, Music Division, Library of Congress).
23. Vincente Minnelli and Hector Arce, *I Remember It Well* (Garden City, NY: Doubleday), 63–65.
24. Minnelli and Arce, *I Remember It Well*, 230.
25. Minnelli and Arce, *I Remember It Well*, 81–82.
26. MV *Georgic* passenger list (www.familysearch.org).
27. YH to IG, October 19, 1935 (GTLC).
28. IG to YH, June 12, 1936.
29. GG to Archie Selwyn, June 22, 1936 (GCLC).
30. Arthur Lyons to GG, April 29, 1936; Arthur Lyons to GG and IG, May 14, June 10, and June 27, 1936; GG and IG to Arthur Lyons, June 11, 1936 (all GCLC).
31. William Daly to GG, September 13, 1936 (GTLC).
32. Jablonski and Stewart, *The Gershwin Years*, 241, 252.
33. Jablonski and Stewart, *The Gershwin Years*, 260.
34. IG, *LOSO*, 248.
35. GG to MS, September 1, 1936 (GCLC).
36. IG to John Fischbach, September 3, 1948 (GTLC).
37. IG to Charles Jackson, November 22 and 24, 1944 (Charles Jackson Papers, Rauner Special Collections Library Repository, Dartmouth College).
38. IG to VD, October 6, 1936.
39. "Gershwin Brothers Give New Bruin Song to Associated Student Body," *Daily Bruin*, September 24, 1936.
40. IG to VD, October 6, 1936.
41. GG to Gregory Zilboorg, October 26, 1936 (GCLC).
42. Transcript of IG conference with Robert Rossen, August 13, 1941.
43. GG to Gregory Zilboorg, October 26, 1936.
44. IG to VD, October 6, 1936.
45. GG to MS, October 28, 1936 (GCLC).
46. GG to Henry Spitzer, October 24, 1936 (GTLC).
47. IG to AMW, December 5, 1936 (GCLC).
48. Contract with Samuel Goldwyn, December 3, 1936 (GCLC).
49. IG to AMW, December 5, 1936.

50. RG affidavit, May 1938 (LDSGTLC).

51. GG to MS, n.d. [January 4, 1937] (GCLC).

52. IG to EP and LP, January 12, 1937 (GTLC [money lost]); Peter Moruzzi, *Palm Springs Holiday: A Vintage Tour from Palm Springs to the Salton Sea* (Salt Lake City, UT: Gibbs Smith, 2009), 38–42 (Dunes); Jim Heimann, *Sins of the City: The Real Los Angeles Noir* (San Francisco: Chronicle, 1999), 68 (goons).

53. IG to EP and LP, January 12, 1937.

54. IG to Morrie Ryskind, "Thursday" [September 23, 1943] (Ryskind Papers).

55. Ewen, *George Gershwin*, 271.

56. IG financial documents.

57. IG to EP and LP, January 12, 1937.

Chapter 11

1. IG to LSS, May 31, 1968 [draft] (LDSGTLC).

2. Eileen Creelman, "Picture Plays and Players: Ira Gershwin Tells of Collaborating with His Brother on 'Damsel in Distress,'" *New York Sun*, December 22, 1937.

3. GG to Zena Hannenfeldt, January 8, 1937 (GCLC).

4. IG to EP and LP, January 12, 1937. The novelist, screenwriter, and producer Pincus Jacob Wolfson (1903–1979) was not credited on *A Damsel in Distress* but was involved in its original stages.

5. IG to EP and LP, January 12, 1937.

6. Jablonski and Stewart, *The Gershwin Years*, 288–89. It remains unclear on which of these days the two incidents occurred.

7. Dr. Philip M. Lovell, "Clinical Report on Mr. George Gershwin," February 27, 1937 (GTLC). Lovell was the owner of the Lovell Health House, designed in 1929 by the modernist architect Richard Neutra.

8. HB, affidavit, 1937 (LDSGTLC).

9. Ewen, *George Gershwin*, 287; Jablonski and Stewart, *The Gershwin Years*, 284.

10. GG to EP, March 16, 1937 (GCLC).

11. IG to VD, May 5, 1937 (Duke Collection).

12. IG, *LOSO*, 258.

13. Teichmann, *George S. Kaufman*, 92.

14. LDS, journal transcripts, February 9, 1965, and June 19, 1962.

15. IG to VD, May 5, 1937.

16. IG to VD, May 5, 1937.

17. IG to Bernard Taper, February 8, 1963 (GTLC).

18. IG to VD, May 5, 1937.

19. GG to RG, June 10, 1937 (GCLC); IG diary, March 5, 1955.

20. Gabriel Segall to Gregory Zilboorg, October 12, 1938 (GCLC).

21. IG, notes, 1937 (GTLC); Ewen, *George Gershwin*, 279.

22. Ewen, *George Gershwin*, 279.

23. Gabriel Segall to Gregory Zilboorg, October 12, 1938.

24. IG, notes, 1937.

25. Gabriel Segall to Gregory Zilboorg, October 12, 1938.

26. GP to Irene Gallagher, Wednesday [July 27, 1937] (GCLC).

27. Louis Carp, "George Gershwin—Illustrious American Composer: His Fatal Glioblastoma," *American Journal of Surgical Pathology* 3, no. 5 (October 1979): 473–78.

28. IG, notes, 1937.

29. P. G. Wodehouse to Leonora Cazalet, July 13, 1937, in P. G. Wodehouse, *A Life in Letters*, ed. Sophie Ratcliffe (New York: W. W. Norton, 2011), 268.

30. IG to Bernard Taper, February 8, 1963.

31. Document shown in Feinstein, *The Gershwins and Me*, 337.

32. IG to ISGO, July 25, 1937 (GCLC).

33. Sam Behrman, "The Gershwin Years," in *People in a Diary: A Memoir* (Boston: Little, Brown, 1972), 252–54.

34. Jablonski and Stewart, *The Gershwin Years*, 287.

35. Edward Jablonski, "What about Ira?," in *The Gershwin Style: New Looks at the Music of George Gershwin*, ed. Wayne Schneider (New York: Oxford University Press, 1999), 236.

36. Ewen, *George Gershwin*, 280; IG, undated notes on GG's final illness (GCLC).

37. Behrman, *People in a Diary*, 254.

38. Gregory Zilboorg to GG, June 30, 1937 (GCLC).

39. Duke, *Passport to Paris*, 351.

40. Jablonski and Stewart, *The Gershwin Years*, 292.

41. Behrman, *People in a Diary*, 254–55.

42. IG, note on L. Wolfe Gilbert to GG (?), July 7, 1937 (GCLC).

43. Jablonski, *Gershwin*, 322; IG, undated notes on GG's final illness; GG, power of attorney, January 8, 1937 (GTLC).

44. Ewen, *George Gershwin*, 281; IG, undated notes on GG's final illness.

45. FG to IG, July 8, 1937 (GCLC).

46. GP to Irene Gallagher, Wednesday [July 27, 1937]. Ewen's 1956 biography notes the time as 3 p.m. (p. 300), while his revised 1970 version says it was two hours later (p. 281).

47. Ewen, *George Gershwin*, 281.

48. Fred Astaire to Adele Astaire, July 18, 1937, quoted in Kathleen Riley, *The Astaires: Fred & Adele* (New York: Oxford University Press, 2012), 182.

49. Gabriel Segall to Gregory Zilboorg, October 12, 1938.

50. GP to Irene Gallagher, Wednesday [July 27, 1937]. Ira's 1937 notes indicate "to hospital" but only mention the midnight time.

51. GP to Irene Gallagher, Wednesday [July 27, 1937].

52. "Chronological Events—Saturday—July 10th 1937," a document loaned to Clifford Odets by IG, 1942? (GTLC).

53. "Chronological Events."

54. Gabriel Segall to Gregory Zilboorg, October 12, 1938.

55. "Chronological Events."

56. "Chronological Events." The family and friends were back at the hospital by 1:35 a.m.

57. GP to Irene Gallagher, Wednesday [July 27, 1937].

58. "Chronological Events"

59. GP to Irene Gallagher, Wednesday [July 27, 1937].

60. "Chronological Events."

61. Gabriel Segall to Gregory Zilboorg, October 12, 1938.

62. "Chronological Events."

63. Jablonski and Stewart, *The Gershwin Years*, 296.

64. Ewen, *George Gershwin*, 282–83.

65. "Chronological Events."
66. GP to Irene Gallagher, Wednesday [July 27, 1937].
67. GP to Irene Gallagher, Wednesday [July 27, 1937].
68. Gabriel Segall to Gregory Zilboorg, October 12, 1938.
69. GP to Irene Gallagher, Wednesday [July 27, 1937].

Chapter 12

1. Isaac Goldberg, *George Gershwin: A Study in American Music*, rev. ed., supplemented by Edith Garson (New York: Frederick Ungar, 1958), 350.
2. IG to EA, August 24, 1937 (GCLC).
3. Don O'Malley, "New York Inside Out," *Kilgore [Texas] News Herald*, August 18, 1937.
4. "Chronological Events"; EA affidavit, n.d. (LDSGTLC).
5. GG, California Certificate of Taxpayer Claiming Residence, January 15, 1937 (GCLC); IG note, n.d., on the verso of IG to Frank Colby, August 17, 1948 (GTLC).
6. Court order, July 12, 1937 (GTLC).
7. "Simultaneous Gershwin Services on Two Coasts," *Film Daily*, July 14, 1937.
8. "Gershwin's Classic, 'Rhapsody in Blue,' May Be His Requiem," *New York Post*, July 12, 1937.
9. Duke, *Passport to Paris*, 352.
10. "Gershwin's Brother Arrives for the Funeral Tomorrow," *New York Post*, July 14, 1937.
11. RG, letters of administration, August 15, 1938 (Charles Schwartz Papers, Music Division, The New York Public Library for the Performing Arts).
12. IG note, n.d., on verso of IG to Frank Colby, August 17, 1948.
13. L. Wolfe Gilbert and Sigmund Romberg to Gene Buck, July 12, 1937 (GTLC).
14. "George Gershwin Funeral to Be Held Here Thursday," *Film Daily*, July 13, 1937.
15. Invoice, Berliner-Pollak Funeral Directors, July 19, 1937 (GTLC).
16. "Thousands Attend Gershwin Funeral," *New York Times*, July 16, 1937.
17. MS to EP, July 21, 1937 (GTLC).
18. LDS, "Carnegie Talk," March 9, 1997 (LDSGTLC).
19. "Gershwin Praised by Rabbi Wise at Composer's Rites," *New York Post*, July 15, 1937; "Thousands Attend Gershwin Funeral." A simultaneous service was held at the Temple B'nai Brith in Hollywood.
20. Invoice, Berliner-Pollak Funeral Directors, July 19, 1937.
21. Kate Wolpin interviewed by Vivian Perlis, January 30, 1986.
22. Ewen, *George Gershwin*, 306.
23. MS to EP, July 21, 1937.
24. IG, "Everyman," April 23, 1917.
25. Feinstein, *The Gershwins and Me*, 26.
26. George Gershwin convinced Max Dreyfus to publish one of Arthur's songs—"Slowly but Surely" (lyrics by Edward Heyman)—under the New World Music imprint.
27. LDS, journal transcript, November 9, 1952 (and later note to entry).
28. GG estate, administrative documents, July 1937 (GCLC).
29. "Geo. Gershwin Estate May Total 800G," *Variety*, July 28, 1937.
30. IG to Alexander Smallens, July 15, 1937 (Alexander Smallens Papers, music division, The New York Public Library).
31. Stephen Saxe, interviewed by author, July 25, 2018.

32. EA affidavit, n.d.; IG to EA, September 1, 1937 (GCLC).

33. IG to ISGO, July 25, 1937.

34. IG to RG, July 31, 1937 (GCLC).

35. Duke, *Passport to Paris*, 352.

36. IG to RG, July 31, 1937.

37. KS to IG, August 11, 1937 (GTLC).

38. IG, foreword to *The George and Ira Gershwin Song Book*, x.

39. IG to ISGO, July 25, 1937.

40. B. R. Crisler, "Film Gossip of the Week," *New York Times*, November 14, 1937.

41. IG to EJ, May 18, 1954 (GTLC).

42. Jablonski and Stewart, *The Gershwin Years*, 335.

43. IG, *LOSO*, 106–7.

44. Jablonski and Stewart, *The Gershwin Years*, 335.

45. IG to RG, August 17, 1937 (GCLC).

46. RG to IG, n.d. [after August 9, 1937] (GTLC).

47. IG to RG, August 17, 1937.

48. IG to EA, August 24 and September 1, 1937.

49. EA to AMW, September 20, 1937 (LSSLC).

50. LDS, journal transcript, April 26, 1953.

51. IG to EP, October 8/9, 1937 (GTLC).

52. IG to EA and Abe Rosenthal, October 20, 1937 (GCLC).

53. IG to Albert Sirmay, September 11, 1937 (GCLC).

54. IG to GP, December 18, 1937 (GTLC).

55. IG to EA and Abe Rosenthal, October 20, 1937.

56. IG to HB, October 26, 1937 (GTLC).

57. IG to FG, April 2, 1949 (GTLC).

58. IG to GP, December 18, 1937.

59. IG to GP, December 24, 1937 (GTLC).

60. Creelman, "Picture Plays."

61. IG, *LOSO*, 65–66.

62. IG to GP, January 4, 1938 (GTLC).

63. IG to Alexander Smallens, September 11, 1941 (Smallens Papers).

64. IG to ISGO, April 13, 1938 (GCLC).

65. IG to VD, December 8, 1938 (Duke Collection).

66. IG to GP, January 30, 1938 (GTLC).

67. *Daily Variety*, January 26, 1938; *Hollywood Reporter*, January 26, 1938.

68. IG, *LOSO*, 139–40.

69. IG, *LOSO*, 140.

70. IG to ISGO, April 13, 1938.

71. IG to FG, April 2, 1949.

72. Edward Wolpin to IG, April 29, 1938 (GTLC).

73. IG to DE, n.d. (quoted in Ewen, *George Gershwin*, 269). Hermes Pan won the Best Dance Direction award for *A Damsel in Distress*, one of the movie's two nominations.

74. IG to ISGO, April 13, 1938.

75. Agreement dated March 28, 1938 (GCLC).

76. IG, document justifying biopic, ca. 1938 (GTLC).

77. IG to EA, December 23, 1938 (GCLC).

78. IG to AMW, October 24, 1938 (GCLC).

79. IG to YH, January 27, 1935.

80. LSG to HB, April 27, 1938 (GTLC).

81. IG to ISGO, April 13, 1938.

82. IG to AMW, April 7, 1938 (GCLC).

83. Robert Kimball, interviewed by author, April 10, 2018.

84. Deena Rosenberg, interviews of EP, May 18 and June 7, 1978 (GTLC).

85. Jablonski and Stewart, *The Gershwin Years*, 306–10.

86. IG on his role in his brother's career, ca. 1952, during the making of *Give a Girl a Break* (LSSLC).

87. IG to ISGO, April 13, 1938.

88. Jablonski and Stewart, *The Gershwin Years*, 318.

89. IG to EA, July 1, 1938 (GCLC).

90. IG to EA, October 18, 1938 (GCLC).

91. LSG to EP, n.d. [ca. July 4, 1938] (GTLC).

92. IG to HB, July 26, 1938 (GTLC).

93. IG to ISGO, April 13, 1938.

94. LDS, note ca. 1996 to his January 6, 1956 journal entry (LDSGTLC).

95. IG to Elsie Goldberg, August 5, 1938 (GCLC).

96. ISGO to GG, September 12, 1935; ISGO to IG, July 27, 1937 (both GTLC).

97. ISGO to IG, August 22, 1937 (GCLC).

98. IG to ISGO, April 13, 1938.

99. VD to IG, October 21, 1936 (GTLC).

100. GG to RG, June 10, 1937; *Boxoffice*, October 1, 1938; Chester Paul, "Filmdom to Frolic for War Victims," *Los Angeles Times*, October 2, 1938. Home movie footage from this party can be seen at the YouTube page of the Library of Congress: https://www.youtube.com/watch?v=X-ECLduZTNI.

101. *Variety*, March 30, 1938.

102. "Liberal Factions Line Up Schedule," *Boxoffice*, October 8, 1938.

103. IG to AMW, December 3, 1938 (GCLC).

104. "Film Leaders Launch Demand for U.S. to Sever Economic Ties with Germany," Associated Press, December 9, 1938.

105. IG to Alfred Simon, June 19, 1968 (GTLC).

106. IG, "Everyman," May 22, 1918 (GTLC).

107. IG to CW, December 28, 1938 (GTLC).

108. IG to Alfred Simon, June 19, 1968.

109. IG to John Cacavas, August 29, 1967 (GTLC).

110. IG to FG, draft, n.d. [after October 17, 1938?] (GTLC).

111. Max Wilk, *They're Playing Our Song: Conversations with America's Classic Songwriters* (New York: Atheneum, 1973), 196.

112. VD to IG, December 3, 1938 (GTLC).

113. IG to VD, December 8, 1938.

114. IG to AMW, October 24, 1938.

115. IG to RG, May 12, 1939 (GCLC).

116. IG to AMW, May 22, 1939 (GTLC).

117. IG to AMW, April 20, 1942 (GCLC).

118. FG to IG, June 26, 1938 (GTLC).

119. LDS, journal transcript, April 26, 1953.

120. EA to IG, January 9, 1939 (GCLC).

121. IG to EA, January 13, 1939 (GCLC).

122. IG to EA, January 13, 1939.

123. IG to FG, April 2, 1949.

124. IG to LSS, September 15, 1950 (LSSLC).

125. IG to AMW, August 22, 1939 (GCLC).

126. IG to HB, May 4, 1954 (GTLC).

127. IG to VD, August 7, 1939 (Duke Collection).

Chapter 13

1. IG to VD, August 5, 1939.

2. IG to VD, February 26, 1940 (Duke Collection).

3. IG, *LOSO*, 325.

4. IG to YH, "Monday" [February 19, 1940] (Harburg Collection).

5. LSG to EP, February 20, 1940 (GTLC).

6. IG, *LOSO*, 315.

7. IG diary, May 1, 1954. Gallahadion was a 36-to-1 long shot.

8. IG to SNB, February 19, 1940 (Behrman Papers).

9. IG, "Recollections of Kurt Weill," a portion of an audio disc included with *The Two Worlds of Kurt Weill* (RCA Victor, 1966). The recording was made at Ira Gershwin's home on November 3, 1965.

10. IG to EJ, August 10, 1944 (GTLC).

11. LDS, "Notes for an essay on *LOSO*," January 21, 1996 (LDSGTLC).

12. IG to EP, July 4, 1940 (GTLC).

13. Sheridan Morley, *Gertrude Lawrence: A Biography* (New York: McGraw-Hill, 1981), 145.

14. "U.S. Classics Pack Stadium," *Life*, July 29, 1940.

15. IG to MD, August 21, 1941 (GTLC).

16. IG to MD, July 11, 1945 (GTLC).

17. IG to CW, August 30, 1940 (GTLC).

18. IG to VD, September 27, 1940 (Duke Collection).

19. FG to IG, "Sunday" [November 26, 1939] (GTLC).

20. IG to FG, April 2, 1949.

21. Margaret Hayden Rector, "You Can't REALLY Tell about People until You've Seen Their Homes," *House Beautiful*, June 1940.

22. LDS, GTSF photo database, June 19, 1995.

23. Kimball, *CLIG*, xii.

24. KW to IG, September 2, 1940 (GCLC).

25. IG, *LOSO*, 207.

26. IG, *LOSO*, 207–8.

27. IG, *LOSO*, 208.

28. IG, *LOSO*, 208.

29. IG, *LOSO*, 50.

30. IG to YH, December 23, 1940 (Harburg Collection).

31. IG, undated note for Library of Congress (LDSGTLC). *Life* changed formats after being purchased by Henry Luce in 1936 and became celebrated for its photography.

32. IG, *LOSO*, 187.

33. IG, *LOSO*, 208–9.

34. LDS, journal transcript, February 24, 1954.

35. Brooks Atkinson, "Gertrude Lawrence Appears in Moss Hart's Musical Drama, 'Lady in the Dark,' with a Score by Kurt Weill and Lyrics by Ira Gershwin," *New York Times*, January 24, 1941.

36. IG, *LOSO*, 201–2.

37. IG, *LOSO*, 219.

38. IG, "Gertie Refused to Sign," July 21, 1967 (GCLC).

39. IG to Donald Klopfer, April 15, 1941 (GCLC).

40. IG, note, July 18, 1967, regarding KW to IG, June 10, 1941 (LDSGTLC).

41. IG, *LOSO*, 220.

42. IG, "Gertie Refused."

43. IG to AMW, March 1 or 4, 1941 (GCLC).

44. IG to YH, December 23, 1940.

45. KW to IG, February 20, 1941 (GCLC).

46. IG to CW, August 27, 1943 (GTLC).

47. KW to IG, April 11, 1941 (GCLC).

48. Moss Hart to IG, May 6, 1941 (GTLC).

49. Felix Manskleid to IG, January 25 and March 18, 1941 (both GTLC).

50. IG to Felix Manskleid, January 22, 1942 (GTLC).

51. Jane Sherman to IG, May 29, 1942 (GTLC).

52. Felix Manskleid to IG, February 16, 1943 (GTLC). Manskleid visited Ira in California in 1955.

53. IG to Fred Thompson, May 31, 1941 (GTLC).

54. IG to LSS, April 30, 1964 (GTLC).

55. IG to EJ, May 29, 1941 (GTLC).

56. IG to Albert Sirmay, October 21, 1941 (GTLC).

57. IG to LSS, April 30, 1964.

58. IG to KW, September 29, 1941 (GCLC).

59. IG to Joseph Losey, October 2, 1941 (GTLC).

60. IG to EJ, September 30, 1942 (GTLC).

61. *Santa Ana Register*, June 21, 1941.

62. IG to KS, September 1, 1941 (GTLC).

63. Agreement with Warner Bros., August 1, 1941 (GTLC).

64. IG, justification of income document, 1952.

65. IG to KS, September 1, 1941.

66. IG to Elsie Goldberg, October 6, 1942 (GTLC).

67. Transcript of IG/Rossen sessions, August 1941 (GTLC).

68. Memo from Robert Rossen to unknown, September 1941 (Warner Bros. Archives, USC School of Cinematic Arts).

69. IG, note accompanying donation of *Rhapsody in Blue* outline to Library of Congress, May 13, 1966 (GCLC).

70. IG to EP, August 6, 1941 (GTLC).

71. IG to Elsie Goldberg, October 6, 1942.

72. IG to Albert Sirmay, October 1, 1941 (GTLC).

73. IG to EP, August 6, 1941.

74. IG to KW, September 29, 1941.
75. IG to Warren Munsell, August 25, 1941 (GTLC).
76. IG to LSS, July 5, 1951.
77. IG to Alexander Smallens, November 26, 1941 (Smallens Papers).
78. IG to Alexander Smallens, December 15, 1941 (GTLC).
79. IG to Alexander Smallens, January 21, 1942 (GTLC).
80. IG to CW, August 27, 1943.
81. IG to EJ, March 13, 1942 (GTLC).
82. IG to KW, January 15, 1942 (GCLC).
83. IG to EA, December 10, 1941 (GCLC).
84. IG financial documents.
85. IG to KW, January 15, 1942.
86. Cheryl Crawford to IG, May 13, 1942 (GTLC).
87. IG to EA, October 30, 1943 (GCLC).
88. IG to Warren Munsell, January 30, 1942 (GTLC).
89. IG to Warren Munsell, May 4, 1942 (GTLC).
90. IG to Warren Munsell, April 8, 1942 (GTLC).
91. IG, note accompanying donation of *Rhapsody in Blue* outline to Library of Congress, May 13, 1966.
92. IG to Elsie Goldberg, October 6, 1942.
93. IG to EJ, November 10, 1942.
94. IG to LSS, March 31, 1967 (GTLC). Ira is mentioned in *Flim Flam*, Paul's 1956 book about his adventures in the movie business.

Chapter 14

1. LSG to EP, "Emily's birthday" [March 22, 1943] (GTLC); IG, note on DE galleys, n.d. (GTLC).
2. Drutman, *Good Company*, 219–20.
3. LDS, journal transcript, March 8, 1954.
4. LDS, journal transcript, May 19, 1967.
5. LDS, journal transcript, March 30, 1953.
6. IG to EJ, February 24, 1944 (GTLC).
7. Alton Cook, "North Star Just Short of Great," *New York World-Telegram*, November 13, 1943.
8. IG to Aaron Copland, November 22, 1943 (GTLC). The Harburg/Kern number was written for *Song of Russia*, MGM's contribution to the propaganda effort.
9. IG to Alfred Simon, June 19, 1968.
10. IG to LP and EP, May 10, 1944.
11. MD to IG, April 4, 1944 (GTLC).
12. IG to EJ, April 19, 1944 (GTLC).
13. IG to EJ, May 31, 1944 (GTLC).
14. IG, *LOSO*, 274–76.
15. IG, *LOSO*, 314.
16. IG, *LOSO*, 15.
17. IG to KW, October 22, 1941 (GTLC).
18. IG, note, July 28, 1967.

19. *Billboard*, July 31, 1943.
20. IG, note, July 28, 1967.
21. KW to LL, April 8, 1942, in Lys Symonette and Kim H. Kowalke, eds. and trans, *Speak Low (When You Speak Love): The Letters of Kurt Weill and Lotte Lenya* (Berkeley: University of California, 1996), 320–21.
22. Jean Dalrymple, *September Child: The Story of Jean Dalrymple* (New York: Dodd, Mead, 1965), 215.
23. IG to LSS, August 8, 1951 (LSSLC).
24. IG to CW, September 15, 1953.
25. IG to LP and EP, May 10, 1944 (GTLC).
26. IG to EJ, November 10, 1944.
27. IG to EJ, November 16, 1944 (GTLC).
28. "Abel" [Green], *Variety*, May 23, 1945.
29. David Farneth, Elmar Juchem, and Dave Stein, *Kurt Weill: A Life in Pictures and Documents* (Woodstock, NY: The Overlook Press, 2000), 231.
30. KW to LL, August 14, 1944.
31. IG to Albert Sirmay, May 8, 1954 (GTLC).
32. IG diary, October 1, 1955. When Mickey Rooney repeated his performance as Danny in 1951 stage performances of *Girl Crazy*, the score was augmented by the addition of "I've Got a Crush on You" and "Someone to Watch Over Me."
33. IG to Herman Starr, April 19, 1948 (GCLC).
34. IG, *LOSO*, 50.
35. George S. Kaufman to IG, January 22, 1944 (GTLC).
36. IG, galley notes to DE, ca. 1970 (LDSLLC).
37. IG to Billy Rose, April 1, 1944 (GTLC).
38. IG to EJ, May 31, 1944.
39. "News and Gossip of the Rialto," *New York Times*, March 18, 1945.
40. Irving Drutman, "Ira Gershwin Waited 25 Years before Attempting an Operetta," *New York Herald Tribune*, April 15, 1945.
41. KW to LL, June 28, 1944 (in Symonette and Kowalke, *Speak Low*, 374–75).
42. KW to LL, July 7, 1944 (in Symonette and Kowalke, *Speak Low*, 383–84).
43. KW to LL, July 10, 1944 (in Symonette and Kowalke, *Speak Low*, 384–85).
44. KW to LL, July 12, 1944 (in Symonette and Kowalke, *Speak Low*, 387–89).
45. KW to LL, July 20, 1944 (in Symonette and Kowalke, *Speak Low*, 396).
46. KW to LL, July 23, 1944 (in Symonette and Kowalke, *Speak Low*, 399).
47. KW to LL, September 13, 1944 (in Symonette and Kowalke, *Speak Low*, 444).
48. KW to LL, August 9 and 12, 1944 (in Symonette and Kowalke, *Speak Low*, 415, 417–18).
49. KW to LL, August 27 and 30, 1944 (in Symonette and Kowalke, *Speak Low*, 432–33, 435–36).
50. Max Gordon to KW, October 9, 1944 (reproduced in Farneth et al, *Kurt Weill*, 233).
51. IG to Charles Jackson, November 22 and 24, 1944.
52. IG to Hal James, February 25, 1966 (GTLC).
53. "Elie.," "Plays Out of Town," *Variety*, February 28, 1945.
54. Drutman, *Good Company*, 63.
55. "'Much Ado' 25G," *Variety*, March 14, 1945.
56. IG to EJ, April 9, 1945 (GTLC).
57. Wilella Waldorf, "'Firebrand of Florence' Strikes Very Few Sparks," *New York Post*, March 23, 1945.

58. KW to LL, July 17, 1944 (in Symonette and Kowalke, *Speak Low*, 393).

59. "Inside Stuff-Legit," *Variety*, March 28, 1945.

60. George Jean Nathan, "When There Is Little Left for the Critic to Say," *New York Journal-American*, April 2, 1945, quoted in Ronald Sanders, *The Days Grow Short: The Life and Music of Kurt Weill* (Los Angeles: Silman-James Press, 1980), 341. Ira was not the only member of his family to suffer at the hands of the critics in 1945: there was also *A Lady Says Yes*, Arthur Gershwin's debut, and sole credit, as a Broadway composer. Partially set in sixteenth-century Venice—a coincidence given Ira's work on *Firebrand?*—the musical marked the only Broadway appearance for the ill-fated movie actress Carole Landis. *A Lady Says Yes* ran for eighty-seven performances, outdoing *Firebrand* by 50 percent.

61. IG to EJ, April 9, 1945. Ira's contribution to the book, if any, is unclear.

62. Drutman, "Ira Gershwin Waited."

63. The page was played by a young Billy (Dee) Williams, fourteen years before he made his movie debut.

64. IG, *LOSO*, 131.

65. IG to CW, August 27, 1943.

66. IG, note accompanying donation of *Rhapsody in Blue* outline to Library of Congress, May 13, 1966.

67. IG to EJ, September 1, 1943 (GTLC).

68. John C. Tibbetts, *Composers in the Movies: Studies in Musical Biography* (New Haven: Yale University Press, 2005), 95 (quoting Rudley from Warner Bros. pressbook).

69. Warner Bros. trade ad for *Rhapsody in Blue*, 1946.

70. Bosley Crowther, "The Screen," *New York Times*, June 28, 1945.

71. George S. Kaufman to IG, December 14, 1945 (GTLC).

72. IG to EP, January 31, 1946 (GTLC).

73. IG to CW, April 14, 1946 (GTLC).

74. IG to EJ, May 27, 1946 (GTLC).

75. IG to "Jo," June 17, 1946 (GTLC).

76. Arthur Kober to IG and LSG, July 16, 1946 (GTLC).

77. *Billboard*, October 5, 1946.

78. IG, *LOSO*, 80–81.

79. IG to KS, October 1, 1946.

80. IG to EJ, October 16, 1946 (GTLC).

81. *Billboard*, November 23, 1946.

82. IG to EJ, April 5, 1947.

83. IG, *LOSO*, 349–50.

84. IG to CW, January 29, 1947 (GTLC).

85. IG, *LOSO*, 123–24.

86. IG, *LOSO*, 312.

Chapter 15

1. IG to Charles Jackson, June 18, 1945 (Jackson Papers).

2. IG to EJ, July 5, 1945 (GTLC).

3. IG, *LOSO*, 70.

4. IG to EA, April 9, 1938.

5. IG to EJ, June 18, 1942 (GTLC).

6. Philip K. Scheuer, "Gershwin Left Unused Hit Legacy," *Los Angeles Times*, January 20, 1946.

7. Agreement between IG, RG, and 20th Century Fox, July 23, 1945 (LSSLC).

8. Kimball and Simon, *The Gershwins*, 66.

9. KS to IG, February 4, 1955 (GTLC).

10. IG to LSS, February 22, 1952 (GTLC).

11. IG to CW, January 29, 1947.

12. IG to EJ, September 17, 1945 (GTLC).

13. IG, *LOSO*, 21.

14. IG, *LOSO*, 220.

15. *Billboard*, November 23, 1946.

16. LDS to Philip Furia, June 16, 1995 (LDSGTLC).

17. "Movie Figures Flying to Washington Hearing," *San Bernardino County Sun*, October 26, 1947.

18. IG to EJ, November 26, 1947 (GTLC).

19. "Film Figures Subpoenaed," *Santa Rosa Republican*, February 14, 1948.

20. Leonard Lyons, "The Lyons Den," *The Huntsville [Alabama] Times*, February 18, 1948.

21. California Legislature, *Fourth Report of the Senate Fact-Finding Committee of Un-American Activities, 1948: Communist Front Organizations*, March 25, 1948, 211.

22. "Red Link Is Denied by Ira Gershwin," *New York Times*, February 20, 1948.

23. IG to EJ, March 11, 1948 (GTLC).

24. LDS, journal transcript, February 24, 1953.

25. IG diary, June 15, 1954.

26. IG to VD, October 6, 1947 (Duke Collection).

27. IG to EJ, November 26, 1947.

28. IG to Milt Cohen, August 25, 1951 (GTLC).

29. IG to Moses Smith, January 5, 1948 (GTLC).

30. IG to DE, May 28, 1948 (GTLC).

31. Arthur Schwartz to IG, December 30, 1946 (GTLC).

32. IG to CW, March 16, 1948.

33. IG to GP, June 9, 1931 (GTLC). A third number, "Sweet So-and-So," originally in *That's a Good Girl*, was sung in early performances.

34. IG, *LOSO*, 222.

35. Scott Schechter, *Judy Garland: The Day-to-Day Chronicle of a Legend* (Lanham, MD: Taylor Trade Publishing, 2006), 152–53.

36. IG to EJ, September 14, 1948 (GTLC).

37. IG to LSS, May 5, 1954 (LSSLC).

38. David Berger, affidavit of services rendered in support of claim to estate, July 18, 1949 (LSSLC).

39. RG will, November 21, 1948 (GCLC).

40. IG to FG, April 2, 1949.

41. Stephen Saxe, interviewed by author, July 25, 2018.

42. LSS journal, December 19–20, 1948; IG to LSS, December 20, 1948 (GTLC).

43. IG to Moses Smith, April 28, 1949 (GTLC).

44. IG to LSS, July 11, 1949 (LSSLC).

45. LSS journal, December 22, 1948.

46. IG to LSS, November 27, 1949 (LSSLC).

47. IG et al., agreement with Loew's, December 27, 1949 (GTLC).

48. IG to LSS, February 14, 1949 (LSSLC).
49. IG to FG, April 2–4, 1949 (GTLC). Millionaire Jock Whitney purchased *The Absinthe Drinker* in 1950 for $15,000.
50. IG to FG, April 2–4, 1949.
51. FG to IG, March 22, 1949.
52. IG to FG, April 2–4, 1949 (GTLC).
53. IG to EJ, April 27, 1949 (GTLC).
54. *Daily Variety*, April 11, 1949.
55. IG, *LOSO*, 290.
56. IG, *LOSO*, 61–62.
57. IG, *LOSO*, 62.
58. George S. Kaufman to IG, September 12, 1949 (GTLC).
59. IG to Lawrence Langner, August 18, 1949 (GTLC).
60. IG to LSS, September 10, 1949 (GTLC).
61. IG to LSS, November 1, 1949 (LSSLC).
62. IG to LSS, "Monday night" [November 7 or 14, 1949] (GTLC).
63. IG to LSS, "Friday" [December 9, 1949] (LSSLC).

Chapter 16

1. IG to LSS, January 15, 1950 (LSSLC).
2. IG to LSS, December 4, 1949 (GTLC).
3. IG to LSS, June 19, 1950 (LSSLC).
4. IG to LSS, September 15, 1950.
5. LSS journal, May 4 and 17, 1950.
6. IG to LSS, July 17, 1950 (GTLC).
7. IG to LSS, April 20 and 21, 1950 (both LSSLC).
8. IG to LSS, July 17, 1950.
9. IG diary, August 29, 1950.
10. IG to EJ, December 14, 1954 (GTLC).
11. IG to Arthur Freed, September 2, 1950 (Michael Feinstein collection).
12. IG to LSS, September 15, 1950.
13. IG diary, September 23–24, 1950.
14. IG diary, September 24–October 1, 1950.
15. IG to EJ, September 17, 1941 (GTLC); LDS, note in GTSF photo database, April 24, 1995.
16. IG to Lucy and English Strunsky, November 27, 1967 (GTSF).
17. LDS, journal transcript, July 19, 1968; IG diary, October 3, 1950.
18. IG diary, October 7–9, 1950.
19. IG diary, October 10–11, 1950.
20. IG to DE, October 4, 1956 (GTLC).
21. IG diary, October 11, 1950.
22. IG to LSS, November 1, 1950.
23. IG to CW, February 15, 1951 (GTLC).
24. IG to EJ, January 23, 1951 (GTLC).
25. IG diary, November 9, 1950.
26. IG to Arthur Freed, September 2, 1950; IG to Vincente Minnelli, September 2, 1950 (Profiles in History auction, 2018).

27. IG to LSS, November 1, 1950.
28. LSS journal, January 12, 1951.
29. IG to LSS, February 23, 1951 (LSSLC).
30. IG to LSS, March 27, 1951 (LSSLC).
31. IG to Goddard Lieberson, March 14, 1951.
32. IG to LSS, March 27, 1951.
33. IG to LSS, July 23, 1951 (LSSLC).
34. IG to DE, March 29, 1951 (GTLC).
35. EJ to IG, March 16, 1951 (GTLC).
36. IG to SNB, April 19, 1951 (GTLC).
37. Jablonski and Stewart, *The Gershwin Years*, 242.
38. "Black and Kostelanetz, as Arbiters, Rule 'Says My Heart' a Plagiarism," *Variety*, August 23, 1939.
39. Jablonski and Stewart, *The Gershwin Years*, 242.
40. IG diary, May 10, 1954.
41. IG diary, October 11, 1954.
42. References scattered throughout 1954/1955 diary; LDS, journal transcripts, April 13, 1956, and July 19, 1968.
43. IG to LSS, July 10, 1951 (GTLC).
44. IG to LSS, July 5, 1951.
45. IG to LSS, July 10, 1951.
46. LSS journal, January 14, 1952.
47. IG to LSS, January 23, 1952 (GTLC).
48. IG to LSS, May 23, 1952 (LSSLC).
49. IG to DH, December 26, 1951 (LSSLC).
50. IG et al., agreement with Blevins Davis, January 9, 1952 (LSSLC).
51. DH to IG, March 27, 1952 (GTLC).
52. LSS journal, April 14 and April 22, 1952.
53. IG to John Rumsey, December 13, 1956 (GTLC).
54. IG to LSS, January 23, 1952.
55. IG, *LOSO*, 171.
56. LSS journal, March 20, 1952.
57. IG to MD, March 7, 1951 (GTLC).
58. IG to EA, October 30, 1943.
59. IG to LSS, March 27, 1951.
60. Herman Levin to IG and Morrie Ryskind, June 27, 1951 (LSSLC).
61. Agreement, July 10, 1951 (LSSLC).
62. LSS journal, October 22, 1951; IG to LSS, October 23, 1951 (LSSLC).
63. IG to LSS, February 5, 1952 (LSSLC).
64. IG diary, August 5, 1954.
65. Vernon Rice, "Few Changes Made in 'Of Thee I Sing,'" *New York Post*, May 1, 1952.
66. IG to Melvin Parks, September 11, 1967 (GTLC).
67. IG, *LOSO*, 308.
68. Lillian Ross, "Twenty Years After," *New Yorker*, May 17, 1952.
69. IG to EJ, "Sunday" [May 11, 1952] (GTLC).
70. Gilbert Gabriel, "A Gershwin Musical Is a Gershwin Evening, after All," *Cue*, May 17, 1952.
71. Louis Calta, "Pulitzer Musical to Quit Tomorrow," *New York Times*, July 4, 1952.

72. IG to CW, November 29, 1952 (GTLC).
73. IG to CW, November 29, 1952.
74. IG to LSS, June 10, 1952 (LSSLC).
75. IG to LSS, June 13, 1952 (GTLC).
76. Robert Breen to IG, August 4, 1952 (GTLC).
77. LSG to Irving Drutman, August 1, 1952 (Michael De Lisio and Irving Drutman Papers. Yale Collection of American Literature, Beinecke Rare Book and Manuscript Library).
78. IG to LSS, September 2, 1952 (LSSLC).
79. IG to Brother Matthew [Doc McGunigle], December 10, 1952 (GTLC).
80. IG to DH, November 18, 1952 (GTLC).

Chapter 17

1. IG to DH, November 18, 1952.
2. Harold Arlen to IG, December 5, 1952 (GTLC).
3. Sid Luft, *Judy and I: My Life with Judy Garland* (Chicago: Chicago Review Press, 2017), 259, 285.
4. Contract between IG and Transcona Enterprises, January 14, 1953 (LSSLC). The $7,500 was never received.
5. Jablonski, *Happy*, 174.
6. Jablonski, *Happy*, 175.
7. IG, *LOSO*, 243–44.
8. Kimball and Simon, *The Gershwins*, 243.
9. IG to LSS, March 8, 1953 (LSSLC).
10. Jablonski, *Happy*, 179.
11. LDS, journal transcript, March 22, 1953.
12. IG to EP, March 29, 1953 (GTLC).
13. IG diary, May 20, 1953.
14. IG diary, July 20, 1954.
15. IG to EJ, November 4, 1953 (GTLC).
16. IG to LSS, September 21, 1951 (LSSLC).
17. "Plush Gershwin Festival Set for '53 Longhair Tour with Blessing of Family," *Variety*, January 23, 1952.
18. IG to LSS, September 14, 1953.
19. IG to HB, October 31, 1953 (GTLC).
20. Agreement, June 20, 1953 (LSSLC); "Composer's Mother Leaves Million Dollar Estate," *Albuquerque Journal*, June 17, 1953.
21. Luft, *Judy and I*, 284–85.
22. LDS, journal transcripts, November 14, November 19, December 5, and December 10, 1953.
23. LDS, journal transcript, October 8, 1953.
24. IG to LSS, October 15, 1953 (LSSLC); agreement between IG and Paramount, November 23, 1953 (GTSF).
25. IG to Paul Miller, November 8, 1953 (GTLC).
26. "33 Songwriters Sue Radio BMI," *New York Daily News*, November 10, 1953.
27. IG diary, April 12, 1954.
28. IG to EJ, November 9, 1953 (GTLC).
29. IG to LSS, October 4, 1952 (LSSLC).

30. IG to Brother Matthew, December 10, 1952.

31. IG to EJ, July 24, 1952 (GTLC); IG to EJ, September 18, 1952 (Edward Jablonski Papers, Music Division, Library of Congress); IG to EJ, November 5, 1952 (GTLC).

32. IG to LSS, February 18, 1953 (LSSLC).

33. IG to EJ, September 20, 1953 (GTLC).

34. IG to EJ, July 29 and September 15, 1953 (GTLC); IG to LSS, September 14, 1953 (LSSLC).

35. IG to EJ, February 10 and April 10, 1954 (GTLC).

36. IG to EJ, April 27, 1955 (GTLC).

37. IG to EJ, May 18, 1954; IG to LSS, February 8, 1954 (LSSLC).

38. IG to EJ, November 8, 1954; LSS to IG, November 4, 1960 (LSSLC).

39. IG to Robert Israel, August 15, 1953 (GTLC).

40. IG to LL, April 9, 1953 (GTLC).

41. IG to Mrs. Charles E. Bohlen, February 8, 1956 (GTLC). The same recordings, along with *The Firebrand of Florence* demos done with Weill in October 1944, were released as part of the double-LP *Ira Gershwin Loves to Rhyme* on the Mark 56 label in 1975.

42. LDS, journal transcript, November 3, 1953.

43. IG to CW, September 15, 1953.

44. IG to LL, April 9, 1953.

45. "Popular Records," *New Yorker*, November 28, 1953.

46. IG to Brother Matthew, December 18, 1953 (GTLC).

47. IG to Irving Drutman, November 24, 1952 (Loeb Music Library).

48. IG to EJ, December 9, 1953 (GTLC).

49. IG, *LOSO*, 256.

50. IG to Brother Matthew, December 10, 1952.

51. Kimball, *CLIG*, 368.

52. IG to Ben Bagley, August 25, 1971 (GTSF).

53. LDS, journal transcript, January 20, 1954.

54. LDS, "Notes for an essay on *LOSO*."

Chapter 18

1. IG to EJ, February 2, 1954 (GTLC).

2. LDS, journal transcript, January 20, 1954.

3. IG diary, January 18, 1954.

4. IG diary, January 24, 1954. "Liebermeyer Beer" was rejected by the producers; Ira instead wrote a series of lyrics to the tune of "London Bridge Is Falling Down."

5. IG to William Perlberg and George Seaton, February 22, 1954 (GTLC).

6. IG diary, January 7, 1954.

7. LDS, journal transcript, January 15, 1954.

8. IG diary, February 24, 1954.

9. LDS, journal transcript, March 26, 1954.

10. IG to EJ, March 30, 1954 (GTLC).

11. IG to EJ, April 10, 1954.

12. IG to Harold Arlen, April 19, 1954 (GTLC).

13. IG to LSS, May 5, 1954 (LSSLC).

14. IG diary, May 3, 1954.

15. IG diary, May 7, 1954.

16. IG diary, May 17, 1954.
17. IG diary, August 2, 1954.
18. Kimball, *CLIG*, 376.
19. IG to SNB, June 22, 1954 (GTLC).
20. SNB to IG, July 1, 1954 (GTLC).
21. Lawrence D. Stewart, "L'Envoi: *Lyrics on Several Occasions: Its Why & Wherefore; and Matters Associative*," in *Lyrics on Several Occasions* (New York: Limelight, 1997), 367.
22. IG diary, November 15, 1954.
23. IG diary, November 19, 1954.
24. IG diary, December 7, 1954.
25. IG to Blanche Knopf, January 7, 1955 (GTLC).
26. LSS to IG, December 23, 1954 (LSSLC).
27. IG diary, May 18, 1953.
28. LDS, journal transcript, January 13, 1954.
29. IG to LSS, June 9, 1954 (LSSLC).
30. LSG to IG, November 3, 1954 (GTLC).
31. IG to EP, December 12, 1954 (GTLC).
32. IG to Max Liebman, August 16, 1954 (GTLC). The reference is to *Roget's Thesaurus* (1852) and *The American Thesaurus of Slang*, by Lester V. Berrey and Melvin Van den Bark (1942).
33. IG diary, September 29, 1954.
34. IG diary, September 17, 1954.
35. Luft, *Judy and I*, 298. A restored, if still incomplete, version of *A Star Is Born* premiered at Radio City Music Hall in 1983, just a month before Ira's death.
36. IG diary, October 11, 1954.
37. LSS journal, September 21, 1963.
38. Lena Horne to IG, telegram, September 13, 1963, in Kimball, *CLIG*, 375.
39. IG diary, December 24, 1954.
40. IG diary, January 29, 1955.
41. John Steinbeck, *Travels with Charley in Search of America* (New York: Penguin, 1997), 5.
42. LDS, "L'Envoi," 365.
43. Ralph Barton, "Theatre," *Life*, February 7, 1930.
44. IG to MD, November 30, 1954 (GTLC). Alajálov got the job after Ralph Barton's suicide in 1931.
45. IG diary, September 9, 1954.
46. IG diary, November 13, 1954.
47. George Beiswanger, "Lyrics at Their Best," *Theatre Arts*, October 1935.
48. IG to MD, November 30, 1954, and an undated draft of same.
49. IG to Blanche Knopf, January 7, 1955.
50. IG to LSG, December 24, 1954 (GTLC).
51. IG, *LOSO*, 316; IG diary, April 18, 1955.
52. IG to Brother Matthew, November 19, 1954 (GTLC).
53. IG to LSG, December 24, 1954.
54. John Rumsey to IG, December 14, 1953 (GTLC).
55. Agreement between Dorothy Heyward, Blevins Davis, and Robert Breen, December 14, 1953 (GTLC).
56. IG to LSS, January 26, 1954 (GTLC).
57. IG diary, February 9, 1954.

58. IG to LSS, May 8, 1954 (LSSLC).
59. IG to LSS, December 13, 1954 (GTLC).
60. LSG to IG, February 25, 1955 (GTLC).
61. LSG to IG, March 2, 1955 (GTLC).
62. DH to IG, November 28, 1954 (GTLC).
63. IG diary, November 29, 1954.
64. IG diary, March 16, 1955.
65. IG diary, February 7, 1955.
66. IG diary, March 23, 1955.
67. IG to Eva Jessye, February 5 [1955] (Eva Jessye Collection, University of Michigan).
68. Blevins Davis to Hugo Pollock, March 21, 1955 (GTLC).
69. IG to DH, April 1, 1955 (GTSF).
70. IG diary, April 5, 1955.
71. DH to IG, April 5, 1955 (GTLC).
72. IG diary, April 14, 1955.
73. IG to LSS, April 7, 1955 (GTLC).
74. IG diary, April 21, 1955.
75. Lawrence Langner to IG, May 9, 1955 (GTLC). Langner's claim cannot be verified, as George Gershwin's 1926 letter is not extant.
76. IG to DH, May 19, 1955 (GTLC).
77. IG to EJ, December 14, 1954 (GTLC).
78. IG to LSS, February 17, 1955 (LSSLC). "Three Coins in the Fountain" received the award.
79. IG diary, June 20, 1954.
80. IG to LL, November 25, 1954 (GTLC).
81. IG, *LOSO*, 48. *The Country Girl* also picked up the award for George Seaton's adaptation of Clifford Odets's play.
82. IG diary, May 24, 1955.
83. IG to DE, August 9, 1955 (GTLC).
84. DE to IG, August 11, 1955 (GTLC).
85. IG to DE, October 11 and 12, 1955 (GTLC).
86. IG diary, May 24, 1955.
87. LDS, "L'Envoi," 371.
88. IG to Martin Dibner, August 3, 1955 (GTLC). The Good Neighbor Policy was an effort of the US government under President Franklin D. Roosevelt to be friendlier to the nations of Central and South America via the use of "soft power" rather than military action.
89. LDS, "L'Envoi," 373.
90. Schumach, "Hollywood Recall."
91. IG diary, September 26, 1955.
92. IG to Blanche Knopf, October 5, 1955 (GTLC).
93. IG diary, October 19, 1955.
94. IG to LSG, August 31, 1955 (GTLC).
95. IG diary, November 10, 1955.
96. IG to Herman Starr, October 14, 1955 (GTLC).
97. IG to LSS, October 28, 1955 (GTLC).
98. IG diary, October 30, 1955.
99. IG diary, November 3, 1955.
100. Robert Breen to Irving Lazar, November 18, 1955 (GTLC).

101. Jablonski, *Harold Arlen*, 270.
102. IG to Brother Matthew, December 21, 1955 (GTLC).

Chapter 19

1. IG diary, January 6, 1956.
2. IG diary, January 7, 1956.
3. IG diary, January 8, 1956.
4. IG diary, January 9, 1956; IG to Brother Matthew, March 20, 1957 (GTLC).
5. IG diary, January 9, 1956.
6. IG diary, January 10, 1956.
7. LSS journal, March 27, 1960.
8. IG to Brother Matthew, March 20, 1957.
9. IG diary, January 10, 1956.
10. Robert Breen to IG, September 15, 1956 (GTLC).
11. Truman Capote, *The Muses Are Heard* (New York: Vintage, 1956), 136.
12. LDS, "Something about Leonore."
13. IG diary, January 14, 1956.
14. IG diary, January 11, 1956.
15. IG diary, January 15, 1956.
16. IG diary, January 12, 1956.
17. IG diary, January 13, 1956.
18. IG to Arthur Freed, n.d. [ca. January 14, 1956] (Freed Collection).
19. IG diary, January 14, 1956.
20. IG, *LOSO*, 187–88. Glière died five months later.
21. IG diary, January 17, 1956.
22. IG diary, January 18, 1956.
23. IG to Brother Matthew, March 20, 1957.
24. IG diary, January 19, 1956.
25. IG diary, January 20, 1956. In November 1957, the airplane crashed at the Norrköping Airport in Sweden and was destroyed in the ensuing fire.
26. LDS, journal transcript, January 30, 1956.
27. LDS, "Notes for an essay on *LOSO*."
28. LDS, journal transcript, March 21, 1956. Only LSG's initials made it into the book.
29. LDS, "L'Envoi," 377–78.
30. LDS, journal transcript, June 13, 1956.
31. LSS journal, February 2 and 6, 1956.
32. DH to IG, January 27, 1956 (GTLC).
33. IG to LSS, February 10, 1956 (GTLC).
34. LDS, journal transcript, February 28, 1956.
35. LSS to IG, March 9, 1956 (GTLC).
36. IG to LSS, March 12, 1956 (GTLC).
37. IG to LSS, June 11, 1956 (LSSLC).
38. IG to LSS, May 14, 1956 (LSSLC).
39. IG to LSS, November 21, 1956 (LSSLC).
40. IG to LSS, May 10, 1956 (GTLC).
41. IG to LSS, August 24, 1957 (GTLC).

42. Blevins Davis to Robert Breen, December 3, 1956 (GTLC).

43. IG to LSS, June 3, 1960 (GTLC). Davis's fortune came from his widow, a railroad heiress.

44. IG to LSS, December 13, 1956 (GTLC).

45. DH to IG, February 1, 1957 (GTLC).

46. IG to DH, February 8, 1957 (GTLC). The option expired on December 14, 1958.

47. IG to LSS, February 8, 1957 (LSSLC).

48. IG to LSS, March 1, 1957 (GTLC).

49. IG to LSS, March 19, 1957 (GTLC).

50. IG to LSS, December 6, 1962 (LSSLC).

51. IG to LSS, April 26, 1957 (GTLC).

52. Robert Breen's agreement with Samuel Goldwyn Productions, May 6, 1957 (GTLC); Thomas M. Pryor, "Goldwyn to Film 'Porgy and Bess,'" *New York Times*, May 9, 1957.

53. LSS journal, August 1, 1957.

54. LSS journal, August 13, 1957.

55. IG to LSS, May 5, 1955 (LSSLC).

56. LSG to Peggy Martin, January 31, 1956 (LDSGTLC).

57. Marika Gerrard, "Film Stars Found a Classic Architect for Their Homes," *Los Angeles Times*, September 29, 1980.

58. IG to LSS, June 21, 1956 (LSSLC).

59. IG to LSS, July 28, 1956 (GTLC).

60. IG to SNB, September 6, 1956 (Behrman Papers).

61. IG to Brother Matthew, March 20, 1957.

62. LDS, journal transcript, September 5, 1956.

63. IG to LSS, October 17, 1957 (LSSLC).

64. LSS journal, December 24, 1956.

65. IG to Brother Matthew, March 20, 1957.

66. LDS, journal transcript, September 14, 1956.

67. IG to LSS, September 17, 1956 (GTLC).

68. IG to CW, September 15, 1953.

69. IG to Brother Matthew, March 20, 1957.

70. IG to Alan Schneider, July 27, 1955 (GTLC).

71. *Jackson [MS] Clarion-Ledger*, June 20, 1957.

72. "Alan Gershwin" to IG, June 20, 1957 (GTLC).

73. IG to LSS, June 23, 1957 (GTLC).

74. IG to LSS, September 6, 1958 (GTLC).

75. LSS to IG, September 22, 1958 (GTLC).

76. IG to LSS, October 8, 1958 (LSSLC).

77. IG to LSS, September 29, 1958 (GTLC).

78. LSS journal, October 16, 1958.

79. "Gershwin 'Claimant'" document, September 11, 1958 (GTLC).

80. Albert Alan Schneider, draft registration card, December 30, 1945 (Ancestry.com).

81. Joe Cohn to Ed [Edward Mahar?], July 23–25, 1957 (GTLC). Cohn worked for the tabloid *New York Evening Graphic*; Mahar was the city editor of the *New York Journal-American* from 1955 to 1963.

82. Belle Levy, report on "Alan Schneider," November 28, 1958 (GTLC).

83. 1964 VA Claim Report (GTLC).

84. George Hubbard to LSS, April 14, 1959 (GTLC).

85. IG to LSS, March 31, 1959 (GTLC).

86. LDS, journal transcript, August 19, 1957.

87. LDS, journal transcript, October 1, 1957.

88. IG to LSS, October 7, 1957 (LSSLC).

89. IG, notes written on the reverse of Irving Drutman to IG, August 10, 1955 (GTLC).

90. IG, *LOSO*, 37. The book's epigraph—"How these curiosities would be quite forgott, did not such idle fellowes as I am put them downe!"—came from a 1949 first edition of the Cresset Press (London) printing of John Aubrey's *Brief Lives and Other Selected Writings*; Drutman to IG, March 1, 1959 (GTLC).

91. IG to LSS, November 21, 1957 (LSSLC).

92. IG to LSS, December 27, 1957 (GTLC).

93. LSS journal, January 3, 1958.

94. IG death certificate, 1983 (GTSF).

95. LSS journal, January 5, 1958.

96. IG to Mascha Strunsky, January 15, 1958 (GTLC).

97. IG to LSS, February 5, 1958 (GTLC).

98. Kimball, *CLIG*, 224 ("slit of light"); LDS, journal transcript, March 17, 1958.

99. IG to MD, April 8, 1958 (GTLC).

100. IG to Brother Matthew, December 10, 1952.

101. IG diary, November 15, 1954.

102. IG diary, October 18, 1954.

103. IG to LSS, May 29, 1958 (LSSLC).

104. LDS, journal transcripts, July 11 and 25, 1958.

105. IG to Horace Sutton, October 20, 1958 (GCLC).

106. LDS, "L'Envoi," 380. The delivery was made by Ira and Lee's nephew, Mike Strunsky.

107. Blanche Knopf to IG, February 4, 1959 (GTLC).

108. Rick Du Brow, "Geo. Gershwin Still Controversial," *Pomona Progress-Bulletin*, April 30, 1959.

109. LSS journal, April 28, 1959.

110. LSS journal, May 6, 1959.

111. LDS to LSS, May 6, 1959 (LSSLC).

112. "Paul Muni, Gershwin Quit Hospital," *Los Angeles Times*, May 9, 1959.

113. IG to LSS, May 13, 1959 (GTLC).

114. IG diary, June 2, 1963.

115. John Tynan, "Portrait of Ira," *Down Beat*, July 23, 1959.

116. IG to Madge Rogers, July 14, 1958 (GTLC).

117. IG to DH, April 4, 1960 (GTLC).

118. IG to LSS, October 27, 1958 (GTLC).

119. IG to Blanche Knopf, February 10, 1959.

120. IG to LSS, May 21, 1959 (GTLC).

121. Frank Lee Donoghue, "Ira Gershwin's Home Still Glorifies George."

122. "'Porgy & Bess' on Shelf in U.S.," *Variety*, March 22, 1961.

123. IG to LSS, April 1, 1966 (GTLC).

124. Hollis Alpert, *The Life and Times of Porgy and Bess: The Story of an American Classic* (New York: Knopf, 1990), 280.

125. DH to IG, March 31, 1960 (GTLC).

126. John G. Fuller, "Trade Winds," *Saturday Review*, November 21, 1959.

127. William Koshland to IG, April 30, 1959; LSS to IG, May 27, 1959 (both GTLC).

128. IG to Irving Drutman, July 24, 1959 (GTLC).

129. Irving Drutman to IG, July 20, 1959 (GTLC). Ira completed a short essay on lyric writing that was not published until 2009, when it appeared in Robert Kimball's introduction to *Ira Gershwin: Selected Lyrics* (Library of America).

130. IG to Irving Drutman, April 19, 1960 (GTLC).

131. LDS, journal transcript, September 17, 1959.

132. IG diary, October 21, 1959.

133. IG diary, October 15, 1959.

134. IG diary, October 19–20, 1959.

135. Knopf advertisement, October 18, 1959.

136. LSS to IG, December 27, 1959 (GTLC).

137. Newman Levy, "Remembered Joys: The Gershwin Words," *New York Herald Tribune Book Review*, February 7, 1960.

Chapter 20

1. IG to Lillian [Carter?], ca. June 4, 1966 (GTLC).

2. William Koshland to LDS, April 20, 1961 (GTLC).

3. IG to LSS, July 16, 1962, and January 19, 1963 (LSSLC).

4. IG to MD, April 23, 1959 (GTLC); LDS, GTSF photo database, March 13, 1995.

5. IG to Albert Sirmay, November 5, 1959; IG to DE, May 15, 1959 (both GTLC).

6. IG to LSS, February 26, 1960 (GTLC). Ira also prepared the contents and provided New York-centric titles for a *Gershwin in New York* piano folio in the 1960s but dropped the idea.

7. IG to P. G. Wodehouse, March 11, 1959; IG to LSG, April 15, 1960 [quote] (both GTLC).

8. IG to LSS, April 9, 1964 (GTLC).

9. IG to SNB, May 17, 1961 (Behrman Papers).

10. IG to P. G Wodehouse, January 21, 1960 (GTLC).

11. IG to LSS, January 10, 1961 (LSSLC).

12. IG to LSS, January 4, 1962 (LSSLC).

13. IG to LSS, December 29, 1961 (LSSLC)

14. LSG to IG, March 12, 1960 (GTLC).

15. LSG to IG, April 19, 1960 (GTLC).

16. IG to SNB, April 14, 1960 (GTLC).

17. LSS journal, June 21, 1960.

18. IG to DH, draft, n.d. [after May 17, 1961] (LDSGTLC). May never have been sent.

19. LSS to IG, December 28, 1961 (GTLC).

20. IG to St. John Terrell, October 9, 1959 (GTLC).

21. IG diary, May 25–26, 1963.

22. IG diary, May 27 and 30 and June 5, 1963.

23. IG diary, June 4, 1963.

24. George S. Kaufman to IG, May 19, 1956 (GTLC) (*Lipstick War*); LDS, journal transcripts, October 17 and November 5, 1956 (*Shop* and *Whoop-Up*). The Kaufman and Fain projects were not produced; *Whoop-Up*, with a score by Moose Charlap and Norman Gimbel, closed after fifty-six performances.

25. LDS, journal transcripts, January 28, 1957, and January 19, 1959. *On the Twentieth Century* arrived on Broadway in 1978, with music by Cy Coleman and lyrics by Betty Comden and Adolph Green.

26. LDS, journal transcript, June 28, 1961. Levin and Kurnitz teamed with Noël Coward for the adaptation, which opened on Broadway in 1963 as *The Girl Who Came to Dinner*.

27. LDS, journal transcripts, January 29, February 8, and February 18–19, 1957. Saul Chaplin (music) and Johnny Mercer (lyrics) wrote the songs for *Merry Andrew*.

28. Jablonski and Stewart, *The Gershwin Years*, 319.

29. Jablonski and Stewart, *The Gershwin Years*, 321.

30. IG to LSS, November 27, 1963 (GTLC).

31. IG to LSS, November 27, 1963.

32. Kimball, *CLIG*, 383.

33. IG to Albert Sirmay, March 19, 1964 (GTLC).

34. Jablonski and Stewart, *The Gershwin Years*, 314.

35. IG to FG, February 28, 1964 (GTLC).

36. IG to LSS, March 13, 1964 (GTLC). The contract also included a payment for the use of "'S Wonderful," which Martin sings in the opening sequence of the movie.

37. IG to LSS, February 13, 1964 (LSSLC).

38. Jablonski and Stewart, *The Gershwin Years*, 326.

39. IG to Albert Sirmay, June 1, 1964 (GTLC). Martin's take on "Sophia" saw the light of day on a 2001 Bear Family Records compilation of his Reprise recordings; Ella Fitzgerald's recordings of "Livelong Day" and "I'm a Poached Egg" appeared on a 2003 compilation of her rare material for the Verve label.

40. IG to EJ, April 17, 1964 (GTLC); IG to Andre Kostelanetz, August 10, 1964 (LSSLC).

41. IG to Louis MacLoon, February 20, 1964 (GTLC).

42. IG to LSS, February 2, 1965 (GTLC).

43. IG diary, May 25, 1928.

44. IG to LSS, July 6, 1955 (GTLC).

45. LSS journal, April 5, 1966.

46. LSS journal, October 11, 1961.

47. LSS journal, August 1, 1962.

48. LSS journal, August 1, 1962.

49. IG to LSS, June 15, 1962 (GTLC).

50. IG to LSS, December 6, 1962.

51. IG diary, June 11, 1965.

52. IG diary, June 1, 1965.

53. LSS journal, August 11, 1965.

54. LSS journal, September 9, 1965.

55. LSS journal, September 10, 1965.

56. LSS journal, September 16, 1965.

57. LSS journal, February 12, 1966.

58. LSS journal, February 23, 1966.

59. IG diary, June 5, 1965.

60. LSS journal, June 26, 1965.

61. Nadia Natali, interviewed by author, August 14, 2018.

62. IG diary, June 25, 1965.

63. IG diary, June 13, 1965.

64. IG to LDS, June 9, 1965 (LDSGTLC).

65. IG to LSS, March 7, 1962 (GTLC).

66. IG diary, June 18, 1965.

67. IG to Albert Goldberg, February 28, 1949 (GCLC).
68. IG to Chet Shaw, September 27, 1944 (GTLC).
69. LSS to IG, July 7, 1965 (GTLC). The amount is equivalent to $3.6 million in 2021.
70. IG, *LOSO*, 282. The singer in question was Morgana King.
71. LDS, journal transcript, January 31, 1954.
72. John Tynan, "Portrait of Ira."
73. IG to MD, April 8, 1958.
74. IG to EJ, May 18, 1954.
75. IG to Ella Fitzgerald, August 10, 1959 (GTLC).
76. Stan Stanley to IG, March 20, 1963 (GTLC)
77. IG to LSS, September 10, 1964 (GTLC).
78. IG to Stan Stanley, December 6, 1964 (GTLC).
79. IG to Victor Blau, December 9, 1965 (GTLC).

Chapter 21

1. Leonard Lyons syndicated column, *Oakland Tribune*, June 16, 1966. Honorary doctorates were also given that day to author Katherine Anne Porter; Dr. John Alfred Hannah, the chairman of the Commission on Civil Rights; and Thomas Bourne Turner, the dean of the Johns Hopkins School of Medicine.
2. IG to Dr. Franklin Cooley, June 22, 1966 (LDSGTLC).
3. IG to Erle Krasna, March 2, 1966 (GTLC).
4. IG to Lillian Hellman, June 15, 1966 (GTLC).
5. IG to Wilson Elkins, May 24, 1967 (GTLC).
6. IG to Marian and Eliot Corday, June 17, 1966 (GTLC).
7. LDS to Harold Spivacke, September 15, 1966 (LDSGTLC).
8. Sam Pearce to IG, February 8, 1967 (GTLC).
9. IG to LSG, March 16, 1967 (GTLC).
10. LDS to EP, June 5, 1967 (GTLC).
11. Edwin Bolwell, "City Museum Wins a Scramble for Memorabilia of Gershwins," *New York Times*, June 7, 1967.
12. LDS to Harold Spivacke, July 13, 1967 (LDSGTLC).
13. Edwin Bolwell, "Theater Collection Is a Mass of Confusion," *New York Times*, September 13, 1967.
14. Melvin Parks to LSG and IG, September 5, 1967 (LDSGTLC); IG to Melvin Parks, August 1, 1967 (GTLC).
15. LDS to Melvin Parks, October 2, 1967 (LDSGTLC).
16. IG to SNB, January 22, 1968 (Behrman Papers); IG to GP, February 21, 1968 (GTLC); LDS to Sam Pearce and Melvin Parks, February 1, 1968 (LDSGTLC).
17. LDS to Sam Pearce and Melvin Parks, January 15 and 23, 1968 (both LDSGTLC).
18. IG to Harold Spivacke, March 11, 1968 (LDSGTLC).
19. LDS to Sam Pearce and Melvin Parks, April 9, 1968 (LDSGTLC).
20. LDS to Sam Pearce and Melvin Parks, November 24, 1967 (LDSGTLC).
21. LDS to Sam Pearce and Melvin Parks, January 2, 1968; Sam Pearce to LDS, January 12, 1968 (both LDSGTLC).
22. LDS, note, May 2, 1968 (LDSGTLC).
23. Elaine Godowsky, interviewed by author, July 30, 2018.

24. Donal Henahan, "Ira Presides at Gershwin Show," *New York Times*, May 6, 1968.
25. LDS, note added 1995 to journal transcript, November 16, 1953; LDS, journal transcript, June 20, 1968.
26. Melvin Parks to IG, June 10, 1968 (LDSGTLC).
27. IG to Felix de Cola, May 20, 1968 (GTLC).
28. LDS to EP, May 31, 1968; LDS to EP, June 6, 1968 (both GTLC).
29. LDS, journal transcript, June 20, 1968.
30. LSS journal, June 7, 1966.
31. IG to LSS, February 21, 1968 (GTLC).
32. LDS to Sam Pearce and Melvin Parks, July 3, 1968 (LDSGTLC).
33. IG to SNB, September 16, 1968 (GTLC).
34. LDS, journal transcript, July 3, 1968.
35. Ron Blanc, interviewed by author, August 6, 2018.
36. "Gershwin Manuscripts Sought," *Los Angeles Herald-Examiner*, July 7, 1972; documents relating to the payment, November 1972 (GTSF).
37. LDS to MS, August 8, 1968 (LDSGTLC).
38. LDS, journal transcripts, July 19 and 25 and August 28, 1968.
39. LDS to IG, November 19, 1968 (GTLC).
40. LDS, journal transcripts, June 6 and August 28, 1968; IG to DE, October 4, 1968 (GTLC).
41. LDS to Sam Pierce and Melvin Parks, November 26, 1968 (LDSGTLC).
42. LDS to MS, December 26, 1968 (GTLC); LDS, note, April 22, 1969 (LDSGTLC).
43. LDS, journal transcript, December 2, 1968; LDS note, September 1, 1969 (LDSGTLC); LDS to English Strunsky, September 10, 1990 (LDSGTLC).
44. IG to HB, n.d. [after June 18, 1969] [draft; never sent?] (GTLC).
45. IG to Stan Stanley, March 4, 1970 (GTLC).
46. IG to Paul Palmer, June 8, 1970 (GTLC).
47. IG to LSG, December 24, 1969 (GTLC).

Chapter 22

1. Robert Kimball, interviewed by author, April 10, 2018.
2. IG to LSS, March 28, 1968 (GTLC).
3. IG to Peter van de Kamp, January 13, 1970 (GTLC).
4. IG to Andre Kostelanetz, September 25, 1963 (GTLC); IG to George Balanchine, March 13, 1964 (GTLC).
5. IG to Stan Stanley, March 3, 1970 (GTLC).
6. Undated (ca. 1970) document (GTLC).
7. IG to Harold Spivacke, July 24, 1970 (GTLC).
8. IG to DE, February 16, 1970 (GTLC).
9. IG to DE, October 14, 1970 (GTLC).
10. Ewen, *George Gershwin*, xvii.
11. IG to GP, April 22, 1971 (GTLC).
12. IG to EJ, November 9, 1970 (GTLC); IG to EJ, March 31, 1971 (Jablonski Papers).
13. 1971 Daily Reminder [calendar] (GTLC).
14. IG to Max Wilk, October 12, 1971 (GCLC); IG to Ron Blanc, May 21, 1971 (GTSF).
15. EP to IG, December 2, 1971 (GTLC).
16. Mayor Tom Bradley declared "Ira Gershwin Day" for the lyricist's eightieth birthday.

17. Household calendar, March 2, 1972 (GTLC).

18. Ron Blanc, interviewed by author, August 6, 2018.

19. Kimball, *CLIG*, xv.

20. IG to Brother Matthew, July 1, 1972 (GTLC). "AK" stands for "alte kocker," Yiddish for "crotchety old man."

21. Robert Kimball, interviewed by author, April 10, 2018.

22. IG to LSS, January 14, 1960 (GTLC).

23. IG to LSS, February 26, 1964 (GTSF).

24. William Koshland to LSS, August 19, 1964 (GTSF).

25. IG to William Koshland, January 21, 1972 (GTLC).

26. William Koshland to IG, July 16, 1971 (GTLC).

27. IG to Madge Rogers, August 24, 1959 (GTLC); IG to LSS, December 22, 1959 (LSSLC); LSS to IG, January 27, 1960 (GTLC).

28. Viking Press royalty statements (GCLC).

29. IG to Paul Vandervoort II, January 30, 1973; medications listed on ca. early 1970s document (both GTLC).

30. IG quoted in Rosenberg, *Fascinating Rhythm*, xv.

31. "Gershwin Recovering from Surgery after Fall in Home," *Los Angeles Times*, April 12, 1975.

32. Alpert, *The Life and Times*, 296.

33. Michael Feinstein, *Nice Work If You Can Get It: My Life in Rhythm and Rhyme* (New York: Hyperion, 1995), 47.

34. Michael Feinstein, interviewed on *Fresh Air* (National Public Radio), July 29, 2002.

35. Feinstein, *Nice Work*, 76.

36. KS to Eva Jessye, n.d. [April 8, 1981] (Jessye Collection).

37. Elaine Godowsky, interviewed by author, July 30, 2018.

38. Feinstein, *The Gershwins and Me*, 45.

39. Death certificate, August 23, 1983 (GTSF); Jerry Cohen, "Ira Gershwin, Giant among Lyricists, Dies," *Los Angeles Times*, August 18, 1983.

40. Todd Purdom, "The Street Where They Lived," *Vanity Fair*, April 1999.

41. Frank E. Campbell funeral chapel, invoice, September 23, 1983 (GTSF); Michael Feinstein, interviewed by author, March 9, 2018; Mike and Jean Strunsky, interviewed by author, July 11, 2018.

42. Jablonski and Stewart, *The Gershwin Years*, 316. Parker's epitaph was included in "A Group of Artists Write Their Own Epitaphs," a piece published in the June 1925 issue of *Vanity Fair* that also included George Gershwin's questioning of his status as an American and as a composer.

43. Quoted in Richard Corliss, "Lyrics by 'the Other One,'" *Time*, August 29, 1983.

CREDITS

Images

Ira and Leonore Gershwin Trusts: cover, 10, 53, 57, 62, 67, 77, 83, 91, 103, 108, 124, 138, 194, 203, 229, 237, 247, 264, 271, 282, 284, 292, 297, 299, 305; George and Ira Gershwin Collection, Music Division, Library of Congress, Washington, DC: 48, 133, 277; Lawrence D. Stewart Papers, Music Division, Library of Congress, Washington, DC: 257; author's collection: 13.

Lyrics

"Applause, Applause" (from *Give a Girl a Break*): Words by Ira Gershwin; Music by Burton Lane. Copyright © 1952 (Renewed) Ira Gershwin Music and EMI Feist. All Rights for Ira Gershwin Music Administered by WC Music Corp. All Rights Reserved. Used by Permission of Alfred Music.

"Aren't You Kind of Glad We Did?": Words and Music by George Gershwin and Ira Gershwin. Copyright © 1946 (Renewed) Nokawi Music, Frankie G. Songs, Ira Gershwin Music and George Gershwin Music. All Rights for Nokawi Music Administered in the U.S. by Steve Peter Music. All Rights for Frankie G. Songs Administered by Downtown DLJ Songs. All Rights for Ira Gershwin Music and George Gershwin Music Administered by WC Music Corp. All Rights Reserved. Used by Permission. Reprinted by Permission of Hal Leonard and Alfred Music.

"The Ballad of Baby Face McGinty" (from *Ziegfeld Follies of 1936*): Music by Vernon Duke; Lyrics by Ira Gershwin. Copyright © 1936 (Renewed) Ira Gershwin Music and Kay Duke Music. All Rights on behalf of Ira Gershwin Music Administered by WC Music Corp. All Rights Reserved. Used by Permission of Alfred Music and Kay Duke Ingalls.

"Bidin' My Time" (from *Girl Crazy*): Music and Lyrics by George Gershwin and Ira Gershwin. Copyright © 1930 (Renewed) WB Music Corp. and Ira Gershwin Music. All Rights Administered by WC Music Corp. All Rights Reserved. Used by Permission of Alfred Music.

"Blah, Blah, Blah" (from *Delicious*): Music and Lyrics by George Gershwin and Ira Gershwin. Copyright © 1931 (Renewed) WC Music Corp. All Rights Reserved. Used by Permission of Alfred Music.

"But Not for Me" (from *Girl Crazy*): Music and Lyrics by George Gershwin and Ira Gershwin. Copyright © 1930 (Renewed) WC Music Corp. All Rights Reserved. Used by Permission of Alfred Music.

lishing Corp., New York, NY, and Ira Gershwin Music. All Rights on Behalf of Ira Gershwin Music Administered by WC Music Corp. International Copyright Secured. Made in U.S.A. All Rights Reserved Including Public Performance For Profit. Used by Permission of Alfred Music and Hampshire House Publishing Corp.

"There's a Boat Dat's Leavin' Soon for New York" (from *Porgy and Bess* ®): Music and Lyrics by George Gershwin, DuBose and Dorothy Heyward and Ira Gershwin. Copyright © 1935 (Renewed) Nokawi Music, Frankie G. Songs, DuBose and Dorothy Heyward Memorial Fund Publishing, Ira Gershwin Music and George Gershwin Music. All Rights for Nokawi Music Administered in the U.S. by Steve Peter Music. All Rights for Frankie G. Songs and DuBose and Dorothy Heyward Memorial Fund Publishing Administered by Downtown DLJ Songs. All Rights on Behalf of Ira Gershwin Music Administered by WC Music Corp. All Rights Reserved. Used by Permission. Reprinted by Permission of Alfred Music and Hal Leonard LLC.

"They All Laughed" (from *Shall We Dance*): Music and Lyrics by George Gershwin and Ira Gershwin. Copyright © 1936 (Renewed) Nokawi Music, Frankie G. Songs, George Gershwin Music and Ira Gershwin Music. All Rights for Nokawi Music Administered in the U.S. by Steve Peter Music. All Rights for Frankie G. Songs Administered by Downtown DLJ Songs. All Rights for Ira Gershwin Music Administered by WC Music Corp. All Rights Reserved. Used by Permission of Alfred Music and Hal Leonard LLC.

"They Can't Take That Away from Me" (from *The Barkleys of Broadway*; from *Shall We Dance*): Music and Lyrics by George Gershwin and Ira Gershwin. Copyright © 1936, 1937 (Copyrights Renewed) Nokawi Music, Frankie G. Songs, Ira Gershwin Music and George Gershwin Music. All Rights for Nokawi Music Administered in the U.S. by Steve Peter Music. All Rights for Frankie G. Songs Administered by Downtown DLJ Songs. All Rights for Ira Gershwin Music Administered by WC Music Corp. All Rights Reserved. Used by Permission. Reprinted by Permission of Alfred Music and Hal Leonard LLC.

"Time Marches On" (from *Ziegfeld Follies of 1936*): Music by Vernon Duke; Lyrics by Ira Gershwin. Copyright © 1936 (Renewed) Ira Gershwin Music and Kay Duke Music. All Rights on behalf of Ira Gershwin Music Administered by WC Music Corp. All Rights Reserved. Used by Permission of Alfred Music and Kay Duke Ingalls.

"Tschaikowsky (and Other Russians)" (from the Musical Production *Lady in the Dark*): Words by Ira Gershwin; Music by Kurt Weill. Copyright © 1941 (Renewed) TRO-Hampshire House Publishing Corp., New York, NY, and Ira Gershwin Music. All Rights on Behalf of Ira Gershwin Music Administered by WC Music Corp. International Copyright Secured. Made In U.S.A. All Rights Reserved Including Public Performance For Profit. Used by Permission of Alfred Music and Hampshire House Publishing Corp.

"The Union League": Music and Lyrics by George Gershwin and Ira Gershwin. Copyright © 1933 (Renewed) WC Music Corp. All Rights Reserved. Used by Permission of Alfred Music.

"Union Square" (from *Let 'Em Eat Cake*): Music and Lyrics by George Gershwin and Ira Gershwin. Copyright © 1933 (Renewed) WC Music Corp. All Rights Reserved. Used by Permission of Alfred Music.

"Who Cares? (So Long as You Care for Me)" (from *Of Thee I Sing*): Music and Lyrics by George Gershwin and Ira Gershwin. Copyright © 1931 (Renewed) WC Music Corp. All Rights Reserved. Used by Permission of Alfred Music.

INDEX

Page numbers in *italics* indicate illustrations.